SALMON WARS

SALMON WARS

The Battle for the West Coast Salmon Fishery

DENNIS BROWN

HARBOUR PUBLISHING

Published by
Harbour Publishing Co. Ltd.
P.O. Box 219, Madeira Park, BC V0N 2H0
www.harbourpublishing.com

Cover and page design by Martin Nichols
Photos courtesy the Fisherman's Publishing Society unless otherwise noted
Edited by Betty Keller and Mary Schendlinger
Cover image by Lonnie Wishart
Back cover author photo by Sean Griffin
Printed and bound in Canada

Harbour Publishing acknowledges financial support from the Government of Canada through the Book Publishing Industry Development Program and the Canada Council for the Arts, and from the Province of British Columbia through the British Columbia Arts Council and the Book Publisher's Tax Credit through the Ministry of Provincial Revenue.

THE CANADA COUNCIL | LE CONSEIL DES ARTS
FOR THE ARTS | DU CANADA
SINCE 1957 | DEPUIS 1957

BRITISH
COLUMBIA
ARTS COUNCIL
Supported by the Province of British Columbia

Library and Archives Canada Cataloguing in Publication

Brown, Dennis, 1950–
    Salmon wars : the battle for the west coast salmon fishery / Dennis Brown.

    Includes bibliographical references and index.
    ISBN 1-55017-351-0

    1. Pacific salmon fisheries—Northwest, Pacific. 2. Pacific salmon fisheries—Government policy—Canada. 3. Pacific salmon fisheries—Government policy—United States. 4. Pacific salmon fisheries—Government policy—British Columbia. I. Title.

SH349.B69 2005   333.95'656'09795   C2004-907468-7

To Kathy

Contents

Acknowledgements 8

Preface 9

Chapter 1: On the Brink of a Disaster 15

Chapter 2: The Hundred Years War. 28

Chapter 3: Fish Wars and Missing Salmon. 44

Chapter 4: The Great Experiment. 63

Chapter 5: Too Many Fishermen 81

Chapter 6: The Tragedy of the Commons. 88

Chapter 7: Stop Your Snifflin', We'll Make Ya Love Mifflin!. 116

Chapter 8: Tangled Lines and Torpedo Tirades. 144

Chapter 9: The Battle of Prince Rupert. 176

Chapter 10: Canada First? 196

Chapter 11: Please, Prime Minister 217

Chapter 12: Coping with the Coho Crisis 243

Chapter 13: The Full Mifflin and the Full Retreat. 263

Chapter 14: The Blockade of Seymour Narrows 278

Chapter 15: A Question of Balance 295

Chapter 16: A Time of Hunger 315

Chapter 17: It Was All Lies! 334

Chapter 18: Returning to the Adams River 359

Endnotes. 376

Bibliography 391

Index. 396

Acknowledgements

I regret that I cannot acknowledge everyone who helped me with this project, or all the wonderful people that I have known in the fishing industry over the years. But I would like to offer special thanks to locals 5, 9, 3 and 1 of the UFAWU for generously providing the financial support to pay for professional editing of my original manuscript.

For reading the many drafts, in part or in full, I also thank: Kathy Bonitz, Alan Brown, Tara Brown, Bob Burkoski, Parzival Copes, John Cummins, Stephen Drymer, Dan Edwards, Sheila Fruman, Sean Griffin, Donna and Richard Gross, George Hewison, Guy Johnston, Rolf Knight, David Lane, Bruce Logan, Terry Lubzinski, Ralph Matthews, Doug McArthur, Leo McGrady, Kenn McLaren, Geoff Meggs, Charles Menzies, Jack Nichol, Des Nobels, Kim Olsen, Les Priest, Don Sananin, Mike Shepard, Joe Smith, Dal Triggs, Pierrette Vezina, Darlene Wulff and Bob Wulff.

Grant Snell of the BC Salmon Marketing Council, Don Kowal of the Pacific Salmon Commission, Bob Grant of the BC Council of Professional Fish Harvesters and John Sutcliffe of the Canadian Council of Professional Fish Harvesters provided critical data when I needed it. Special mention should also go to Sandy Argue of the Department of Fisheries and Oceans. Sandi Brice of the UFAWU–CAW organized the original electronic draft of the manuscript and helped me to select photographs from the archives of *The Fisherman* newspaper. My editors Betty Keller and Mary Schendlinger deserve fulsome praise for making my script more concise and readable. Above all, this book owes its very existence to John Radosevic, who offered friendship and encouragement when I needed it most. Finally, I thank Norah and Alan Brown for instilling in me a reverence for the past, and Connor and Brendan Dell for giving me hope for the future.

Preface

In June 2001 I was fired from my job as a special fisheries advisor to the province of British Columbia. At the time it seemed the world had come to an end. But the apocalypse had not arrived; the BC New Democratic Party had simply suffered the most humiliating defeat in its history.

I had been appointed to my position four years earlier by then Premier Glen Clark, who had been elected to office by a very narrow margin in 1996. Clark's left-wing government had faced hostility from many BC voters, and he was keen to improve his popular support. A wily politician, he sensed that most British Columbians felt alienated within Canadian confederation; thus, an aggressively pro-British Columbia stance vis-à-vis the federal government should enhance his political fortunes, and no issue seemed to arouse British Columbians' anti-Ottawa feelings more than the mismanagement of the West Coast fishery.

Just before Clark's election, the federal government had embarked on a massive program to restructure the commercial salmon fishery, throwing thousands of people in coastal communities out of work. At the same time, reports that some salmon stocks were approaching extinction had sent shock waves through the public. To add insult to injury, in violation of the Pacific Salmon Treaty, the United States of America was stealing millions of BC salmon. All of this was grist for Clark's mill, and he struck a sympathetic chord with the public when he declared his intention to wrest control of the fishery from Ottawa. This gambit would culminate in what later became known as "The West Coast Salmon War." It was a war highlighted by a bitter showdown between Clark and Liberal David Anderson, BC's senior federal cabinet minister. On the international front, the salmon war also featured a spectacular confrontation between a ragtag but heroic group of commercial fishermen and the world's only superpower.

I was in the eye of that political hurricane, and this book is an attempt to untangle the wreckage it left behind.

I worked for the United Fishermen and Allied Workers' Union (UFAWU) for almost 20 years, first as a staff worker and later as an elected officer. Back then, I believed I would spend my entire working life with the union. But then along came the federal Pacific Salmon Fleet Restructuring Program, or the Mifflin Plan, as it was generally known, and in short order the West Coast fishery was in a shambles and the union's future in question. When the invitation to work for the provincial government came, I sincerely believed it was an opportunity to carry on the fight to save the industry as much as a chance to secure a future for myself.

I never really felt I was part of the government service. I wasn't welcome in the cozy little club of senior bureaucrats, nor was I a part of the inner circle of elected politicians. Instead, as a political appointee, I occupied the shadowy zone between politicians and bureaucrats. But the experience gave me a sobering look at how our so-called democratic system really works. I was struck by how much power the senior bureaucracy wields, and how little control over events our elected politicians actually have.

When I worked with the government, I was too busy coping with daily problems to come fully to terms with the larger events of the Mifflin era. Only after I was fired did I have the time to take a long hard look at things, and to write this book. I was born into a fishing industry family that spans three generations. My mother's parents immigrated to British Columbia from Ireland just before the First World War. My grandfather, William Binns, worked as a bookkeeper for BC Packers at several North Coast canneries, and my mother Norah was born in Port Essington, near the southern entrance of the Skeena River. My mother left the village as a child, never to return, and since then time and economic change have conspired as relentlessly as the fierce currents of the Skeena River to render Port Essington a ghost town. Its ruins have long since disappeared into the dark underbelly of the rain forest.

My uncle Paddy Binns—my mother's brother—was the first person in the family to be a fisherman. His training as an amateur boxer prepared him for the rigours he would later face as a troller. My father, Alan Brown, came to fishing via the navy. He had served as a stoker aboard the corvette HMCS *Hespler* in the north Atlantic during World War II, and his apprenticeship in its engine room prepared him for a post-war career as a steam engineer. But it seems he was not cut out for the nine-to-five routine, and after a few years ashore he scraped together enough for a down payment on an old gillnetter. Back in the early fifties it took only a few hundred dollars to purchase a fish boat, and commercial fishing served as an ideal form of employment for returning veterans. My father started his gillnetting career in Rivers Inlet in the heart of BC's central coast. He learned fast and became a good producer, but like most fishermen, he was always trying to get out from under the control of the canning companies. There was not much money to be made, but for my father, adventure and tall tales were plentiful.

Dennis Brown at Beaver Cannery, Rivers Inlet, 1954. Photo by Norah Brown

Indeed, my earliest memories—though vague and fleeting—are of fishing in Rivers Inlet. I can still recall my fascination as a three-year-old as I watched my father haul the glistening salmon over the stern rollers of the boat. Their scales would flicker with bright rainbow hues as their tails flapped amid the tangle of jellyfish and kelp that fell between my father's giant black gumboots. The boat would be heaving in the swells, it was usually raining, and seasickness always seemed to prevail. I was haunted by the sad eyes of the salmon as they lay dying underneath the dripping hulk of the wooden gillnet drum, around which the linen net with its black-tarred wooden floats and heavy lead line was tightly wrapped.

Years later, I read letters that my young mother had written to my grandmother describing her life with two small children aboard a 9 m (30 ft) gillnetter. There was seldom any fresh food, no place to hang diapers, little respite from the monotonous routine and never any money.

As youngsters my brother Kerry and I occasionally joined my father when he trolled for winter chinooks in the Gulf of Georgia. We'd leave early on a weekend morning and be out all day. At that time of year the only buyer for my father's fish was Pete Sainas, an old Greek fishmonger who owned The Seven Seas, a fish store in Vancouver's pre-gentrified Kitsilano. It was always dark by the time we came back under the Burrard Bridge, plying the oily black waters of False Creek between shores lined with a maze of ramshackle old warehouses, marine ways and other industrial detritus. My old man would place what few chinooks or "smilies" he'd caught in a sack, and we'd drive up to old Pete's place. Pete had constructed a special chute at the back of the store, through which we'd slide the day's catch after hours. The fish would land with a slap on the pile of ice that he'd put there before locking up.

As I grew older, I turned against fishing and became what my father contemptuously referred to as a landlubber. Once he offered to help me buy a fish boat; in my youthful arrogance I disdained the idea, but he did persuade Kerry, who operates a gillnetter to this day. As far as I was concerned, the less I had to do with gillnets, fish slime or greasy mechanical toil, the better. I was into psychedelic music, radical politics and all of the other countercultural activities of the late sixties.

In 1968, without a clue what I wanted to do with my life, I enrolled at the University of British Columbia, joining the host of long-haired, anti-establishment rebels that flourished on campus at the time. Four years later I was no closer to a secure career than when I had started, but I put all such concerns aside while I travelled around Europe—a lifestyle that I resolved would last forever, if I could finance it.

I returned from Europe in 1974—penniless—and found myself on the deck of a herring packer operated by Seafood Products Ltd. of Port Hardy, a job that had come my way because my father had fished for the company for several years. With seasonal work, I had decided, I could support the bohemian life. Yet surprisingly I found the work almost enjoyable. I was thrilled by the spectacular scenery and took a keen interest in all facets of coastal navigation.

As the years passed and my journeys abroad continued, I found myself returning each summer to work on fish packers, and now I had a growing stake in the industry.

But it wasn't until the three-week salmon strike of August 1975 that my eyes were opened to the harsh economic realities of the industry, and I was drawn to the UFAWU and in particular its charismatic president,

Homer Stevens. My first volunteer assignment with the union was in 1976, as chairperson of the Combines Defence Committee, a rank-and-file group that supported members charged under the Combines Investigation Act during the strike of 1975. Some disgruntled non-union fishermen who had opposed the strike had decided to launch a federal combines investigation into the union's affairs, claiming that union picket lines amounted to a "conspiracy" designed to restrain free enterprise in the industry. Despite the fact that the Fisheries Association of BC, an organization of fishing companies, had inflicted considerable damage on the UFAWU during that strike, and that the Combines Act was originally intended to bust corporate monopolies, investigators descended on the union and seized its files. To make matters worse, neither federal nor provincial law recognized the right of commercial fishermen to strike like any other workers.

When called before the Combines Branch, UFAWU officers Homer Stevens, Jack Nichol and George Hewison refused to testify. A protest rally was organized to prevent the investigation from proceeding behind closed doors, and charges were laid against the UFAWU's three officers and four rank-and-file activists. Harry Rankin, the union's lawyer, got most of the charges dropped, but two men, tenderman Ken Robinson and fishermen Dave McIntosh, were forced to stand trial. A rank-and-file committee, which I chaired, set out confidently to defend them, yet these two individuals—whom I considered working-class heroes—were found guilty of obstructing justice. Although they were later granted a full pardon, I never again held the Canadian justice system in the same esteem.

Throughout all of this I was impressed with the integrity and intellectual power of men like Stevens, Nichol and Hewison, and for the first time I saw my youthful idealism manifest in real human beings—men who were prepared to sacrifice everything they had in the name of the working class. Some of them, like Homer Stevens, were members of the Communist Party of Canada and had spent time in jail for their beliefs. The UFAWU became the focal point of my life.

Over the years, more than a few stars were knocked out of my eyes, but my affinity with working people never diminished. I continued to be involved in the fishery—as the skipper of a fish packer, among other things—until I went to work full time for the UFAWU as its Fraser Valley organizer in 1980. I loved my job of organizing the gillnetters and trollers based in the Lower Mainland and relished the opportunity of interacting with the hundreds of interesting characters in the small boat fleet.

In 1990 I was elected an officer of the union, replacing the retiring Bill Procopation, and in this new role I enjoyed something of a media reputation during the many public campaigns and issues the union took on, not the least of which was the protracted struggle to secure an equitable salmon interception treaty with the United States of America. I made a lot of noise in the media about how the Yankees were stealing our fish, and in 1994 the flamboyant young federal fisheries minister from Newfoundland, Brian Tobin, appointed me one of the four commissioners representing Canada on the Pacific Salmon Commission. That summer, negotiations with the Americans collapsed, and Tobin announced that Canada would embark on an aggressive fishing strategy to reduce American interceptions of BC salmon. A master at handling the media, he earned the moniker of "Captain Canada" with his pro-Canada stand. Tobin's theatrics were being carefully observed by another young politician, Glen Clark, who aspired to be the premier of BC. He, too, went on to take up the cudgels against the Americans.

This book is not about salmon—as magnificent, mysterious, poetic and awe-inspiring as they may be. Rather, it is about people. It is also about money and power, and how the seemingly simple process of harvesting and selling salmon affects the lives of all those involved.

Everyone in this story depends in one way or another on the salmon: some for their prestige, some for their wealth, some for their culture, others for their survival. But equally so, the salmon depend on the outcome of those human struggles, which are far from over. It is the voices of those who appear to have lost those struggles that I am—in the words of the great British historian E.P. Thompson—"seeking to rescue from the enormous condescension of posterity."[1]

On the Brink of a Disaster

A historical understanding is what I am after,
not agreement, approval, or sympathy.

Eric Hobsbawm, *Interesting Times*

Every story has a beginning, and this one starts in 1994, when the West Coast fishing industry changed forever. That year critics alleged that commercial fishermen had fished BC's precious salmon stocks to within 12 hours of disaster, and that year Canadians went to "war" with the United States of America over Pacific salmon.

My most vivid memory of that time, however, is personal. It is of my father, Al Brown, struggling to loosen a rusty sprocket from the propeller shaft of his gillnetter/troller, the *Sea Deuce*. A few days earlier he had been gillnetting for Fraser River sockeye in Sabine Channel, when the shaft bearings had seized. Now he was desperately trying to fix the damage so he could get back out fishing, but no matter what he did, the sprocket wouldn't move. He tried to loosen it by heating it with a blowtorch, and even to weld a steel bar directly onto the sprocket and lever it with a six-tonne hydraulic jack. But that sprocket would not budge.

When he was building the boat in his backyard in the years between 1963 and 1967, he'd anticipated engine failure, as all fishermen do, and created a unique system: a main engine supplemented by an auxiliary motor, both connected to a single propeller shaft. He'd designed a heavy sprocket, over 30 cm (12 inches) in circumference and 7 cm (3 inches) wide, to fit onto the shaft. When necessary, the clutch on the main engine could be disengaged and the more fuel-efficient auxiliary, connected to the sprocket gears by a series of chains, would drive the propeller. Now, after many years, the sprocket had rusted and the shaft could not be pulled out for repairs.

That day, August 28, 1994, while he toiled in the cramped engine room of his boat, I was in Vancouver at a meeting at the Department of Fisheries and Oceans (DFO) on behalf of the United Fishermen and Allied Workers' Union (UFAWU). I was a member of a DFO advisory committee waging an "aggressive" fishing strategy to force the US to renew the expired annexes of the Pacific Salmon Treaty. After the meeting, I called my father to let him know the DFO was planning to open the Gulf of Georgia the next day to all commercial salmon licence holders to troll for sockeye. For decades he had trolled in the Gulf every year, and commented that it was "nice fishing"—as if there were such a thing. But in 1981 DFO had instituted an area-licensing policy that limited access to only 300 trollers, and he had been shut out ever since.

When my father first began fishing in 1950, commercial fishermen took pride in fishing on a full-time, year-round basis, and he often cursed the "moonlighters" who came along at the peak of the season to compete with the "bona fide" fishermen. In those days anyone could become a commercial fisherman, for all species of fish, by simply paying a one-dollar licence fee. The lives of bona fide fishermen had changed irrevocably when the federal government began to impose a host of regulations and restrictions to "modernize" the salmon fishery and make it more "efficient" and "rational." Yet despite this constant meddling, the West Coast fishery had not become more viable. In fact, ever since the limited-entry licensing scheme had been introduced in 1969, fishermen had faced a steady erosion of their fishing privileges. At the same time they had been forced to fish much harder to get out of debt, which they had incurred because they had had to buy a separate fishing licence, often worth thousands of dollars, for virtually every species.

Now, for the first time in almost a quarter century, the DFO was about to reverse its habit of restriction—although very briefly—because the bilateral Pacific Salmon Commission (founded in 1985 to supervise fisheries in BC, the northwestern states and Alaska) had predicted an enormous buildup of late-run sockeye in the Gulf of Georgia over the next few days. The DFO's decision was made to satisfy Ottawa's short-term political needs rather than the needs of the fishermen. But the battalions of experts who try to make commercial fishing a more economically rational enterprise seldom consider the problem from the fisherman's point of view.

The Legendary 1958 Adams River Run

While he worked on his boat that day in 1994, my father was thinking about the 19 million sockeye forecast to return to the Fraser, some of which he would catch the next day if he fixed the propeller shaft in time. Where would the main schools be concentrated? How would the tides and the presence of such a large fishing fleet affect their movements? Each run of Fraser River salmon—which this year would include the dominant cycle of the famous Adams River run—had its own unique behaviour. Some runs moved up the river quickly; others stayed outside the mouth for weeks. Pinks and other species have two-year spawning cycles, but sockeye return to spawn on four- or five-year cycles, and my father chased many cycles of Adams River sockeye during his 45-year fishing career. He remembered the famous Adams River run of 1958 and about the canners who had decided to cut their price to fishermen because there was such a glut of fish. The UFAWU, armed with a 90.26 percent rejection vote by its membership, had stood its ground.[1] A strike deadline was set for August 9, and the canners agreed on August 16 to pay the previous year's prices—28 cents per pound—or better.

Then, during the week of August 22, the unexpected happened: millions of sockeye bound for the Fraser River poured through Johnstone Straits, just north of Campbell River. A "northern diversion" like this one sometimes occurs because of Vancouver Island, a rugged 300-mile barrier. Salmon returning to the Fraser River must get around the island by passing through either the Strait of Juan de Fuca to the south—a strait shared by the US and Canada—or through Johnstone Strait at the northern end of the island. For reasons that are not entirely clear or predictable, but that may have to do with ocean temperatures and salinity levels, some races of Fraser sockeye in some years choose to migrate en masse via the "northern diversion." This has been viewed as an advantage to Canada, as far fewer fish migrate through American waters. Thus, in 1958, the forecast for the run had been good but no one had expected the bonanza that occurred because of the northern diversion, and despite an unprecedented fishing effort, millions of sockeye evaded the commercial fleet and entered the Gulf of Georgia. Thousands of part-time fishermen joined the rush for the spoils, and the government responded by imposing a series of licence policies that wreaked havoc on the lives of bona fide fishermen—not to mention the salmon—in the years to come.[2]

The record run also triggered a bitter response from American fishermen who were on strike to obtain prices similar to those won by fishermen in Canada: the US canners managed to divert the strikers' wrath by accusing Canadian fishermen of catching more than their share of sockeye in Johnstone Strait. By treaty, Canada and the United States were required to share the harvest of sockeye and pinks equally in the Strait of Juan de Fuca, Puget Sound and the lower Gulf of Georgia. However, the International Pacific Salmon Fisheries Commission (IPSFC)—a body set up in 1937 to monitor those fisheries—did not have jurisdiction over Canadian fisheries in Johnstone Strait. The editors of the *Vancouver Sun* took up the American fishermen's complaint: "Agitation among US fishermen for changes in the system of dividing Fraser River sockeye catches deserves a fair hearing. It would seem wise to work out techniques to share the catch fairly..."[3] Homer Stevens, then secretary treasurer of the UFAWU, rejected this idea, saying, "Fish that pass through the waters of only one country to spawning grounds in that same country are absolutely no concern of the other. That is the case in Johnstone Strait..." He added, in response to the *Sun*'s fear of US retaliation, "Your editorial suggests the Americans may break the treaty and 'catch every Fraser sockeye they could find in US waters.' Your readers should know the Americans did just that on both sockeye and pinks for many years. They learned, painfully, that was only a case of cutting off their noses to spite their faces. They also learned that two can play such a silly game which reduces fish populations very quickly."

By the end of August 1958, BC canneries were plugged with a massive inventory, 1.8 million cases of canned sockeye. They were relieved when the DFO imposed a closure throughout most of September to protect the Adams River sockeye, which normally delay for more than a month before entering the Fraser. However, before the closure ended, the canners announced they didn't want to buy any of the millions of surplus sockeye still milling around in the Gulf of Georgia. James Sinclair, formerly the federal minister of fisheries and now a spokesperson for the Fisheries Association of BC, claimed that "the tail-end sockeye are not fit to can" and could only be fed "to Eskimos and Native Indians." The canners, however, said they would reconsider their position if the fishermen agreed to cut the price from 28 cents to 17 cents per pound.

The union membership refused to accept the cut and voted to boycott any company paying less than the contract price agreed to in August. In return, the canners called Homer Stevens a "dictator" and imposed a lockout, and millions of salmon in excess of the spawning goal headed up the river. In an attempt to salvage the season, the UFAWU offered to "discuss alternative proposals" if the sockeye were of poor quality, but the canners refused to negotiate. The union found buyers in the US and petitioned Ottawa to allow them temporarily to export unprocessed sockeye and pinks, after the American fishermen's strike was over. In the meantime, however, Ritchie Nelson of BC Packers Ltd. had met secretly with the US buyers and threatened retaliation if they purchased the Canadian catch.

On that day in 1994, my father told me his story of the 1958 lockout. "That was a tough year," he said. "When the lockout started, we knew we couldn't fish for the prices the canners wanted. I mean, how could we? It would have meant working for slave wages! So we swore we would never give in. That we would fight until the last man standing and 'til the last dog was hung, as we used to say during the war. The hell of it was, though, the canners could afford to wait it out, while a lot of the fishermen couldn't. Plenty of guys went broke that winter. And even though most of the Adams River run was wasted, the company boys were still drivin' fancy cars and puffin' big cigars."

'Til the last dog was hung, I thought. An interesting turn of phrase I'd often heard fishermen use. Usually it meant staying out on the fishing grounds, despite bad weather and diminishing returns, until the bitter end of the season. It struck me how much this bit of slang symbolized

the stoic grit and determination of commercial fishermen, that rare and remarkable breed of men and women who make their living from the sea. Appropriate also, I thought, in its military context, connoting struggle, conflict and sacrifice, things a veteran like my father knew all too well but seldom spoke about, the very stuff that had shaped his life and prepared him for the difficult, often lonely, and widely misunderstood profession he had chosen.

After the canners' lockout in 1958, no further fishing occurred that year, and by mid-October no one was sure how many fish were headed up the river. The federal fisheries department estimated the number to be as high as 4 million; the canners claimed more than 10 million sockeye would go to waste and blamed this on the actions of the UFAWU. On October 10 the union demanded that federal Fisheries Minister Angus MacLean buy the excess salmon as part of a humanitarian food program. MacLean and the rest of the Ottawa bureaucracy dodged the issue, and the press claimed the "greed" of UFAWU members had caused the company lockout, which in turn had resulted in an over-escapement on the spawning beds.

The union leadership replied on October 24, in an editorial in *The Fisherman*, the UFAWU newsletter: "The truth of the tragic situation is that the Salmon Commission made an error in judging the number of fish available for spawning, waited too long to clean up the situation, the canners washed their hands of the responsibility and in so doing broke their signed agreement with the union, and the federal government through its minister of fisheries refused to help find a solution. In all this mess, the fishermen and the public were the real victims, and many thousands of valuable food fish were wasted."

On October 30, the IPSFC met to discuss the large surplus escapement flooding the spawning grounds. The commissioners voted unanimously to install an electric fence at the mouth of the Adams River on Shuswap Lake to ensure the more than 1.7 million "prime quality" spawners already in the river were not disturbed by the mass of late arrivals. "This unprecedented action appears essential if we are to forestall a serious decline in the returning run in 1962," said Canadian Senator Tom Reid, chair of the commission. However, four years later, in the spring of 1962, the IPSFC announced that adverse "estuarial conditions" in the brood year had resulted in a poor return to the Adams River. Consequently, the 1962 season—thanks to the canners' lockout—was a disaster instead of a record return as in 1958. Eventually the IPSFC was forced to admit that "the total Adams River escapement [in 1962] is not expected to meet maximum requirements…"

But that was 1958 and this was 1994, and my father would either repair the shaft bearings in the next few hours or he would miss the chance to drop his lines for one last time in the Gulf of Georgia. When he took a break, I watched him run his gnarly weathered hands through his hair as he stared ahead stoically and cursed the bloody sprocket. Then he said, quite unexpectedly, "Do you know who first started trolling for sockeye?" I had heard the story before but encouraged him to continue. "No bullshit now," he said, "but it was your uncle Paddy Binns and me. Most guys won't believe that if you tell 'em, but it's true. We heard some old-timers say that sockeye will strike at anything red, so we thought, what the hell, let's try it. And we cut up an old red hot water bottle Paddy had and made some homemade lures. And you know, it worked. We caught some sockeye. The guys in the fish camp couldn't believe their eyes when we delivered them."

Regardless of whether my father actually caught the first sockeye on trolling gear, his story had a fortuitous connection to the following day, when more than 1,000 trollers were slated to fish in the Gulf of Georgia at the behest of federal Fisheries Minister Brian Tobin, who was waging a "fish war" against the Americans. The public, most of whom cannot distinguish a salmon from a tommy-cod, were nonetheless fascinated by a Canadian politician with the nerve to stand up to the Yanks. Officially the DFO was simply allowing the trollers to take the share of the catch they'd missed offshore earlier in the season. However, everyone including the Americans knew the trollers were being deployed as part of Tobin's audacious political brinkmanship.

This was ironic because trollers, as my father's story suggests, were at one time not able to catch sockeye.

There are three primary methods of harvesting salmon commercially in British Columbia: trolling, gillnetting and purse-seining. Trollers fish with a number of deep lines suspended from long poles fastened to the sides of their vessels. Shorter lines, or leaders, with hooks and lures at

Fisheries Minister Brian Tobin briefs the Minister's Advisory Panel on tactics designed to pressure the US into renewing the annexes to the Pacific Salmon Treaty, June 1994.

the end are attached to these main trolling lines. The lines and lures can be raised or lowered depending on the location of the fish. Gillnetters fish with a net, usually about a quarter of a mile long. The meshes of the gillnet are almost invisible to the approaching salmon, particularly after dusk. Once a salmon enters the net, it is usually ensnared by its gills and cannot back out. Both trollers and gillnetters operate smaller-sized vessels—traditionally between 9 and 15 m (30–50 ft) long—and seldom employ more than a single deckhand. Purse-seiners are much larger—17 to 24 m (55–80 ft) long—and employ five- or six-person crews. They attach one end of a deep, small-meshed net to an adjacent shoreline or a skiff, and tow it in a very large circle. The two ends are then joined and closed by pulling a purse-line attached to the bottom of the net, trapping whatever salmon have entered the circle. Until the Mifflin Plan was introduced in 1996, there was also a fourth method, combination fishing, in which a fisherman—usually on a small boat—used both net and troll gear.

BC trollers have traditionally roamed far offshore in search of chinook and coho, which do not travel in large schools. Therefore, the troll fishery was once considered much less efficient, and trollers were allowed to fish seven days per week throughout most of the season. Gillnetters and seiners, on the other hand, who traditionally targeted large, concentrated schools of sockeye, chum and pinks, were restricted to tightly regulated, time-limited fisheries closer to shore. With the advent of new lures and new technology, trollers learned to harvest sockeye and other "net species" with great efficiency, and by the late 1970s the troll share of the sockeye catch had grown to almost 30 percent of the total allowable catch (TAC). In the absence of sharing arrangements, this expanding troll harvest posed serious problems for DFO bureaucrats. Besides being forced to contend with infuriated net fishermen, they could no longer maintain an accurate in-season accounting of the offshore troll harvest. They were considering a plan to limit the trollers when in 1983 negotiations to limit US interceptions of Canadian salmon reached an impasse. In the absence of regulations curbing the trollers, the DFO sent the entire Canadian troll fleet off the west coast of Vancouver Island to intercept Fraser-bound sockeye and pinks before those stocks passed through US waters. In a matter of days the trollers landed a huge catch. Naturally the Americans complained, but it was not long afterwards that the Pacific Salmon Treaty was signed.

West Coast purse-seiners.

"Screw it! Let's go home," my father announced. It was getting dark and the damned sprocket had not budged. I agreed reluctantly. I had hoped to join him as deckhand the next day. Instead, I attended yet another meeting at the DFO offices. When I arrived, a small group of officials were already poring over reams of statistical information. The chair was Dave Schutz, a quiet-spoken fellow whose job it was to keep track of all salmon fisheries along the coast. At his side was Wayne Saito, a Fraser River sockeye specialist, Bud Graham, director of fisheries management, and several others. In short order I discovered that the "hails" from the troll fishery that morning, August 29, 1994, were far below expectation. Before starting the telephone conference call with the staff of the Pacific Salmon Commission and the American side of the Fraser panel, the Canadian contingent caucused. Given the poor results, we were apprehensive about allowing the Gulf troll fishery to continue, but a Vancouver Island fisheries manager spoke vociferously over the speakerphone against curtailing the net fishery in Johnstone Strait. "Don't forget the Gulf of Georgia is a huge bloody area," he cried. "When those Adams sockeye go deep they're really hard to find, even if there are over a thousand damned trollers out there!" He also reminded everyone that in 1993 the DFO had underestimated the largest run of sockeye on that cycle since 1913, so fisheries off northern Vancouver Island and in Johnstone Strait had been curtailed while millions of surplus sockeye were wasted.

When the bilateral conference call began, Jim Woodey, chief biologist for the Pacific Salmon Commission, reported a catch of approximately 111,000 sockeye for the first day of the Canadian troll fishery—not a bad catch, but nowhere near what had been expected. Unless there was a sudden surge of fish, he warned, the Fraser run might be in danger. Woodey also reported that the bulk of the early run of sockeye—ushered past the commercial fleet in July—was now inexplicably delayed in the Fraser Canyon. Hundreds of thousands of them were trapped and dying along the banks of the river due to a lethal combination of warm and turbid water conditions. Before this meeting, no one had suspected that the 1994 Fraser sockeye run would be substantially below forecast.[4] The Canadian Fraser panel concluded that it was best to close the troll fishery the following day, though the DFO did leave open the option of fishing again if more sockeye appeared. I agreed with the decision, but I was also thinking of the old man staring at that rusty sprocket, and I was secretly hoping more fish would show up in a day or two.

My father, meanwhile, was returning the hydraulic jack he'd rented, and learning that the proprietor had mistakenly rented him a jack with only a fraction of the promised lifting power. My father returned to his boat with a better jack, and gave it one mighty push. The sprocket screeched and, like some giant Jurassic vertebrae, it rotated slowly on the propeller shaft. Unbeknownst to my father, however, it was too late. The fish war of 1994 was already over, and his attempt to troll one last time in the Gulf of Georgia had been foiled. For him an era had ended without ceremony, but for the West Coast fishery as a whole, an era of turmoil had just begun.

American Revenge

On August 31, 1994, the DFO announced that all Canadian salmon fisheries were closed for the balance of the season for conservation reasons. (The only exception was a minor gillnet fishery in Johnstone Strait, which continued until 8:00 a.m. on September 2.) At this point DFO managers claimed there were still enough sockeye left to ensure that optimum escapement targets were met—assuming that the Americans stopped fishing. However, because of Tobin's "aggressive fishing strategy" and the high diversion of the run through Johnstone Strait and wholly Canadian waters, the Americans had had poor catches all season. So now they insisted they would continue to fish until they caught their rightful share, and the sockeye of the Adams River run, which were still lying just across the border off Point Roberts, only a few miles from the river's mouth, were an easy target. US commercial fisheries continued all through the week ending September 3 and into the week of September 10. These included the Washington State Treaty Native fishery, which was open for 113 hours during the week ending September 3 and another 20 hours during the week ending September 10; the non-Native purse-seine fishery, open for 25 hours; the gillnet fishery, open for 30 hours; and the reef net fishery, open for 105 hours. Thus, from August 28 onward, the Americans harvested some 736,500 Fraser River sockeye, a catch that made the difference between a reasonable escapement and a disaster.[5]

When the fish finally entered the river at the end of September, the test fishery revealed that the total 1994 sockeye run was almost 2 million less than predicted. This prompted *Vancouver Sun* reporter Mark Hume to write that the legendary Adams River sockeye run had been "wrecked." A host of so-called fisheries experts—including John Fraser—claimed that the debacle had been caused by "attitudinal anarchy" in the DFO and the "grab-all" behaviour of BC's commercial fishermen. No mention was made of the slaughter just across the international boundary line at Point Roberts. Scores of scientists, "independent" fisheries experts, environmentalists, government officials and journalists clamoured to have the commercial fishing fleet slashed. In response, in 1996 Ottawa introduced the Pacific Salmon Fleet Restructuring Program—generally known as the Mifflin Plan—followed by the Anderson Plan in 1998. In short order, the fleet was reduced by more than half, fishing privileges were concentrated in ever fewer hands, and coastal communities were thrown into profound turmoil.

A Scapegoat Found

In another era, the problems facing BC fishermen might have aroused public sympathy, but not now, on the heels of the East Coast cod collapse, which to many Canadians symbolized the wanton plunder of the natural environment. The participants were seen as looters bent on "fishing the last fish." Consequently, saving "endangered" salmon became a *cause célèbre* for the dominant elites and vilification of commercial fishermen an easy substitute for changing the ways society as a whole threatens the salmon resource. Ottawa claimed it had acted in the name of conservation, but it can be argued that the subsequent dismantling of the West Coast commercial salmon fishery had more to do with the interests of powerful fishing companies than with the health of the resource. Reflecting on the plight of commercial fisheries around the world, as the cultural anthropologist James R. McGoodwin notes: "The major problems in the fisheries today [worldwide] are not the biological depletion of fish stocks, economic overcapitalization, and so forth.

Rather, they are the deleterious consequences of these conditions for the human participants in a fishery...Many fisheries problems are merely a small but connected part of more pervasive problems in the world political and economic order."[6]

This certainly holds true for the West Coast fishing industry: its collapse was caused by government mismanagement, but it was working people, not politicians, who paid the price. And although the turmoil that ensued was often described as the death rattle of an outmoded industry, it was in fact symptomatic of a much greater sickness afflicting our contemporary society.

CHAPTER 2

The Hundred Years War

*I still say the history of Canada is in
shoe boxes under people's beds.*

—Joyce Beaton, *Early Canadian Life*

To comprehend why two countries that claim to enjoy the world's longest undefended border would go to "war" in 1994 over something so seemingly trivial as salmon or how a conservation crisis in a relatively small regional industry could expose the harsh nature of power politics in contemporary Canadian society, one may go back to the earliest days of the West Coast salmon industry.

Silver and Gold:
The Earliest Days of the West Coast Fishery

When gold was discovered in the mountains of California in 1849, western North America was changed irrevocably. According to the eminent British historian Eric Hobsbawm, that discovery was also the spark that exploded the bonds of European mercantilism and thrust the forces of modern industrial capitalism and trade upon the world.[1]

In 1858 another major gold rush occurred in the wilds of colonial British Columbia, and as the miners worked their way up the Fraser River, "they were unaware of the great riches represented in the silvery sockeye, coho, pinks, chum, steelhead, and spring salmon which annually struggled up the same waterway."[2]

Native people have harvested salmon since the beginning of human settlement on the Pacific coast. University of Colorado anthropologist Gordon Hewes estimates that at least half the caloric intake of aboriginal people in the "Pacific Salmon area"—Alaska, BC, the Pacific Northwest and California—was derived from salmon. He calculates that before European contact aboriginal societies consumed approximately 123 million pounds of salmon per year, based on a per capita consumption of 365 pounds[3]—about 15 percent of the modern commercial catch in Hewes' study area.

According to some contemporary writers, traditional aboriginal harvesting customs were a paradigm of resource husbandry, superior to current industrial fishing methods. However, social geographer Martin W. Lewis, in his book *Green Delusions*, provides historical evidence to repudiate this view,[4] and James R. McGoodwin shows that one of the earliest recorded cases of overfishing happened in ancient Peru some three thousand years ago. "Cultures develop as ongoing experiments. Thus there was nothing inherent in pre-industrial cultures assuring that they would live in a state of harmonious equilibrium with nature...Most of the earliest human societies had neither the numbers nor the technology that would have enabled them to deplete all their food resources. So these people's harmonious coexistence with nature seems to have been essentially a consequence of their simple inability to overtax their important ecosystems..."[5] Hewes points out that after European contact, aboriginal societies suffered significant population decline, especially between 1820 and 1860, the period in which the commercial salmon fishery began on the west coast of North America: "The high initial productivity experienced on nearly every salmon stream in the commercial era may therefore be explained in part by the 'resting period' which set in with the sharp drop in the rate of the native subsistence fishing. The subsequent declines in the commercial salmon fisheries (1900–1920) may represent a partial return to fish population levels which had prevailed during the many centuries of aboriginal fishing..."[6]

Mike Shepard and Sandy Argue, in their study *The Commercial Harvest of Salmon in British Columbia, 1820–1877*, state: "Without any agriculture, the traders and their staffs depended on their Indian clients for food and, in particular, on the salmon the Indians dried for their winter existence."[7]

In a study for the International Pacific Salmon Fisheries Commission (IPSFC), Philip Gilhousen reported that the earliest commercial harvests were by Native Indians using dip-nets in the Fraser Canyon. Few sockeye were caught in the river below Hope, "possibly because salmon were so easily dip-netted in the Fraser canyon."[8] Commercial fishing activity changed decisively after the introduction of the drift gillnet, which seems to have been the invention of William Vianen of the Hudson's Bay Company, and which was eventually adopted as the only legal salmon fishing gear.[9]

After British Columbia became a colony in 1858, the Hudson's Bay Company lost its exclusive trade monopoly in the region. This made possible the establishment of the first crude cannery at Annieville in 1865, marking the beginning of the commercial salmon canning industry in BC.

"From this feeble beginning with a total pack of perhaps 1,300 cases of one- and two-pound cans laboriously made by hand and cooked in boiling vats, the industry grew rapidly. Four canners put up 18,719 cases in 1874. A quarter century later in 1901, 73 canners, two-thirds of them on the Fraser, canned a million and a quarter cases, virtually all of it sockeye."[10]

At first the fishery was confined mainly to the mouth of the Fraser River, where a huge fleet of vessels operated. It was hard and dangerous work pulling the heavy linen nets by hand and, judging by the prevalence of labour disputes at the time, not very financially rewarding. Yet by the turn of the century, concern was already being raised about the ability of the resource to sustain such fishing pressure.

Across the border, the first American cannery had been built in 1877 at Mukilteo on Puget Sound. By 1894, canneries had been established at Friday Harbour in the San Juan Islands and Point Roberts, the tiny peninsula that juts across the 49th parallel a few miles south of the Fraser's mouth. Most of Washington state's commercial fishery was dependent on Fraser River stocks.[11]

Point Roberts also became the site of one of the first fish traps in Washington state, and by 1900 there were 13 of them in that area. The fish were caught in vast fence-like nets known as "jiggers" staked out along known salmon migration routes. The Point Roberts trap was linked to a large cannery, so that the fish literally swam to its doorstep. This technology allowed the Americans to intercept the Canadian catch of Fraser salmon, and Canadians began to complain. After years of rancour, the first International Fisheries Commission for Fraser River sockeye was established in 1908, and Canada was represented by two officials from Great Britain. The regulations that were established were to apply for four years, but there was no proviso for "in-season" adjustment in the event of run-size variations.[12] The US senate ratified the treaty, but opposition from Washington state lobbyists led to an impasse, which left Canada no choice but to rescind the deal, a pattern that would recur repeatedly over the next century.

Hells Gate

For millennia the water draining from the 218,400 square km (84,000 square mile) Fraser basin has reached the sea by pounding through one of the longest and narrowest canyons on the continent. Simon Fraser, forced to portage around it on his journey down the river in 1808, called it "the gates of hell" and it became "Hells Gate" to all who came after him. Of necessity, the ancient Native trade routes had followed this canyon, as did the early European explorers whom the Natives guided, and more modern forms of transport. The first of these was the Canadian Pacific Railway (CPR), designed to link British Columbia to the rest of Canada. An American, Andrew Onderdonk, won the contract to build the section that would follow the canyon, and work began there on May 15, 1880. But construction in the canyon caused many landslides, and an unknown amount of rock debris was deliberately dumped into the river. When the Canadian Northern Railway (CNR) began building its own mainline through the canyon in 1913–14, the contractor saved time and money by illegally dumping more rock into the river. Then in February 1914, while a tunnel was being built at the narrowest section of the canyon—a gap only 110 feet wide—a huge landslide occurred that narrowed the channel and changed the water flow. The extent of the damage done by the slide was not fully appreciated until the following year, when an enormous return of sockeye was blocked at the site. In his history of the IPSFC, John Roos notes, "Large numbers of sockeye were observed in creeks and rivers many miles downstream from Hell's Gate... included among the sockeye were large numbers of pink salmon...And the stage was set for a staggering decline in future production."[13] The federal government began to remove the debris and transport salmon above the canyon, but according to Roos, "in eight days of operation only 16,500 sockeye and 850 chinook were captured."[14]

In the area next to the slide, the river had dropped more than 15 vertical feet in a stretch of only 75 feet. Dominion and provincial crews removed some of the rock there, but the rapids still posed a formidable barrier to salmon. Yet John Babcock, provincial fisheries commissioner, cited overfishing as the prime cause of the sudden decline in the stocks, and he advised the government that further repairs at the site were unnecessary.

The Quest for a Treaty

After the Hells Gate slide, in 1917 Canada and the US made another attempt to negotiate a treaty, but despite Canadian approval of a new draft agreement, on October 21, 1919, Washington state officials stonewalled the deal. They complained that US federal negotiators had infringed on the state's constitutional right to control fisheries. The Canadian side then began contemplating retaliatory measures to combat the interception problem. In what John Roos describes as a "bizarre concept," the Canadian government even considered blocking off the southern channels of the Fraser to encourage salmon smolts to adopt northerly migration patterns on their seaward journey.[15] It was believed that adult salmon would thus avoid US waters completely. The plan was never implemented, and during the next decade, despite the industry's near collapse, American purse-seiners moved farther seaward to intercept what few stocks remained. This reduced Canada's share to about one-third of the total catch, which explains why some Canadians were for the first time willing to consider a US proposal to split the catch equally. The two federal governments finally reached a tentative agreement on May 29, 1930, but the treaty was vetoed in the US senate after a fierce lobby by Washington state's Governor Roland Hartley.

After four more years of hostility and declining stocks, BC's Premier Duff Pattullo and Washington state's Governor Clarence D. Martin requested that a conference of eminent scientists and government officials be convened. Several contentious issues were resolved at this conference in Seattle in 1934, including the urgent matter of repairing the damage caused by the Hells Gate slide. Shortly afterwards, Washington state voters voted to ban the use of fish traps, which by this time were accounting for as much as 75 percent of the annual American catch of Fraser River sockeye. This move had as much to do with conserving Washington's resident salmon stocks and appeasing fishermen as it had to do with granting a favour to Canada, but a new spirit of co-operation prevailed, and in 1936 a tentative deal to split the catch of Fraser sockeye on a 50–50 basis was reached. The agreement applied to an area thereafter known as "convention area waters," which included the Strait of Juan de Fuca, the southern portion of the Gulf of Georgia and the Fraser River.

Roos notes that after Washington state's fish traps were eliminated in 1935 the Canadian catch of Fraser sockeye jumped to 83 percent compared to 35 percent the year before, but he points out that the majority of the 1936 sockeye run had by chance gone through Johnstone Strait, not the Strait of Juan de Fuca: "This fortuitous event convinced the Americans that 50/50 was a pretty good deal...Who knows what might have happened if the diversion of 1936 had not occurred or if the US had realized what had happened?"[16] An agreement leading to the establishment of the International Pacific Salmon Fisheries Commission was ratified by both countries on August 4, 1937, and the modern era of fisheries management of the Fraser River's salmon had begun.

Neither side was pleased. The Canadians feared they would lose sovereignty and the Americans would demand increased catches, so federal officials tied the issue of joint salmon enhancement to the idea of catch equity, as they do today. The Americans, on the other hand, were suspicious that Canada would avoid the terms of the agreement by accelerating fishing activity outside the convention area. Nonetheless, to most observers the agreement was better than nothing. Some people on both sides, particularly the American side, believed that artificial propagation of salmon would offset declining stocks. This had been the case on the Columbia River, where it was believed that the building of fish ladders and hatcheries was going to compensate for the negative impact of dozens of hydroelectric dams. A Washington state Department of Fisheries document even declared that these devices, when used carefully, could "provide the reality—salmon without rivers."[17] In the meantime, although many fisheries "experts" still believed overfishing was the prime cause of declining Fraser salmon stocks, an American biologist named Arthur Einarsen was insisting that the Hells Gate slide was the main problem.[18] He did not believe that the slide had been properly cleared, as the Canadian government had claimed, and he had discovered that not all races of Fraser sockeye were declining at the same rate.[19] John Pearse Babcock, the provincial commissioner of fisheries, had also discovered that certain Fraser runs were faring better than others, but he surmised this was the result of some primitive hatcheries the provincial government had constructed. According to Roos, "It appears that he [Babcock] was cognizant of a very important biological distinction but did not fully comprehend the significance of the observation."[20]

Fortunately, the founders of the IPSFC rejected the Washington state "salmon without rivers" approach and insisted that wild salmon could regenerate naturally if the effects of dams, pollution and problems such as Hells Gate could be overcome. Thus, between 1936 and 1944, the primary focus of the IPSFC was habitat restoration and research. This was important, as neither side was prepared to commit fully to the treaty until it was clear all management decisions were based on "science." Indeed, some innovative research was done during this period, including the first comprehensive high-seas salmon-tagging program, which provided valuable insight into the migratory patterns of both juvenile and adult salmon. Above all, the IPSFC played a crucial role in the construction of the Hells Gate fishways in 1944, and Einarsen was able to confirm his theory.

The fishways were enormously successful, and some races of sockeye soon returned to high levels of abundance. However, the Canadian government later regretted its parsimonious decision to split the $1,470,333 cost of the fishways with the American government. For what is a pittance by today's standards, the Americans established a permanent claim on Fraser sockeye and pinks. Catch records show they have reaped hundreds of millions of dollars in return for their initial investment. Thus, it became the policy of subsequent Canadian government officials and industry stakeholders never to participate in a joint salmon enhancement program again.

IPSFC research between 1936 and 1944 led to other important developments. For the first time, scientists studied the complex fresh-water habitat of juvenile sockeye and attempted to determine the optimum carrying capacity of the lakes and river systems that produced the various runs, and some came to believe that salmon runs, especially sockeye, could be engineered to unprecedented levels to become a renewable source of industrial wealth. Today most fisheries managers are less enthusiastic about this, believing that the engineering of runs for commercial purposes poses a serious threat to the biodiversity of any river system. For one thing, enhanced runs are suspected of competing with and displacing other wild stocks. As well, commercial fisheries on large enhanced runs sometimes lead to "weak stock" management concerns due to the increased harvest rates.[21]

However, the IPSFC concluded that over-escapement could be as damaging to stocks as under-escapement. Indeed, it had been found in some cases escapements resulted in substantially lower brood-year returns. The dominant view on the subject of establishing optimum escapement goals was pioneered by W.E. Ricker, who believed that the spawning targets of all runs should be increased gradually until its natural productivity limit was reached, whereupon the stock rebuilding curve would "break."[22] Ricker's theory would be later taken in an unintended direction by politicians who believed that runs of salmon could be rebuilt at minimal cost by severely restricting commercial harvests.

After the Hells Gate fishways were finally constructed in 1944, three decades after the slide, the Fraser sockeye runs began the long process of recovery. By this time World War II was about to end, ushering in 30 years of unprecedented economic growth. At the same time, Canada was about to make permanent changes to its economy. The Abbott Plan, crafted by the federal finance minister of the day, committed Canada to closer economic ties with the US. Certainly the influence of the IPSFC on domestic fisheries management was consistent with the increasingly continentalist nature of Canadian affairs.

Ever since the Dutch jurist Hugo Grotius had published his opus *Mare Liberum* (Freedom of the Seas) in 1609, it had been assumed that the world's oceans were an inexhaustible source of bounty, free for all nations to exploit as they saw fit. This belief was reinforced after World War II, when global fish stocks reached levels of great abundance after a major hiatus in world fishing activity during the war.

There was, however, an extraordinary increase in demand for protein at this time. Local fisheries could not meet it, and "distant water" fishing fleets were established. Many nations took part in the high-seas fishery, which was dominated by Japan and the USSR. But these fisheries posed a serious threat to the stocks, and in 1945 US President Harry Truman declared sovereignty over the high seas contiguous to the coasts of the US, ostensibly to protect fish stocks. Even before the war, American fishermen had complained about the Japanese interception of salmon originating at Bristol Bay, north of the Aleutian Islands, and now the problem intensified. By 1951 the Japanese salmon catch was estimated to be 4.4 million, and it climbed to a staggering 52 million by 1957. Homer Stevens, then secretary-treasurer of the UFAWU, declared, "Obviously they are taking somebody's salmon and the figures indicate that some of it is ours."[23]

In 1952 despite overlapping claims with Canada over fisheries within the continental shelf zone, the US joined with Canada in establishing the International North Pacific Fisheries Commission (INPFC), which also included Japan. For the first time, as part of both the IPSFC and the INPFC, Canada enjoyed a measure of certainty in the management of its fish stocks. In theory, members of the INPFC could not intercept stocks fully used by another country (the Abstention Principle), or fisheries undergoing conservation or rebuilding programs (the Conservation Principle). Both principles were later enshrined in the United Nations Convention on Law of the Sea. However, establishment of the INPFC did not stop US interception of Canadian salmon, nor did it control interceptions by non-INPFC nations. George North notes, "As early as 1946 the UFAWU was campaigning for the 12-mile limit, calling on the federal government to establish offshore fishing zones over which Canada would have full jurisdiction."[24]

The Pink Salmon Accord of 1956

The 1937 IPSFC agreement had limited the American interception of Fraser sockeye, but no measures were in place to protect other species or stocks elsewhere on the coast, and during the 1950s the American interception of the Fraser's prolific pink salmon became a matter of acute concern. Pinks are deemed to be of lesser value because of the quick deterioration of the flesh, but they are good for canning, and in the early years of the fishery, canners had realized their greatest profit margin from pinks, which they always bought from fishermen at very low prices. After the Hells Gate slide, pink salmon stocks had declined, but they had rebounded much faster than the sockeye because of their two-year spawning cycle and higher rate of productivity. Since then the American seine fleet had dominated the harvest of pinks, taking 70 percent of the catch in convention waters between 1945 and 1951.[25] James Sinclair, Canada's fisheries minister, set out to make changes. He believed a fish war was the only way to force the Americans to limit the interception of Fraser pinks, and by 1953, at his behest, Canadian fishermen were taking 47 percent of the convention pink catch in the Strait of Juan de Fuca seine fishery.

Sinclair's aggressive approach dovetailed nicely with the interests of the canners, who had invested in an expanded seine fleet suitable for fishing farther offshore. Naturally this did not sit well with Canadian gillnetters based in the Fraser River. The UFAWU tried to play a mediating role between the various competing interests. According to George North:

> The union arranged an historic three-hour meeting [on April 19, 1955] at White Rock, attended by 148 representatives of salmon fishermen and vessel owners from both sides of the border. While US seine boat owners blocked united action on the principle of equal catch division, the meeting set in motion the movement which culminated in the "protocol" under which the International Pacific Salmon Commission is responsible for conservation, rehabilitation, and equal catch division of Fraser pink runs…The policy favoured by

James Sinclair as Minister of Fisheries of out-fishing the Americans by moving out into the Pacific was never endorsed by the UFAWU, which saw the danger this posed for salmon stocks. In fact, the union wanted a return to the river fishery on which so many old-time fishermen depended.[26]

Nevertheless, a new IPSFC pink salmon protocol was finally signed on July 3, 1957, by acting External Affairs Minister Davie Fulton. It assured each country an equal share of the Fraser pink catch in convention area waters. Here, as in almost every "fish war" conducted by Canada, maximizing the catch has taken precedence over allocating it to the various fleets. This has led to internal disputes that undermined the Canadian effort. The IPSFC protocol of 1957 was no exception; once again the DFO failed to balance the catch within the Canadian fleet, and the infighting escalated.

The Surfline Agreement of 1957

As vessel design and technology improved, the fleets of both Canada and the USA continued to move farther seaward, and each country deployed vessels in the territory of the other. In 1957 the two governments agreed to what later became known as the Surfline Agreement, which restricted all net fishing inside of a line running point to point along the outermost headlands of the continent. During the negotiations Alaska claimed it needed more time to determine the precise coordinates of the line. Alaska became a state in 1959, and drew the line three miles seaward of the point-to-point line agreed to by Canada, arguing that it was a state's right under the US constitution to regulate all waters out to the three-mile limit. Although the other northwest states chose not to go this route, the Alaskans initiated major intercepting fisheries off Noyes Island at the lower end of the panhandle, where many returning Fraser River and northern BC salmon sometimes make "landfall" on their return from the north Pacific. Canada complained but nothing was ever done, and the Noyes Island seine fishery later became a major flashpoint.

Despite these aggravations, the two countries continued to jointly promote the basic principles of the United Nations Convention on Law of the Sea (UNCLOS), particularly Article 66, which declares that "States in whose rivers anadromous stocks originate shall have the primary interest in and responsibility for such stocks."

After the 12-mile limit was established in 1970, the US expelled Canadian trollers from the waters of Washington and Oregon, and BC halibut fishermen lost access to the Gulf of Alaska. Concurrently, Canadian fishermen demanded Ottawa reduce the US take of Fraser sockeye and pinks, not only for reasons of equity but because British Columbia had sacrificed the enormous hydroelectric potential of the Fraser to protect its salmon runs. It was understandable that W.A.C. Bennett, Social Credit premier of BC, would resurrect the plan to build the Moran Dam, just upstream from Lillooet, but a vast coalition of conservation, wildlife and commercial fishing groups—including the UFAWU, a leading voice—fought the proposal to a standstill.

Without doubt, the threat of the Moran Dam highlighted the importance of Fraser River salmon for the commercial industry in both countries. Washington state was reaping the financial benefits of the Columbia hydro-dams, but the dams had devastated the salmon runs and the commercial fishermen had come to depend on Canadian salmon.

In 1970 Canada stepped up efforts to negotiate a new reciprocal salmon interception agreement. The Liberal majority government's plan for a major initiative, the Salmom Enhancement Program (SEP) as part of the recently announced Davis Plan made it even more urgent to apply interception controls.

In their official history of the PST, Shepard and Argue note, "Negotiations for a new treaty began in March 1971. By June 1 of that year, negotiators from the two countries had agreed upon a set of *ad referendum*, principles that they hoped would provide a framework for the future relationships regarding salmon interceptions." The basic principles were:

> a)...each country should fish the salmon bound for its own rivers and should seek to avoid interception of salmon bound for their rivers of origin in the other country.

b) Recognizing, however, that it is not possible to harvest some stocks without at the same time catching salmon bound for rivers of the other country…it is agreed that there shall be an equitable balance between the interceptions by the two countries…It is further agreed that this equitable balance should be achieved, where possible, by reducing rather than by increasing interceptions, and that each country shall seek to make adjustments in the techniques and economics of its fisheries which will make reduction of interceptions possible. These adjustments must take into consideration the overriding requirements of conservation.[27]

But all efforts to finalize a new treaty failed, and another decade of strife began.

The Lynnwood Accord

Hopes for a new treaty were revived in 1981 with the signing of yet another framework agreement that became known as the "Lynnwood Accord." It was little more than a reiteration of the principles of 1971, but it did result in a series of interim arrangements to limit interceptions during the 1981 and 1982 seasons, and the two countries hoped to convert it into a lasting comprehensive treaty. Once again Alaska served as the spoiler in the negotiations, with the new governor demanding that a special advisory committee examine the draft treaty. There was also considerable resistance to the draft agreement in BC, whose fishermen believed they had been cheated out of the long-sought goal of equity.

Another setback occurred in November 1983, when scientists announced that chinook stocks throughout the Pacific coast were on the verge of extinction. Efforts to save the chinooks would depend on the co-operation of Alaska, which intercepts stocks originating in BC, Washington, Oregon, and Idaho rivers. But Alaska balked, and the tentative deal on the treaty collapsed. The northwest states were loath to conserve and enhance chinook runs simply to have them caught by Canadian fishermen, and Canada would reduce its interception of salmon bound for the northwest states only in exchange for an equivalent reduction in Alaskan interceptions.

The chinook crisis of the early 1980s was a difficult period for BC commercial fishermen. In 1981 the DFO banned gillnetting for chinooks on the Fraser River, and had imposed an area-licensing provision in the Gulf of Georgia that severely curtailed access by most trollers and combination boats to Gulf of Georgia and Fraser River chinook. In addition, trollers had to use a limited number of lines and catch a limited size of chinooks. On the other hand, for virtually the first time, sports fishermen were required to accept some restrictions.

The Fish War of 1983

The man responsible for carrying out the huge chinook conservation program was Wayne Shinners. Born, raised and educated in the Maritimes, Shinners had worked in biochemistry in the DFO's Halifax research laboratory. He then moved into the field of fisheries management, and soon became the director of field services, maritime region. A few years later he transferred laterally to direct field services for BC and the Yukon. He knew very little about the West Coast fishery but was excited by the challenge.[28]

The situation Shinners inherited would have been a test for the most battle-hardened West Coast bureaucrat, let alone a neophyte from the east. Not only were commercial fishermen opposed to the chinook conservation plan, but the anger of sports fishermen had been aroused as well. They had daily catch limits and a four-month winter closure, and he also told them that it wasn't particularly "sporting" to use commercial gear in the recreational pursuit of chinook. A great number of recreational fishermen

Wayne Shinners, Pacific Regional Director of DFO, 1983.

were employing the latest technological gadgetry, including high-speed seaworthy vessels, radar and sonar. Of particular concern was the use of "down-riggers," power winches that permit the easy deployment of several lines to almost any depth. (A ban placed on them at this time was later rescinded, so long as quick-release mechanisms were employed to release undersized chinooks.)

The owner of the Oak Bay Marine Group, Bob Wright—nicknamed "Mad-Dog" by many in the industry—emerged as the champion of the sports fishing sector. Having built a multimillion-dollar sports fishing empire, he understood backroom politics, and he travelled to Ottawa on several occasions to lobby cabinet ministers and other powerful figures. At one point, he became so irate about the restrictions imposed on the recreational sector that he threatened to lead "250,000 bedouins" in a war against the DFO.[29]

While fending off this sort of pressure at home, Shinners also had to lead the Canadian delegation at IPSFC negotiations. There was no agreement in place for the 1983 Fraser sockeye fishery, and a lot was at stake. When Shinners demanded that the Americans accept a permanent reduction in the interception of BC salmon, they refused and instead asked for more. And when he warned that the DFO would intervene to prevent the bycatch of endangered chinooks in any IPSFC-managed sockeye fisheries, everyone at the table was astounded, including IPSFC staff, who generally managed sockeye and pink fisheries in isolation from other stocks.

Shortly after that, Bill Wilkerson, who led the American delegation, refused to curtail the American catch of chinook, and Shinners declared, "If you fish, then we're going fishing, too!" The Americans had heard such threats before and knew that Ottawa usually backed down, but Shinners was not bluffing. He intended to put pressure on the Americans by having the Canadian fleet catch as many Fraser sockeye as possible before they entered US waters. However, it was one thing to deprive the Americans of sockeye and quite another to do it without jeopardizing endangered chinooks. And it would be profoundly challenging to conduct a fish war while satisfying the conservation and allocation demands of all Canadian stakeholders. Nonetheless, Shinners authorized a major escalation in Canada's outside troll fishery, and the trollers' sockeye catch climbed to the highest percentage level in history. Meanwhile, the seine fleet was enjoying mediocre catches, and the gillnetters—especially those in the Fraser River—had their lowest catch on record. When all the smoke had cleared, Canada had achieved its primary goal: the Americans had been held to only 469,000 sockeye out of a total catch of 3,886,000, their lowest catch percentage in history.

Shinners' gambit had a great impact on the northwest states, though it was helped by the fact that the Northwest Treaty Tribes had at the same time launched a lawsuit designed to shut down Alaskan interceptions of chinooks. Not long after, the US government returned to the bargaining table, and during the winter of 1983–84 a comprehensive agreement was finally reached.

Nowadays, the term "fish wars" has strong negative connotations, especially with environmental lobby groups. Canada's diplomatic approach had proved completely unsuccessful. In the final analysis, had Shinners not taken a combative stance in 1983, Pacific chinook would likely be much closer to extinction today.

Fish Wars and Missing Salmon

It is not accidental that the fishery has been, and remains, Canada's most contentious foreign affairs issue.

—Michael Harris, *Lament for an Ocean*

When US President Ronald Reagan and Prime Minister Brian Mulroney met in Quebec City on March 18, 1985, an array of agreements was announced with great fanfare. Reduced trade tariffs, a new air transport agreement, revised copyright laws and a new Pacific Salmon Treaty were all initiatives that paved the way for the controversial Canada–US free trade agreement (FTA) that was signed by Mulroney in 1988. The media hailed this "Shamrock Summit" as a great day for Canada and swooned when the two leaders and their wives locked arms and sang "When Irish Eyes Are Smiling," with Mulroney singing the lead solo. It was in this atmosphere that the Pacific Salmon Treaty (PST) was signed. Perhaps caught up in the excitement and bonhomie, federal Fisheries Minister John Fraser put his signature on the US side of the treaty, foreshadowing the tumult and humiliation that lay ahead.[1] The Mulroney Tories hoped the new deal would mark the beginning of an era of co-operative salmon management, but in its infringements of the PST, the US repeatedly abused its "special relationship" with Canada.

The Terms of the New Treaty

The principles of the Pacific Salmon Treaty, although few, are rich in significance. Many tenets of the voluminous statutes of the United Nations Convention on Law of the Sea (UNCLOS), including the conservation, abstention and ownership or equity principles, are contained in the PST. For example, Article III, the equity principles, states that each of the two countries shall be entitled to receive the benefits of an amount of salmon equivalent to that originating in its own waters.

The PST provides for the establishment of two national sections, which meet regularly under the auspices of an independent bilateral secretariat called the Pacific Salmon Commission (PSC). Each country appoints four commissioners and four alternates to the PSC. In addition, three sub-panels oversee the bilateral aspects of fisheries in the north, south and Fraser River regions. The initial regional annexes were established for eight years (1985–92), to allow the parties to evaluate the treaty's effectiveness over two successive four-year spawning cycles. In addition, an assortment of joint scientific working groups was established. The PST dealt with all five species of Pacific salmon: chinook, coho, sockeye, pink and chum.

Under the auspices of the southern panel, Canada's troll catch off the west coast of Vancouver Island was limited to 360,000 chinooks and 1.8 million coho each year, a significant reduction—Canadian trollers had taken over 2.2 million coho off the west coast of Vancouver Island just one year earlier. Under the Fraser panel, Washington state net fisheries were granted a fixed annual percentage (about 25 percent) of the Fraser River sockeye and pink catches during the first four years (1985–89). This formula was based on past American catch levels and a recognition of the US contribution to recent Fraser River enhancement programs, whose results had yet to come on stream. Thus, in the southern panel area the arrangements constituted a sort of rough equity balance since BC fishermen intercepted chinook and coho bound for the US and Washington state fishermen intercepted Fraser River stocks. But on a coast-wide basis the PST came nowhere close to ensuring that Canada would receive its share. In fact, at the time the PST was signed, Ottawa estimated the annual interception imbalance favoured the US by at least 1.5 million "sockeye equivalents."(The DFO uses the average value of a sockeye as the standard

45

measurement unit for all other species landed in a given season.) However, because the two sides never agreed on a method of calculating interception value, Canadian estimates were always rejected by the US.

The Americans complained when their percentage of the Fraser River catch appeared to decline under the new treaty, but the new Fraser panel covered the harvest of Fraser sockeye "wherever caught," instead of the former IPSFC method of only counting the catch taken in the old convention area of Puget Sound, the lower Gulf of Georgia and the Strait of Juan de Fuca. The Americans had a smaller percentage but of a bigger piece of the pie.

Nonetheless, to safeguard their position the Canadian negotiators insisted that a different sharing formula apply during the second four years (1989–92) of the Fraser panel's eight-year agreement. The Americans were allocated 7 million sockeye instead of the usual fixed annual percentage, guaranteeing their catch regardless of any fluctuations in the stocks during that period. If the Fraser runs stayed at 1985 levels—20 to 30 million sockeye over a four-year cycle—there would be little difference between the 7 million "cap" and an annual percentage. In fact, when the deal was first signed, American negotiators boasted that they had secured the better deal.[2]

Canadian negotiators believed that the cap was a strategic victory for Canada, because this country could reap the exclusive benefit of all increases above the American limit. DFO biologists believed that Fraser sockeye runs could be enhanced to produce 60–90 million sockeye during each four-year cycle, and at first they appeared to be right. Sockeye runs improved dramatically over the next few years, reaching nearly 60 million between 1986 and 1991. The fact that BC fishermen and shore-workers were enhancing those runs by forgoing significant earnings was never understood by the public, especially after adverse ocean conditions in the late 1990s caused a temporary downturn in the stocks.[3]

Everything hinged on escapement goals, and the PST granted Canada the exclusive right to determine the escapement goals for Fraser salmon after 1985. Before the PST, the four-year (1981–1984) cumulative escapement of spawners had been 7.4 million. But during the treaty years of 1985–88, that number climbed to 9.6 million. Between 1989 and 1992 it soared to 12.3 million, almost double the pre-treaty levels. This was made possible by the use of "escapement add-ons" and/or increased escapements through reduced harvests. Had a strict percentage-sharing formula been in place as it was between 1989 and 1992, the Americans would have harvested an additional 1.5 million in 1989, 1.3 million in 1990, 1.4 million in 1991 and 600,000 in 1992—facts that were not lost on the fishermen of Washington state.

Meanwhile, on the North Coast the provisions of the 1985 PST agreement were more nebulous than in the south. The northern panel was assigned to oversee Canadian troll fisheries in Dixon Entrance, Canadian net fisheries directed at Nass and Skeena river stocks, Canadian fisheries on passing Alaskan stocks and several Alaskan fisheries targeting Canadian stocks. The northern panel was also responsible for the trans-boundary fisheries on the rivers that intersect the eastern coast of the Alaska panhandle. Although these rivers—which include the Stikine, Taku and Alsek—lie mostly in BC, under the PST Canada gained almost no equity credit for their production because they flow into the sea just inside Alaskan territory, and the vast majority of the salmon originating in them are taken by Alaskan fishermen.

However, despite its many shortcomings, the PST did for the first time ensure a limit on some of the key intercepting fisheries in the northern boundary area. For example, both Alaskan and Canadian fisheries were held to a harvest of 263,000 chinooks per year in the northern panel area. Canada also agreed to limit its catch of Alaskan pink salmon to approximately 1.9 million pieces each year, despite the fact its own production of pink salmon was increasing.

However, relatively few restrictions were imposed on the Alaskan interception of BC stocks. By virtue of its geographical location and the fact that most Pacific salmon stocks migrate in a southerly direction, Alaska was well positioned to intercept many stocks bound for both BC and the northwestern states. The equity clause (Article III) clearly says that each country should manage its fisheries to avoid interceptions, but the Alaskans continually avoided this by citing an obscure PST provision that "traditional fisheries" not be unduly disrupted. The US federal government was unwilling to upset the Alaskans by enforcing the agreement and the Alaskan government maintained that federal law gave it veto power over all provisions of the PST.

From a Canadian perspective, the one significant benefit of the northern annex was the agreement to limit the Alaskan seine fishery in District 104 (Noyes Island) near the southern tip of the Alaskan panhandle to 120,000 sockeye (all of Canadian origin) before the end of July each year. Assuming that most Canadian sockeye would be clear of District 104 by the end of July, Canadian officials placed no limitations on Alaskan fishermen in that area after July. But ocean conditions changed after the PST was signed, altering the migration schedule of many salmon stocks. Increasing numbers of BC salmon passed through Alaskan waters later in the season and became vulnerable to Alaskan interception.

When the new Pacific Salmon Treaty was first signed, the UFAWU pointed out that it failed to achieve Canada's long-standing goal of catch equity. In response, Canada's negotiators acknowledged the PST's shortcomings. They explained that the initial annexes had been the best that Canada could achieve at that time, and described them as temporary "bridging measures" that would lead to full equity in the future. In fact, a separate Memorandum of Understanding (MOU) on Equity, attached to the 1985 agreement, obliged the two parties to negotiate and implement Article III—the equity clause—before the eight-year annexes expired. Jack Nichol, president of the UFAWU, rejected Ottawa's claim that future salmon enhancement programs would compensate Canada for past American interceptions. He warned, "I'm sure that in a few years the Americans will come along and make further demands for more fish and we'll give in again and say to everyone: 'Well, that's the best we could do,' just like we did this time."[4] Paddy Greene of the Prince Rupert Fishermen's Cooperative, one of the new Canadian commissioners, was critical that Alaskan fisheries were largely exempt from the terms of the new treaty. Although the provisions of the PST dramatically reduced the traditional troll catch on the west coast of Vancouver Island, the Pacific Trollers Association (PTA)—which always maintained close ties with the DFO—approved the deal. Ron Fowler, vice-president of the PTA, said, "We've needed a treaty for a long time. Neither side was interested in enhancement as long as the other side might take the fish. Now we can rebuild our stocks." Rather than joining the UFAWU, which had launched a campaign to scrap the PST, the leaders of the PTA decided to struggle for a bigger share of the Canadian allocation. "What we're doing," explained Fowler, "is looking to make up the shortfall by catching pink and sockeye in the Fraser."[5] On the American side—despite loud complaints—Alaska Governor Bill Sheffield acknowledged, "This is far better than those negotiations two years ago..."

The PST became a victim of its own success even before the first eight-year annexes had expired. Increased Canadian salmon production between 1985 and 1992, combined with a serious decline in Washington state chinook and coho stocks, prompted the Americans to take more than their share of Fraser River salmon, and in spring 1992 Canada warned the US that its four-year 7-million-sockeye cap had already been taken in the previous three years, so the Americans could take only 360,000 sockeye in the 1992 season. American officials made it plain they intended to take twice that amount, even though the run was forecast to be very weak. Washington state complained that growing interceptions in southeast Alaska, primarily in District 104, had inflated US catch totals at Washington state's expense. Canadian officials reminded them that the PST obliged them to count all Fraser River sockeye "wherever caught." The Alaskans shrugged off the issue, though the catch of Fraser sockeye in District 104 had gone from a four-year average of 7,075 during 1985–88 to 151,000 in 1989–92.[6]

The dispute was complicated by the US government's legal obligation to ensure that the Northwest Treaty Indian tribes were allocated 50 percent of the catch in Washington state waters. The state claimed that the 7-million cap upset its ability to satisfy both the tribal fishery and the all-citizens fisheries. The tribes, meanwhile, refused to reduce their catch to accommodate the US government's obligation to Canada under the PST. Instead, they suggested the all-citizens fishery be reduced. Canadian officials pointed out that this US internal allocation problem should not be allowed to override the terms of the PST, but during the 1992 fishing season Washington state allowed the 7-million sockeye cap to be exceeded by 361,000 pieces—and, at the same time, asked Canada to cut back its treaty share of US-bound chinook and coho for conservation reasons.

Thus, the 1992 season, which ended the first eight-year period of the PST, concluded with the Fraser River annex of the PST in a shambles and the Canadian government vowing to demand repayment of the unauthorized catch. As it turned out, the debt was never repaid.

On Skipper John's Watch

When the Americans breached the terms of the Pacific Salmon Treaty in the summer of 1992, John Carnell Crosbie—or "Skipper John" as the author Michael Harris nicknamed him—was Canada's minister of fisheries. Despite his reputation in Canadian politics as the rowdy man from the "Rock," Crosbie did not leap into a rumble with the Yankees over West Coast salmon. Indeed, he had enough problems back home. On December 18, 1992, he had announced that the northern cod fishery—the mainstay of Atlantic Canada for almost 500 years—was to be

Tory Fisheries Minister John Crosbie confronted by UFAWU protestors, 1992.

completely closed. It was the end of a fishery that produced 20 percent of the GDP of the Atlantic region, employed 100,000 people and supported 1,500 communities.[7] As Richard Cashin, former leader of the Newfoundland Fisheries, Food and Allied Workers Union, put it, "We are dealing with a famine of biblical scale—a great destruction."[8]

The first signs of decline in the northern cod stocks had been detected in the 1980s, yet the offshore trawl fleet had continued to expand, and the number of processing plants increased from 109 in 1974 to over 220 in 1981, 167 of them for groundfish alone. In fact, during the four years between 1983 and 1987, the freezer capacity for groundfish had grown by over 40 percent.[9] Michael Harris dubbed it "the ecological disaster of the century [and] the political scandal of a decade."[10] Inshore fishermen blamed the offshore trawlers, the provinces blamed the DFO and Ottawa blamed the provinces for subsidy programs that encouraged too many participants in fishery. It was even suggested that the root of the crisis went back to the early 1960s, when Premier Joey Smallwood introduced his schemes to "modernize" the fishery, and Ottawa encouraged him because it was a way to promote regional development while asserting sovereignty within Canada's 200-mile exclusive economic zone.[11]

Tom Siddon was federal fisheries minister in January 1990 when the first cuts in the northern cod total annual catch (TAC) were announced, from 235,000 to 197,000 tonnes.[12] The reduction would have been greater had not Crosbie persuaded Siddon to resist the even harsher cuts proposed by some DFO scientists. "We couldn't suddenly cut the TAC by more than half," Crosbie wrote later in his memoirs. "If we did, for historic and political reasons, we would have had to give priority to inshore fishermen or accept the death of their communities. Cutting the TAC overnight would have wiped out the offshore fishery...We were walking a very thin line between scientific advice and economic reality.[13]

Bernard Valcourt, who succeeded Siddon as fisheries minister, provided $584 million in aid in 1990 through the Northern Cod Assistance and Readjustment Program (NCARP) to Atlantic Canada and Quebec. But Crosbie, after being set upon by an angry crowd of fishermen in Bay Bulls, Newfoundland, on July 1, 1992, threatened to quit the Tory cabinet if more aid was not forthcoming. Mulroney agreed to it for fear of losing every Tory vote in Atlantic Canada.

A year later Crosbie, now fisheries minister himself, found himself grappling with the true magnitude of the northern cod stocks decline. So, when efforts to renegotiate the Pacific Salmon Treaty broke down on June 18, 1993, he had little time for the problem. He told the *Vancouver Sun*, "They wanted us to give with respect to coho and other stocks on their way to Washington state, and after we had done that they wanted us to give them the right to take more Fraser River sockeye."[14] David Johnson, US consul general, retaliated by announcing, "We will be fishing at what level we believe is an appropriate level, not at what Canada believes is an appropriate level." As it turned out, that "appropriate level" was 28 percent of the 1993 Fraser sockeye run. This marked a return to annual percentage-sharing (eliminated in the 1985 sockeye cap) and escalation of American catch averages—the 1993 sockeye return was forecast to be one of the best in history.

Ambassador Fortier Appointed

"Skipper John," preoccupied with the East Coast cod crisis, now turned to Yves Fortier to sort out the PST mess. Fortier had served as Canada's ambassador to the United Nations and a member of the Security Council, and he had successfully handled two fisheries arbitrations for Canada. Crosbie planned to have him conduct negotiations between federal governments to get around the de facto veto that various state authorities were wielding at the Pacific Salmon Commission.

In May 1993 Fortier met with David Colson of the US State Department, and after more than 30 days of meetings and negotiations, they agreed on a controversial interim deal for the 1993 season. Washington state's 7-million sockeye cap would be lifted. A new system, known as marginal sharing, gave the Americans 20 percent of the total Fraser River catch if the run was between zero and 12.06 million. If the run was between 12.06 million and 15 million, they would receive 2.412 million plus 10 percent of any incremental allowable catch. And if the run exceeded 15 million, they would receive 2.7 million plus 5 percent of any incremental catch to a limit of 2.8 million. The Americans were jubilant, as this was a giant step closer to the open-ended sharing of Fraser sockeye that they had surrendered in the 1985 treaty. But Fortier attached an important caveat to this interim arrangement, warning Colson that he did not want to make any more short-term temporary arrangements without making significant progress on the long-term equity question, as agreed in the MOU in 1985. In this context the term *equity* implied that American interceptions would be reduced to allow Canada to receive benefits equivalent to the production of salmon originating in its waters. Fortier pointed out that Canada had reduced its interceptions to help resolve the US's problems with chinook and coho stocks, but that "it would not be equitable to look to Canada, and Canada only, to solve those problems...The essence of the Treaty is not that problems encountered by one nation should be solved exclusively by the other nation." He added, "We will find solutions more easily if we don't leave the equity principle dangling up there in the air...until the 21st century."[15]

The 1993 season passed without Fortier making progress on the matter of long-term equity. In the election of October 25, 1993, Jean Chretien's Liberals slaughtered the Conservatives, led by Mulroney's successor Kim

Campbell, and won 166 seats and 43 percent of the popular vote. However, in British Columbia the Liberals took only six seats and the Reform Party won 24. Chretien appointed Brian Tobin, a Newfoundlander, as the new federal minister of fisheries. This minister, like others, turned his attention first to the East Coast. With John Crosbie's extension on the Northern Cod Assistance and Readjustment Program (NCARP) about to expire and hundreds of East Coast fishing communities in chaos, Tobin needed some way to deflect the political heat. On March 15, 1994, he announced he would enforce the Coastal Fisheries Protection Act passed in the House of Commons two days earlier, an act that gave Canada the right to protect its endangered fish stocks from "foreign pirates" beyond the 200-mile territorial limit. After the introduction of the limit, foreign fishing had been confined to two small areas of the Grand Banks known as the "nose" and the "tail," outside the Canadian boundary. Now the DFO claimed this was a vital nursery zone for "straddling stocks" of turbot and insisted that all foreign fishing there should stop.

Brian and the Pirates

The test case was a rusted, storm-battered trawler called the *Kristina Logos*. For more than a month her Portuguese crew had been setting their gear in the frigid swells of the North Atlantic just 365 km (228 miles) off the east coast of Newfoundland, doing backbreaking, dangerous work in indescribably foul living conditions. Then, on April 3, 1994, two armed Canadian patrol vessels appeared on the horizon and escorted Captain Antonio Tavaras and his crew of 22 back to St. John's, Newfoundland. The *Kristina Logos* was discovered to be carrying more than 100 tonnes of frozen cod, turbot and redfish—all considered endangered species by the DFO—valued at $250,000.

The "foreign pirates" were a hapless group of exploited Portuguese crewmen fishing for endangered Canadian fish on a trawler flying a Panamanian flag but owned by Ulybel Enterprises of Medway, Nova Scotia, whose primary shareholder was Jose Pratas. The DFO had been monitoring its activity for months and, upon learning that the ship had been improperly registered in Panama, had taken action. As a Canadian citizen, Jose Pratas now faced charges under Canadian law for illegally fishing during a conservation closure. "The pirates are the boys in the blue suits who sit in the corporate boardrooms and own these vessels," said Fisheries Minister Brian Tobin with satisfaction. His words were warmly received by both outport fishermen and media pundits. On April 1, 1994, the *Globe and Mail* reported, "In the seizure of the vessel in international waters on Saturday the Chretien government fired a shot across the bow of those flouting the cod moratorium and sent a signal to Newfoundlanders that it takes their plight seriously."

There was, however, a major legal technicality: the *Kristina Logos* had not been fishing in Canadian waters when it was arrested. For years Canada had been using diplomatic channels to press for an international consensus to control fishing outside the 200-mile limit, and the Northwest Atlantic Fisheries Organization (NAFO) was poised to lower the total turbot catch there from 60,000 tonnes to 27,000 tonnes. Tobin, however, had convinced a narrow majority of NAFO members to agree to a larger Canadian quota at the expense of the European fleets. Then, just as a 16-year diplomatic effort to negotiate a new multilateral agreement was about to enter the critical stage, Tobin ordered that the *Kristina Logos* be seized, and in one fell swoop aroused the anger of the international fishing community.

When Evelyn Meltzer, a Halifax-based law of the sea expert, questioned Tobin's abandonment of the traditional diplomatic approach, he replied, "We have conducted diplomacy down to the last few pounds of fish."[16] In response, John Beck, the European Union's ambassador to Canada, warned that any attempt to harass European vessels outside the 200-mile limit would be "dangerous." Meanwhile, although the "famine of biblical proportions" continued for East Coast cod fishermen, Tobin claimed that outport residents were giving thanks over their Easter supper for his bold arrest of the "pirates."

UBC sociologist Ralph Matthews believes that Tobin's unilateral move was more than a desire to protect endangered fish. Today's politicians, he says, operate in a "risk society" culture, and that unlike the sovereigns of old, they must constantly justify their claim to and use of power because they are no longer trusted. Matthews contends that "there is a growing belief that society is the enemy of the environment," and that "In Canada as elsewhere, pro-environmentalism is rapidly becoming the dominant 'moral' ideology taught in our schools, serving increasingly like a state religion..."

Normally governments resist such powerful popular convictions. But when the Canadian state suffered a profound crisis of legitimacy after the collapse of the northern cod stock, Brian Tobin's actions, Matthews suggests, "constituted one of the first times that a modern nation state has used the 'risk society' mentality of post-modern society for its own power interests rather than being on the defensive with respect to that mentality." More simply put, pious platitudes about endangered species or the environment can be good for political ratings. Certainly a talented politician like Brian Tobin sensed both the political threat and the opportunity posed by the northern cod collapse. He diverted public attention from the DFO's mismanagement of the domestic fishery by focusing on the threat of foreign overfishing, and the Canadian state, according to Matthews, gave "itself permission to engage in such actions by appealing to its moral rights to protect nature. In doing so, it used, not the legal courts, but the 'theatre of public opinion.'" The incident, says Matthews, marked a dramatic shift in Canada's approach to fisheries diplomacy. The DFO's domestic policy goals would no longer be "aimed at ensuring marginal employment for the largest number of people"; instead, the DFO would be increasingly driven by the imperatives of "environmental politics."[17]

Captain Canada Rattles His Sabre

While Brian Tobin was becoming a national celebrity in Atlantic Canada, the quest to renegotiate the Pacific Salmon Treaty was reaching a hopeless impasse. The various bilateral panels of the PSC had been meeting all through the winter of 1993–94 but had failed to agree, and Yves Fortier broke off negotiations in May 1994. He turned to Ottawa for direction, and Brian Tobin took personal responsibility for the file. On May 27 Tobin and David Zirnhelt, BC's minister of fisheries, travelled to Washington, DC, in an attempt to break the PST log-jam. That same week, US president Bill Clinton had declared the salmon fishery in Washington and Oregon a natural disaster and provided $15.7 million in relief to US coastal communities. Tobin and Zirnhelt believed this crisis offered an important opportunity to jump-start the PST talks. "This is a last ditch attempt to get them to the realization that the best hope for conservation is a treaty," explained Zirnhelt.[18]

However, Tobin and Zirnhelt came home empty-handed. "I'm beat, beat, beat," Tobin told reporters. "We made no progress. It's impossible—the US has no unified negotiating position." As for working out another "one-off" interim deal with Washington state as in 1993, Tobin curtly replied, "We don't negotiate with state legislatures. We negotiate country to country." Then he cryptically warned he would take "unilateral action" if a settlement was not negotiated.[19]

In early June, Tobin announced he had abandoned hope of reaching a PST settlement in time for the 1994 salmon season. Instead, he declared that Canada would develop a "stand-alone" fishing plan to limit the number of Canadian salmon intercepted by the Americans. To assist the DFO in formulating the details of this "aggressive fishing" strategy, Tobin established an advisory group known as the Minister's Advisory Panel, which included representatives from the Native, recreational and commercial fishing sectors; I became one of five commercial sector advisors. Our guiding principles were: 1) ensure that the spawning targets of all major stock groups were guaranteed; 2) ensure that the constitutionally protected fishing rights of Native groups were honoured; 3) ensure that the Canadian catch was shared as equitably as possible by all users; and 4) ensure a minimum bycatch of chinook, coho and steelhead.

In the first week of June, Prime Minister Jean Chretien called Bill Clinton about the West Coast salmon deadlock, but Clinton gave Chretien little comfort. He ignored the clear obligations of the PST and insisted that the problem could only be sorted out at the state level. Tobin, therefore, used the Coastal Navigation Protection Act to impose a $1,500 transit fee on all US fishing vessels travelling to Alaska through BC's Inside Passage. The US was outraged. Alaskan Congressman Don Young declared that it was a gross violation of international law, and before long, television newscasts showed DFO patrol vessels escorting furious American seiners into various West Coast Canadian ports. "I would expect the telex lines to Congress will be lit up before the day is out," Tobin said.[20]

Over the many years I worked for the UFAWU, I met a succession of fisheries ministers, but the first one to call me at home, on the Canada Day long weekend, was Captain Canada himself.

"How's it goin', bye?" he asked cheerfully, mimicking a stage Newfie accent. "Look," he said with sudden earnestness, "I need your help. I just received a call today from the White House." Vice-President Al Gore had called him about the transit fee, expressing official outrage over the harassment of innocent American citizens by the DFO, but indicating he was amenable to solving the PST impasse—if Tobin dropped the transit fee immediately. How could he remove the transit fee without appearing to have caved in to the Americans? Especially since Gore had not promised to settle the PST deadlock before the 1994 fishing season and had only offered vague promises about reviewing the American approach in past negotiations. "Let's see some proof before we lift it," I told Tobin.

He shared my feelings, he said, "but let's give this a chance to work. The majority of the Alaskan fleet has already gone up there, so the transit fee has already served its purpose. But we've got their attention now, and it won't hurt to make a gesture of goodwill. I can always reinstate the levy in the fall before they head back home, if there's no progress."

The following day all the members of the Minister's Advisory Panel publicly endorsed Tobin's decision. After the transit fee was lifted on July 2, Alaska Senator Frank Murkowski told the *Vancouver Sun*, "I'm glad to see Canada has finally come to its senses and removed a highly illegal and inflammatory transit fee." Then he suggested that Tobin was an upstart punk. Not to be upstaged, Captain Canada shot back, "Murkowski is the equivalent of a gnat flying around a horse."

The War of 1994

After the transit fee was dropped and the 1994 season began, Alaskan fishermen shamelessly increased their interception of BC salmon, despite Vice-President Gore's promises. Both their net and troll fisheries in the lower panhandle region were extremely productive for all species, with a staggering 5.7 million coho being landed—almost five times the 32-year historic average. Survey programs conducted by the PSC had shown that 40 percent of the coho caught in Alaska are of Canadian origin, and coho were considered on the brink of extinction in both BC and Washington state.[21] In the absence of binding treaty annexes, Canada tried to put pressure on Alaska by increasing its catch of salmon in the trans-boundary rivers, but this only amounted to a catch of 100,000 pieces. Canada also increased its troll catch of Alaskan pinks, but these retaliatory measures had little effect.

Canada had much more clout on the South Coast, where technically this country's fishermen could have hammered Washington state chinook and coho stocks and still remained well within the legal parameters of the PST. But they did not—Canada cut back on its harvest of US coho and chinook, a fact never acknowledged by some critics of the 1994 "fish war." The Canadian side hoped to win favour with the northwest states and perhaps drive a wedge between them and the Alaskans.

Meanwhile, they would maximize the catch of Canadian-bound sockeye at Washington state's expense by launching a virtual non-stop fishery for most of July in the southern approach route of the Strait of Juan de Fuca. This strategy raised two tricky problems. First, so few sockeye were migrating through Juan de Fuca, and it is so expensive to operate a seiner on a prolonged basis, that the seine fleet in the area grew frustrated. Second, the small but unavoidable bycatch of Canadian chinook and coho sparked an explosion from Canadian recreational fishermen, and on August 13, the recreational fishing representatives on the Minister's Advisory Panel resigned en masse. "We support the minister's position on pursuing equity with the US," griped Craig Orr of the Steelhead Society of BC, "but not at the cost of wiping out our coho."[22]

The total commercial catch of coho in Juan de Fuca for the 1994 season, however, was only 131,023 pieces, well below the 1970s' ten-year average of 365,319, and the 1980s' average of 169,857 pieces.[23] Still, commercial fishing critics inundated the press with terms such as "body count," "slaughter" and "extermination." Native politicians such as Ernie Crey, of the Lower Fraser Fishing Authority (LFFA), also attacked Tobin's plan, claiming that it devastated the fragile early Stuart sockeye run. He did not mention the fact that the Natives were the only group fishing during the peak of the early Stuart run during 1994.

Meanwhile, the Americans' catches were so low that some US officials began to call Tobin a terrorist. Washington state Senator Slade Gorton demanded retaliation, including sending out the US Coast Guard to escort American fishermen.

The PSC Miscalculates the Fraser Run

Based on the huge escapements of Fraser River sockeye in 1990, the DFO had forecast a record return of 30 million in 1994, then reduced it to 19 million after fewer brood-year smolts than estimated migrated out of the river in 1991. Traditionally, however, managers from both Canada and the US rely on the in-season run-size estimates of Pacific Salmon Commission biologists before opening sockeye and pink fisheries, and despite the breakdown in the PST talks, the PSC had to make the in-season estimate of the 1994 Fraser sockeye run. Normally these estimates are based on a number of test fisheries along the coast: if the samples from these test fisheries are good, PSC biologists recommend that commercial fisheries occur. The most reliable indicators of in-season abundance, however, are the commercial net fisheries that usually occur simultaneously in Johnstone Strait and the Strait of Juan de Fuca, both being located far enough from the mouth of the Fraser to allow the PSC time to gauge the size of the run before it migrates up the river.

Had the run divided itself equally between Johnstone Strait and the Strait of Juan de Fuca in 1994, as had been forecast, Tobin's "aggressive fishing" strategy might have proved quite successful. But more than 90 percent of the sockeye appeared unexpectedly in Johnstone Strait—exactly as they had during the legendary run of 1958. The DFO, expecting an equal split, had decided to keep Johnstone Strait closed to fishing for the first part of the season to ensure spawning escapements and had dispatched the seine fleet to the southern approach route in the Strait of Juan de Fuca. The seiners there caught very few sockeye in two weeks of almost non-stop fishing, yet the media, along with a number of commercial fishing critics, denounced the fishery and later blamed it for the conservation crisis that emerged later in 1994.

This aside, the absence of a commercial fishery in Johnstone Strait forced the PSC to depend exclusively on test fishing samples to determine the size of the 1994 sockeye run—a much less reliable means of assessing stock abundance than a one-day commercial fishery, where the fleet is spread out over the entire area. The limited data seemed to confirm that the run was very large, so DFO managers believed they had to open Johnstone Strait. By now the run was peaking, and an unprecedented 1,581,000 sockeye were landed in a single 24-hour period. The DFO decided to allow another two and a half days' fishing in Johnstone Strait (a normal occurrence when fishing is good) and a total catch of 6 million sockeye was eventually landed.

The hundreds of individual races of Fraser River sockeye are divided into three basic groups, based on their migration timing: the early summer run, the midsummer run and the late run. Normally the midsummer run reaches its peak in Johnstone Strait in late July, and the late run arrives in mid- to late August. Quite unexpectedly, the two runs overlapped in 1994, likely because of the effect of warm water currents off the West Coast, and the lack of commercial catch data in Johnstone Strait throughout the early part of the season partially obscured this fact. When the DFO finally opened the Johnstone Strait fishery that year, it was not clear that the peak of the late-run Adams River sockeye were migrating through Johnstone Strait at almost the same time as the peak of the midsummer run.

In other words, the huge catch taken in Johnstone Strait that year came about not because of Brian Tobin's aggressive fishing strategy, but because both the PSC and the DFO believed the Fraser sockeye run was much larger than expected. In fact, the total number of days fished in Johnstone Strait in 1994 was among the lowest on record.

Meanwhile, in light of the apparent abundance in Johnstone Strait, the DFO also decided to lift the Gulf troll area-licensing regulation for the first time in decades, in an attempt to restrict the American catch at Point Roberts as well as to balance the catch between the Canadian troll and net fleets. It was this fishery, in August 1994, that my father tried in vain to take part in.

On August 29, more than 1,000 trollers massed in the Gulf of Georgia for a two-day fishery. Their catch—166,000 sockeye—erased the trollers' outstanding domestic allocation imbalance and limited the Americans' catch at Point Roberts, but it was nowhere near what the DFO had expected. On August 30 the DFO closed all commercial fishing for sockeye in Canadian waters for the balance of the season.

The Americans would not comply with Canada's request to close all fishing for the balance of the season. They had a right to continue fishing until they reached their "historic" share of the catch, they said, through a series of openings at Point Roberts that were timed to catch the bulk of the late-run Fraser sockeye as they arrived in the Gulf of Georgia in late August and early September. These fisheries, by both the Treaty Indian tribes and the all-citizens fishery, occurred during the weeks ending September 3 and September 10 and harvested an unprecedented 736,000 sockeye.[24]

The Case of the Missing Salmon

On September 15, 1994, after a preliminary investigation, the DFO announced that at least a million early Stuart and early summer-run sockeye had failed to arrive on the spawning grounds. This sparked an immediate outcry. The *Globe and Mail* reported, "Most troubling for the fisheries regulators is that they say there is no evidence of natural or industrial environmental devastation of the vital spawning stocks. That raises the spectre of poaching on a grand scale or a profound failure of the management systems that are supposed to track and safeguard the stocks." Bud Graham, the DFO's director of fisheries operations, declared, "I'd hate to call it a mystery. We believe there are potential sources of escapement error."[25] Brian Tobin reacted to the problem on September 26 by announcing the appointment of a four-person scientific panel to review "the discrepancy between the number of sockeye counted in-river and the total that finally reached their spawning grounds."[26]

The worst fears of the DFO's managers were realized in early October—the late Adams River run escapement was also short by 1.9 million pieces, bringing the number of "missing fish" to a total of 3.2 million. The *Globe and Mail* declared that DFO could not even count the fish,[27] and DFO officials confessed they could not explain it. "The whole situation has taken me by surprise," said Assistant Deputy Minister Pat Chamut. "…This makes me ask whether we can rely on the [Pacific Salmon] Commission when estimates are so far out."[28]

Meanwhile, Ian Todd, executive director of the PSC, declared that there was no mystery. The lack of long-term data for such a high diversion through Johnstone Strait, combined with unusual efficiency in the seine fishery, had caused the Salmon Commission staff to briefly overestimate the size of the run. "Put the fault here, if you want to," he said candidly. "…the so-called aggressive fishing strategy had nothing to do with it."[29] A month later Brian Tobin vowed, with no mention of American marauders, "We will take in the coming season whatever measures are required to ensure conservation is first and foremost."[30] After the season, the PSC reported, "The preliminary post-season estimated Fraser sockeye run is 15,753,000 fish compared to the pre-season forecast of 19.0 million. The post-season estimated gross escapement past Mission is 3,573,000 fish. The US caught 1,830,000 Fraser sockeye in Washington fisheries… An additional 225,000 Fraser sockeye are estimated to have been caught in the Alaskan District 104 seine fishery…The commercial catch was 11.2 million sockeye, of which 9.1 million were caught by Canada."[31]

Tobin announced that there would be a public inquiry into the missing fish. "We have neither the time or the money to hold a [judicial] inquiry," he said. "…We are in the middle of negotiations with the US to try and restore the Pacific Salmon Treaty. I need a process that is fast and effective."[32] He turned to an old Tory adversary and ex-fisheries minister for help and announced in early November that the Honourable John Fraser would lead the six-member Fraser Sockeye Public Review Board, which would consist of Dr. Lee Alverson, Dr. Paul LeBlond, Dr. Rick Routledge, Dr. Joe Scrimger and David Brander-Smith, QC.

CHAPTER 4

The Great Experiment

Native issues are almost never just Native issues.
Native issues are human issues.

—Buffy Sainte-Marie

Despite all the controversy in 1994, this was not the only time—before or since—that salmon have "gone missing" in the Fraser River. In 1992, just after Tory Fisheries Minister John Crosbie had made major cuts to the DFO budget and simultaneously introduced the controversial Aboriginal Fishing Strategy (AFS) pilot sales program, 800,000 sockeye mysteriously disappeared. Ever since, many in the commercial fishing sector have maintained that poaching under the guise of the AFS is the prime cause of missing fish. Native leaders refute this charge, and DFO officials blame warm water in the Fraser River for increased "pre-spawn mortality" rates.

In 2004, as many as 2 million Fraser sockeye went missing, and at this writing a multitude of DFO experts and members of the Pacific Salmon Commission are still scrambling to explain why. Answers must be found, and the volatile debate over the AFS pilot sales program must not inhibit the search for long-term solutions. This is not to blame Native fisheries for the recurring problem of missing fish, but the struggle for political justice for aboriginal people should not blind us to the problems associated with the Native fishery and DFO's enforcement capacity in recent years.

The North Vancouver shipyard in which my father, Al Brown, was trying to repair his boat during the fish war of 1994 was located on the Squamish Indian Reserve. He had spent a great deal of time there over the years, working on boats, and had become good friends with the late Frank Rivers, Harold Nahannie and other members of the Squamish band. As a result, back in 1986, when he set about building a fish boat, he had been granted the rare privilege of using reserve land—free of charge—to build it. The boat was to be donated to the people of San Juan del Sur, a poverty-stricken fishing village in Nicaragua that my father had visited with UFAWU activists Scotty Neish and Don Sananin. The project was officially sponsored by the Tools for Peace organization, but my father did most of the work and donated all of his labour over the next eight years.

This collegial relationship of Native and non-Native people was not exceptional in the commercial fishing industry, which has a higher percentage of Native participants than any other industry in Canada. But that changed dramatically after the federal government launched its controversial Aboriginal Fishing Strategy (AFS) in 1991, ostensibly to honour its fiduciary responsibility to Native people. Like most other non-Native fishermen, my father recognized that the AFS was a misguided policy for which he blamed the government, not aboriginal people. But inevitably, the AFS drove a wedge between Native and non-Native people as a whole in BC.

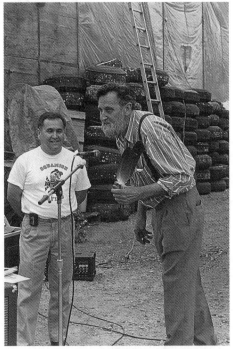

Gerry Nahannie (Squamish First Nation) and Alan Brown at the launch of the boat built by UFAWU volunteers, on the Squamish reserve in North Vancouver, for the village of San Juan del Sur Nicaragua, 1995.

The Sparrow Case

On May 25, 1984, Ron Sparrow set his gillnet in the Fraser River under the auspices of a Musqueam Band food-fishing permit. At the time the DFO limited the length of the nets used in the Native food fishery to 25 fathoms, and as Sparrow's net was 37 fathoms long, he was arrested by DFO and charged with using an illegal net. This seemingly inconsequential incident led to a six-year court battle, and finally, on May 30, 1990, the Supreme Court ruled that the DFO had acted improperly in charging Sparrow because the Musqueam Band had "an existing right to fish for food and social and ceremonial purposes."[1]

More importantly, the court decreed that the Musqueams' right to fish was second only to the requirements of conservation and that the Crown had a fiduciary duty to ensure that right was granted in a liberal and generous fashion.

The Sparrow decision did not determine whether Native people had a constitutionally protected right to sell fish obtained in a Native food fishery, but this landmark decision rocked the very foundations of the West Coast commercial fishing industry and was hailed as an unprecedented breakthrough for Native rights in Canada. Before the Sparrow case, the provincial government had claimed that aboriginal rights had been extinguished by the Royal Proclamation of 1763. Now the province's position might be untenable. "The whole provincial regulatory scheme of things is in question," said Joe Mathias, vice-chief of the Assembly of First Nations. "We have a long way to go...But from this point on we'll be talking about the Sparrow Case."[2]

Native people have fished for salmon in the area now known as British Columbia for thousands of years—as far back as 9,000 years ago, according to some archaeological evidence.[3] Before 1877 there were no regulations governing or restricting fisheries in BC. That year the Crown enacted the Dominion Fisheries Act, and in 1879 the Act was amended to read: "Indians shall at all times have liberty to fish for the purpose of providing food for themselves, but not for sale, barter, or traffic..."[4] In 1910 Ottawa amended the regulations again, requiring that Native fishermen obtain official permits prior to fishing. The regulations remained virtually unchanged from that time until 1981.

Under the Pacific Salmon Treaty, Canada was allowed to deduct the equivalent of 400,000 sockeye from its annual sharing arrangement with the US, a deduction known as the Indian Food Fishery (IFF) exemption. IPSFC records show that until the 1960s the IFF sockeye catch on the Fraser averaged only about 150,000 pieces, and it rose slightly to 200,000 during the 1970s. On a coast-wide basis, the total annual catch for all Native bands was approximately 450,000 pieces between 1951 to 1981.[5] But after 1981 there was a dramatic increase in reported IFF landings—just under a million salmon in 1981, with the catch in the Fraser River alone totalling almost 450,000. According to the IPSFC, this was a tenfold increase over the historic catch levels, yet Fraser River runs had not increased by a factor of ten.[6]

Many things may account for the IFF increase, including the fact that Native communities had become the fastest growing segment of the Canadian population. Far more important was the legacy of the 1975 Boldt decision in the US federal court, which had provided the Northwest Treaty tribes with a 50 percent share of the total catch in Washington state waters. That landmark decision—which some authors have described as the beginning of "the era of modern salmon management"[7]—had served as a catalyst for increased catch demands by Native people in BC.

During the 1980s, the DFO became increasingly concerned about its ability to manage and control the IFF. Ottawa had introduced a regulation requiring that the snouts of all salmon caught in a Native food fishery be removed to prevent illegal sales. The Native community made it clear that this was demeaning, and the regulation was eventually dropped. At the same time, Natives and DFO officers began to clash—sometimes violently—over the alleged illegal sale of salmon.

Then, as part of his 1982 Royal Commission, Peter Pearse made a series of sweeping recommendations to reform the management of the Native fishery. He recommended that each Native band be given a specific allocation to manage and use as they saw fit, which would relieve the government of the cost of monitoring the Native fishery. The Liberal government of the day declined to implement Pearse's proposal. In 1985 the new Tory government offered Native bands specific allocations but did not implement Pearse's proposal for self-management. This failed to placate Native leaders, and more violent clashes occurred along the banks of the Fraser River in 1986 and 1987. Around this time, the DFO mounted a major "sting" operation to crack down on alleged illicit sales of IFF catches. Many non-Native commercial fishermen applauded the move, but the sight of Native people being taken from their homes during late-night raids upset the public. Therefore, instead of accused Native "poachers" coming under fire, it was the DFO that was condemned by the media for its heavy-handed tactics, and the DFO responded by raising the IFF ceiling to 500,000 sockeye.

At the same time, Ottawa conducted a task force inquiry into Native land claims. The chair, Murray Coolican, recommended that the pace of negotiations be accelerated, and that interim measures, such as encouraging self-government by Native people, be implemented immediately.[8] For its part, the DFO released a document entitled "Policy Proposal for a BC Indian Community Salmon Paper," which proposed Native "co-management" of the fishery. Commercial fishermen responded by forming the Pacific Fishermen's Defence Alliance, which included all commercial fishing industry organizations except the UFAWU and the Native Brotherhood of BC. The Alliance launched a number of court actions designed to prevent the proliferation of Native fishing rights, and when the courts continued to rule in favour of Natives, tensions in the industry increased. Dr. Scott Parsons of the DFO observed, "The government faced a dilemma given these court rulings and non-Native groups' opposition to change. The situation was exacerbated by the lack of agreement at the First Ministers' Conference on Aboriginal Rights in March 1987. This led many Natives to think that they must provoke the government to recognize their rights."[9]

In 1988, Minister Tom Siddon's Pacific Area Regional Advisory Committee (PARC) consulted briefly with Native leaders, but nothing was accomplished, and on August 20 Native fishermen across the province staged a "day of protest" against DFO regulations. "We're just sick and tired," Richard Watts, vice-chair of the BC Aboriginal Fisheries Commission, had told the *Vancouver Sun* on August 3. "It's not the law we are breaking. It's the narrow interpretation of the law. There will be hundreds more court cases and a lot more confrontations."[10]

The Great Experiment

Then on May 30, 1990, the Supreme Court handed down its landmark ruling in the Sparrow case, and just two weeks later, an obscure back-bench MLA named Elijah Harper stood up in the Manitoba legislature, waved an eagle feather and said "no" to the Meech Lake Accord, which he believed did not properly address the rights of First Nations people. Technically the Accord needed every sitting member of Parliament and the provincial legislatures to be passed, which was unlikely to happen. This aside, during the Meech Lake process the Tories had been preoccupied with placating Quebec and paid little attention to the discontent festering in Native communities.

Section 35(1) of the Canadian Constitution affirms aboriginal rights, yet no one could say what it really meant. In 1982, when then Minister of Native and Northern Affairs Jean Chretien had introduced the Constitution Act, he had declared that the courts would decide the full extent of aboriginal rights. However, the legal system had proved almost as difficult and frustrating for Native people as the negotiating table.

Now, with the demise of the Meech Lake Accord, the question of aboriginal rights was left in limbo. Mulroney announced that his government would accelerate negotiations and settle all outstanding land claims by the year 2000, but critics charged that his priority was to eliminate the nuisance of Native road blocks and protests, rather than to ensure justice for Native people.

The next crisis was a dispute over a golf course development on the Kahnawake reserve near Oka, Quebec, that led to a standoff between the Canadian army and a group of Mohawk warriors. The confrontation lasted the entire summer of 1990, and became a flash point for Native grievances across the country—even in BC, where several major roads were blocked in a gesture of solidarity with the Mohawks.

Fishing rights were still the central concern of West Coast Native protestors, but the Sparrow decision had changed that landscape. In his book *Dead Reckoning: Confronting the Crisis in the Pacific Fisheries*, Terry Glavin wrote:

> DFO couldn't simply boss the Indians around anymore.
> Without extensive consultations or pre-season agreements

involving almost all the two hundred Indian bands in BC—almost half of which are situated within the Fraser Basin—it was going to be next to impossible to plan fisheries. In this increasingly complex approach DFO was going to be hard-pressed to make decisions unless DFO staff knew what would happen in the tribal fisheries—how many fish Native people would catch, when Native people would be going fishing, which fish, exactly they intended to catch, where people would be catching the fish and how many people would be fishing.[11]

Fisheries Minister John Crosbie turned to Bruce Rawson, a veteran troubleshooter in the senior civil service, to concoct a solution to the crisis. Rawson flew to the West Coast and quickly convened a three-day "summit" at the Dunsmuir Lodge near Victoria. It was attended by a number of Native leaders and commercial fishing representatives, including Jack Nichol, then president of the UFAWU. Nichol recalled:

> He begged us to get the Tories through the next couple of years. They were embarrassed by Oka…The Indians were getting sympathy around the world for being abused by Canada. It was clearly an embarrassment to the government and Rawson was sent here with the express purpose of getting us to go along with them to cool the thing down. He wanted us to agree to commercial allocations for the Indians. Well, that would have been fatal to the commercial industry, and we had no authority to do that. I could go back to my own union membership and take my lumps, but I couldn't speak for the entire industry, nor could anyone else. Then the Indians found themselves in exactly the same position and that's why it finally ended at the end of the second day, because they said, "We have no mandate to make any decisions whatsoever."[12]

Nichol made an interesting point when he said that the West Coast fishery had become a disproportionately prominent part of Mulroney's campaign to quell Native discontent across the country. The only natural resource under federal jurisdiction is fish; all other resources that would be part of potential land claims settlements are under provincial control, and Ottawa's only other bargaining chip is cash. Thus, given its declining interest in managing commercial fisheries, the federal government was quite willing to put generous amounts of fish on the bargaining table. Significantly, the transfer of fish affects a relatively small segment of the Canadian work force, so the government would not have to upset the whole country by forcing it to shoulder more of the cost of settling land claims. Throughout the debate over this issue, commercial fishermen repeatedly stated that they would pay the same amount per capita as other Canadians, but not a disproportionate share, and not at the cost of their livelihood. In a study commissioned by the Commercial Fishing Industry Council in 1992, Dr. Edwin Blewett determined that a 50 percent allocation of the salmon resource to the Native sector would require $5.5 billion compensation to the commercial fishing sector for future lost earnings.[13] Over the next year, Bruce Rawson served as the chief architect of Ottawa's Aboriginal Fishing Strategy (AFS), one of the most controversial policies ever imposed on the West Coast fishery. And in the spring of 1991 John Crosbie was able to announce that an initial $11 million would be invested in the AFS to cover 150 agreements across the country. Another $1.1 million was earmarked for a series of pilot programs in aboriginal fisheries co-management. "The BC fishing industry is a profitable, relatively stable fishery that supports a substantial commercial and sports fishery." Crosbie declared. "I believe that what we are doing here today will increase that stability without impairing the profitability or the predictability or the jobs of fishermen and plant workers."[14]

The following summer, Crosbie unveiled the full AFS program, including $140 million to be spent over seven years, 70 percent of it in BC. He also announced a new Native fisheries guardian program and the launching of a pilot sales program. For the first time in 100 years aboriginal people were to be allowed to sell the fish obtained in Native fisheries. According to Scott Parsons, Crosbie believed that relations between the DFO and aboriginal groups "would continue to be characterized by confrontation and conflict unless the prohibition on sales was lifted."[15] Senior DFO bureaucrats explained the new policy to the Standing Committee on Forestry and Fisheries by saying, "So in the interest of the whole industry, the commercial and recreational fisheries, and stability, and to try to keep the industry profitable, we're trying [pilot sales] as an experiment…Rather than wait for the courts to decide whether you can sell a fish or can't sell a fish, wouldn't it be better for governments and the groups involved to devise a system that satisfies everyone and that will be reasonable? That's why we're trying these experiments."[16]

Long before the introduction of the AFS, Natives had played a role in the West Coast commercial fishery proportionately much larger than their numbers in the general population. And for most of the century Natives worked in the commercial fishery under the same rules and restrictions that applied to non-Natives. This is not to suggest that Native people were always treated fairly. Rather it is to refute the notion that the AFS pilot sales program was a noble attempt by Ottawa to eliminate racial barriers keeping Natives out of the commercial fishery.

It can be argued that many Native fishermen suffered economic hardship over the years because they were unable to forge lasting alliances with non-Native fishermen and join forces against the canners. The union always enjoyed the support of a large number of Native shoreworkers, some 9,000 of them in the 1920s. Changing technology reduced this number to about 1,500 by the 1970s.[17] But although the UFAWU always claimed that Native fishermen were welcome, the union was much less successful in recruiting them. Several UFAWU locals were established in Alert Bay, Kitkatla, Port Simpson, Kincolith and Kitwanga, but most organized Native fishermen supported the Native Brotherhood. There were serious tensions between the two organizations, but most of the time they did manage to work co-operatively in negotiating price agreements with the canners.

Some Native politicians tried to undermine this alliance. In 1969, for example, NDP MLA Frank Calder complained that Native unemployment was caused by the stranglehold that resource industry unions had over hiring practices. "Unions are kicking the Indian one way and another," Calder declared. "…Companies regard Indians as the best workers but can't employ them [because of union seniority provisions]." Homer Stevens, president of the UFAWU, said, "Such remarks open the door to further attacks on labour…[which] would tend to segregate Native Indians away from the trade unions and would be contrary to laws aimed at preventing discrimination and the very fight for equality which Calder espouses."[18]

Responding to claims that Natives had been marginalized in the industry, Ottawa introduced a series of affirmative action programs, including the special Indian-only (A-I) salmon licence category, the Indian Fishermen's Assistance Program (IFAP) and the Indian Fishermen's Emergency Fund. In addition, Ottawa purchased 300 gillnet vessels and licences from BC Packers Ltd. and gave them to three North Coast tribal councils. Thus, by 1985 Natives owned and operated 923 West Coast salmon licences out of 4,497.[19] In 2003 Michelle James, a former DFO economist and spokesperson for the canners, wrote a report commissioned by the provincial government in which she said that Native-owned or -operated licences accounted for 26.9 percent of the fleet.[20] However, it is a well-known fact that a great number of these Native licences were leased out to non-Native fishermen, thus providing rentier-style income for a privileged group of Native licence holders but considerably less employment in their communities than the figure might suggest.

In an effort to diminish opposition to the AFS by the non-Native sector, Crosbie had also provided $7 million for a licence buyback to compensate for the 400,000 Fraser River sockeye transferred to the pilot sales program. However, most of the boats surrendered to the buyback were owned by less than average producers who likely caught nowhere near that amount, so the commercial sector was not properly compensated. Nonetheless, the DFO's Scott Parsons believed the AFS represented a fundamental reform of the federal government's approach to aboriginal fisheries, because Native groups had sometimes taken "unpredictable numbers of fish," but now the catch "would be counted and the fishery closed when the limit was reached."[21] The "experiment" with the AFS that followed soon proved the department's optimism was entirely unfounded.

800,000 "Missing" Salmon

Certain pundits apparently believed the entire commercial fishing fleet had reacted to the AFS with intense anger right from the start. Journalist

Terry Glavin wrote, "The commercial fishing industry has waged a campaign against the minority of AFS agreements with pilot sales provisions that in many ways matches the worst of the industry's previous excesses in its opposition to aboriginal fishing rights."[22] In fact, initial criticism of the AFS within UFAWU circles was quite muted. Some UFAWU members did believe the AFS threatened their livelihood, but many others, who supported aboriginal rights, were reluctant to complain. Consequently, the UFAWU leadership held its fire and hoped that the AFS would encourage better management of the Native fishery, as the DFO had pledged.

This tenuous situation changed dramatically when the DFO announced on August 24, 1992, that the entire South Coast sockeye fishery would close for the season because of a drastic shortfall in the spawning escapement. The Pacific Salmon Commission had forecast a return of 5.9 million sockeye to the Fraser River,[23] set a spawning goal of 1.5 million and left a potential commercial catch of 3.7 million to be shared by Canada and the US. The PSC's hydro-acoustical salmon counter at Mission indicated that sufficient numbers entered the river, but very few spawners were reported to be making it through the Fraser Canyon. As many as 800,000 to 1.2 million sockeye had gone "missing." DFO Deputy Minister Bruce Rawson told the *Vancouver Sun* on August 29, 1992, that "There isn't any choice but to close it because our responsibility first is to conservation."

Upon hearing this, about 200 fishermen formed a flotilla on the river not far from the DFO's New Westminster office. They were convinced that poaching under the guise of the AFS pilot sales program had caused the fiasco, and that the DFO had failed to enforce the program. Mike Forrest of the Pacific Gillnetters Association declared that the DFO had failed to enforce the program. Edgar Birch, a UFAWU veteran, said, "They should start over again with the commercial fishermen involved. This is the first time in 44 years fishing this river that I've seen 800,000 fish go missing." And Phil Eby of the Fishing Vessel Owners Association pointed out that because of Tory budget cuts, "[The DFO have] doubled their requirements for enforcement, but they haven't doubled their enforcement staff."

But even as the closure was cutting the Fraser River commercial gillnet quota short by at least 100,000 pieces, Native leaders were complaining that they had not received their share either. Ernie Crey of the Sto:lo Band vehemently denied that Native fishermen had over-fished and called upon Ottawa to conduct a full inquiry into the "missing salmon." Meanwhile, the *Vancouver Sun* reported on August 24 that Joe Becker of the Musqueam Band considered the protests of non-Native fishermen to be "the same old racist cant." He added, "We have scrupulously observed our quotas as spelled out in the pilot program adopted this year."

Other Native fishermen used ethnic chauvinism to deflect public criticism from the fact that they were profiting individually from a program supposedly designed to benefit Native communities as a whole. As a result, many Native people complained that the AFS pilot sales program was depriving them of their food fish. On September 8, 1992, Chief Nicholas Prince of the Necoslie Band in Fort St. James wrote, "I have told my people many times that once permission is granted to commercially net the spawners in the Fraser River, the salmon would be finished. I know the traditions of my people, and I also know the greed that governs these people. It seems that those of us who are trying to protect the spawning grounds get the short end of the stick. We must go without our traditional foods because of the greed of the First Nations of the Lower Mainland."

Not a Disaster

Following the closure of both the commercial and Native fisheries on August, 25 1992, the number of spawners passing through the Fraser Canyon rose dramatically, and some months later, in its Eighth Annual Report, the Pacific Salmon Commission announced that the total recruitment of sockeye spawners in 1992 was 1.1 million. This was well below the escapement target of 1.9 million, yet reasonably close to the 1998 escapement of 1.4 million. However, most of that escapement was made up of late-run stocks, and the early Stuart and early summer runs remained low. Most non-Native participants in the industry favoured a judicial inquiry into the matter of the "missing" 800,000 sockeye. Ottawa turned instead to Peter Pearse—a choice that appalled most non-Native fishermen, given that Pearse had long advocated an expanded, commercialized Native fishery.

Nevertheless, in his report of November 1992, *Managing Salmon in the Fraser*, prepared with the scientific and technical advice of Peter A. Larkin, Pearse wrote, "In June 1991 the Department issued new national guidelines for enforcement, forbidding fishery officers from laying charges until they obtained authorization in advance from both their headquarters and the Department of Justice. This requirement was cumbersome and frustrating. Approvals were inconsistent and sometimes no

Peter Pearse, University of BC economist.

response was forthcoming before the court appearance...Enforcement was therefore weak and fishery officers felt powerless, frustrated by an apparent lack of support from their superiors. They also say they were harassed by some Native leaders."[24]

Pearse also noted that several bands refused to sign AFS agreements, and many of those that did demonstrated questionable enforcement and catch reporting practices: "Upriver, beyond the agreement area, surveillance and enforcement effort was abandoned altogether. Faced with cuts in staff and instructions not to lay charges the Department's staff threw up their hands. Major enforcement problems developed. Formerly rare illegal practices such as drift gillnet fishing were observed. Up to 75 percent of the nets inspected were not properly marked."[25]

Even Terry Glavin, a strong defender of the AFS, was compelled to write, "There were increasing numbers of community members joining the fishery without proper skills or knowledge. There was a growing lack of respect for traditional fishing sites. There were increasing numbers of nets in the river. And there was potential of adverse impacts posed by the decriminalization of sales upon a variety of Sto Lo fishing traditions. Overall people felt things were going too fast."[26]

However, Pearse did not lay the entire blame for the "missing" fish on the Native fishery. He proposed at least two other possible explanations. The first, vigorously endorsed by Ernie Crey of the Lower Fraser Fishing Authority, was that the PSC hydro-acoustical salmon counter at Mission had overestimated the numbers of fish migrating upstream. Pearse and Larkin eventually rejected this theory, claiming that the salmon counter functioned accurately enough. The second theory was that many salmon had died in the Fraser Canyon because of unusually high water temperatures, and they preferred this theory even though very few carcasses were found floating downstream.

In the conclusion to his report, Pearse wrote, "It is important to keep the 'missing fish' in proper perspective. It is cause for concern when large numbers of salmon seemingly disappear from the river. But 1992 was by no means a disaster."[27]

The Second Survival Coalition

In the aftermath of the controversy in 1992, a large group of fishermen gathered at the Fraser River boat shop of Joe Smith, a UFAWU gillnetter, to discuss what to do about the AFS. Dal Triggs, a widely respected gill-netter who first began fishing on the Fraser in 1936, expressed the feelings of many fishermen when he said that the AFS pilot sales program was a form of racial discrimination against non-Native fishermen, rather than a means of alleviating past injustices to Native people.

Not long afterwards, two prominent Fraser River gillnetters, Bob McKamey and Don Reid, met with Jack Nichol and myself to discuss the prospect of the UFAWU playing a greater role in the battle against the AFS. The union had not joined the Pacific Fishermen's Defence Alliance because it had disagreed with the strategy of blocking Native rights in the courts and supported a negotiated political solution to the question of Native fishing rights. Now, given that the major abuses occurring within the AFS program posed a serious threat to the resource, the union had no choice but to speak out. More and more UFAWU members pressured the leadership to take a stand against the AFS pilot sales program. The union's officers agreed to get involved, but made it clear that the UFAWU was opposed to a flawed Tory fishing policy, not the advancement of Native rights.

Over the next several months, I served on a steering committee, consisting of several industry representatives, which grappled with the problem. In January 1993 this committee sponsored a conference in Richmond, which was attended by more than 2,000 fishermen, and where the BC Fisheries Survival Coalition was formed. Unlike its namesake—the BC Fishermen's Survival Coalition, set up in 1983 to fight the Pearse Report—this coalition had no base in the Native commercial fishing sector.

Meanwhile, the AFS pilot sales program continued to be dogged by controversy. A year later BC Reform MP John Cummins released a "leaked" DFO enforcement branch memo titled *Enforcement Plan Fraser River, 1993*, reporting that DFO monitoring was "completely inadequate and unable to address under-reporting of catch and poaching by unauthorized fishers and fishing during closed times…Enforcement of most fisheries was sporadic, and in many areas was inadequate to the point where it can be viewed as virtually 'non-existent'."[28]

Cummins seized on the memo as an opportunity to attack the government and to demand an independent inquiry into the management of the West Coast fishery. Cummins was quick to condemn Native

Fishermen rally outside hearings of the Parliamentary Standing Committee on Fisheries on the Aboriginal Fishing Strategy, Vancouver, 1992.

poachers, but did not emphasize an important passage in the memo: "This [poaching] has happened because current resources available have not allowed DFO staff to be on the grounds to properly complete pre-fishery or post-fishery clean up patrols." During this period the DFO was in the process of chopping 40 percent of its workforce in the context of a federal budget reduced to $950 million from $1.9 billion. Sadly, Cummins' Reform Party was very much in favour of "downsizing" government.

The Court Rules

The reaction of BC's commercial fishing industry to the AFS belies the fact that members of the UFAWU and other industry participants supported the settlement of Native land claims. They objected to the AFS—particularly the pilot sales program—because it does not follow the comprehensive land claims settlement process. It is not paid for equitably by all Canadians. It was an "interim measure," introduced at the expense of one small industry. A great many fair-minded Canadians genuinely believed that the program was a major step toward social justice, not realizing that so few people actually benefitted from it or that it put the salmon resource at risk.

In instituting the AFS pilot sales program, senior DFO bureaucrats had assumed the courts would rule in favour of the aboriginal right to sell fish taken in the Native food fishery. But they have not, and in 1996 the BC Supreme Court denied that there is an aboriginal right to sell fish. In the case of Dorothy Van der Peet, a Sto:lo Band member charged with selling several Fraser River sockeye, the court's judgement said in part:

> Section 35(1) should not be interpreted as having the purpose of enlarging the pre-1982 concept of aboriginal rights; instead it should be seen as having the purpose of protecting from legislative encroachment those aboriginal rights that existed in 1982. Section 35(1) was...enacted so as to protect "traditional" aboriginal practices integral to the culture and traditional way of life of the Native community...the commercial sale of fish is different in nature and kind from the aboriginal right of the Sto:lo

to fish for sustenance and ceremonial purposes, with the
result that the appellant could not be said to have been
exercising an aboriginal right when she sold the fish.[29]

Many Canadians who supported the AFS pilot sales program assumed
that the controversy could have been avoided had commercial fishermen been willing to reach a compromise with Native leaders. This
would have been next to impossible. Ever since the Constitution Act
of 1982, if not before, it has been maintained that Native land claims
(including fishing rights) can only be dealt with on a nation-to-nation
basis. This may be legitimate in a formal sense, but it has caused practical difficulties, such as some Native leaders' belief that it is inappropriate for them to deal directly with "third parties" on matters of natural
resource tenure. For example, in 1993 a number of fishing industry leaders—including myself—persuaded the DFO to set up an independently
facilitated forum in which non-Native fishermen could discuss fishing
issues directly with Native representatives. The initiative was later known
as the "Vista process," after the name of the consulting firm that facilitated the sessions. We met for many months and exchanged interesting ideas, but the process arrived at the same sort of stalemate that had
beset the Dunsmuir summit in 1992 because the Native representatives
insisted they had no mandate to work out deals with "third parties." As
well, the nation-to-nation negotiating format is, by government design,
bureaucratic. Native and non-Native communities therefore encounter
each other as "two solitudes" divided by fear, economic insecurity and
cultural estrangement. The structure presumes that the interests of all
third parties will be protected by the government agents sitting at the
bargaining table. In no other context is it assumed that civil servants
will look after people's wishes. And in no other context is the right to
disagree or criticize so limited.

Toward a New Salmon Commons?

In his book *Salmon: The Decline of the BC Fishing Industry*, Geoff Meggs
envisions the creation of a new salmon commons, secured by an alliance of Native and non-Native fishermen, working in concert to protect

and enhance BC's salmon runs. Such a vision could not be realized by the AFS, and the continuing tension between Natives and non-Native commercial fishermen engendered by the AFS can scarcely be considered a step in that direction.

Many non-Native fishermen believe that an ambitious government-funded program to encourage more Native participants in the existing commercial fishery would be far preferable to carving out a second, separate Native commercial fishery. In such a context the two groups could forge new alliances in the struggle against the massive environmental assault—and penurious government budget cuts—that currently threaten the salmon.

Too Many Fishermen

Truth I have no trouble with;
it's the facts I get all screwed up.

—Farley Mowat

The initial terms of reference for the Fraser Sockeye Public Review Board specified that it was to 1) determine the accuracy of the Mission sounding program; 2) assess the accuracy of the in-river catch-reporting data; 3) consider the relationship between high-water temperatures and pre-spawn mortalities; 4) assess the accuracy of spawning-ground enumerations; 5) assess the methods used by the Pacific Salmon Commission to estimate run sizes; and 6) assess DFO stock management, surveillance, monitoring and enforcement activities.[1] After more than six months of deliberations, on March 7, 1995, the report was finally released. In it, John Fraser wrote, "[W]e must conclude that there is no single explanation for the 1994 problem. While a number of factors likely interacted in the missing salmon issue, the Board sees no reason to assign proportional weights to any of them…no one, including the authorities, the experts and this board, knows precisely what happened or exactly how it happened."[2]

In this respect Fraser's report echoed Peter Pearse's inquiry into the missing Fraser River salmon of 1992. Yet Fraser insinuated that the catching power of the BC commercial fishing fleet was to blame. In particular he condemned the Minister's Advisory Panel for its "less than prudent attitude growing out of the aggressive fishing strategy" and said it had acted "to the detriment of conservation."[3] He also suggested the aggressive fishing strategy contributed to a "'grab-all' attitude in the Canadian fleet," which led to a "corresponding removal of any moral responsibility for conservation on the US side."[4]

Although he was aware of the Pacific Salmon Commission's difficulty in estimating the size of the 1994 sockeye run after the Pacific Salmon Treaty negotiations had collapsed, Fraser did not accept that a simple mistake had been made. On March 8, 1995, he told the *Globe and Mail*: "One more 12-hour opening could have virtually eliminated the late-run of sockeye." (Such hyperbole was not new: in 1979, A.W.H. Needler of the DFO had argued that the commercial fishing fleet was hypothetically capable of harvesting 98 percent of BC's salmon in just six days.[5]) Fraser's report implied that "attitudinal anarchy" during the aggressive fishing strategy had blinded the DFO to the fact the run was at risk, in spite of the fact that the DFO had closed the Johnstone Strait fishery at the first sign of trouble. He described the Gulf of Georgia troll fishery on August 29, 1994, as a "disaster waiting to happen" by comparing it to the Johnstone Strait seine fishery that had taken a million fish in 12 hours earlier in the season. However, in the narrow Johnstone Strait, concentrated schools of migrating salmon are very vulnerable to net fisheries; the sockeye available to the Gulf of Georgia troll fishery were dispersed from Campbell River in the north to Puget Sound in the south—almost 200 miles. Additional net or troll fisheries were not necessarily justified when the run was in jeopardy, but Fraser's declaration was more hyperbole than fact.

In its submission to the Fraser Sockeye Public Review Board, the PSC had been remarkably candid in its belief that two factors had led to the overestimation of the 1994 run. First, the early summer-run stocks encountered some of the highest water and most extreme temperatures ever recorded in the Fraser River. Dr. Jim Woodey, the PSC's chief biologist, believed that this caused an enormous—yet unexpected—en-route mortality of the run in the Fraser Canyon, but not until 1998, when a similar pattern occurred, could the link be made conclusively for 1994.[6]

Other industry participants suspected that poaching under cover of the Aboriginal Fishing Strategy pilot sales program was another contributing factor.

Former federal Fisheries Minister John Fraser at the time of the Fraser Sockeye Public Review Board hearings, Vancouver, 1995.

The PSC also noted that the Fraser sockeye run had behaved unpredictably in 1994. Warmer temperatures in the Pacific Ocean had caused most Fraser sockeye to migrate through Johnstone Strait rather than Juan de Fuca, which made stock assessment very difficult in the absence of regular commercial fisheries. The problem was compounded by a peculiar overlap in the timing of the summer and late-run stocks, and by an unforeseen heightened effort of the seine fleet during an unusually short Johnstone Strait seine fishery in mid-August—only three and a half days, compared to 15 to 20 days each season a decade earlier.

PSC officials certainly did not dismiss the severity of the 1994 sockeye shortfall, but they did attempt to explain why the Johnstone Strait seine fishery had been so efficient:

> The shorter durations [12 or 24 hours in 1994] of Johnstone Strait purse seine fisheries in recent years of high diversion rates have affected the behaviour of fishermen leading to increased harvest rates in the available open period. We understand…that fishermen do fish

more intensively [more sets per unit time] when time is limited. The need to pace themselves is absent, such as would be the case with multiple-day fisheries, and the opportunity to change location does not exist. Also with a larger fleet, the shorter duration fisheries do not allow purse seines to wait in line for preferred tie-off spots, but new technology advances permit open setting offshore. This allows each vessel to make more sets in a given opening.[7]

The PSC made a series of recommendations to improve future run-size estimates, with particular emphasis on slowing the pace of commercial fisheries. Unlike some critics of the commercial sector, the PSC did not call for the elimination of the Johnstone Strait mixed-stock fishery or a reduction in the size of the fleet, as Fraser's review panel did. Instead, the PSC insisted that the Johnstone Strait fishery be continued as a vital and irreplaceable source of catch data: "Improving the quality of in-season catch and racial data, stabilizing the fisheries, and improving the run-size models will reduce the likelihood of errors...We urge the adoption of the view that fisheries serve two purposes. One is to provide the economic gains derived from harvesting the fish. The second is to provide the data that is necessary to manage the fisheries with enough precision to meet both spawning escapements and catch goals without compromising the conservation of the stocks."[8]

Fraser's pronouncement that we had come "within a few hours of wiping out the famed Adams River run" was much more dramatic than the PSC's sober analysis. The media focussed on Fraser's 131-page report with its 35 recommendations, which included his call for radical structural change in Canada's commercial fishing fleet, but which did not include any criticism of US violations of the treaty Fraser had personally signed into law while minister of fisheries. Nor did Fraser take a strong position on the question of poaching. He made a mild criticism of the Aboriginal Fishing Strategy pilot sales program, but did not recommend that the program be scrapped. About the DFO's declining budget to prevent poaching, he said, "The scenario has its roots in the 1992–93 DFO Pacific Region reorganization. Cutbacks and budget reductions were made to the extent that the Department was left in charge without clear lines of accountability or necessary tools to enforce its regulations with any credibility."[9] Fraser himself was a member of the Tory government that had made those cutbacks, and he did not recommend that the ruling Liberals restore the DFO's budget. "Since the fiscal situation is likely to prevail for some years," he wrote, "DFO must examine alternative approaches to do more with less."[10] The public could only conclude that commercial fishermen had operated with wanton disregard for conservation, even though it is the DFO, not commercial fishermen, that decides when, where and how all fisheries in BC take place. It is also significant that Fraser completely ignored Ian Todd's acknowledgement that the PSC's miscalculation of the 1994 run size had nothing to do with the "aggressive fishing plan."

Minutes after the release of the Fraser Report on March 7, 1995, Brian Tobin held a video press conference in Ottawa and took the BC media by surprise by enthusiastically accepting every recommendation contained in the report. In a front-page story in the *Vancouver Sun* the following day, Mark Hume marvelled, "It's unheard of for government to accept all recommendations in a report like this." Tobin even denounced his own department for "managing on the edge" during the 1994 season. This was an astounding bit of revisionism: when it had been politically expedient to wave the flag and conduct "fish wars," Tobin had been happy to do so. Now he said, "It is evident that the existing management program can no longer effectively cope with the complexity imposed by a large and increasingly efficient commercial fleet..." It was a turning point in Ottawa's fight with the Americans over the PST. Instead of standing up to them, Canada now circled the wagons and took aim at its own fishermen.

A Radical Program of Change

The media analyst David Taras notes that in shaping its headlines and ten-second sound bites, the mass media thrive on grand statements such as those made by John Fraser. Such alarmist oversimplification causes the "ultimate corruption of our democracy" because the media does not present in-depth, multi-sided discussions about most problems facing contemporary society.[11] The people of Canada could have no detailed understanding of the complexities of the BC salmon fishery during the fateful 1994 season, and the publicity on Fraser's report gave the overwhelming impression that commercial fishermen had wilfully overfished and that the solution to the problem lay in reducing their numbers. This, in spite of the fact that on February 3, 1995—just a month before the Fraser Report was due for release—DFO Assistant Deputy Minister Pat Chamut had told Miro Cernetig of the *Globe and Mail* that after post-season spawning ground surveys, the total number of "missing" sockeye had dropped from 1.3 million to 800,000, and that at least 466,000 sockeye had died because of water temperatures in the Fraser River, a calamity beyond the control of both the DFO and the fishermen. Chamut also said that the Native fishery had "under-reported" its catch by at least 169,000 pieces. The tally of "missing" summer-run sockeye was now about 300,000 pieces, compared to an earlier projection of more than a million, and "There are still plenty of sockeye to lay eggs…even if it is a setback in plans to increase the number of spawners." When Fraser released his report, he responded by writing, "senior DFO officials seem to have been in a state of denial regarding the dysfunction within their organization and continue even today to assert there was no crisis in the 1994 salmon fishery."[12]

In his book *Solving History*, Canadian fisheries analyst Raymond A. Rogers notes that governments have constructed multi-stakeholder round-table processes, public inquiries and a host of other environmental institutions purportedly to address environmental issues. But official "green" initiatives seldom succeed, Rogers says. "[N]ation states are entirely incapable of promoting an environmental agenda, given their preoccupation with promoting the global economic agenda…The contradiction that these [green] initiatives face is that while the environmental policy process is becoming more inclusive, the corresponding economic and technological realities linked to privatization, deregulation, and free trade—which these increasingly ambitious environmental policy forums are supposed to address—are becoming less and less accountable to the public sphere."[13]

The 1994 "missing salmon," the Fraser Report and the media coverage were fortuitous for both government and industry. Ottawa had to respond to the crisis, and in the context of global political and economic pressure, combined with severe budget cuts, it was easier for government to reduce the commercial fleet than to take a balanced look at all the factors threatening BC salmon. Canadians would only support cuts to the fleet if they were afraid of environmental catastrophe, even though the federal government was taking no comprehensive steps to stop the ongoing damage to the environment. As it happened, the persistent notion of "too many fishermen chasing too few fish" was also useful to the canners and those interests who favoured privatization of the fishing industry. In his testimony to the Fraser Sockeye Public Review Board, Fisheries Council of BC President Mike Hunter had declared, "I think that there are many people in the industry, including the Minister, who have recognized that—not just the power of the fleet in its physical terms but the economic implications of having that many units of capital out there—is probably not the most efficient way to do business. And I think that the industry will find or have imposed upon it a solution for the next few years to that problem."[14]

Clearly the Fraser Inquiry was not just about protecting salmon, but also about making "units of capital" more profitable. According to Hunter, a smaller, more efficient fleet would automatically be more profitable and therefore able to assume the cost of most fisheries management programs through the payment of catch royalties. By turning management of the fishery over to industry, Hunter said—meaning the canners and a small group of wealthy quota holders—government costs would be reduced. It was a tempting prospect to the Treasury Board, and the plan to dismantle the West Coast fleet gained momentum rapidly.

Through it all, few people asked the question: why are there too many fishermen chasing too few fish? And how did this problem come about? The answer lies in the DFO's licensing policies.

The Tragedy of the Commons

These two extremes—absolute government control of a common property fishery and absolute privatization—exemplify classic positions in a grand scale philosophical debate concerning the best way to organize human societies and economies.

—James R. McGoodwin, *Crisis in the World's Fisheries*

When my father first started commercial fishing in 1950, a commercial fishing licence cost one dollar. He paid $500 for his first gillnetter. In those days, from such a nominal investment the industrious—or the lucky—could earn a modest annual income by fishing the entire coast for nearly all species of fish. In contrast, in 2004 my brother Kerry, who owns a modern gillnet vessel, estimates the value of his boat and licence to be at least $100,000. Yet despite this financial commitment, he is now entitled to fish only one area of the coast (Area C: northern gillnet), and because of DFO restrictions, he may harvest only one species of fish: sockeye salmon. Salmon prices have fallen dramatically over the last ten years, so it is increasingly difficult for a single-licence salmon fisherman to make ends meet.

Fishermen like my brother have experienced profound financial insecurity in recent years, and their stressful economic circumstances have intensified within the last generation. They have been forced to fish harder and harder—with less and less return—because of the accelerating, yet unnecessary, overcapitalization of the fleet.

Geoff Meggs identifies five distinct periods in the history of commercial fishing licence systems in BC. First, between 1860 and 1889 the salmon fishery was essentially "open" to all, with the canners assuming most of the capital risk. During this period fishermen invested little and were essentially piece-rate workers. Second, between 1889 and World War I, the government's first licensing system awarded most fishing privileges to commercial canners, which resulted in "attached licences," used mostly by Native and Japanese fishermen. The canners had almost exclusive control and could pay prices far below the market value of the fish.

Third, from World War I to 1969 the grip of the canners diminished gradually as Ottawa encouraged more fishermen—most of them white—to enter the industry. Concurrently, fishermen had to absorb a greater share of the financial risk through ownership of their vessels and gear. Fourth, in 1969, for the first time, the government restricted the number of vessels participating in the fishery. By this point virtually all of the capital costs of harvesting the fish had been transferred to the fishermen, on the ideological premise that fishermen were "independent businessmen" as opposed to "workers."

The fifth stage is still underway as, one by one, fisheries for various species have been reorganized around the individual transferable quota (ITQ) system. This latest phase is qualitatively different from all past ones. Previously, governments tried to control fishing by limiting the numbers of individuals who were allowed to fish, and catches were left entirely to chance and to the skill of the fishermen. The ITQ system, however, confers on a quota owner the private ownership rights to a given quantity of fish even before they have been caught, so that it is often more profitable to lease a quota than to engage in the physical act of fishing. The entire investment risk—which is considerable in the blackcod and other fisheries—appears to fall to the quota holder. But this can be deceiving: many quota holders have off-loaded the cost of acquiring or leasing their quotas onto their crews. Thus, in exchange for their jobs, crew members must deduct the cost of quotas (or stackable area licences in the case of the roe-herring fishery) from the gross value of the catch in a given fishery, though they receive no ownership equity in the quotas held by vessel owners and fishing companies.[1]

The Right to Fish

An intense controversy swirls around the apparently simple question of who should be entitled to make a living catching fish. But the conflict is not really about fish; it is about money. And, those who have the most money have the most influence over the political process.

In her book *Uncommon Property: The Fishing Industry and the Fish Processing Industry in British Columbia*, UBC sociology professor Patricia Marchak discusses fishing privileges or licences in the context of the history of private property rights in western civilization. Before European contact, aboriginal people on the West Coast considered salmon to be a form of communal property, notwithstanding the hierarchies of power within tribal societies. This attitude appeared to dovetail nicely with the belief, in keeping with English common law, that fish are a resource owned by all Canadians. But Marchak asserts that ever since European contact, Canada's marine resources have actually been subject to state or Crown ownership. As a result, over time a complex and highly political system of granting fishing privileges to private interests has evolved. According to Marchak, "the central difference between communal property owners and contemporary commercial fisheries is that the users are not catching fish to eat; they are catching them to sell. Fish are commodities." She adds, "Once accumulation rather than subsistence is the reason for catching fish (or cutting trees or any other activity), there is a need to define and defend property rights" to ensure that the rights holders benefit from their investments and activities. They could defend their property by force, but a superior method has evolved that uses "a system of laws ultimately backed up by a single institution with monopoly of force [the state] ... "

The government of Canada claims that it grants "privatized" fishing rights or licences to promote the "public good," but as Marchak notes,

"Governments...must satisfy an electorate while ensuring the continued economic viability of the system...And they must act, appear to act, and satisfy themselves that they are acting, to the best of their ability, in the public interest." She continues: "The power of large corporations necessarily affects and structurally constrains the choices governments make...A capitalist system by its intrinsic nature is perpetually changing because the cycles of accumulation and reinvestment persistently alter the nature of technology, the conditions of production and the actors. To protect the system of property rights, then, means protecting the accumulation process even when the process adversely affects the particular property holders of a previous cycle."[2]

In other words, privileges that governments may grant can also be taken away.

Marchak's claim that the Canadian government has routinely intervened in the West Coast fishery to maintain the dominant economic system is echoed in an East Coast context by sociologist Miriam Wright. In *A Fishery for Modern Times: The State and the Industrialization of the Newfoundland Fishery*, Wright states: "The state has a larger role—to appease and control conflicts within civil society, while still creating the best environment for economic structures...The rise of the interventionist State in the twentieth century was in part a response to a series of crises that were afflicting industrial capitalism in the late nineteenth century."[3]

In the BC fishing industry at the end of the nineteenth century, a savage battle for survival had been waged by both large and small players. Often the struggle played out along class lines, as fishermen waged strikes against canning companies over the price of salmon. Other conflicts broke out between fishermen of various racial and ethnic groups who tried to restrict potential competitors. At the same time, the United States and Canada were locked in a deadly duel over the "ownership" of Pacific salmon.

Licensing Fishermen

The first licensing system in the BC fishing industry was introduced on the Fraser River by the federal government in 1889. The government expressed concern about overfishing and limited the number of commercial salmon licences to 500, of which 350 went to the canners, giving them an overwhelming advantage both in controlling the harvest and setting the price. According to Scott Parsons: "The major flaw in the initiative appeared to be the failure to recognize the resource rent or excess profit accruing to the licensees [mostly canners], which resulted in demands from other independent fishermen for the right to fish the river. Cannery capacity increased significantly. In 1892, the licensing system was terminated and by 1893 the number of vessels involved in the fishery had more than doubled."[4]

In 1908 the provincial government imposed a licence system, this time on the North Coast, and once again organized around the financial interests of the canning companies, which were given allotments of fishing licences for their exclusive use. During World War I the demand for salmon rose, and in 1923 the cannery licence system was dropped in order to encourage more entrants into the fishery. The government of Canada made no further attempt to restrict access to the fishery until 1969, and save for the provincial commission conducted by Judge Gordon Sloan in 1939, which banned the use of fish traps in BC waters, neither Ottawa nor Victoria appeared to take much notice of the West Coast fishery. And the canneries did not object to the unlimited entry system, especially after World War II, when the demand for fish grew steadily.

It was not until the legendary Adams River run of 1958 enticed a vast influx of moonlighters into the fishery, with devastating effects on the incomes of "bona fide" fishermen, that there was pressure for change. It came from the United Fishermen and Allied Workers Union, which lobbied for a limited-entry licensing scheme to protect those for whom the fishery was "the primary means of earning a livelihood." In response, in 1959 Ottawa commissioned Dr. Sol Sinclair, a professor of agricultural economics and farm management at the University of Manitoba, to study the problem. Sinclair concluded in his report that "as long as there is free entry to the fisheries, a condition of excessive capital and labour will persist in them, and the consequence will be a low return to these inputs." He agreed with the UFAWU that the number of fishing licences had to be limited, but not just to improve fishermen's incomes: he also wanted to reduce the number to the point where those remaining could afford to pay "economic rent" to the Crown. Sinclair recommended that Ottawa auction all existing licences to the highest bidder, to issue no new salmon licences for five years and, after the moratorium, to make all salmon licences fully transferable. Such trade in licences would "utilize as far as possible the automatic forces of economics to bring about necessary adjustments to the changed condition in the fishery."[5]

The minority government of the day did not act on any of Sinclair's recommendations. The UFAWU, not content with this lack of progress, began formulating its own licensing recommendations, and in February 1966 the delegates to the union's annual convention endorsed a nine-point licensing program, including these provisions: 1) that a five-year moratorium be imposed on licences (1966–71) except for those who fished in 1964 and 1965 and derived 30 percent of their income from fishing; 2) that licence holders use licences as their primary means of earning a livelihood—at least 30 percent of their income to start with and gradually increasing; 3) that people engaged in other full-time employment surrender their licences; 4) that each licensed fisherman hold a licence-book with an annual $10 book fee and $1 licence fee; 5) that after the five-year moratorium all unused licences go to people on a waiting list; 6) that licences be non-transferable; 7) that Native participation in the industry be maintained; 8) that company financing of boats and gear be eliminated; and 9) that an impartial licence appeal board be established. The Canadian government did not respond to these recommendations.

The Davis Plan

In 1968 the federal Liberal Party swept to power on a tide of "Trudeau-mania." BC MP Jack Davis was appointed minister of fisheries, and Trudeau instructed him to tackle the perennial problem of licensing in Canada's fisheries. It happened that Davis and his team of DFO planners followed the teachings of James Crutchfield, the economist from Washington state who in 1969 had published *The Pacific Salmon Fishery: A Study of Irrational Conservation*.[6] Crutchfield argued that because of its open access the salmon fishery was vulnerable to overfishing, and that economic contrivances, rather than traditional management constraints, were the best way to protect the resource. His position was consistent with Michael Graham's 1943 "Great Law of Fishing," stating that unregulated commercial fishing activity will eventually expand to the point of collapse, or "bio-economic equilibrium." The problem of overfishing, Crutchfield said, would disappear if fisheries were privatized. But another controversial American writer, Garrett Hardin, in his 1968 essay "The Tragedy of the Commons,"[7] condemned common property resource management—a metaphorical catchphrase that would have a much more lasting and pernicious influence on future fisheries policy. Hardin did not focus specifically on fisheries but referred mostly to the management of sheep grazing on the English commons of the eighteenth century, yet his theories were seized on by writers such as Crutchfield and applied to fish harvesting. The social geographer Martin W. Lewis suggests that Hardin's views are "eco-fascist"—Hardin actually suggested mass starvation as a cure for overpopulation[8]—but Hardin's influence could be felt in the work of Peter Pearse and his acolytes at DFO's Economics and Planning Branch as they prepared Canada's first limited-entry commercial fishing licensing system.

Davis introduced the plan into the BC salmon fishery in 1969. Contrary to UFAWU advice, the scheme licensed fishing vessels rather than fishermen by establishing two vessel licence categories: those with landings over 10,000 pounds of salmon in 1967 or 1968 (freely transferable "A" licence) and those with less than 10,000 pounds (non-transferable "B" licence). According to Geoff Meggs, "Davis hoped that by forcing thousands of boats into the 'B' category, where their licences would expire, he could concentrate the buyback on the core of only 2,500 vessels which accounted for 80 percent of the landings."[9]

The Davis Plan was to be carried out in four distinct phases: freeze the fleet at a stable level, gradually reduce the fleet, improve the standard of vessels and introduce economically optimal gear and area regulations. The system would purportedly increase fishermen's incomes, reduce excess fleet capacity and improve fisheries management. And, echoing Sol Sinclair, Davis made it clear that once fishermen's incomes improved, Ottawa intended to introduce a catch royalty system to ensure that economic rent was paid to the government.

The UFAWU, fearing corporate control of the harvest, strongly opposed the transferable licences and called for non-transferable licences that would be "placed on the man." The union believed that licences should only be held by owner-operators to prevent licence leasing. A union licensing committee then worked out a detailed program in which licences were non-transferable, only bona fide fishermen were eligible, inactive licences reverted to a general pool and new entrants obtained licences through a waiting list based on seniority. Special provisions would be given to children of existing licence holders, and a pension plan would compensate licence holders upon retirement.

However, on February 14, 1969, *The Fisherman* reported that Jack Davis had rejected the union's proposal because "licensing the man" would lead to a union-dominated closed shop. He told delegates to the UFAWU annual convention that "No younger person wanting to get in as a commercial fisherman could in fact get in. I did not like to think of an industry with an aging workforce, with no new entrants." Decades later, the Davis Plan would lead to this very outcome as the prohibitive capital costs associated with West Coast salmon licences barred most younger fishermen from entering the fishery.

Meanwhile, UFAWU Secretary-Treasurer Homer Stevens warned Davis that the real threat to new entrants was corporate control of salmon licences. "If our assumption is correct, then at the very minimum the freeze allows the major companies to control 2,094 boats…We disagree with any scheme which produces inflated price tags for licences and in which the right to fish is sold to the highest bidder."

In response, Davis said, "If a company starts to buy up a significant numbers of boats, I will be on the phone to its president in a hurry." Then, despite the fact the UFAWU and most of the industry opposed his plan, he declared, "If it happened at some time that two-thirds of the fishermen didn't think it was the best scheme in the world, I would still be concerned about putting it in. Because I think it is the best and in the end will turn out to be the very best."[10]

Throughout the debate, he insisted that fishermen would become "members of a elite club" and their licences would be passports to a comfortable retirement.[11]

Later that spring an extraordinary surge in boat building occurred as fishermen rushed to upgrade their vessels before the moratorium. In a brief on licensing, the UFAWU wrote, "Because [Davis] has indicated further measures to reduce the fleet...the pressure on each owner to see that all licensed vessels engage in the salmon fishery is extremely heavy. When we warned experts in the federal fisheries department 12 years ago that herring would be depleted by overfishing, we were practically told that as fishermen we knew nothing. When we warned of the decline of halibut resources when the eastern Bering Sea was opened to the Japanese, our protests were ignored. The experts were wrong. Fishermen had to suffer the consequences."[12]

On December 18, 1970, *The Fisherman* reported that Ken Fraser, an official with BC Packers Ltd., welcomed the Davis Plan. "There is no place in the industry for poor or average fishermen who can barely make a living," he said.

Phase II of the Davis Plan began in 1970, when the government initiated the first licence buyback, and continued until 1973. Over 350 vessels (seven percent of the fleet) were retired and subsequently resold. Under pressure, Ottawa introduced rules ostensibly to limit corporate control of licences to 12 percent. However, the DFO reneged on the earlier understanding that "B" licence-holders could retain their (non-transferable) licences until retirement, and limited such licences to 10 years. Meanwhile, despite the moratorium on new licences, owners of non-salmon vessels lobbied hard to be included in the plan, and the DFO eventually granted salmon licences to several of them. According to Scott Parsons of the DFO, "This modification seriously undermined the objectives of the licensing program. Although only a few vessels (160 at most) were added to the fleet, many of these were large groundfish trawlers and halibut longliners. This created a large pool of unused capacity which could fish salmon."[13] At the same time there was a spate of new vessel construction as owners replaced their older, smaller vessels to qualify for "A" licences, and the DFO reacted by introducing vessel replacement rules based on gross tonnage. These provisions failed to stop a rash of "licence pyramiding": a loophole allowed large capital holders to combine a number of smaller gillnet licences into seine licences. The results of the federal government's efforts to reduce the fleet can be seen in the numbers: in 1968 there were 397 licensed seine vessels; by 1977 there were 514, an increase of 29.5 percent.

A New Form of Property Rights

By the mid-1970s the fleet had been transformed. According to sociologist Brian Hayward, the Davis Plan had served to create "a new form of property rights…Because no more licences were to be created," he wrote, "all that had to occur was for conditions in the salmon industry to appear lucrative and the demand for the scarce commodity would rapidly inflate its value."[14] This demand came with the spectacular expansion of the post-World War II Japanese economy, which reached its apogee in the 1970s. And the introduction of the new roe-herring fishery in 1972 along with the huge Japanese demand for salmon fuelled a dizzying cycle of licence speculation. Hayward points out, "The effect of this economic dynamic on fleet capitalization has been profound…The estimated market value of the salmon fleet has increased from $73.8 million in 1968 to $273 million in 1977, a 270 percent increase in 10 years." Contrary to Jack Davis's claims, the new system forced fishermen's income into a downward cycle: "in 1960, while landings were one million pounds less than in 1975, the rate of return on total investment was 24.23 percent higher." As well, "Some new entrants clearly paid excess prices for licences. These individuals may actually be worse off than in a situation of free entry."

This new information directly contradicted Hardin, Crutchfield and others who held that open access was the source of the industry's problems. All was not well, and in 1973 Ottawa instructed the West Coast Fleet Development Committee to review the Davis Plan. This group consisted mostly of DFO and industry representatives, but Peter Pearse, the UBC resource economist (and an unsuccessful federal Liberal Party candidate) was added "to represent the public." According to Meggs, "The majority report [of the committee], largely drafted by Pearse, was to provide the framework for future industry development. An endorsement of the Davis plan, it urged continued fleet reduction, continued buy-back programs, and catch royalties or a landing tax. Pearse also urged elimination of fishermen's unemployment insurance…"[15]

By 1977 the DFO had carried out most of Phase III of the Davis Plan, requiring higher vessel inspection standards to improve fish quality. In addition, the DFO belatedly ended licence pyramiding. Phase IV, designed to introduce area licensing and catch royalties, was put on hold.

The Davis Plan succeeded in reducing the number of commercial fishermen from 9,600 to 8,600, but it nonetheless left a bitter legacy. In 1978, when Dr. Sol Sinclair wrote another report on licensing for the DFO, he was vigorously critical of the Davis Plan. He wrote, "the reduction of the total number of licences increases the inherent incentive…to increase fishing capability,"[16] and he reiterated his call for a catch royalty to curtail overinvestment in the fleet.

In another independent licensing study commissioned by the DFO in 1982, Don Cruickshank, a former fish processor, wrote, "When the limited entry program was initiated in 1969 there were 6,104 vessels in the salmon fleet; today there are 4,707. This would appear to represent a reduction in fleet capacity; but to consider only the number of vessels is misleading. The salmon seine fleet has actually increased over 40 percent from 369 to 532 during this period, while the troll and gillnet fleets have decreased from 5,737 to 4,175."[17]

Geoff Meggs explained, "The value of the licences, which had been nil in 1969, [by 1980] stood at $150 million. The debt load, which had stood at $13.4 million in 1969, now was at least $300 million. In sum, the industry had produced a fleet worth about $600 million, financing at least half of that cost with debt. By 1981 when salmon and herring revenues were $180 million, fishermen had paid out $45 million in interest."[18] Yet, as DFO economist David Reid wryly observed, "This debt didn't catch any more fish."[19]

The Prophet of Privatization

In 1981, when Pierre Elliott Trudeau was returned to the office of prime minister, he faced the challenge of salvaging the Canadian economy. The post-World War II boom had ended, and Canada was increasingly affected by the crisis-ridden US economy. Oil prices were skyrocketing, interest rates were rising and North American manufacturing was experiencing serious competition from Europe and Japan.

Trudeau commissioned the Economic Council of Canada (ECC), under the direction of Sylvia Ostray, to survey all sectors of the Canadian economy. A group of about 30 experts produced a report cryptically entitled *Reforming Regulation*, which included a brief analysis of the economic performance of Canada's fisheries. The primary contributor on fisheries was Peter Pearse. "The [commercial fishery] system is not ideal," the report said, "and has led to poor economic performance in the fisheries; redundant labour and capital; unstable income and employment prospects; and consistent pressure on fish stocks." The ECC experts went on, "With open access to a common property resource, an individual or group of individuals cannot legally exclude others. Under such conditions, the fishery would attract more capital and labour than necessary to harvest the catch efficiently. In the past the government has intervened to reduce excess fishing capacity and to conserve fish stocks... At some point the reduction in the size of the catch would mean that the extra fishing effort would not be worthwhile, and a 'bio-economic equilibrium' would be achieved."

The report was critical of fishermen for overcapitalizing their fishing operations: "In the Pacific salmon fishery, for example, when limitations were set on the number of boats in order to control the total catch, fishermen increased the size of their boats. Regulations were then adopted to limit the total tonnage, and fishermen responded by using more powerful boats. Measures were then introduced to fix the haulage power; fishermen reacted by augmenting their speed..."[20]

Thus the ECC laid all the blame for the fisheries crisis on the fishermen, rather than on government policies such as the Davis Plan. The report proposed five options to restructure the fishery: 1) limited entry/licence buy-outs; 2) gear control; 3) sole-ownership rights or enterprise allocations for companies; 4) landing taxes or catch royalties; and 5) stinted landing rights or individual transferable quotas (ITQs). The report said that private ownership would allow "the federal government [to]... exercise its sole ownership right" to capture the rent from fishing, by, for example, auctioning the right to catch a certain tonnage of fish, which would generate "an economic incentive to minimize [bidders'] expenditure on labour and capital." The report continued candidly: "Sole ownership [by fishing companies] would clearly be superior to comprehensive controls on fishing effort; however, there would be political and social problems with this solution."

The ECC then settled on the next best option: Individual Transferable Quotas. "Stinted landing rights [ITQs] have the advantage that unlike the landing tax or comprehensive control options, the fisherman makes the decision on how best to harvest his allotted share. Thus many gear [enforcement] regulations could be abolished, but at the same time there would be no incentive to increase rent-dissipating capital and labour...We recommend that the DFO adopt a series of measures aimed at regulating individual ocean fisheries through a system of transferable, quantitative stinted landing rights...We recommend that the DFO consider the use of a tax (or catch royalty); licence fees, and/or buy-back schemes as supplements to the introduction of transferable quantitative stinted landing rights."[21]

The ECC's recommendations were forwarded to the federal cabinet for action, though the report had at least one dissenter. Harry W. Arthurs, a law professor from Osgoode Hall, York University, wrote, "At the heart of my discontent, perhaps, is my preference for a vocabulary of analysis and a system of social priorities that is different from the report. Where the report seeks to translate common property in fish or the environment into marketable private rights in order to maximize rent, I would prefer to give more careful consideration to the disruption of a traditional way of life or the dangers to future generations."

Turning the Tide

Just prior to the release of the ECC's report, the DFO commissioned Peter Pearse and Fernand Doucet to conduct a quick study of the problems facing the West Coast commercial fishery. In October 1980 they came back with recommendations such as increased licence fees, a catch royalty, area licensing, a new licence buyback and the removal of "perverse subsidies" to the industry. The report also called for an expanded inquiry into Pacific fisheries, and as it turned out, Peter Pearse had written his own job description: he was named chief commissioner of a two-year Royal Commission. Given his past involvement with the Davis Plan, many fishermen questioned his objectivity, and at the opening session of the Royal Commission, UFAWU president Jack Nichol asked Pearse if he would listen to the views of working people in the industry or simply impose his "preconceived ideas" and succumb to the influence of the canners. Pearse was indignant at suggestions that he had a hidden agenda. "I want to emphasize that this is an independent commission," he said, "and it is important that it be totally independent of all the influences—of all other influences—other than those that are properly brought to bear in the course of this inquiry."[22]

UFAWU Secretary-Treasurer George Hewison identified two serious weaknesses in the inquiry's terms of reference: "The Pearse commission will be unable to recommend solutions to the problems confronting working fishermen unless it deals with the degree of corporate concentration in the BC fishing industry and the repercussions of the Canada/US treaty."[23] Pearse said that his workload was already too heavy to do anything about it. "I could not deal with that question now, although it is an important and urgent problem, unless I stopped being a domestic inquirer," he said. "The whole structure of this commission would have to change."[24]

Despite the public hearings that followed, Pearse's final report, *Turning The Tide: A New Policy for Canada's Pacific Fisheries*, simply reiterated the ECC's report of 1981 with some interesting policy embellishments. Pearse's prime concern was the common property nature of the fishery. He called for better conservation, integrated management, long-term planning and enforcement, though in this period of austerity, such recommendations were largely cosmetic. And although Pearse made much ado about protecting salmon habitat, his call for a "no net loss of habitat" policy was a pernicious legacy since it accepted habitat destruction as inevitable. He proposed cash payments to support habitat restoration programs, rather than holding developers to the stringent regulations in the Fisheries Act. To make matters worse, he insisted that all salmon enhancement programs be subject to a rigorous cost-benefit analysis before being approved. According to Geoff Meggs, "By 1982, enhancement production was just coming on stream. Despite unexpected cost overruns and sharp funding cuts, the program had returned $1.30 to the economy for every dollar expended... While Pearse was content to let market forces determine the value of fish habitat, he was determined to have proof of profit before endorsing the salmon enhancement program."[25]

The crux of the Pearse Report was his recommended licensing policy. He proposed to reduce the fleet by 50 percent within 10 years through a complex competitive bidding process. He also suggested that the proceeds of this bidding process, in tandem with a catch royalty system, pay for a major licence buyback program. Looking back on it years later, Scott Parsons of the DFO observed that "any successful [fleet reform] program would have to be: 1) administratively feasible; 2) politically acceptable; and 3) publicly defensible. It is debateable whether Pearse's proposals were administratively feasible. They engendered a storm of public debate over the next five years which made it clear they were nei-ther politically acceptable nor publicly defensible."[26]

The scheme met with fierce opposition, and a grassroots movement called the Fishermen's Survival Coalition, representing dozens of coastal communities, was formed in December 1983. (This coalition had no di-rect links with the coalition formed in 1992 to fight the Tories' Aboriginal Fishing Strategy.) In a keynote speech at the founding conference, Jack Nichol, president of the UFAWU, told the assembly, "We believe that the fisheries are being sacrificed to other resource developments—min-ing, timber, double-tracking of railways, offshore drilling." About 200 delegates endorsed a "fishermen's charter of rights," which included the right to an industry with a future; the right to decent income (that is, fish-ermen's bargaining rights), the right to a job (that is, protection of bona fide owner–operator fishermen), the right to maximize the full potential of the resource for all Canadians (that is, an equitable interception treaty with the USA) and the right to a meaningful advisory process.

On December 14, 1983, the *Vancouver Sun* reported that Pierre De Bane, the Liberal fisheries minister appointed in September 1982 to re-place Romeo LeBlanc, had declined to meet with the Survival Coalition. He met instead with Native leaders in Port Alberni and suggested he was interested in using the fish resource as "a springboard for Native eco-nomic development." UFAWU business agent Bill Procopation warned, "Not only do [De Bane's] actions directly threaten the economic survival of all fishermen, they open the way for a fratricidal, race-oriented split in the fishing industry that will pave the way for Pearse." And he noted that Native and non-Natives had for decades united against other industries that would "mine, drill, and saw their way through the last of our renew-able resources—fish."[27]

A confidential memo prepared by De Bane's staff proposed that Na-tive fishermen be given 43.6 percent of the salmon catch—an astounding increase over the 14.5 percent of the total catch at the time. The figure was based more upon the US federal court's granting of 50 percent of Washington state's commercial harvest to its Native tribes than on traditional Canadian Native food fishery landings. It was also predicated on a traditional Native per capita annual consumption of up to 1,000 pounds of salmon, well above the estimate of anthropologists such as Gordon Hewes who calculated a maximum of 365 pounds.

Meanwhile, the Coalition—representing the UFAWU, Pacific Trollers Association, the Gulf Trollers Association, and the Pacific Salmon Seiners Association—had raised over $50,000 to send a large delegation to Ottawa, and hundreds of fishermen attended the send-off rally in Vancouver. On February 6, 1984, dozens of fishermen donned bright orange survival suits to protest on the snowy lawn in front of the House of Commons in Ottawa. Tory MP John Fraser turned out to champion the Survival Coalition's cause, but Pierre De Bane simply ignored them. That day the *Vancouver Sun* reported that De Bane's political assistant Terry O'Reilly and Deputy Minister Art May were at work on a secret plan to reduce the fleet by 50 percent, just as Pearse had recommended.

But while Pearse had been at work on his report, another report had been in the making. In the spring of 1982, then Liberal Fisheries

Fishermen don survival suits on Parliament Hill, Ottawa, to protest Pearse Royal Commission Report, 1983.

Don Cruickshank, former owner of Seafood Products Ltd., of Port Hardy BC. In two separate reports, Cruickshank provided DFO an alternative blueprint for the fishing industry designed to enhance salmon stocks and to protect coastal communities.

Minister Romeo LeBlanc had commissioned a parallel industry task force on fleet rationalization, led by Don Cruickshank. The Fleet Rationalization Committee recommended a voluntary licence buyback, designed to preserve a balance between the large and small boat fleets, and Cruickshank wrote, "The Department of Fisheries and Oceans permitted and condoned, even encouraged, the present status through their commissions and omissions. The Department issued more licences than the resource can reasonably support. The pyramiding of 'A' licences was allowed to continue despite industry recommendations to the contrary, and inadequate current vessel replacement rules have contributed to fleet growth and overcapitalization. The abrogation of established rights of fishermen by naked economic forces would remove the burden of mismanagement from the Department by placing excessive, inhumane hardships on fishermen."[28]

In particular, Cruickshank was alarmed that Pearse believed ITQs would encourage conservation."Please recognize that the implementation of a quota system is virtually irreversible," he wrote to De Bane. "If you are truly intent on determining the viability of quota systems, scrutinize our present abalone fishery. There are only 26 licences to police in this fishery, yet our staff members admit privately they have no control."[29] The abalone fishery was the first West Coast fishery subject to ITQs. Within a very short time the stock approached extinction due to quota-busting and poaching, and it has never fully recovered.

Cruickshank proposed that a volume-based catch royalty be the fishermen's contribution, equally matched by government, to a fund to support both licence retirement and expanded salmon enhancement. He also called for all licence holdings to be made public to properly measure corporate ownership of salmon licences, and he suggested that all licences not held by individual owner-operators be extinguished. His recommendation was not adopted. Over the next 15 years, unusually good ocean survival condi-tions resulted in some of the largest returns of salmon in modern history, and a royalty system would have generated enormous revenue for use in rebuilding the runs and gradually reducing the fleet. Cruickshank's system also required fishermen to foot at least half the bill, covering the "eco-nomic rent." However, in the eyes of the canners and the mandarins in Ottawa, the report's fatal flaw was that it left the common property nature of the salmon resource intact. Cruickshank wrote:

> Behind the statistics and official concepts were the shad-ows of the boats and the people for whom decisions will be made that mean either the continued life or death of an industry in a form that we know. Fishermen are pri-mary protein producers, but the fish could be harvested with far less effort and manpower if mere production was the only value. The men, and even a few women, who go to sea have chosen a sometimes lonely, more physi-cally demanding life than most of us who sit in offices. It would be a sadder and poorer place without them, and the view of the sea without fishing vessels is beyond our comprehension. Yet this is what is actually at stake: we could save the fish and abandon the fishermen; or we can implement measures that will save them both.[30]

A New Direction for Canada's Economy

When Brian Mulroney and his Tories were swept to power on Septem-ber 4, 1984, John Fraser was appointed the new minister of fisheries. However, all of their alluring election promises to BC fishermen—$100 million for a voluntary buyback, $100 million for salmon enhancement and a major overhaul of the DFO's policy-making system—were soon abandoned. Scarcely a month after the election, Michael Wilson, the new minister of finance, unveiled the document *A New Direction for Canada: An Agenda for Economic Renewal*. In it he declared, "A major rea-son for our poor performance has been the failure of the Government of Canada to deal with real problems... For too long it has allowed its fiscal situation to deteriorate and debt to increase. Through excessive regulation and intervention, it has substituted the judgements of politicians and regulators for the judgements of those in the marketplace."[31] In a section on West Coast fisheries, he added, "The crisis in the BC salmon fishery requires urgent attention. The regulatory system has failed to control over-investment in fishing vessels and gear, resulting in an excessively large fleet. For the stocks to rebuild and for fishermen to make a decent living, there must be a significant reduction in the size and fishing power of the fleet."

By March 1985 Fraser had already reneged on his election promise to fund Phase II of the Salmon Enhancement Program (SEP)—it would be "impossible," he said.[32] The existing Phase I program was to be slashed as well. The 1985 budget of $37 million was to be cut to $20 million and the SEP staff of 235 reduced to 215. Then in June, DFO Deputy Minister Art May told the annual meeting of the Fisheries Association of BC that the Pearse Report was not dead. "I would think that he [Pearse] ought to be very pleased that over a short period so many recommendations were accepted and acted upon," said May.[33]

Fraser failed to rein in his zealous deputy, or to do much of anything else. On October 18, 1985, *The Fisherman* reported, "Between September and December 1984 Fraser was away from his office for 43 days consecutively. Between January and April he was absent for 23 days consecutively. Little wonder then that May could boast of his determination to drive through the Pearse Report without fear of Fraser's interception."

May replaced Pacific regional director Wayne Shinners with Patrick Chamut, who hailed from DFO's Ontario region and who would go on to oversee the complete restructuring of the West Coast fishery. Fraser himself lasted less than a year as minister of fisheries before having to resign over the infamous East Coast Tuna Scandal. *The Fisherman* reported: "John Fraser is gone. The man who pledged to fight for new programs for the fishing industry will be written up in history books as a failure. He ultimately became the victim of his decision to put the profits of one tuna company ahead of the interests of the industry and the public."[34]

In late 1985 Mulroney appointed Erik Nielsen to lead a task force to review all government programs and expenditures at the same time as he was given the job of interim minister of fisheries and oceans. As part of his task force report, Nielsen recommended that the fishermen's unemployment insurance program be cut in order to placate US fish processors, who claimed that the program was an unfair subsidy. He also recommended that DFO staff be cut by 20 percent, that DFO make aquaculture research a priority and that more salmon be allotted to the sports fleet. He called for the privatization of the Salmon Enhancement Program, more cuts to DFO habitat staff, the termination of the fishermen's loan program, the granting of enterprise allocations to fishing companies, the relaxation of Canada's salmon export regulations, and the privatization of small craft harbours. To realize this grim agenda the Tories appointed Peter Meyboom, a neo-conservative from the Treasury Board who knew nothing about fish, as deputy minister of fisheries. Then, just before handing over the fisheries portfolio to Tom Siddon on November 20, 1985, Nielsen cancelled Phase II of the salmon enhancement program.

Armchair Fishermen

Through the remainder of the 1980s the West Coast fishing industry was left to languish. Tom Siddon, Bernard Valcourt and John C. Crosbie all introduced DFO policy initiatives, but nothing was done to help the salmon or commercial fishermen. Certainly, none of them even considered the industry plan developed by Cruickshank's Fleet Rationalization Committee. Thanks to a brief period of buoyant export prices in the Japanese market during the mid-1980s, the Tories could claim that all was well, but it was not. Scott Parsons points out, "Taking inflation into account, between 1969 and 1988 the capital value of the seine fleet had increased by a factor of 3.6. The overcapacity problem was masked by higher-than-average salmon abundance and prices...Increased capital investment, however, left the fleet more vulnerable to cyclical catch and declining prices."[35]

The crunch came in 1989 just after the introduction of the Free Trade Agreement, when a series of factors plunged the industry into economic crisis. The Japanese demand for herring roe and fresh-frozen salmon had only temporarily inflated the value of the catch, thus disguising the deep structural problems caused by the Davis plan. In the late 1960s, the DFO—after repeated warnings from the UFAWU that herring stocks were in decline—had closed the "reduction" herring fishery (roe herring used to produce fertilizer) in order to conserve stocks. By 1971 stocks had improved sufficiently for the DFO to initiate an "experimental" roe fishery. Two years later the wholesale value of the roe herring catch had risen to $35 million; by 1979 it had ballooned to $170 million. The fishery had what Parsons describes as "gold fever," with BC processing companies temporarily enjoying a "virtual monopoly" in the Japanese market.

At the outset, the DFO believed that setting licence fees ($200 per gillnetter and $2,000 per seiner) would somehow control activity, so they licensed roe herring fishermen instead of vessels. But the system was a perversion of the non-transferable "licence-on-the-man" proposal made by the UFAWU years earlier, and by the late 1970s speculation in herring licences was out of control. The DFO tried to take command by introducing area licensing to the herring fishery in 1981, and soon afterwards required fishermen to "stack" licences to access more than one area. Licence stacking, according to DFO economists, is an effective way to control fishing by reducing the number of participants, and it gives the illusion that the reduction of licences occurs voluntarily.

But in the licence stacking system, there is an immediate increase in licence values as those still fishing have to buy or lease licences from others in order to access a given fishery or area. The system also encourages the rise of a new class of armchair fishermen, who can sit back and collect a personal resource rent by leasing their licences. Furthermore, some licence holders sell their licences for exorbitant sums even though they never paid a cent to acquire them in the first place.

Don Cruickshank observed, "During the 1991 roe herring fishery, 160 individual seine vessels physically fished the 252 active licences. Ninety-two licences were leased at fees ranging from $80,000 to $100,000. Of the 1,327 roe herring gillnet licences, a knowledgeable source at Fisheries and Oceans estimates that about half were leased at up to $15,000 each."[36]

The GATT Ruling and the Strike of 1989

By 1980 several new suppliers had entered the Japanese roe market, forcing the wholesale price downwards, and BC processors began to slash the price paid to fishermen. The Prince Rupert Fishermen's Co-op tried to lower costs by buying roe herring from non-unionized Alaskan fishermen, who traditionally got lower prices. Then, on April 1, 1986, the Alaskan processors launched a complaint before the trade dispute panel of the General Agreement on Trade and Tariffs (GATT), claiming that Canadian regulations forbidding the export of unprocessed herring, sockeye and pink salmon put them at a disadvantage. The Alaskans were really seeking to get access to superior quality BC fish. Canadian government officials offered to negotiate an informal settlement, but the Alaskans refused and the matter ended up before a special tribunal panel of the GATT.

Ottawa had good arguments in its defence: the export regulations had been in effect since 1908, long before the GATT came into effect,[37] and many other countries—including the US with its Magnussen Act—had similar regulations protecting their processing sectors. Nonetheless, on November 3, 1987, the GATT panel upheld the US complaint. The ruling was non-binding, but Ottawa chose not to exercise its veto in order to avoid upsetting the Americans during the critical stages of Free Trade Agreement (FTA) negotiations. Indeed, as part of the FTA agreement the Tories had agreed that all previous GATT rulings between the two countries would become permanently binding. Thus, on March 22, 1988, the full GATT council upheld the earlier panel decision regarding the West Coast fisheries export regulations.

Ironically, Ottawa had made special provisions to protect the export of unprocessed fish on the East Coast, where fishermen's voting power is much greater than in BC. When questioned about this glaring discrepancy, External Affairs Minister Joe Clark said, "BC's fish processing industry will be a loser in the free trade deal with the US…you are not going to be able to win on every front."[38]

The GATT ruling left the West Coast industry in an extremely vulnerable position. The UFAWU feared that thousands of shoreworkers would lose their jobs if the canners relocated their operations to the US. But the Pacific Trollers Association and other groups welcomed the decision, naïvely believing the increased competition would lead to higher dockside prices for salmon. Don Cruickshank responded, "The landed value of a fisherman's catch represents only half the wholesale value of that same catch. The shoreworkers are not the only ones who stand to lose. Are there still a few rednecks who think that they will receive high fish prices as a result of the GATT ruling?...Fish mongers, on either side of the border, have never been noted for their benevolence. You will get exactly what the buyers feel they must pay, while maximizing their profits and not a penny more."[39]

On February 19, 1988, the UFAWU executive launched a campaign to fight the GATT ruling, including a 50-person lobby to Ottawa and a one-day strike by over 3,000 shoreworkers. Soon after that, Trade Minister Pat Carney and Fisheries Minister Tom Siddon announced that all Canadian salmon and herring would have to be landed and processed in Canada for "scientific purposes." However, the US immediately vetoed this proposal, and a year later John Crosbie would announce that all attempts to defend the export regulations had been abandoned.

The issue came to a head during a three-and-a-half-week strike in the summer of 1989. The canners claimed the world market now forced them to cut wages and benefits as well as drastically reducing the dockside price of salmon, and they and the DFO would also claim that expanding competition from salmon farms had caused a worldwide price collapse. In fact the markets for wild and farmed salmon were not always identical, so aquaculture could only account for part of the price decline. It was ironic that in the past, canners had promoted aquaculture as a way to make the industry more profitable.[40]

The canners' price cuts were devastating for fishermen. For example, in 1984 the total commercial catch of salmon was 19,028,402 pieces, worth $45,976,779. A nearly similar catch in 1995 of 20,775,915 pieces only fetched $40,686,840.[41] Given inflation, debt servicing and other spiralling costs, the fishermen were indeed in a jam. The strike was a brutal affair with the new "open border" policy giving the canners a huge strategic advantage. Fishing industry strikes had once been relatively brief, as the shortage of processing capacity put a limit on strike breaking by non-union fishermen. Now, given easy access to plants in Washington state, the canners could encourage a large portion of the fleet to fish during the strike.

On July 30 the Native Brotherhood broke ranks with the strikers and signed an agreement with the canners, even though drastic price cuts were still on the bargaining table. But at the same time the Brotherhood executive insisted on a "me-too" clause that ensured their membership the same terms the union would eventually win. Such activity demoralized UFAWU members who remained on the picket lines. The peak of the fishing season was so short that they had lost most of the season's earnings during the three-week struggle, while non-union fishermen enjoyed reduced competition on the fishing grounds. On August 2 the UFAWU leadership released the union fleet in a "plug and jam" operation, ostensibly to deprive the scabs of their catch, and shortly afterwards the strike ended. The union had beaten back the worst of the price cuts, and shoreworkers had made history by winning the industry's first pension plan, but the 1989 strike marked a profound shift in the industry's balance of power.

The Same Old Snake Oil

Early in 1990 Tory Fisheries Minister Tom Siddon and his deputy minister, Peter Meyboom, instructed Al Wood, head of the Pacific Region Economic Programs and Planning Branch (EPPB), to draft an emergency response to the industry's alleged overcapacity crisis. The EPPB worked feverishly to produce a discussion paper, *Vision 2000*, which was leaked to the media on February 9, 1990. *Vision 2000* contained some radical—but familiar—recommendations: reduction of the fleet by 50 percent; elimination of "mixed-stock" fisheries; restriction of seine fisheries to "terminal" areas; drastic reduction of the troll fleet; catch royalties to pay costs of all fisheries management; privatization of all fishing rights; cuts to government management costs; increased Native participation in the fleet; expansion of aquaculture; consolidation of the processing sector; use of area licensing, enterprise allocations and ITQs to reduce the fleet; and restriction of DFO consultative processes to holders of licences, quotas or enterprise allocations. Geoff Meggs, then editor of *The Fisherman*, wrote, "*Vision 2000* was nothing more than a new version of the same snake oil."[42]

Just before *Vision 2000* was leaked, the DFO had begun limiting access to a number of fisheries—crab, shrimp, prawn—that had formerly been open to all salmon "A" licence holders. While many fishermen rallied in Nanaimo on January 22, 1990, to protest the change in policy, a smaller group of fishermen were working with the department to develop new eligibility criteria based on past landings. Those who had not participated in fisheries for the various species, for whatever reason, were now unexpectedly deprived of their privilege to do so, as articulated by Peter Pearse in the ECC paper of 1981.

Fishermen reacted bitterly. At a protest rally, troller Bob Ostrom declared, "It all started with the Davis Plan. It did nothing to limit the fleet. It created licences that could be sold...Licences should not be a thing that can be sold. It should be a right to fish—the licence should be on the fisherman."[43] Richard Tarnoff, a Gulf troller, rejected the notion that privatized fishing rights reduced the capital costs of fishing. "In DFO's policy document, the section on individual quotas lists benefits and problems, but there is no evidence to back it up," he said. "...There will be increased costs from buying quota; there will be extra costs if fishermen have to pay for enforcement; there may be royalties or higher fees for fisheries management."

Bob Carpenter, a Nanaimo halibut fisherman, was alarmed by rumours that some underhanded skippers planned to recover the new costs of private quotas by passing on the costs to their crews: "All these halibut fishermen who want to have quotas—they don't stop to think what's good for everybody or what's good for the industry. There are some who now have a large quota on a halibut boat, that own the boat, and can't even dress a halibut or bait a hook. What about the crew? What are they going to get? Do you think they didn't pay the fuel bills and the grub bills? They worked the gear and worked their fingers to the bone—but where is their quota?"

On June 1, 1990, the UFAWU sponsored an industry conference on the implications and impacts of *Vision 2000* at the University of British Columbia. The keynote speaker was Dan MacInnes of the Department of Sociology and Anthropology at Saint Francis Xavier University, Antigonish, Nova Scotia. As part of its privatization campaign, the DFO, with the help of the Fraser Institute, a right-wing think tank, had claimed that ITQs had produced miraculous benefits for fishermen in New Zealand. MacInnes, an expert on the subject, reported that speculation in quotas in New Zealand had disrupted fishing communities and was pushing some fisheries to the point of collapse. Speaking about the DFO's plans to privatize Atlantic fisheries barely a year before Ottawa's official confession about the northern cod catastrophe, MacInnes warned, "The Atlantic coast crisis is rooted in fishing practices that have raped and pillaged ocean resources and the marine environment. It is rooted in government mismanagement of access and participation that has encouraged rather than eliminated or controlled the rape. It is rooted in greed and political deal making."[44]

MacInnes then suggested that quotas be granted in perpetuity to fishing communities, to be used by individual local working fishermen. He also emphasized the need for selective fishing practices that placed a premium on the quality, not quantity, of the catch. Above all, he asserted that "livelihood" fishing, as opposed to monopolized industrial fishing, was the only way for the world's fish stocks to survive.

The Fishermen's Vision of Licensing

In 1990 eight fishermen's organizations banded together to develop a practical and responsible alternative to *Vision 2000*. They were the Deep Sea Trawlers Association, the Fishing Vessel Owners Association, the Gulf Trollers Association, the Pacific Gillnetters Association, the Prince Rupert Fishermen's Co-operative Guild, the Prince Rupert Fishing Vessel Owners' Association and the UFAWU. They commissioned Don Cruickshank to again tackle the thorny issues facing the fleet. Cruickshank was retired but agreed to the gruelling task—and he declined remuneration. Moreover, he conducted formal hearings in 23 coastal communities between April 22 and June 6, 1991, and informal discussions in 17 more.

In the end he produced a 113-page document, simple and pragmatic, that reconciled the antinomies that had plagued the industry for over a century. Cruickshank was a veteran businessman, not a theoretical economist, so he designed a realistic business plan to fix the problems. He addressed both conservation and budgetary concerns without compromising the socioeconomic needs of working fishermen. Early in the report, he warned fishermen that they would have to embrace change or be destroyed by it. At the same time, he admonished the bureaucrats at the Economics and Planning Branch of the DFO for relying on brutal market forces to solve the industry's problems:

> The Department maintains that the British Columbia fishing fleet is valued at slightly more than $1.2 billion, a sum that is used to support the contention that the industry is overcapitalized. There is no supportive documentation for this figure, but, assuming that it is close to accurate and that *Vision 2000* planners adhere to their stated aim of consistency with the 1982 Commission, then the fleet is to be cut in half through the use of area licence combinations and stackable quotas. Under Pearse's fleet reduction proposal, one half of the fishermen, their boats, gear and licences, would be bought out by the remaining half. The sellers retire, the buyers remain in the industry.
>
> The value of the assets of fishermen leaving the industry would be about $600 million, half the total market value estimated by the Department. As a consequence, the investment of those fishermen remaining in the industry must increase by $600 million. The first question is: Who goes and who stays? Marginal producers, those that have had the least impact on the resource, will be the first to offer their boats, licences and quotas for sale. These are the fishermen least financially capable of bidding on additional area licences or stackable quotas. As in the past, Native coastal communities will be stripped of fishermen; the highliners, big producers and corporations will remain.
>
> The second question is: What share of the total allowable catch will this latter group have acquired with their $600 million investment? Presumably only the share that had been caught by the marginal fishermen—30 percent, maybe 40 percent. Certainly less than half, or those that sold would not have been marginal. According to this plan, the fishermen of the future will have

doubled their investment but increased their catch only slightly.[45]

As an alternative, Cruickshank reiterated the solutions he had put forward in 1983: a voluntary, phased buyback program financed in part by a volume-based catch royalty system. In addition, he recommended that royalties—matched by equal contributions from government—be administered on a regional basis, rather than disappearing into the general revenue fund in Ottawa. Most important of all, Cruickshank—unlike Pearse—proposed a way to slay the dragon of licence leasing. He believed that millions of dollars were being collected each year by armchair fishermen who leased herring, blackcod and halibut quotas. In his opinion this "rent" did nothing to help the resource, and those collecting it didn't turn a wheel to earn it. He recommended that the ownership of all licences be made public to determine how much control the canners enjoyed. Cruickshank hoped to put an end to the speculative and usurious trade in licences by introducing an owner–operator clause. In one fell swoop a large portion of the fleet's overcapacity could be eliminated. Aware that the canners and licence leasers would react negatively, Cruickshank suggested that they retain their licences as non-owner–operators for 10 more years, so long as they paid much higher licence fees.

Most working fishermen supported Cruickshank's recommendations. For the second time in a decade he had offered the DFO a practical way out of the overcapitalization morass created by Jack Davis, and he offered coastal communities their last, best hope of keeping fishing employment in their local economies. He believed that protecting owner–operators, many of whom resided in coastal communities, was the most practical way to ensure those communities maintained a stake in the commercial fishery.

Cruickshank's alternatives were ultimately rejected by Ottawa, as they had been in 1983.

Stop Your Snifflin', We'll Make Ya Love Mifflin!

Try as I might and give them a fight,
But they say, "We will bend ya to the corporate agenda."

I scream and I moan as they give me the bone,
But they say, "Stop your snifflin', We'll make ya love Mifflin."

I fished mighty hard at a dollar a pound,
but the corporate agenda was grinding me down.

And all of my licences stacked up the coast
at 100 grand plus were hurting me most.

Now I sit on the dock where I look out to sea
and all I have left are my gumboots and me.

They said, "Stop your snifflin', We'll make ya love Mifflin.
And then we'll bend ya to the corporate agenda."

—Song by A.S. "Snuffy" Ladret, written aboard his gillnetter
Wild Thing in the fall of 1997

On April 20, 1995, in response to the recommendations of the Fraser Report, the DFO established the Pacific Roundtable on Fleet Restructuring. In charge was Louis Tousignant, the DFO's new Pacific regional director-general, hand-picked by Brian Tobin for the task of dismantling the West Coast salmon fleet. Describing his role, Tousignant told the *Vancouver Sun*, "Mr. Fraser's report deals with the 1994 season. My job basically is to look at the 1995 season and see that the problems shall not recur. This may mean closures. This may mean exploitation rates lower than 80 percent [which had been standard]. Our main priority is to see that the fish reach the [spawning] grounds...As regional director-general I have the power of applying sanctions—that is, removing licences—rather than going through the courts. I intend to use that authority. In fact, I've removed one licence already this year."[1]

The Disastrous 1995 Season

The Pacific Roundtable accomplished very little during its initial round of meetings in spring 1995, and it was put on hold when the salmon season got underway. The PSC had predicted that 10.7 million sockeye and 18 million pinks would return to the Fraser River that year because of a record spawning escapement in the brood year of 1991, but by mid-August only 3.3 million Fraser sockeye had arrived. El Niño and adverse ocean conditions, not overfishing, were responsible for the poor runs, though in the aftermath of the Fraser Report the public was convinced otherwise.

Based on a forecast of 10.7 million Fraser sockeye, the 1995 spawning escapement goal had been set at 2.9 million, which should have left a total catch of about 8 million. But when it was determined that only 3.3 million sockeye had returned by mid-August, the DFO announced that the commercial fishery would be closed so that as many sockeye as possible could reach the spawning grounds. South Coast commercial fishermen supported the closure, stipulating only that recreational, aboriginal and American fishermen make the same sacrifice. Yet once again the burden of conservation was not shared equally. By the end of the season, 438,000 Fraser sockeye had been taken by the Americans, compared to only 798,000 by the entire Canadian commercial fleet, and another 775,000 by the Native fishery. These numbers were wildly out of whack with the pre-season allocation target of 1.5 million for the Americans, 4.8 million for the Canadian commercial catch and 1.3 million for the Native fishery, and BC commercial fishermen paid by far the greatest price to protect the run. For the first time in history, the aboriginal catch was the same size as the entire South Coast commercial harvest, generating extreme bitterness toward the AFS pilot sales program.

Following the imposed South Coast closure, the UFAWU demanded that Ottawa provide BC fishermen and shoreworkers with the same sort of relief given to East Coast cod fishermen under The Atlantic Groundfish Subsidy (TAGS). Tobin, having been criticized for the cost overruns incurred by the TAGS program, offered BC fishermen only a few pious platitudes. "What we are seeing today is not the result of overfishing," Tobin acknowledged. "Yet I don't have today nor will I ever have a clean and easy answer, some assurance, that I can give this gillnetter or his family, and that is regrettable."[2]

Meanwhile, Tousignant and the Economics and Planning Branch were busy preparing the blueprint for the radical restructuring of the fleet. And when the roundtable reconvened that fall, Brian Tobin said he would take action unilaterally if no consensus had been reached by December 7, 1995.

The roundtable was divided into four "panels," one for each gear sector in the commercial fleet, in addition to a "main table" with equal representation from the commercial, recreational and aboriginal sectors. I sat at this main table as the UFAWU representative. The sociologist Raymond A. Rogers notes, "The round-table process can create the temporary illusion that those sitting at the table are on a 'level playing-field,' whereas there is a profound difference in economic and political power of the participants, and, indeed, the table is tipped at a precipitous angle."[3] This round table was tipped at a precipitous angle by those representing big business, such as Mike Hunter of the Fisheries Council of BC, who represented the canners, and Bob Wright of the Oak Bay Marine Group, who represented the recreational fishing industry. Hunter declared:

> We see [fleet reduction] as a very important part of the
> future. This industry has had to cope with two significant

Mike Hunter, president of the Fisheries Council of BC.

changes in the last 10 years. One is the rise of aquaculture. The second change was the removal of the process-in-Canada regulations, which meant the end of an era when processors had to have enough capacity as the peak harvest required. That has resulted, together with technology, in a smaller processing sector. The downsizing that occurred because of those two economic facts didn't reach the harvesting sector... Everybody had talked about too-many-boats-chasing-too-few-fish for 25 years, but it never became an economic issue until now, when short harvests didn't result in higher prices. Alaskan seine boats and gillnetters deliver five and ten times as much fish as a BC unit. What you can't get in price you have to make up in volume, and that argues for a smaller, more efficient fleet.[4]

In a special paper prepared for the roundtable, DFO economists agreed with the canners' perspective: "The processing industry does not have security of supply of raw material at a known price. The industry pays for the raw material based upon market expectations that may or may not be realized. Industry bargaining associations have bargained minimum prices with little flexibility to respond to market conditions. As raw cost of fish represents over 60 percent of the value of BC fish products, this makes it difficult for industry to stay competitive with world seafood producers."[5]

Such analysis was typical of DFO economists, who often saw eye to eye with the canners. In fact, Michelle James of the Economics and Planning Branch went to work as a spokesperson for the Fisheries Council of BC immediately after the Mifflin Plan had been imposed. However, the DFO's claim was questionable. The union had made price agreements with the canners through collective bargaining, an arduous process for commercial fishermen, and when markets were poor, the canners always had the option to cease buying salmon. On the other hand, when the market price of salmon had soared above the union-negotiated minimum, the canners had seldom shown "flexibility" by voluntarily increasing the amount paid to the crews and non-licence holders who depended exclusively on the minimum price agreement.

The Blueprint

The roundtable's progress was painstakingly slow in the autumn of 1995, because the industry's problems were complex and the possible solutions diverse. Two basic ideological camps were represented at the roundtable. One was the canners and their allies, who believed that there were too many fishermen and favoured the use of harsh market forces, such as stackable area licensing, to reduce the size of the fleet. Their broader objective was to maximize profit by privatizing the resource. The other was the UFAWU, which believed there were too few fish and demanded that Ottawa rebuild stocks by expanding the salmon enhancement program. The union also called for a voluntary, government-funded licence buyback to reduce the excess fishing capacity created by the DFO's earlier schemes. The UFAWU maintained that salmon should remain as a common property resource, and that licences should be granted only to those who considered them a means to earning a living rather than an investment opportunity. Meanwhile,

Ottawa had instructed Tousignant and the Economics and Planning Branch to shoot down any fleet reduction proposals that would increase government costs. Given these diametrically opposed views, the roundtable could not reach a genuine consensus, but given that the DFO was not a neutral player in the process, it was bound to win the ideological battle. John Sutcliffe, a former UFAWU small boat organizer, recalled:

> There was a cluster of events at this time. You had increasingly shrill political demands being made upon the government for access to the salmon resources [from the Native and recreational sectors]. You had some conservation "red-flags" popping up for all the Canadian public to view. And you had massive capacity reduction [in DFO staff] to manage these issues…This for DFO clearly was a crisis. So some "rocket scientist" decides on an overall response. The blueprint was there, the problem was in getting some process to validate DFO's plan for down-sizing.[6]

DFO representatives at news conference called to give assurances on 1995 escapements. Left to right: Mike Henderson, Louis Tousignant, Paul Sprout.

If the DFO had a "blueprint," clearly it was the one drafted by Peter Pearse while he was a member of the West Coast Fleet Development Committee that advised Jack Davis back in 1969. But a process by which the DFO could enact privatization had proved elusive. Even Pearse, with the power and prestige of a Royal Commission, had failed to convince the industry or the public that privatizing the resource was the solution. Now, with the release of Fraser's report and the public's fear of ecological disaster, the DFO had an opportunity to try again.

So, although the roundtable participants discussed habitat protection, salmon enhancement, better science, more effective monitoring of fisheries, and other topics, the main debate focused on reducing the size of the fleet through stackable area licensing. An influential group of vessel owners proposed that the coast be divided into fishing zones or areas and that fishermen be allowed to buy more than one licence should they choose to fish in more than one area. The Fisheries Council of BC had proposed this plan two years earlier:

> A smaller fleet would mean the sharing of available harvests by fewer participants. Traditional approaches to this problem have been to suggest a government-funded vessel and licence buyback program. With one slight exception to address Native issues, FCBC rejects this approach because it requires significant public funds in impossibly tight fiscal times. FCBC, therefore, proposes that DFO implement an area and gear licensing policy in the salmon fisheries...The policy must permit vessel owners to buy existing licences from those who wish to retire, and permanently place the resulting licence on the one vessel."[7]

Fishermen had mixed opinions on the question of area licensing. Some believed it would reduce competition on the fishing grounds, but most feared being confined to a single area during poor runs. They remembered the herring fishery experience and the usurious licence leasing that had accompanied it. A group of multi-licence holders, led by Greg Taylor, a manager from Ocean Fisheries Ltd., campaigned aggressively for stackable area licensing, but none of the three roundtable gear panels could agree to the concept. Concerned that his December 7, 1995, deadline would pass without consensus, Brian Tobin travelled to Vancouver to light a fire under Louis Tousignant. He also extended the deadline for a second time, to December 16.

Throughout the roundtable process, the public was barraged with declarations that the commercial salmon fishery was no longer viable, having produced a landed value of only $80 million in 1995, down more than 65 percent from a four-year average of $205 million.[8] And they were told that low salmon returns in 1996 would exacerbate the situation, because fishermen might put too much pressure on the resource. To complicate matters, Eric Malling of CTV—whom Linda McQuaig described as "one of the most effective salesmen for 'the elite'"[9]—broadcast a program that claimed DFO subsidies to fishermen were bleeding the taxpayer to death. Malling proposed that all Canadian fisheries be privatized to make them more profitable and to eliminate government costs. He pointed to Iceland and New Zealand as countries where the fishery had rebounded after being privatized. He did not mention the many fishermen in those countries opposed to privatization, or the decline in stocks after the introduction of individual transferable quotas (ITQs).

In fact, the DFO's Pacific regional operating budget was anything but excessive. The DFO oversees a host of programs—including the Coast Guard service, scientific research, habitat protection, hydrography, oceanographic surveys and small craft harbour maintenance—that benefit a much greater portion of society than commercial fishermen. Malling implied that the DFO's entire Pacific Region budget of $180 million had been squandered on a bankrupt commercial fleet, but in truth only $49 million had been spent on managing the salmon resource in 1995, $30 million of which was for salmon enhancement, which benefits Native and sports fishermen as well as the commercial fleet. So the direct cost of supervising the commercial salmon fishery in 1995 was a mere $19 million.[10] In other words, the fishery had been a net producer into the economy.

Doing the Deal

Despite the DFO's best efforts, the three roundtable gear panels did not reach a consensus by Tobin's new deadline of December 16, 1995. Two days before, the UFAWU organized a protest rally of more than 700 fishermen in Richmond. Infuriated by Tobin's threat to impose unilateral change, David Secord of the Pacific Gillnetters Association warned the DFO, "We want to be part of the process [of change], but we'll be damned if we'll jump to your timetable!"[11] Tobin announced that the roundtable would reconvene to make a last-ditch attempt to come up with an agreement, and Louis Tousignant and his staff set to work. According to John Sutcliffe of the UFAWU:

> Tousignant dispatched Paul Sprout [Director of Operations branch], Steven Wright [Director of Policy and Economics Branch], and Wayne Saito [the DFO's salmon coordinator] to push the troll panel along. DFO anticipated that the troll panel would be the one to give them the breakthrough they needed. An opening of the door anyway, for some industry group to agree to area licensing, which was critical to their fleet reduction plan. And they eventually got it!
>
> I had been out of town, so I missed the social and reception held the night before the last round of panel meetings. I'd heard from another panel member that DFO's Paul Sprout, specifically, and Wayne Saito met with the PTA crowd of trollers. They came there—and this was quite clever—with a suite of options, some acceptable, some not...At the round table meetings the next day, it was very hard for me and any others that had criticism of what was going on to get through to most of the panel members.
>
> As usual, they were buying into the belief DFO was working with them and not against them. So they thought they had an omnibus package that would work. But they didn't see the devil in the details.

Without Lorne Iverson and Dan Edwards, who opposed area licensing and who were not at the meeting because it had been called on short notice, a majority voted to accept area licensing. Sutcliffe left the room in frustration and ran into a senior DFO official, who was relaying news of the vote to one of his colleagues. One of the men hurried down to the seine panel and Sutcliffe followed him. "And he went into the seine panel," Sutcliffe remembers, "and burst into the room and said: 'The trollers have agreed to area licensing.' I didn't hang around. What I really wanted to do at that moment was to talk to the seine panel...launch into a loud explanation of what had gone on. But it was clear to me that getting that agreement out of that troll panel and delivering it to the seine panel was extremely critical for the DFO. And the seine panel then caved."[12]

The DFO needed all three gear panels to agree in order to present stackable area licensing as a fishermen-approved means of reducing the fleet. When they could report that the troll panel had come to a "consensus," many holdouts on the seine and gillnet panels assumed a *fait accompli* and shifted their focus from trying to stop area licensing to making the deal as palatable as possible. The vote was not unanimous, but the DFO claimed that all three panels had agreed to stackable area licensing.

No one was sure how the new system would actually work, but federal files show that after the initial roundtable report had gone to cabinet, at least one canners' representative had lobbied to have the gillnet and troll fleets confined to three areas as opposed to two,[13] and the area-licensing system was eventually structured in just this way. Therefore, the corporate-dominated seine fleet, which has the greatest catching power, was the least reduced, and the small boat fleet was affected the most, as it had with the implementation of the Davis Plan in 1968. However, Rick Nordstrom, president of the Pacific Trollers Association and chair of the troll panel, denied that the trollers had anything to worry about. He told the *Globe and Mail* on December 16, 1995, that the troll fleet would only be reduced by 10 percent in 1996 and only 30 percent over the longer term.

The roundtable also submitted a report to DFO containing 27 other recommendations designed to revitalize the West Coast salmon fishery: "Reducing the size of the fleet is not in and by itself sufficient to renew the commercial sector and fulfil the conservation, economic and partnership objectives set by the Minister of Fisheries and Oceans for renewal of the commercial Pacific salmon fishery...There exists deep concern about the potential impact of departmental plans respecting expenditure reduction on the department's continuing ability to manage the resource."[14]

Among other things, the report called for a major increase in funding for salmon enhancement and an expanded habitat protection capacity. These recommendations made it easier for many of us to support the roundtable report as a whole. But the DFO did not consider the report to be a "total package," and simply cherry-picked the recommendations.

Even with the advent of the stackable area-licensing system, the DFO knew a licence buyback fund of at least $200 million would be needed if the fleet was to be reduced by 30 to 50 percent right away. Where would the money come from? Despite allotting billions of dollars to the East Coast fishery, Ottawa was reluctant to support West Coast fishermen. And the BC government, which had become increasingly vocal about the fishery, made a hasty retreat when federal officials suggested the province share the costs of a buyback.

Brian Tobin was joyful at the completion of the roundtable process. On December 16 he told the *Globe and Mail*, "You will kill off the resource if you put too much pressure on it, and the industry is recognizing this. This is real work, valuable work, historic work being done here. The industry has decided not only to talk conservation but to walk it as well." But the funding issue was unresolved, and some important fishing constituencies, unhappy with the outcome of the roundtable process, submitted minority reports to the minister. The West Coast Sustainability Association, which represented commercial, aboriginal and recreational fishermen on the west coast of Vancouver Island, wrote:

> The roundtable process was seriously flawed in several respects, among them: the lack of a neutral person in the role of chair for the process; dependant coastal fishing communities were excluded from the process... [which was] both undemocratic and unethical. Considering that over the past 37 years there has been a Royal

Commission, four other Commissions, and countless other committees and workshops wrestling with the complex problem of fleet rationalization, it is beyond comprehension that the sponsors could expect the roundtable process to succeed. Six days of plenary discussion over a three-month period, given the complexity of the issues, is a design for failure.[15]

The UFAWU wrote, "The best approach to fleet rationalization is resource enhancement not fleet reduction. However…An industry controlled buy-back—as opposed to strategies that stack fishing privileges through area licensing or privatized fishing rights through quotas—is the only option that can successfully achieve industry goals, solve current problems, and ensure the continued participation of thousands of individuals who on the basis of considerable personal investment have chosen fishing as a career."[16] The DFO dismissed all such pleas as it implemented policies that had been 20 years in the making.

In the meantime, the canners and Greg Taylor's "dream team" had attached a major caveat to their support for reducing the fleet. Convinced that a smaller fleet would result in a much larger total allowable catch (TAC) for them, they demanded that such catch benefits accrue exclusively to those commercial fishermen who remained, with no reallocation to the Native sector. They believed that Tobin and Tousignant had agreed, and later they claimed the DFO had betrayed them by allowing the Native catch to increase.

As 1995 came to a close, the media celebrated Brian Tobin's "banner year." Not only had he tackled the problem of over-capacity in the West Coast salmon fleet and driven the pirates off the Grand Banks of Newfoundland, Captain Canada had also helped secure a narrow victory (50.6 percent) for the federalist side in the Quebec referendum. The pundits had begun touting him as the successor to Prime Minister Jean Chretien when, on January 9, 1996, Tobin surprised everyone by announcing his intention to succeed Clyde Wells as premier of Newfoundland. On the same day, 4,000 miles away, a 38-year-old upstart named Glen Clark announced his candidacy for the leadership of the BC New Democratic Party. Thus, Tobin was exiting the scene just as the draconian fleet restructuring plan he had set in motion got underway, and Clark was soon to become entangled in the mess that Tobin left behind.

A Cold Glass of Water or a Peanut Butter Sandwich?

Although it was considered next to impossible, the UFAWU set out to stop the DFO from slashing the commercial fleet. Just days before Tobin announced his entry into provincial politics, a rank-and-file committee of UFAWU fishermen met in Vancouver to consider whether it was necessary to reduce all sections of the fleet by 30 to 50 percent. They were also incensed by Louis Tousignant's manipulation of the roundtable process in favour of the canners. "The roundtable delegates were hand-picked by the Department of Fisheries and Oceans," said Bruce Probert, a third-generation gillnetter from Fort Langley. "The fishery is totally run by politics, not reason."[17] The committee decided to democratize the process by allowing all commercial fishermen—not just a hand-picked advisory group—to vote on the issue of fleet reduction. They prepared a ballot that read:

> If fleet reduction occurs, which method is acceptable to you?
>
> A) voluntary, industry-controlled buy-back; or
>
> B) licence stacking, through area licensing, transferable quotas, fractional licensing?

Tobin had promised that the process of dismantling the West Coast fleet would begin by February 1, 1996, so the UFAWU had to move quickly to conduct its vote in remote coastal communities. By January 22, 97 percent of fishermen had voted to endorse a voluntary, government-funded buyback as opposed to stackable area licensing.

The vote had been open to all commercial fishermen, regardless of affiliation, and 70 percent of the 1,091 voters were licence holders, yet the DFO dismissed it, insinuating that most of the ballots had been cast by non-licence holders. The vote was the largest unambiguous opinion sample on a single question that had taken place during the entire roundtable process. The DFO had sent out some mail-out surveys to all salmon licence holders, and they had had more time and money to tabulate their results, but because their surveys contained many, often contradictory questions, the results were inconclusive. The UFAWU vote flew in the face of the official claim that the fleet overwhelmingly supported stackable area licensing. Yet when UFAWU president John Radosevic and I presented the results of the ballot to Louis Tousignant, he said, "Your vote is like asking a man dying of thirst in the middle of the Sahara Desert which he would prefer: a nice cold glass of water or a peanut butter sandwich?" We challenged him to conduct a government-supervised vote solely on the issue of licence stacking, which the DFO had never done despite the thousands of jobs at stake. Tousignant responded that he had already spent $4 million plus six months of DFO staff time on the roundtable, and that was quite enough for him.

Put a Match to My Boat

On March 29, 1996, Mike Emes, a gillnetter, made his way through a crowded press conference in the ballroom of the Sutton Place Hotel in Vancouver, approached a microphone, then stood staring through the glare of dozens of TV lights at Fred Mifflin, Canada's newest federal minister of fisheries and oceans. Rear Admiral Mifflin, a retired Newfoundland navy man who had succeeded Tobin in early January, was visiting Vancouver to announce the details of the Pacific Salmon Fleet Restructuring Plan. He had just finished telling the crowd that $80 million in federal funds had been secured to reduce the salmon fleet by at least 30 percent through a "voluntary" licence buyback, and that the DFO would introduce stackable area licensing before the 1996 salmon season (a move that would, according to the *Vancouver Sun*, put as many as 3,500 people out of work).

Mike Emes is a quiet man. He had been a UFAWU stalwart for many years but was not one to draw attention to himself or make loud speeches at union meetings. As he approached the microphone, reserved for the press, some DFO officials tried to turn him away, but Fred Mifflin leaned forward and gallantly beckoned Emes to speak. Emes hesitated, then said, "Mr. Mifflin, what are you going to do for people like me? I've

Gillnetter Mike Emes confronts Fisheries Minister Fred Mifflin over the issue of stackable area licensing, March 1996.

been in this industry for 22 years. I only have one licence on my boat. I have to fish all areas of the coast in order to make a living. How am I going to come up with $70,000 to buy another licence?"[18] He paused, momentarily overcome.

Mifflin, looking deeply concerned, nodded in a fatherly way and encouraged him to continue, and Emes bellowed, "I might as well go back to False Creek and throw a match to my boat!" A crowd of supporters cheered as camera crews scrambled to record the scene. Mifflin explained that the restructuring plan would help fishermen by ensuring the long-term survival of the salmon, but he seemed uneasy and at one point even apologized to Emes for any inconvenience.

Outside the ballroom Emes was besieged by reporters, and he tried to explain how the Davis Plan had wreaked havoc on the fishery decades before. Most of the journalists seemed more interested in knowing if he really intended to set fire to his boat, but they all nodded sympathetically when he said, "Every time the DFO makes a complete blunder, I end up paying for it."

On the television news that evening, Mike Emes became the spokesperson for thousands of people in coastal BC who were about to be thrust into turmoil. His cry for help also resonated with prairie farmers, loggers, redundant public sector workers, East Coast cod fishermen, unemployed millworkers, and many other Canadians. As the "Mifflin Plan" was being introduced, and a storm of neo-conservatism swept the country, Gordon Thiesen, governor of the Bank of Canada, said, "Canadians...are worried about their jobs as businesses continue to restructure their operations in an effort to become more competitive. In many cases this has meant that jobs have changed or have disappeared completely. While these adjustments are stressful, they are part of a necessary process of change that will result in a more vigorous Canadian economy, with stronger employment creation."[19]

Carving Up the Coast

March 29, 1996, after Mifflin's press conference, the *Vancouver Sun* questioned the DFO about its selective approach to the roundtable recommendations, and communications officer Bill Morrell explained, "The decisions have been based on those recommendations [of the roundtable], but that doesn't mean the federal plan will be a precise copy of the report submitted by the industry." This was a major understatement, as most of the industry's demands for better habitat protection, salmon enhancement and research had been ignored. But the demand for a federally funded $200 million buyback was also ignored. Ottawa had only set aside $80 million, most of which had come from the collection of commercial licence fees that the DFO had earmarked for reducing the fleet after the introduction of the Davis Plan.

On April 3, 1996, the roundtable reconvened to put the finishing touches on the new area-licensing system. At that time it was decided that seiners would operate in two areas and gillnetters and trollers in three, just as the canners had always wanted, and combination fishing—the use of both gillnet and troll gear on the same vessel—would be prohibited. Technically, a combination-boat fisherman who trolled and gillnetted in all areas of the coast—as my father had once done—would now have to own six licences to do so. Few fishermen—as Mike Emes had demonstrated—could afford that option: a licence for a single area could cost as much as $100,000. But the canners, who controlled an abundance of licences, were ideally placed to take advantage of the new stackable area-licensing system.

In face of all this, I decided on April 4, 1996, to resign as the UFAWU's representative on the roundtable's main panel. I told the press, "There is no way we can serve as the undertakers for this industry." My place at the roundtable was quickly taken by Les Rombough, a gillnetter from Campbell River who favoured stackable area licensing. The roundtable then proceeded to assist the DFO in implementing the Mifflin Plan.

Can the Plan

Despite the best efforts of the DFO, the controversy surrounding the Mifflin Plan soon spilled over into the public domain. On April 8, 1996, the editors of the *Vancouver Sun* wrote:

> Unlike Mr. Davis's plan which was intended primarily to increase fishers' incomes, Mr. Mifflin's first priority is conserving the resource. But his approach is wrong-headed. Announcing the plan in Vancouver, Mr. Mifflin said a 50 percent cut in the "capacity of the commercial salmon fleet" is needed. But his plan aims instead to cut in half the number of fishing boats, which is hardly the same thing...While it is impossible to divide [the salmon] up in a way that keeps everybody happy, the Mifflin plan puts virtually the entire burden on the small owner-operators...with little sacrifice being asked of the large-scale fishers or of companies such as BC Packers that hold many of the licences. No wonder the department is trying to ram the program into place before its opponents can get organized.

Even BC's few Liberal MPs were concerned. *Vancouver Sun* columnist Barbara Yaffe reported that Hedy Fry, Herb Dhaliwal, Ted McWhinney, Anna Terrana and Raymond Chan all had misgivings about "the optics of $80 million for BC compared to $1.9 billion for the East Coast." One MP, who refused to be named, complained, "The general plan was endorsed by all these people [on the roundtable]. But none of them came forward in the meeting to defend the minister. He was left on his own and then went back to Ottawa." Yaffe noted that the BC caucus had hoped that Ross Fitzpatrick, a prominent Liberal senator, could get the prime minister's attention on what one of them described as a "public relations disaster in BC."[20]

Indeed, Mifflin seemed to have no support at all—until April 15, 1996, when Peter Pearse entered the fray. "It's an unbelievable imbroglio," Pearse told Yaffe. "I feel sorry for the guy." Pearse insinuated that most of the opposition was being generated by the UFAWU and that a silent majority in the industry supported the Mifflin Plan. "The worst thing that could happen is for this whole effort to be packed in and nothing to be done," he said. "Then we'd have chaos...Our major natural resource is in a desperate situation. The state of our commercial fishery is an economic disaster."

Louis Tousignant began to fear that fishermen would organize a boycott of the area selection process. "Fishermen should be aware that completed licence applications with full payment of fees must be received in a DFO licensing office by May 24, 1996," he warned, "or this will result in licence eligibility being revoked." UFAWU organizer John Sutcliffe deplored this unprecedented move. "It's just another example of how they're trying to stampede fishermen into accepting this," he said.

Early on the morning of April 26, 1996, Ross Wetzel hauled his gillnetter *Terry Lynne* out of the Fraser River, placed it on a trailer, drove it to the DFO's Pacific regional headquarters in downtown Vancouver and parked it, just in time to impede traffic during the morning rush hour. Before long a crowd of over 500 fishermen filled the streets outside the DFO office to protest the Mifflin Plan. The protestors strung a gillnet around the circumference of the office, then started a fire in a rusty 45-gallon drum. When they had a good blaze going, with boisterous exhilaration they pitched hundreds of 1996 salmon licence application forms into the fire.

John Radosevic (president of the UFAWU–CAW), Catherine Stewart (Greenpeace), Rose Davidson (Coastal Community Network), Rick Nordstrom (Pacific Trollers Association), Jacob Nyce (Native Brotherhood of BC), Jim Fulton (David Suzuki Foundation), Dan Edwards (West Coast Sustainability Association), and I climbed onto the deck of the *Terry Lynne* to speak to the huge crowd. But the highlight of the rally

Fishermen burn Mifflin Plan area-licensing application forms outside the Vancouver office of DFO, April 1996.

occurred when Premier Glen Clark, who had just won the provincial NDP leadership, addressed the cheering crowd. "The federal government is stopping BC fishers but it isn't stopping the problems," cried Clark. "They should can the plan and stop it until they get it right!"[21]

On April 28,1996, a large group representing fishermen's organizations, coastal communities and environmentalists travelled to Ottawa. The highlight of the lobby was the appearance before the Parliamentary Standing Committee on Fisheries of the media personality and environmentalist David Suzuki, who had family roots in commercial fishing. He confessed that it was strange for him to work with commercial fishermen, since he had been "beaten up by a few of them a number of times," but he believed he and the fishermen were of one mind. "We know that change must come, and I think the people in this delegation are prepared to pay a price to protect the future—but not by the Mifflin Plan." He went on:

I'm a biologist and I fear for the future of wild organisms that are being shoe-horned into agendas being set by politicians and economics, not biology. What is a biological problem gets fractured into bureaucratic subdivisions that ensure the fish will never be properly dealt with as a single entity and therefore protected properly. We believe local communities will be the unit of survival into the future, communities with a shared stake in the quality of the air, the water, the soil, and bio-diversity...Their future, it seems to me, is our best hope for the planet. Fishers have knowledge that cannot be duplicated by science.

Politicians come and go. Government experts and bureaucrats seem immune from long-term accountability for their decisions. Local communities aren't immune to consequences of these decisions. I believe they must have an opportunity for their knowledge and advice to be heard and acted upon...The concentration of licences in corporate hands at the expense of small boat owners may maximize profitability and the ease of management, but it sure doesn't maximize jobs or the viability of local communities.[22]

The standing committee was impressed, but key Liberal cabinet ministers such as Fred Mifflin and David Anderson were not present. And the lobby came to an abrupt halt when Mifflin decided to travel to the West Coast to consult with the industry that same week. He and his senior staff only agreed to meet the lobbyists in the foyer of the DFO's headquarters for a few minutes. Even the *Vancouver Sun*—which had long criticized the commercial fishery—censured Mifflin: "History encourages the minister to believe that toughness is all that's needed here. The commercial fleet should have been reduced 10 to 15 years ago and the decisions now are much harder. The current plan comes in the midst of the worst crisis in the history of the fishery. But the urgent need to do something does not justify doing the wrong things in the wrong way. Mr. Mifflin should turn this ship around."[23]

Regional Director Tousignant claimed the majority of the industry supported the Mifflin Plan and that the opposition was made up of "ignorant professional muckrakers" in the union who were only "concerned about a loss of membership."[24] He was therefore shocked when an open letter from 27 members of the roundtable, calling for major changes to the Mifflin Plan, was published by the *Vancouver Sun*. It was signed by Robert Strom, Ross Wetzel, Greg Wadhams, Percy Williams, Mike Forrest (gillnet panel chair), Barry Palo, Richard Haugan, Lorne Iverson, Rick Nordstrom (troll panel chair), Brian Lande, Richard Gray, Robert Burkoski, Ron Fowler, John Radosevic, Dennis Brown, Dana Doerksen, Kendall Smith, Clinton Young, Boi Nguyen, John Sutcliffe, Garth Mirau, Robert Carpenter, Dave Christensen, Dan Edwards, Alvin Dixon, Heber Clifton, and Paddy Greene. The letter demanded a secure long-term allocation for the commercial sector, improved habitat protection, a publicly funded voluntary buyback program, tax incentives to encourage voluntary retirement of licences, retraining programs for fishermen and workers voluntarily leaving the industry and preservation of Native participation in the industry.

Tousignant told the press that the remaining 17 members of the roundtable had encouraged him to stay the course.

Louis, Louis

On May 9, 1996, about one hundred fishermen gathered at the Maritime Labour Centre in east Vancouver, then boarded two chartered buses and proceeded to the DFO's downtown office. Tousignant ordered security guards to bar the doors, but the fishermen entered through the fire escape and poured into the DFO's fourth-floor offices. They then headed for the DFO's licence application office, where they would apply en masse for their 1996 salmon licences, ignoring the new area-licensing selection requirement and applying for licences to fish the whole coast as in the past. The clerks in the licensing branch promptly closed the office. The crowd then asked to meet with Tousignant, and settled in to await a response. Before the end of the day, most of them had left the building, but a small, determined group of protestors vowed to stay until they got a meeting with DFO officials. They included Lorne Iverson,

Laurie Ronneseth, Mike Emes, Ross Wetzel, Mike Norum, Cynthia Norum, Walter Groening, Barbara Groening, Buddy Iverson and Ellis Iverson.

At the same time, DFO offices in Prince Rupert, Ucluelet, Nanaimo and Port Hardy were also being occupied. According to Bob Grant, a former UFAWU Vancouver Island organizer, the Nanaimo occupation was so sudden and unexpected that DFO staff left the premises without even turning off their computers. The protestors had a rare opportunity to sabotage hundreds of applications for fishing licences and throw the area-licensing system into chaos for the 1996 season. However, the Nanaimo protestors took the moral high ground and did not tamper with government files.[25]

Occupying a government office for a prolonged period is an arduous experience. It attracts media attention for a day but soon exposes the shortcomings of any battle fought from a fixed position. Such action can only end in full victory or complete defeat. To make conditions as unpleasant as possible, DFO officials shut off the air conditioning and most of the lights. The protestors in Vancouver, Port Hardy and Nanaimo spent more than a week sleeping on thinly carpeted concrete floors at night and living with prison-like monotony during the day. For those on the outside it was a challenge to feed the protestors and maintain their morale. When Louis Tousignant still refused to meet with them, they threatened to escalate their action by blockading the elevators of the

North Island fishermen occupy the Port Hardy office of DFO (Fisheries and Oceans Canada) to protest the Mifflin Plan, May 1996.

Simon Fraser University downtown campus in the adjacent building. This prompted the DFO to seek an injunction, which was handed down by Supreme Court Justice Wally Oppal on May 16, 1996.

A crowd of reporters gathered to watch the authorities serve the injunction, so they also witnessed the protestors' parting shot. Just as they prepared to leave, one of them turned on a ghetto blaster and played the 1960s rock classic "Louie, Louie." Tousignant was enraged when the demonstrators danced in front of the TV cameras, gleefully singing, "Oh Louis, Louis! Oh, Oh! We gotta go now!"

On Your Side

The NDP's campaign for the provincial election scheduled for May 28, 1996, featured the populist slogan "On your side," which Glen Clark had coined atop the *Terry Lynne* at the fishermen's anti-Mifflin rally on April 26. Clark was scorned by mainstream media as a rabid socialist, but he more closely resembled the traditional social democrat intent on propping up the sagging fiscal supports of the post-war social contract through controversial revenue-generating schemes. These included photo radar, gambling casinos and various mega-projects that either never came to pass or, as with the fast ferries, were political disasters.

Early in the campaign, Michael Walker of the Fraser Institute said, "There's motion in the socialist camps all over the world toward more market-oriented policy. But the rhetoric Mr. Clark is using—get the rich, help the little guy—indicates there is a lag in adjustment here. Using class images like that is not the case anymore, certainly not in Britain where the class warriors are gone." Clark confidently replied, "If standing up for the middle class is class war, then we need more of it." Meanwhile, Barbara Yaffe of the *Vancouver Sun* and others were predicting electoral success for the candidate who could tap into British Columbians' seething resentment toward the federal government. And at that time, nothing served as a more potent symbol of BC's hostility toward Ottawa than Pacific salmon.

With the Mifflin Plan wreaking havoc in coastal communities, more than a few pundits criticized the government for its insensitive handling of West Coast issues. Moreover, BC voters—among the most "green" in the country—were alarmed that the DFO had allowed some salmon stocks to approach extinction. And many voters believed that BC was given short shrift within confederation. For example, Ottawa's designation of BC as a "have" province entitled it to much lower federal transfer payments than other provinces, and people thought BC was simply being used as a "cash cow," contributing $1.1 billion each year in equalization payments to the seven "have not" provinces. The BC public was also angry that their province had less than equitable representation in the House of Commons, the Senate and the Supreme Court, as well as at the constitutional talks in Charlottetown the previous year. BC had its separatists, but most of the electorate favoured a better deal for BC within the increasingly decentralized (post-Mulroney) Canadian political milieu. And Glen Clark—his socialist leanings notwithstanding—seemed the right candidate for the job.

International concerns weighed heavily on British Columbians as well. Despite Mulroney's free trade pact, the US had continued to impose tariffs blocking BC softwood lumber exports, and many BC voters thought Ottawa was not treating the problem with the same energy it would devote to a trade issue affecting Ontario or Quebec. There was also the unfinished business of the Pacific Salmon Treaty, dropped abruptly by Brian Tobin. In a meeting with the *Vancouver Sun* editorial board on May 25, Clark said, "I hate to get into constitutional wrangling and I think the last thing we need is another constitutional debate. But they [the federal government] just don't understand BC. They don't understand the consequences of their actions. I refuse to believe they don't care. But they just don't get it."

When Clark had become NDP leader three months earlier, his party was at 25 percent in the polls. By election day his rating had soared, and Liberal leader Gordon Campbell plunged from 50 to 30 percent support. On May 28, 1996, Glen Clark achieved what no one had thought possible: a second consecutive term in office for the BC NDP.

A Song of Mourning

The tiny village of Alert Bay lies in a gently curved bay on the west side of Cormorant Island, not far from storm-swept Queen Charlotte Sound.

The waterfront road is lined by a picturesque agglomeration of piers, old cannery buildings and net lofts. Just south of the main settlement a group of weathered totem poles guards the village cemetery, where on June 4, 1996, some 400 people stood facing the wind, as Namgis Chief Bill Cranmer led them in a special song of mourning. Accompanied by ceremonial drummers, the crowd sang sorrowfully. "We are here to mourn what has happened to our people," Chief Cranmer announced solemnly. "To mourn the way the government of Canada has treated us."

For years the canners had stationed a significant portion of their seine fleet in Alert Bay, and although most of the vessels were old, the fishermen of Alert Bay were an indomitable force on the nearby fishing grounds of Johnstone Strait. Now things were changing.

Ottawa had scheduled the local Coast Guard station for decommissioning and slashed other important community infrastructure programs. Then came the Mifflin Plan, striking like a hurricane, and almost overnight most of the jobs in this predominantly First Nations community had disappeared. The canners had taken advantage of the licence-stacking provisions of the Mifflin plan and reassigned most of the licences from the Alert Bay seine fleet to southern-based vessels. Most of the remaining licences used by Alert Bay fishermen had been sold to the buyback. This tidy arrangement enabled the canners to maintain their cash flow during the "difficult restructuring period," but the fishermen of Alert Bay were simply thrown out of work.

"Normally when we sing our traditional song of mourning, we sing another to shake off our sorrow," said Chief Cranmer. "But we won't do that today—not until we have defeated Mifflin's plan." Many other people spoke, including roundtable seine representative Greg Wadhams, Alert Bay Mayor Gilbert Popovitch, Chief Pat Alfred, UFAWU President John Radosevic and MLA Dave Zirnhelt. "Fred Mifflin has declared war on Alert Bay and other fishing communities on this coast," said Mayor Popovitch. "His plan will turn viable communities into ghost towns."

And *The Fisherman* newspaper observed:

> Four years ago, in June 1992...Fred Mifflin rose in the
> House of Commons to plead with the then Conservative government to consider the plight of people in

Speakers address an anti-Mifflin Plan rally in Alert Bay, BC, June 1996. Left to right: Gilbert Popovitch (mayor of Alert Bay), Greg Wadhams (Native Brotherhood of BC), David Zirnhelt (BC Minister of Fisheries), Bill Cranmer (chief of Namgis Nation), Glen Robertson (MLA), John Radosevic (UFAWU–CAW), Dan Edwards (West Coast Sustainability Association).

fishing communities in Newfoundland who had been devastated by the cod moratorium. He was impassioned in his appeal, even suggesting at one point that he would "bring my guitar and sing a song" if that would get the government's attention. But somehow, none of that sympathy has ever reached the West Coast. For Mifflin...names like Alert Bay, Sointula, Ucluelet, Bella Coola, and Port Hardy apparently don't get the same political rating as Bonavista or Harbour Grace.[26]

An Exaggerated Death

On May 24, 1996, a group of fishermen tried to obtain a court injunction to stop the stackable area-licensing provision of the Mifflin Plan. They were represented by Victoria lawyer Joe Arvey, whose fees were paid by the Clark government. The judge had been sympathetic to the fishermen's plight but ruled that the DFO had the legal authority to

141

implement the program. Stackable area licensing became a reality, and on July 19, 1996, the DFO announced that it had achieved the goals of its Pacific Salmon Licence Retirement Program. The licence buyback underwent two separate rounds: most of the initial 1,100 bids were deemed to be too high and the applicants had to resubmit their licences at a much lower price.

The DFO made much of the $79.2 million it spent on the buyback, though no one mentioned that $65 million of it had been extracted from fishermen's licence fees, collected for this very purpose since the inception of the Davis Plan. In all, 800 out of 4,100 salmon licences were retired at prices ranging from $250,000 to $500,000 for seines, and $40,000 to $120,000 for gillnetters and trollers. And on July 20, 1996, Louis Tousignant triumphantly told the *Vancouver Sun*, "The 1996 Pacific salmon fishing season is opening with 30 percent fewer boats on the water due to a combination of licence retirements, licence stacking and voluntary withdrawals...The plan is essentially working. Reports of its death are greatly exaggerated." Tousignant's barb was aimed directly at me for rashly declaring at the large fishermen's rally outside the DFO's office that the Mifflin Plan was dead.

Those fishermen who surrendered their licences could scarcely plan on a Hawaiian retirement, however, as the proceeds were subject to capital gains tax and other hidden costs. During the Davis Plan buyback, the DFO had bought both the licence and the vessel, but under the Mifflin Plan the fishermen had to dispose of redundant vessels. Without licences, the fishermen no longer qualified for discounted wharfage fees at government-owned small craft harbours. Those who could not find buyers went to considerable expense to scrap their vessels. For older fishermen with no other option but retirement, Ottawa offered no retirement benefits as on the East Coast. Younger fishermen leaving the industry found that their licence retirement money was not enough to invest in career alternatives, and Ottawa declared that those who had received buyback funds were ineligible for some federal support programs. It is worth noting that tendermen—mariners who packed the fish from the fishing grounds to the processing plants—received absolutely no compensation for losing their jobs or for having their vessels made redundant by the Mifflin Plan.

Nonetheless, on the eve of the 1996 salmon season, the Ottawa mandarins were proud of a job well done. The smaller commercial fleet would now be much easier to manage. It had been distributed into eight licence areas. There were 176 seine licences in Area "A," which stretched from Cape Caution north to the Alaska boundary, and 289 seine licences in Area "B" from Cape Caution south to the Washington state boundary. The troll and gillnet fleets were divided into three separate zones: Area "F" (North Coast) had 294 troll licences, Area "G" (West Coast Vancouver Island) 529 troll licences, and Area "H" (Gulf of Georgia) 118 troll licences. Area "C" (North Coast) had a whopping 1,139 gillnet licences, but Area "D" (Johnstone Strait) had 307 gillnet licences and Area "E" (Fraser River) had 529 gillnet licences.

The DFO looked to the 1996 management plan with renewed optimism, but most fishermen did not. A few "enterprising" fishermen had secured the right to fish the whole coast by stacking licences on their vessels, but the vast majority were now locked into a single area.

Tangled Lines and Torpedo Tirades

Doesn't the service of quiet diplomacy require dirty hands?

—Dennis Lee, *Civil Elegies*

On October 21, 1996, in a statement published in *The Fisherman*, Doug Kerley, provincial jobs commissioner for BC, estimated that the Mifflin Plan had eliminated 7,800 jobs in the salmon fishery. He also criticized the DFO for failing to deliver on its promise of transitional programs to help displaced fishermen find other jobs. In response, Fred Mifflin—like Brian Tobin before him—claimed that Ottawa could not afford to provide BC fishermen with the social support programs given to East Coast fishermen. The victims of the Mifflin Plan would have to make do with existing programs such as Employment Insurance (EI). Most fishermen did not qualify for EI, as they had so few insurable weeks' earnings due to the DFO's "risk–averse" management policies. And despite a whopping $12 billion surplus in the EI fund at the time, Human Resources Development Canada (HRDC) bureaucrats also confirmed that the federal government could not afford any special fisheries programs.

Meanwhile, Corky Evans, BC's new minister of agriculture, fisheries, and food, presented the jobs commissioner's report directly to Minister

Mifflin, who had to admit that Kerley's findings were "unquestionable." "I call upon the federal minister of fisheries and BC MPs to accept their responsibility to provide assistance," Evans said.[1] Finally the DFO agreed to a federal–provincial review of the Mifflin Plan. The process was "independently" chaired by John Fryer, a one-time union leader and now a private consultant for various government agencies. Joining Fryer on the review panel were Mike Francino, representing Ottawa, and Bill Lefeaux-Valentine, representing BC.

But on November 7, before "the Three Amigos," as they had come to be known, could release a report, a beleaguered Fred Mifflin promised that emergency funding would be forthcoming at the end of the review process. He told the *Vancouver Sun*, "There is no dollar limit. We will pay whatever it costs to get this done."[2] [This statement naturally raised expectations, and it would later haunt Mifflin when he subsequently failed to deliver on this promise.] The Three Amigos' report, *Tangled Lines*, was released by Fryer and Lefeaux-Valentine on December 16, 1996, at a large press conference in Vancouver. Their key recommendations were the establishment of a conservation council, a catch royalty system, an early retirement program for fishermen, a $15-million salmon enhancement

The "Three Amigos" review the Mifflin Plan, winter 1996. Left to right: Bill Valentine, John Fryer, Mike Francino.

program, a new Salmon Industry Development Board, a vote on licence stacking, a public registry of salmon licences, compensation for combination fishermen whose gear would now be redundant, a professional audit of the DFO's consultation process, a salmon marketing program and development of fisheries for under-utilized species.

The panel's prime concern was whether the stackable area-licensing program should proceed, so the vote they recommended was important. Just before the start of the 1996 salmon season, the DFO had imposed a temporary moratorium on licence stacking, so before they began their work, the Three Amigos asked that this moratorium be extended to January 15, 1997. By that time many fishermen—some of whom had opposed stackable area licensing—had already stacked additional licences on their vessels, and they feared that those who held stacked licences would vote against further stacking in order to safeguard their advantage over single-area licence holders. To make things worse, the panel could not agree on a date for a vote. Francino believed that it should occur in 1998 after completion of the Mifflin restructuring process. Lefeaux-Valentine called for an immediate vote. Fryer apparently split the difference and scheduled the vote for the end of the 1997 fishing season, a compromise that pleased no one.

During the *Tangled Lines* press conference on December 16, Ross Wetzel, one of the gillnet representatives on the roundtable, made an emotional appeal to Fryer. "The roundtable was supposed to make us viable," he cried. "We asked for a vote, and Tousignant said, 'No way!' The union had a vote and it was ignored. Eight months later you say, 'Vote in a year!' We can't wait that long. I don't want compensation. I want to survive as a fisherman!" John Murray, president of the Pacific Gillnetters Association and a fervent supporter of licence stacking, shouted, "I don't agree with the UFAWU. The Pacific Gillnetters Association says you did a wonderful job!" The argument continued and the press gallery seemed dazed and confused. One baffled reporter asked, "Who's the devil here? The DFO or the fishermen?"

Before ending the press conference, Fryer remarked wistfully, "In all my years of public service I've never experienced such a bad relationship between a government agency and the public. I'm not going to speak for the DFO, but a lot of work has to be done on this relationship. Most decisions are made by bureaucrats in Ottawa. You can't have the DFO against the industry. The relationship is just not there now."[3]

Scrap, Can and Deep-Six the Plan!

Just after New Year's Day 1997, Corky Evans boarded a small chartered plane bound for Alert Bay, with the intention of visiting nine coastal communities before January 15 to gain support for extending the licence-stacking moratorium for another year. On the village's tiny airstrip Evans was greeted by a full welcoming delegation, including Mayor Gilbert Popovitch. Around them a committee held up placards that read: "Down with Area Licensing!" and "Mifflin, your job could be next! Start retraining!" and "Scrap, Can and Deep-Six The Plan!" The delegation marched to the Alert Bay Community Hall, where 400 people crowded inside.

Meanwhile, Mifflin was on his way to Vancouver with David Anderson, his BC cabinet colleague. In contrast to Evans' grassroots community tour, Mifflin settled in the DFO offices while releasing *Towards a Sustainable*

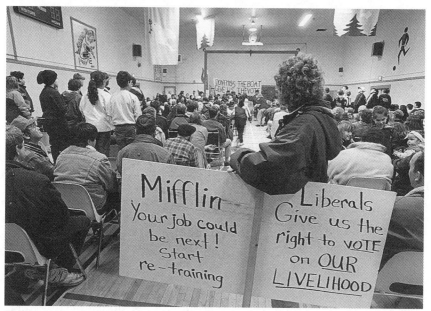

Residents of Sointula, Port Hardy and Alert Bay meet with Corky Evans, provincial minister of agriculture, fisheries and food, to discuss the impact of the Mifflin Plan on coastal communities, January 1997.

Pacific Salmon Fishery: The Federal Response to the Tri-Partite Panel Report.
He then announced that he would lift the licence-stacking moratorium
on January 15 and that a vote on licence stacking would take place at the
end of the 1997 season. He also presented a federal aid package of $35
million to help displaced fishermen. The offer was less than one percent
of the amount spent to help East Coast fishermen.

Mifflin's unexpected visit caught Corky Evans by surprise. His coastal
tour now seemed pointless.

"The federal government saw the tour happening," he said to the
Alert Bay crowd, "and they thought maybe there are people opposed,
that maybe the province is not alone, and they decided to nip it in the
bud...I thought about cancelling the tour, but going home would be
like losing, like abandoning people. I decided to continue and change
the nature of the tour. I've been energized by the people I've met and
their incredible resolve not to be beaten." Then Evans told the cheering
crowd, "People want Victoria to get fisheries management brought out
to the West Coast, but they also told me, 'You'd better come home and
share it with us in the communities!'" And at the end of the meeting he
received a standing ovation when he said, "The provincial government is
now in this scrap and is beginning to take responsibility...And we will
never, never walk away again."

We Won't Stop Until We Get It!

Glen Clark raised his hands in mock surrender and beamed as the
delegates to the 52nd annual convention of the UFAWU gave him yet
another standing ovation. Behind him, occupying a full wall in the
auditorium of the Maritime Labour Centre in Vancouver, was a 1940s-
vintage social realist mural, depicting scenes from BC's resource and
waterfront industries, a fitting backdrop for this working-class premier.

A few months earlier, the province had registered a $1 billion deficit,
and the local scribes had launched a merciless attack on Clark's "tax-and-
spend" NDP government. Without success, Clark had explained that the
downturn in provincial revenues was caused by a sudden decline in BC
resource exports due to slumping Southeast Asian economies, a situation aggravated by cuts to federal transfer payments. Now, scarcely more

than six months into his term, he was plummeting in the polls. So now, on January 31, 1997, Glen Clark was momentarily basking in the adoration of a friendly crowd. For these fishermen, shoreworkers and tendermen, the prospect of a friendly premier was the first sign of hope they'd seen in five years.

"Many people question getting involved in fisheries," Clark said, "but I want you to know: I totally reject this view. I think this industry has a future and the working people in it have a future in it, and I'm not going to give up on it! Provincial governments have usually…supported the forest industry at the expense of the fishing industry," Clark continued to the amazement of his audience. "It's time for the provincial government to stand shoulder to shoulder with this union to fight on behalf of coastal communities. We have to wrest more control of the fishery away from faceless bureaucrats in Ottawa and bring it to BC, not to replace bureaucrats with bureaucrats, but to give some control to fishing communities, and we won't stop until we get it!"

Clark announced that his government would fund a new salmon habitat restoration program and pass a new Fish Protection Act. Then he brought up the unresolved Pacific Salmon Treaty dispute. "The spineless position of the federal government in dealing with the US on the salmon treaty is shameful. I'm proud of the federal government for standing up to the US on Cuba, but the salmon treaty is worth about five times in economic value what trade is with Cuba." Then, to the delegates' delight, Clark declared, "I've told the federal government if there is no progress by March 15th, there will be unilateral action by the provincial government, and we'll make sure it gets the attention of the US before the prime minister meets with the president. I won't tell you what it will be, but it will be controversial and might even be an international incident."[4]

A few months before this I had been asked to join Clark's political staff as a special advisor on the Pacific Salmon Treaty, so I knew that he planned to make good on his pledge to cancel the provincial lease to the seabed at the Nanoose Bay torpedo range. The premier was about to trigger the most dramatic phase in the century-long "salmon war" between Canada and the United States. Unbeknownst to us all, Clark would have to fight on two fronts: one with the Americans, the other with Ottawa.

And sadly, the army he hoped to lead had already lost 7,800 "soldiers" in the "civil war" incited by the Mifflin Plan.

A New US Negotiator

Much besides the Mifflin Plan controversy had happened on the Pacific Salmon Treaty front since the infamous fish war of 1994. In exchange for Tobin dropping the transit fee imposed on Alaskan fishermen, Vice-President Al Gore had appointed James Pipkin as the new US federal PST negotiator. According to Gore, Pipkin had a new mandate not only to negotiate a deal with Canada, but also to forge a consensus between the northwest states and Alaska. First he was to prepare a new US "equity paper" on salmon interceptions, a paper that admitted for the first time that the Americans intercepted more Canadian salmon than they should. However, Pipkin warned that he was not prepared to disrupt "traditional" US fisheries to resolve this problem. Instead he proposed a one-time cash payment to Canada in lieu of the interception imbalance. The cash would finance an enhancement fund for both countries. In return Canada was expected to accept an integrated abundance-based approach to sharing on terms laid out by the Americans.

Yves Fortier believed that Pipkin's offer indicated a new willingness to negotiate. Therefore, the Canadian national section of the PSC agreed to consider some elements of Pipkin's paper—including the cash payment—so long as it led to a significant long-term reduction of US interceptions. On January 10, 1995, Sandy Argue, the DFO's international affairs advisor, prepared a counter-position that included several caveats: 1) conservation needs would be met in an "even-handed" manner by all parties; 2) abundance-based fisheries would ensure that the lion's share of the catch is enjoyed by the country in which the salmon originate; 3) "caps" and "floors" would be put in place to ensure that neither party would exceed or fall short of appropriate harvests; 4) Alaska would take steps to meet Canada's conservation needs as well as reducing the equity imbalance; 5) Washington state would take steps to reduce its catch of Fraser sockeye and pinks in accordance with Canada's reduction in interception of southern coho and chinook stocks; and 6) any cash payment would be twofold to adjust any past and future imbalances.

Back in January 1995 while this Canadian counter-position was being prepared, I had been appointed by the DFO to replace Jack Nichol as a salmon commissioner on the Canadian side. At the first meeting that I attended, Mike Hunter of the Fisheries Council of BC declared that Pipkin's paper was "the last nail in the coffin" for Canada's traditional equity concept. A former DFO economist, Hunter had been on the team that negotiated the 1985 treaty, and was fully aware of the history of Canada's quest for equity. He now argued, however, that the realities of 1985 had been entirely different, and at one point he floated the idea of accepting American cash to support a new regionally based, joint enhancement accord with the Alaskans. He reasoned that if the "pie" was bigger, the equity issue would become less important.

Hunter's approach was consistent with the business interests of the big canners for whom he worked. Ever since the 1988 GATT ruling that struck down Canada's ban on the export of unprocessed sockeye and pink salmon, Canadian canners had become increasingly interested in processing American-caught salmon. Large quantities of cheap Alaskan salmon lowered the canners' overhead and cushioned them from the effects of the DFO's cuts to BC harvests. It no longer mattered to the canners where a salmon was caught so long as the price was right. And now fish wars and arcane squabbles over equity were a nuisance, if not a threat, to their business interests.

An *Amicus Curiae* for the Salmon

Although several treaty meetings occurred in 1995, no substantive progress resulted from Pipkin's appointment. Brian Tobin therefore agreed to submit Canada's equity case to non-binding, third-party mediation, squelching all hope of stopping American interceptions during the 1995 season. That year the DFO reported that BC chinook stocks were on the verge of extinction because of El Niño, and the PSC recommended that all Chinook harvests be reduced by at least 50 percent. BC commercial fishermen agreed with this directive, but the Alaskans did not.

For all its boasting about good fisheries management, Alaska's salmon resource is much less genetically diverse than BC's. Its total catch is much greater than BC's, but most of southeast Alaska's harvest is lower-valued pinks and chums, and almost all southeast Alaskan chinook stocks are produced in hatcheries. DFO data shows that 90 percent of the chinooks that are landed in Alaska originate either in BC or the northwest states. The PST limits both southeast Alaska and northern BC to 263,000 chinooks per year. Yet in spite of Canada's agreement to reduce its 1995 northern chinook catch to 130,000 pieces, Alaska announced that it would only cut its catch to 230,000.

At this point, an internal US National Marine Fisheries Service memo, which confirmed that the Alaskans were overfishing BC chinook, was leaked to the media. This report recommended that the catch be reduced to 138,000 in 1995. Alaska ignored the memo and James Pipkin did nothing, pending the appointment of a mediator. It was left to the Northwest Treaty Tribes in the US to take legal action against Alaska for overfishing. On August 12, 1995, US Supreme Court Judge Barbara Rothstein handed down an injunction halting the Alaskan chinook catch at 177,000 pieces. She stated, "Alaska has violated an agreement to rebuild salmon along with Washington, Oregon, Canada, and Indian Tribes."[5] Thus it was Judge Rothstein, not US President Bill Clinton, who had the temerity to stop the Alaskan overfishing. And Canada, in its role of *amicus curiae* or friend of the court, had provided much of the technical evidence in the Northwest Tribes' case.

The injunction was only temporary, however, and the judge ordered the PSC to meet as soon as possible to work out a compromise. The PSC did so in Seattle on August 27, 1995. Despite the combined pressure of the Canadian and northwest states commissioners, the Alaskans launched an appeal against the injunction. That appeal was overruled on September 9, by which time the 1995 salmon season was effectively over. Although the US Supreme Court subsequently held the Alaskans to 177,000 chinooks, this catch was far above the safe limits set out by the PSC.

There were concerns about coho salmon in 1995 as well. On the North Coast a coalition called the Skeena Watershed Committee (SWC) had advised the DFO to cut back the commercial harvest of Skeena River sockeye in order to reduce the bycatch of coho. This committee was funded largely through the infamous Greenplan slush fund and was basically a sop to the growing political power of the commercial sports lodge operators along the Skeena. When the DFO complied with their rec-ommendation, it led to an over-escapement of a million sockeye, which caused a serious outbreak of Ichthyophthirius disease (ICH), caused by overcrowding on the spawning grounds. The SWC also demanded the DFO curtail the commercial fishery at the mouth of the Skeena to con-serve steelhead and coho—which they would continue to catch at the same rate. These moves hobbled the northern gillnet fishery.

But the recreational fishing lobby had nothing to say about the slaughter of BC coho and steelhead just across the border in Alaska. DFO sources say the Alaskans harvested 3,118,000 coho in 1995, of which 825,000 were of BC origin. At the same time, the DFO was charg-ing Canadian commercial fishermen for having a single coho in their possession. It was too much for the hard-pressed gillnetters. Hundreds of them surrounded the Alaskan ferry MV *Taku* in Prince Rupert harbour for several hours on July 10, 1995.

Nick Stamatiou, a Delta gillnetter, picks a sockeye out of his net near the mouth of the Skeena River, 1995.

The Case of the Missing Mediator's Report

As the 1995 salmon season came to a close, all effort on the PST front shifted to the mediation process. The two countries agreed to have Ambassador Christopher Beeby of New Zealand try to sort out the long-term equity muddle. Canada's chief negotiator Yves Fortier wrote to Beeby:

> The United States has been deriving far greater benefits from its harvests of salmon than its own production would warrant at the expense of Canada and directly contrary to the Treaty…In fact, the United States has rejected Canada's frequent demands that the equity principle be carried out as required by the Treaty and MOU. The result is that year after year the inequity has grown as the United States has ignored both the letter and spirit of its obligations.
>
> The United States arguments opposing, qualifying or otherwise delaying implementation of equity are not due to any misunderstanding of the intent behind the relevant provisions of the Treaty and related understandings. Rather, they stem from the fact that, being in what the MOU refers to as the "advantaged" position in respect to benefits gained as the result of interceptions, to the extent of $70 million annually, the United States is content to preserve the status quo.[6]

Beeby met extensively with stakeholders and government officials from both countries. Early in 1996 he produced a report that was in essence a framework for further negotiation rather than a ruling. He suggested the two parties establish a "base-line" for all interceptions, and that compensation be paid if either party exceeded that level. Yves Fortier welcomed Beeby's proposal, considering it a vindication of Canada's position, and Beeby was so impressed with Canada's case, he surmised that Canada would likely have won, had the matter gone to arbitration.[7]

James Pipkin spurned Beeby's proposal, however, calling it a rehash of the Canadian "theology" on equity. Given Pipkin's intransigence, Beeby concluded there was no hope for further progress and bowed out of the dispute. Canada could not even claim a moral victory, thanks to Brian Tobin's promise to keep the mediator's findings confidential should the Americans dislike the outcome. The Canadian national section of the PST demanded Ottawa release the details of the Beeby Report, but Ottawa refused for fear of jeopardizing future negotiations. This decision marked a turning point in the century-long struggle to achieve sovereignty over Canada's salmon stocks. Rather than using Ambassador Beeby's report as a springboard to binding third-party arbitration, Prime Minister Jean Chretien, External Affairs Minister Lloyd Axworthy and Fisheries Minister Fred Mifflin simply conceded defeat. Axworthy assigned John Fraser the task of finding a "diplomatic solution." Fraser and his US State Department counterpart Eileen Claussen were to review the PST deadlock and seek ways to get negotiations back on track.

There were now so many players in the PST imbroglio that Fraser's appointment only created more confusion. The Pacific Salmon Commission and its various panels were still expected to work out interim fishing plans, though without any reference to long-term equity. Government-to-government negotiations between Pipkin and Fortier were on hold but would continue. And at least three cabinet ministers—Lloyd Axworthy, David Anderson and Fred Mifflin—were tinkering with the file. In the meantime the long-term equity issue was in limbo, and the calamity facing BC chinook salmon was left unchecked. And despite a seemingly interminable round of meetings, the Fraser–Claussen process produced no meaningful results.

Treading in Dangerous Waters

During the 1996 BC election, Premier Glen Clark had challenged Ottawa's handling of the Pacific Salmon Treaty negotiations and on April 17, 1996, had told the *Vancouver Sun*, "We have the federal government taking very drastic action [the Mifflin Plan] to deal with salmon stocks in BC but not taking equivalent drastic action to deal with the Americans." Clark then said at a press conference that if the Americans did not stop overfishing Canadian salmon, he would cancel the US's lease on the large torpedo testing range at Nanoose Bay on Vancouver Island.

"We're not going to sit back and let the federal government misman-age our fish stocks the way they have on the East Coast," Clark declared. "If the Americans won't co-operate on protecting salmon, if they aren't respecting our sovereignty, our resources or our treaties, we should not continue with the [Nanoose Bay testing] agreement." Then Clark took up Captain Canada's cudgel and demanded Ottawa use the Coastal Navigation Protection Act to reinstitute the transit fee on all Alaskan fish boats travelling though BC waters.

The Nanoose Bay threat sparked outrage in Ottawa. External Af-fairs Minister Lloyd Axworthy told the press, "Mr. Clark—to use a bad metaphor—is treading into very dangerous waters if he starts linking issues related to fisheries to other issues." In fact, Clark was concerned about all aspects of BC's resource economy. As the forest industry was increasingly threatened by international boycotts, and a group of Hol-lywood film stars had placed an ad in the *New York Times* attacking the BC lumber industry, Clark referred to environmental extremists as the "enemies of BC," and told the *Vancouver Sun* on May 16, 1996: "We've got to fight this kind of propaganda because is does no good for British Columbia and clearly it's out of synch with what we are doing…on the environment." His attack on environmentalists would appeal to forestry workers and certain converts to the right-wing populism of the Reform Party, but in using it he ran the risk of alienating the "green" wing of the NDP. Clark hoped that a strong public stand to save BC salmon would improve his image with both the public and the more moderate ele-ments in the environmental community.

Although the runs of sockeye to both the Skeena and Fraser were far above forecast in 1996, the DFO still had to deal with a pre-cipitous decline in chinook and coho stocks. On April 19 the DFO's chief chinook biologist, Brian Riddell, had reported that only 15,000 chinooks (just one-third of which were female) were expected to return that year to the Robertson Creek hatchery on the west coast of Vancouver Island, which had produced runs as high as 300,000 in the past. Moreover, the Robertson Creek chinook run was an im-portant "indicator stock" that the DFO had traditionally used to ex-trapolate the returns of hundreds of other smaller runs. "We cannot meet any of our egg requirements for that stock," said Riddell. "We truly believe…we are at risk of losing small populations of chinook throughout the west coast of Vancouver Island."[8]

The DFO responded by banning any harvest of chinook salmon by commercial trollers off the west coast of Vancouver Island and the Queen Charlotte Islands. Minister Mifflin then ordered mandatory catch-and-release of all sports-caught chinooks. He pointedly reassured recreational anglers that they could catch other species of salmon, but Canadian Commissioner Bob Wright, a champion of the sports fishing sector, assigned Velma McColl, executive director of the Sports Fishing Institute of BC, to campaign strenuously against the chinook catch-and-release proposal. She complained the program would cost sports lodge operators $250 million in lost earnings and threaten 2,000 jobs, and on April 16 she told the *Vancouver Sun*, "We don't have an economically viable commercial fishery, but we do have an economically viable sports fishery right now that generates spending in this province." She claimed the recreational sector harvested only four percent of the entire BC salmon catch, but did not mention that this included at least one-third of the chinooks landed each year. "You don't have a sports fishery that's going to within a half-hour or 10 hours obliterate a run," she said, invoking the words of John Fraser, an ardent recreational angler. "Sports fishing isn't like that."

A Pig-Headed Prime Minister

Appalled by the threat to BC chinooks, on June 21, 1996, at the First Ministers' Conference in Ottawa Glen Clark called on Prime Minister Chretien to take action against Alaskan overfishing. At the same time, his deputy minister, Doug McArthur, was trying to negotiate a new federal–provincial accord for West Coast fisheries with Chretien's chief of staff, Eddie Goldenberg. The following day, Peter O'Neil reported in the *Vancouver Sun* that Clark was outraged that Chretien had backed out of an earlier pledge to do more to protect BC salmon. "It's a complete waste of time," Clark declared. "They don't appear to want to work co-operatively, so we're going to have to work in a more confrontational way."

To the astonishment of the Ottawa press gallery, Clark accused Chretien of being "pig-headed." "Arrogance on the part of the federal government, intransigence, bureaucratic inertia, stupidity. I don't know. Ask them," Clark added. "Either the prime minister's sympathetic talk wasn't being translated to the bureaucracy or there wasn't political direction given to the bureaucracy."

The press scolded Clark for his lack of tact. "Not since Brian Peckford punched out the feds in a fight over offshore oil jurisdiction has a premier from English Canada behaved so belligerently toward Ottawa," wrote Barbara Yaffe in the *Vancouver Sun* on June 25.

With the help of the press, the Ottawa establishment turned Clark's concern about sovereignty and conservation into a controversy over political etiquette. For years, BC media pundits had longed for a political leader with the *savoir faire* to take on Ottawa as Quebec's Lucien Bouchard and Alberta's Ralph Klein had done. But this was not quite what they had in mind. Norman Ruff, the political scientist from the University of Victoria, accused Clark of using the fishery issue to divert attention from other problems, including a large provincial deficit. According to Dave Cameron, a University of Toronto political scientist, Quebec premier Lucien Bouchard or even former Newfoundland premier Brian Peckford could get away with "fed-bashing" because the public grudgingly understood their issues.[9] Clark's intervention on salmon, the pundits said, was comparatively trivial and obscure.

Brian Peckford rose to Clark's defence. "It was very important for the premier of BC to establish at the first meeting a strong position," he said. "Then, over time, he develops the details of the position. By osmosis, it becomes part of the body politic, part of public policy debate in the country at large."

Meanwhile, Clark tried to qualify his comments about Chretien. "I didn't call them [the first ministers] stupid," he said. "What I said was that the federal government and the bureaucrats were acting in a stupid fashion when it came to dealing with this issue."[10]

With the long-term equity issue mired in the murky Fraser–Claussen process, Canada's chief negotiator, Yves Fortier, attempted to do something about the chinook crisis by invoking the technical dispute resolution clause of the PST, which states: "Either party may submit to the chairman of the Commission, for referral to a Technical Dispute Settlement Board, any dispute concerning estimates of the extent of salmon interceptions and data related to questions of overfishing...The Board shall make findings of fact on the disputes and other technical matters referred to it." Fortier suggested the two parties refer the urgent question of the 1996 chinook quotas to Ambassador Beeby. However, the US rejected Fortier's proposal, claiming that he had interpreted the clause wrongly. A small team of senior DFO bureaucrats met quietly with Washington state officials to sign a "one-off" Fraser sockeye deal for 1996, which provided great benefit to the Americans and was reached without any input from Canadian commissioners. The parties agreed that because of low forecast returns of Fraser sockeye in 1996, neither party would fish that stock, but that the US could take 16 percent of the total allowable catch if by chance the run went above 2 million pieces. It was yet another step backwards from the 7-million Fraser sockeye cap in the original treaty, but worse, it signalled that Canada was no longer prepared to take the fighting stance that it had in the fish wars of 1956, 1983 and 1994.

Not Our Fish to Give Away

Early in 1997, Regional Director Louis Tousignant solemnly announced that BC coho stocks were seriously endangered and that all Canadian fisheries would be curtailed as a result. No one in the Canadian national section denied there was a coho problem, but many questioned why Tousignant had presented such information on the eve of a new round of PST negotiations, since for years the troll fishery for coho off the west coast of Vancouver Island had been Canada's strongest bargaining lever with the US. The Americans were heartened by the announcement—any Canadian conservation measure represented a gratuitous "pass-through" of US-bound chinook and coho—and Tousignant, having completed his Mifflin assignment, was about to be transferred back to Ottawa.

When the PSC met in Vancouver in January, Alaskan Commissioner David Benton proposed to Yves Fortier that the negotiations be turned over to a select group of "fishermen stakeholders." He suggested that a government-to-government negotiated settlement on equity would not work because Alaska could veto any deal imposed by Washington, DC, but that a deal was possible if these stakeholders negotiated it by themselves.

Fortier gave the idea short shrift at first, but finally agreed to give the idea a try when Benton implored, "Let the stakeholders try it. If they fail to reach a deal, then it will be much easier for me to say, 'You had your chance'."[11]

The new initiative got underway in February, amid great media fanfare in Portland, Oregon. Although the nebulous Fraser–Claussen process was technically pending, the American government appointed yet another federal official, Mary Beth West, to oversee the stakeholder talks. James Pipkin was still very much on the scene as well, so it became extremely hard to know whether Claussen, West, or Pipkin was speaking for the US government on the PST.

During the week-long Portland session, each country nominated two panels of eight stakeholders: Both Canadian panels consisted of legitimate non-governmental representatives, but the Americans named a number of government officials to their panels. The panels were to discuss both northern and southern fisheries—a major concession by Canada, as Ottawa had always insisted that negotiations occur on a national rather than regional basis. The stakeholders made progress on many minor issues but did not have time to address long-term equity.

The panels resumed negotiations in Juneau, Alaska, after the March herring season, but enthusiasm for the new process began to wane as the stakeholders began to bog down in arcane technical disputes. The rest of the PSC delegation had no choice but to stand by and watch.

Not long after, Mike Staley, chair of the southern Canadian stakeholder panel, reported that Washington state seemed willing to reduce its interception of Fraser sockeye in exchange for an abundance-based management system for chinook and coho. This proposal would destroy the traditional troll fishery off the west coast of Vancouver Island, but Gerry Kristianson, a sports fishing representative on the southern stakeholder panel, enthusiastically embraced the concept. It was in his constituents' interest to eliminate the competition posed by commercial trollers, and Kristianson was convinced that securing the trollers a greater catch of Fraser sockeye would be the optimum solution for all. As a prominent Liberal Party campaign organizer and friend of David Anderson, he had a great deal of influence. Years later the *Vancouver Sun* carried a story on

Kristianson in which it was implied that West Coast trollers had been used as pawns to settle the PST dispute.[12]

Believing they could strike a deal, the southern Canadian stakeholders agreed to scrap the coho and chinook entitlements in the original PST agreement. However, as soon as Canada had agreed to adopt long-term abundance-based management instead of fixed quotas, the American stakeholders claimed it would be impossible to reduce the US catch of Fraser sockeye in exchange for Canadian concessions on abundance-based management because the US government did not have the legal right to curtail the catch of the Northwest Treaty Tribes. Their only other option was to reduce or eliminate the non-Native US commercial fleet, and the US stakeholders refused, saying that they would be lynched if they agreed to it. Such a reduction would require federal funding for a buyback, they said, which they could not authorize. Then they appealed to the Canadian section to help them lobby the US Congress for buyback funds.

The Canadian stakeholders were stunned. They had fully revealed their bottom line and received nothing in return. Their situation was truly preposterous: the US government, which *did* have the authority to make such expenditures, was claiming that only the stakeholders had the moral authority to renegotiate the treaty. At the same time, the American stakeholders had brokered a tentative deal, then claimed that only the US government could deliver financially on the deal.

The northern panels spent long, equally frustrating hours arguing over the semantics of terms such as "total allowable catch (TAC)," favoured by Canada, versus "annual allowable harvest (AAH)," favoured by the US. Yet the two sides did agree to some changes in the conduct of the Alaskan net fisheries at Tree Point (District 101) and Noyes Island (District 104). In return, the Alaskans demanded a guaranteed annual allowable harvest of Skeena and Nass river sockeye. From an equity perspective, this was totally unacceptable to the northern Canadians. The adjustments to the District 101 and 104 fisheries, said Joy Thorkelson, Canadian northern stakeholder chair, fell far short of equity. In response, "I have to represent my constituents," Jim Bacon, the Alaskan stakeholder chair, said, "These fish aren't mine to give away."[13] Perhaps inadvertently, Bacon had finally debunked the US officials' line that the stakeholder process could solve the long-festering equity dispute. Instead of making a difficult compromise and living up to their treaty obligations, US politicians stalled, deferring to inconclusive stakeholder negotiations, while chinook stocks in both countries approached extinction.

When Fortier had reluctantly agreed to the stakeholder process in January, he had insisted on a deadline of March 15, 1997, for results. Mary Beth West persuaded Fortier to extend the deadline to May 9, in the hope that two further sessions in Seattle and Vancouver would lead to a settlement. No progress was made on long-term equity by May 9, but the two sides had continued work on short-term fishing arrangements for the 1997 season. In the southern panel talks in Portland, the Americans had demanded a 26 percent share of the Fraser sockeye catch and the Canadians offered 6 percent; now the gap was narrowed to 20 percent versus 13 percent. The northern panel had tentatively agreed on minor adjustments to the District 101 and District 104 fisheries, but there was no progress on reducing the huge number of Canadian salmon taken in Alaska. In fact, the Alaskans—James Pipkin's 1995 equity paper notwithstanding—never agreed that there was an interception imbalance at all, but in "a spirit of friendship and co-operation," they proposed—without prejudice—a US-funded northern-boundary salmon-enhancement program. Canadian salmon commissioners such as Jack Nichol had always rejected joint enhancement activity as a threat to Canadian sovereignty, but the Canadian northern stakeholder panel left the option open. "Salmon enhancement is very popular in the north," Joy Thorkelson explained, "and we must be sensitive to that fact."[14] Still, they made it clear that a US-funded enhancement program was not a substitute for reduced Alaskan interceptions, and Robert Stewart, a Nisga'a representative on the northern panel, bluntly declared, "Our fish are not for sale!"

The equity issue remained unresolved on May 9, and most Canadian national section members—including me—assumed the outstanding issues would be referred to Pipkin and Fortier. The Alaskans rejected this option completely, in spite of Dave Benton's pledge to Yves Fortier in January. The Canadian stakeholders had deliberately stalled, they charged, hoping to send the talks to the government-to-government level, and provincial officials such as myself had forced the Canadian stakeholders to stonewall any potential settlement. In fact, no one had to pressure the Canadian stakeholders to take their stand, and the Alaskans made absurd allegations because they were afraid that Washington, DC, might finally see reason and make a deal at their expense.

No More Mifflin Plans

Just before the PST stakeholder talks collapsed, Prime Minister Chretien called a federal election for June 2, 1997. Premier Clark now had an important opportunity to press Ottawa to satisfy BC demands—in fact, Ottawa had already made a number of concessions to Clark on the fisheries front. On April 17 Chretien and Clark had signed the new Canada–BC Agreement on the Management of Pacific Salmon Fishery Issues, and Clark pronounced it a "historic day for BC." "There will be no more Mifflin plans," he said. "This deal allows us to be proactive, not reactive."[15] Fred Mifflin was more circumspect: "The agreement will mean things will be slower. But perhaps a slower process means better agreements and less animosity," he said.[16]

Public reaction to the agreement was mixed. Reform Party fisheries critic John Cummins dismissed it as nothing more than "fluff," but Mike Hunter of the Fisheries Council claimed it "showed promise." Jim Fulton of the David Suzuki Foundation noted, "The key will be if it opens up fisheries management to public scrutiny." The well-to-do multiple-licence and quota holders in the commercial sector, who had actively promoted the Mifflin Plan, were opposed to any public involvement in fisheries decision-making. On May 9, 1997, midway through the federal election campaign, Clark announced that he would create a new Crown corporation called Fisheries Renewal BC (FsRBC) to rehabilitate West Coast fisheries. It would be funded by a $7.7 million grant from Forest Renewal BC. Clark must have believed that FsRBC would be a major lifeline for commercial fishermen displaced by the Mifflin Plan. In fact, he announced it at the False Creek commercial fishermen's wharf, where he told a cheering crowd that FsRBC would help protect their jobs through "balanced fleet reduction instead of the Mifflin Plan." Several West Coast fisheries interest groups griped that the FsRBC was nothing more than a sop for the UFAWU, and the *Vancouver Sun* went so far as to suggest on May 17 that there was something "fishy" about the new Crown corporation, which should not be a make-work project for unemployed UFAWU fishermen.

But the critics had little to fear. The FsRBC bureaucracy, once established, was tightly constrained by provincial Treasury Board spending guidelines. The modest fund had to be distributed throughout the province—including fresh-water fisheries—and not just to coastal communities. Native, conservation and recreational fishing organizations were also eligible for the FsRBC money, so the amounts earmarked for community projects involving commercial fishermen were limited.

Leaking the Mediator's Report

The stalled PST negotiations gave Clark another opportunity to attack Ottawa midway through the federal election campaign. At the time, I was working closely with a communications team based in the premier's office, including Geoff Meggs, who was now Clark's communications director, and Sheila Fruman, a private media consultant who had been Premier Harcourt's communications director. The Alaskans had outmanoeuvred the Canadian side in the press after the stakeholder process collapsed on May 9, and the government-to-government talks between Yves Fortier and Mary Beth West were slated to resume in Seattle on May 19, so the team decided to leak Ambassador Beeby's report to the media two days before the start of the Seattle meetings. We hoped to show the public how the US had consistently violated the intent of the treaty. We also hoped to strengthen Yves Fortier's bargaining hand by focussing on the deliberations of an impartial analyst like Beeby.

Despite a sour reaction from External Affairs bureaucrats, most members of the Canadian national section, including Fortier, were happy that the report was public. "Beeby doesn't give us everything we asked for," UFAWU President John Radosevic told the *Vancouver Sun* on May 17, "but the bottom line is, the interceptions must stop." Mike Hunter of the Fisheries Council added, "Imbalances in interceptions have to be addressed and that's an obligation the US has not lived up to. If the United States is going to be exposed to what an independent third party and respected mediator concluded, they are going to have to explain how he got it wrong."

I had been invited by Yves Fortier to represent the province—as both Clark's advisor and a Canadian commissioner—at his critical negotiating session with Mary Beth West in Seattle. Fortier hoped to improve the fishing arrangements developed by the stakeholder panels, then sign a one-year deal. He planned to address long-term equity later. He told West that Canada would help the northwest states with their serious coho conservation problem, but that Canada required an equivalent reduction in the US harvest of Fraser sockeye.

West acknowledged Canada's sacrifice, but said, "I cannot alter the stakeholders' last position on Fraser sockeye. I have no authority to do so." Fortier reminded her that they were to negotiate a deal, and West replied that she could amend the US bargaining position only after consulting with all US stakeholders. Fortier replied politely that her stakeholders were here in this hotel, and West said, "But I'm required to consult with many at the regional level who are not here today before I can make changes." Fortier said he was prepared to negotiate further Canadian concessions, and West said courteously that she still had no room to move. "Ms. West, I cannot negotiate with myself," said Fortier in exasperation.

That evening, with the talks again at an impasse, the Canadian commissioners discussed strategy. Fortier said that he'd never before encountered such an outlandish negotiating experience. Everyone at the table agreed, and then Assistant Deputy Minister Pat Chamut declared, "It's time to turn the hounds loose!"[17]

Turning the Hounds Loose

An American fisherman named Tom Millman met the hounds on May 21, and that afternoon he sat hunched at the end of the Port Hardy pier while his 33 m (109 ft) crab boat, *The Four Daughters*, heaved gently in the swells nearby. The vessel was chained to the government wharf, having been arrested by the Canadian Coast Guard while en route from Crescent City, California, to Kodiak, Alaska. Unbeknownst to Millman, the Canadian government had ordered that US fishing vessels travelling through BC's Inside Passage were required to have a special permit, under the Coastal Navigation Protection Act. He failed to produce the permit, and was ordered to appear in court the following day.

A large group of reporters soon gathered at the pier. Russ Hellberg, mayor of Port Hardy, had offered food, shelter and entertainment, but Millman chose to stay on the pier. With the TV cameras on him, he turned and pointed shakily toward his vessel. "That's my home," he said. "To get into my home you have to have a search warrant. They didn't do that."[18] He told reporters that the Canadian authorities had been "walking around all day with weapons, like this is a police state!"

In court the next day, Millman, and the skippers of four other American vessels were found guilty, and each was given a $300 fine. In handing down the sentence, Judge Brian Saunderson remarked, "Someone just turned up the heat under you, gentlemen. And you are the pawns."

The US authorities were not long in responding to an American citizen being "taken hostage" by the Canadian government. On May 22, 1997, the *Globe and Mail* reported, Nicholas Burns of the US State Department said, "Canada has seriously misjudged the situation and has lost, at least for now, the possibility of achieving a long-term agreement." US officials also accused Yves Fortier of walking away from the bargaining table. "It's all a smokescreen," stated Robert Turner, salmon commissioner for Washington state. "There is something else there. It appears this was all disrupted [by Canada] to avoid making an unpopular decision, to avoid criticism." And Ron Allen, representing the Northwest Tribes, said, "I believe it was campaign-related. Some folks were delighted that it broke off so they could go back and stand in their righteousness." Fortier's response was, "Poppycock! That's an outrageous distortion."

US State Department officials cancelled a PST negotiating session tentatively set for May 30. Meanwhile, Alaskan Senator Frank Murkowski wrote to Admiral Robert E. Kramek, commander of the US Coast Guard, demanding an armed escort for all US fishing vessels in BC waters.

On the Canadian side, Glen Clark stoked the flames by asserting, "the time for talk is over." The following day, May 31, 1997, he called another press conference at the False Creek fishermen's dock to announce that he had served 90 days' notice on the cancellation of the Nanoose lease. US Navy officials were very worried about losing the Nanoose Bay torpedo testing range. John W. Douglas, assistant secretary of the navy, wrote to US Senator Diane Feinstein, expressing concern and listing the unique properties of the Nanoose site. On May 23 the *Globe and Mail* reported that the Nanoose range had saved the US Navy $2 billion over a 32-year period, and described Clark's gambit as a "cautious first step" designed to jump-start PST negotiations again. Mere hours after Clark's announcement, US Secretary of State Madeline Albright had called External Affairs Minister Lloyd Axworthy to request that the PST talks resume the following week. In Victoria, Clark crowed, "We got the talks back on track today…It's a good first step, but we're not breaking out the champagne yet and we're not changing our minds about closing Nanoose."

A week before the federal election, I accompanied Premier Clark to a meeting in Seattle with Washington State Governor Gary Locke. It was supposed to be a friendly get-together, following Locke's recent election, but Clark shocked the American media with a blistering tirade against US overfishing. On the way home, we discussed what we would say about the PST dispute at an NDP election rally in Burnaby that evening. A number of former NDP voters were attracted to the federal Reform Party, and I suggested he condemn the party's near total silence on the PST crisis. Preston Manning's only significant comment on the issue had been to demand that Yves Fortier, Canada's chief negotiator, be replaced. The PST was an important topic at the rally, and in the federal election campaign as well. Alexa McDonough, leader of the federal NDP, attacked the Chretien Liberals for "folding like a cheap umbrella" in the face of US overfishing.

Clark's strong nationalist stand may also have contributed to a sudden surge in NDP popular support in BC—10 percentage points in less than a month. Years later, officials in the NDP and elsewhere concluded that Clark's aggressive stance on the PST jeopardized BC's interests. But in the spring of 1997, many leading opinion-makers were praising him for it. CKNW's Rafe Mair, the liege lord of hot-line radio, applauded Clark for standing up to both Ottawa and the US, and on May 26, Mike Smith of the Vancouver *Province* dubbed Clark the "new Captain Canada." "I couldn't believe how David Anderson, our only federal cabinet minister, chickened-out this week by suggesting we should stop arresting US fish-boats," Smith wrote. "'I believe we have their attention now,' Anderson squeaked to CBC radio the other day."Even the editors of the Province, normally hostile to Clark, wrote proudly on May 28 that "Perhaps now the Americans will realize that we're serious and will strike a fair deal." And at the annual meeting of the Coastal Community Network (CCN), 120 delegates voted to "strongly support" the cancellation of the Na-noose lease if US interceptions of BC salmon were not stopped. "I've always been a Liberal," said Russ Hellberg, chair of the CCN, "but you've got to admire Glen Clark for getting tough."[19]

"My hat is off to the Premier for taking a hardline stand with the Americans," BC Senator Pat Carney chimed in. "His response has been much stronger than Ottawa's and the only thing the US responds to is tough negotiating. That's how you get things done. Most politicians in Ottawa don't know a cod from a salmon and they don't care."[20]

Her opinion was shared by the western premiers who joined Clark at a summit in Campbell River on May 30, 1997. The premiers met at the swank Painter's Lodge, owned by Canadian Salmon Commissioner Bob Wright, and there, between fishing sorties, the premiers discussed Ottawa's inept handling of the Pacific salmon file. According to the *Victoria Times Colonist* on May 30, Saskatchewan Premier Roy Romanow declared, "The federal government should invite the participation of the provinces in the defence of Canada's international economic interests whether it's salmon or, in the case of Saskatchewan, agriculture and ag-riculture trade wars that we've had with the United States." Glen Clark smiled happily for the cameras as he showed off the 17-pound salmon that had won him first place in the premier's fishing derby, but landing the political support of the premiers for his PST stand was the biggest catch of all.

On June 2, 1997, the federal Liberal Party managed to hang on to a slim majority in the House of Commons. The Reform Party, which formed the official opposition under the leadership of Preston Man-ning, swept all but six seats in BC, and the media attributed the vote to British Columbians' profound anger toward the ruling Liberals.

The Rally vs. the News

The PST talks, which had been hurriedly scheduled to resume after Premier Clark's Nanoose threat, were cancelled almost as quickly. In addition, Alaska Senator Frank Stevens, chair of the all-powerful Senate Appropriations Committee, threatened to withhold $100 million (US) that had been earmarked for the cleanup of four abandoned US military bases in Canada's far north. Clark responded by threatening to cancel 50 co-operative agreements between BC and the US. BC Opposition Leader Gordon Campbell complained that Clark's tit-for-tat politics were harmful to BC, and federal External Affairs Minister Lloyd Axworthy pronounced the threat to close Nanoose "unhelpful."

On June 5, a major rally on the PST took place in downtown Vancouver. More than 500 people turned out to hear Premier Clark; Buzz Hargrove, president of the Canadian Auto Workers Union; Herb Dhaliwal, BC MP and the new parliamentary secretary for fisheries; Mike Hunter, president of the Fisheries Council of BC; Russ Hellberg, chair of the Coastal Community Network; Barry McMillan, president of J.S. McMillan Fishing Company Ltd.; Jack Nichol, past president of the UFAWU; John Holdstock, president of the BC Wildlife Federation; Jim Fulton of the David Suzuki Foundation; MP Svend Robinson; John Cummins, Reform MP for Richmond–Delta; and Christine Hunt of the Kwagiulth Fisheries Commission. The rally was organized as a festive event that crossed all political lines.

On the day of the rally, Mark Hume of the *Vancouver Sun* declared that the event was a public relations stunt to promote Glen Clark at taxpayers' expense and that $20,000 had been spent to promote the rally. In his work on the PST, Clark had assembled an advisory committee that included representatives of the BC Wildlife Federation, the Fisheries Council of BC, the UFAWU, BC Aboriginal Fisheries Commission, the David Suzuki Foundation, Salmon Watch, Pacific Trollers Association, West Coast Seafood Processors and the Sports Fishing Institute of BC, all of whom supported and attended the Robson Square rally. Yet Hume's story centred on an "anonymous member of the committee" who had said, "I would suggest it [the ad] was 90 percent paid for by the government."

Clark's advisory committee on the PST was broad-based and debates took place regularly. Yet Hume's anonymous source had never raised his concerns with the full committee.

A Plummy Sort of Fellow

On June 12, 1997, David Anderson, the Member of Parliament for Victoria, was named Canada's minister of fisheries and oceans. Chretien was taking a political risk. In 1994 Anderson had brought suit against the federal government because the previous Tory government had terminated his $76,000 per year payment for sitting on the Immigration Appeal Board. Citing Anderson's minister's salary of $140,000 per year, the *Vancouver Sun* declared on January 11, 1994, "Anderson shouldn't have it so plummy!" And Reform MP Chuck Strahl said, "If Anderson and his colleagues are serious about cleaning out the pork barrel, they shouldn't be standing in it." Anderson insisted it was a matter of principle. The government dispatched Chretien's special advisor on ethics, Mitchell Sharp, to talk to Anderson, who eventually dropped the lawsuit. Not long afterwards, Anderson supported a federal plan to de-staff BC lighthouses. To the people of the coast, the loss of the light keepers was an emotional symbol of how Ottawa mistreats this province. The issue might have come and gone, but when Anderson returned from a Hawaiian vacation aboard his yacht and encountered bad weather, he had to call the Bamfield lighthouse keeper to help him navigate to safety. Anderson insisted that he had not really been rescued but had only asked the light keeper for directions, and he said that he had hiked along the West Coast Trail the day after the storm to give the light keeper a bottle of champagne. But the light keeper told a public hearing on lighthouses that Anderson had been travelling without the appropriate nautical charts and had to be guided into port over the radiophone.

On August 6, 1994, Peter O'Neil reported in the *Vancouver Sun* that Chretien considered Anderson a political liability but did not have a suitable replacement for him within the BC Liberal caucus. The editors of the *Vancouver Sun* wrote that Anderson's appointment, coming at the height of the Mifflin crisis, "signals two things: 1) Ottawa has renewed confidence in Anderson, 2) West coast issues deserve more attention." They went on to suggest that Anderson's cabinet profile might help curtail Clark's "unprecedented interest in this small industry."

Six days after Anderson was appointed minister, he met with Clark in the premier's office to discuss the PST issue. Anderson's assistant, Brian Bohunicky, and I were the only others present in the room. Clark proposed that Anderson follow Brian Tobin's lead and launch an "aggressive fishing strategy" to pressure the Americans. Anderson was not averse to the idea, but his prime concern during the meeting was to get Clark to drop the Nanoose threat. Clark said he would make a strategical retreat on Nanoose if Victoria and Ottawa worked together to secure a new salmon treaty, and if Anderson would refrain from publicly attacking him on the Nanoose issue.

Anderson seemed to agree with Clark's request, and the two politicians held a joint news conference, declaring their mutual resolve to secure a new PST deal. Anderson said, "I think Mr. Clark and I both understand if we don't hang together, the Americans will hang us separately." But the very next day, on a Vancouver hot-line radio show, Anderson did an about-face and condemned Clark's Nanoose tactics. The two men never again saw eye to eye.

In the meantime, a 14-member industry advisory panel had prepared a confidential report for Anderson on a "Canada First Strategy," with a series of far-reaching recommendations. They included: 1) allow extra seine-fishing in the Strait of Juan de Fuca; 2) increase Canadian trans-boundary river sockeye and coho harvest shares while maintaining Canadian escapement targets by fishing up to seven days per week; 3) terminate trans-boundary sockeye enhancement; 4) initiate Portland Canal chum gillnet and seine fisheries and increase fishing opportunities in selected portions of approach routes to the Skeena River; 5) initiate a North Coast winter/spring troll fishery for chinook but stay within overall area ceiling; 6) initiate a winter/spring troll fishery for chinook on the west coast of Vancouver Island but stay within the overall area ceiling; 7) apply a disproportionate catch-up/makeup for the northern troll fleet; 8) give high profile to the Alaskan overharvest/bycatch of coho, steelhead and chinook; 9) stop illegal US sport charter operations in Canada; 10) move trollers into fisheries in Queen Charlotte Sound, west coast of the Queen Charlotte Islands, Strait of Juan de Fuca and Strait of Georgia and effect a vigorous troll fishery on the west coast of Vancouver Island, consistent with the troll consensus; 11) allow additional fisheries for northern trollers for Fraser sockeye within their existing licensed areas, consistent with the troll consensus; 12) maximize gillnet fishing capacity at the Fraser apex by allowing movement of certain gillnetters on a voluntary basis; 13) allow additional northern gillnet fisheries for Fraser sockeye.[21]

The main purpose of the "Canada First" fishing plan was to harvest as many Canadian salmon as possible before they became vulnerable to US interception. It was meant to apply to all areas of the BC coast, but its greatest leverage lay in drastically limiting the Washington state catch of Fraser-bound sockeye while meeting spawning escapement goals for all stocks. The plan was also designed to avoid catching threatened stocks of US chinook and coho as they passed through Canadian waters, but numerous "fish war" critics within the media—not to mention those in the recreational, aboriginal and environmental sectors—characterized the "Canada First" fishing plan as a reckless slaughter.

A few weeks after his meeting with Clark, David Anderson announced that the US and Canada would meet again to sort out the PST impasse. In his meetings with the governors of the concerned states, he said, his efforts had helped to close the gap between the two sides. (Others believed it was Clark's threat to close the Nanoose range that had brought the Americans back to the table.) Meanwhile, Mary Beth West had consulted with her US stakeholders and met again with Fortier, and despite Anderson's claim that the Americans had promised to negotiate in good faith, West's position had not changed. The *Vancouver Sun* reported on June 27 that one DFO official had said in dismay, "She came in and we're sitting and waiting because it's in their court...They didn't change their coho position by one scale. And on sockeye they had been at 20 percent and they [now] have this generous offer of 19.76 percent. A reduction of one quarter of one percent!"

Fortier made several attempts to negotiate with West, but finally broke off the talks and headed to Denver, where Prime Minister Chretien and President Clinton were attending a G-8 summit. Fortier was convinced that the two leaders were the only ones who could break the log-jam. In Denver he told Chretien that Canada's last offer on Fraser sockeye in May had been 16 percent, and the Americans demanded 20 percent, so Fortier had hoped for a compromise at 17 or 18 percent, leaving the issue of long-term equity for another day. Chretien made the same pitch to Clinton, who apparently agreed, but his decision was subsequently overruled by the US stakeholders' lobby.

Chretien had an embarrassing moment later on, at a North Atlantic Treaty summit in Madrid. He inadvertently chatted before a live microphone and was overheard gossiping with Belgian Prime Minister Jean-Luc Dehaene about Clinton's inability to control the US stakeholders. After the international press reported this faux pas, Chretien said nothing more to Clinton about the PST.

The Bullies and the Pipsqueak

From the start of the 1997 fishing season, BC salmon were exposed to a pincer attack from the Americans. According to the *Juneau Empire* of June 24, 1997, the Alaskans intended to take 277,182 chinooks, almost five times the limit set by the PST Chinook Technical Committee the year before. In the south, Washington Fish and Game Department (WFGD) officials authorized a commercial fishery on the early Stuart sockeye run in the first week of July, despite the reservations of both DFO and PSC biologists.

This prompted Glen Clark to place political advertisements in Washington state media, which read, "Your state's commercial fishing interests have failed the first test of salmon conservation: You don't fish until you are certain the stocks can take it…The decision is a blot on the conservation record of your state." The ads urged Washington residents to write to President Bill Clinton, Senator Slade Gorton, Senator Patty Murray and Governor Gary Locke about the conservation crisis. But the ads only inflamed the American public, and several Washington state radio stations refused to air them. Even some BC media objected. Barbara Yaffe described the ads as "capricious, foolhardy, and counterproductive."[22]

As this issue faded from view, another more serious problem emerged. On July 16, 1997, the public learned that Alaskan seiners at Noyes Island had taken 375,000 Canadian-bound sockeye, three times the legal limit allowed under the North Annex of the PST. The run had not yet reached its peak, and the Alaskans showed no sign of stopping. According to the *Globe and Mail* on July 17, Alaskan Commissioner David Benton said, "If Canada has trouble with that, they should have remembered it before they walked away from the table." It was a remarkable accusation, given

Mary Beth West's refusal to negotiate with Yves Fortier. The Alaskans claimed they were not targeting Canadian sockeye anyway, merely fishing for Alaskan pinks. At that time of year there were few pink salmon off Noyes Island. In fact, the 1997 southeast Alaskan pink run was one of the lowest on record. The seiners were openly preying on the much more valuable Canadian sockeye in the area, which was worth at least $4 US per fish compared to 28 cents for a pink. Few pinks were being landed in this "pink fishery," yet Alaskan fish managers—who routinely boasted about their "conservation-based principles"—ordered several extensions in the Noyes Island seine fishery that July.

Premier Clark accused the Alaskans of piracy. "The conduct of the Alaskan fishery marks a new stage in this dispute," he wrote to Prime Minister Chretien on July 16, 1997. "Until now, we faced a US refusal to negotiate fishing plans which implemented the principles of the treaty. Now we see a direct attack on those principles through increased interceptions of our stocks. Canada, in contrast, has carefully refrained from fisheries which would threaten the conservation of any stocks, regardless of the country of origin." He urgently requested a meeting with David Anderson and Foreign Affairs Minister Lloyd Axworthy. He demanded that Anderson temporarily lift the Mifflin area-licensing scheme so that northern fishermen could help southern Canadian licence holders harvest as many surplus Canadian sockeye as possible in South Coast waters. Then he called upon Axworthy to follow Brian Tobin's lead and institute a series of "non-fishing" measures to pressure the US.

Axworthy rejected Clark's call for the use of "non-fishing" measures, and Anderson told the *Vancouver Sun* on July 19, "As long as I'm minister, we will still have conservation first, second, and third among the objectives of the Department. Therefore I won't countenance any fishery that would impact on any American coho stocks in a manner that might endanger them in any way." At no point had anyone—least of all Glen Clark—advocated intercepting endangered US coho, or compromising basic conservation principles. In fact, everyone had agreed to leave the US coho alone, despite Canada's legal right under the expired annexes of the PST to conduct a coho fishery off Vancouver Island.

Clark demanded that Ottawa convene an emergency summit to address the PST crisis, but David Anderson vetoed the idea. "Anderson is trying to keep the heat down," an anonymous federal official said later. "A face-to-face meeting is an automatic photo-op and a chance [by Clark] for grandstanding which won't help resolve the issue."[23] Instead, Minister Axworthy sent a "strongly worded" diplomatic note to the Americans, condemning US overfishing. The silence on the US side was deafening. Clark could only say in disgust, "Is that not a pathetic attitude? What are we supposed to do—throw up our hands and go home?"[24]

The Battle of Prince Rupert

The Luddites weren't against progress, they were against their exclusion from progress.

—William Greider, *One World Ready or Not!*

Navigating the aisles of the Prince Rupert Safeway store on July 18, 1997, Darlene Wulff had a great deal more on her mind than the price of groceries. After "grubbing up" her gillnetter, she had many other chores to complete before meeting her husband Bob at the airlines terminal. He was returning on the evening flight from Vancouver after participating in a gillnet fishery on the Fraser River.

Meanwhile, Darlene had been fishing sockeye with the Skeena River gillnet fleet almost non-stop since the beginning of the month. This fishery had run for two or three days in a row, then the exhausted fishermen would return to port just long enough to refuel and do repairs, then they went back and worked almost around the clock. But the worst part of this gruelling routine was that there were so few fish. Like her husband, Darlene was a third-generation fisherman. She had deep roots in the industry and she loved the work. But ever since the Mifflin Plan had been brought in, fishing was a much tougher way to make a living, and so far the 1997 season was one of the worst she had ever seen. And that day, at a union meeting at the Fishermen's Hall, she had learned that the down payment for sockeye had been cut.

The reduction had been recommended by Joe Weiler, a UBC law professor and arbitrator. A few years earlier he had assisted the UFAWU–CAW and the Fisheries Council of BC toward an agreement on a "market-sharing" formula, designed to set the price of sockeye. In theory the system would prevent costly strikes. It provided fishermen with a reasonable down payment at the beginning of each season, and later the companies would share a percentage of the market value with them. However, this year the canners were complaining that the world market for fresh salmon was flooded with farmed fish, and that the huge salmon runs forecast to return to Alaska in 1997 would further depress the canned salmon market. It didn't help matters that the non-unionized fishermen in Bristol Bay, Alaska, were having to accept prices dramatically lower than those paid to Canadian fishermen the year before.

At the start of the season, the canners wanted to drop the down payment from $1.20 to 90 cents per pound, though they had paid a final price of $2.25 per pound for sockeye in 1996. Weiler acknowledged their arguments but recommended a down payment of $1.05. Just as he did so, the gigantic run to Bristol Bay, forecast at 25 million sockeye, collapsed. It was too late to change the ruling.

Nevertheless, the fishermen who gathered in the Fishermen's Hall on July 18, 1997, were in no mood to accept the cut. To complicate matters, over the previous three weeks Alaskan seiners had intercepted at least 325,000 Canadian sockeye, 10 times the average catch of sockeye in southeast Alaska over the previous 16 years—and, more importantly, three times the limit established in the PST.

After the meeting, Darlene Wulff and a large number of other fishermen headed for the local DFO office to get more information, but as they approached, security guards barred the entrance. Garth Mirau, a UFAWU–CAW organizer, tried to force his way in, and one of the guards shouted, "You can't come in here! This is a public building!"

A group of frustrated fishermen then attempted to pry the door off its hinges, and UFAWU–CAW leaders restrained them. John Radosevic, president of the UFAWU–CAW, called Fisheries Minister David Anderson on his cell phone and got Velma McColl, Anderson's political assistant, who said that Anderson was away on holiday and would not be returning calls.

The Safeway Caper

Now, in the Safeway, Darlene Wulff spotted her brother Dave Sandve talking with fellow fishermen Al Mearns and Eric Taylor. "I can't afford to fish for these prices," Taylor said. "A pound of wieners costs more than I get for my sockeye!"[1] Sandve said he had not fished for prices this low in twenty years, and Taylor commented that the Alaskans were catching the Canadians' fish and the government was doing nothing.

Several other fishermen stopped to listen, and someone said, "Maybe we should occupy the DFO office."

"Ahh! I was just up there," another man said, "and they locked the doors on us."

Darlene reminded them that the fishery would open soon. "Time's a-wastin'!" she said.

"What's the hurry?" Taylor countered. "There's no goddamned fish out there anyway."

"Well, if you feel that way, why don't we all just stay in?" she said. "Maybe that would wake the companies up."

"That's a hell of a good idea," Taylor said. "But that's assuming we all stuck together."

A shoreworker from the Oceanside cannery approached the group. "You guys know there's another big packer coming in from Alaska tomorrow?" she said.

This news infuriated the group. "Here we are going broke," said Taylor, "and Jimmy Pattison is filling his warehouse with cheap Alaskan fish."

Someone else pointed out that they were Canadian fish, not Alaskan, and that the canners were buying fish in Alaska because the local fleet was not producing enough.

"You shoreworkers should refuse to handle that stuff!" one of the fishermen said.

"We can't do that by ourselves," the woman shrugged.

The group continued to talk out in the parking lot, and more fishermen—including John Stevens, Jim Chislett, Pat Olson, Walter and Barbara Groening, Heather Mearns, Thor Kristianson and Nick Stevens—joined them. Before long the group had resolved to return to the docks and organize a "tie-up" to prevent any Alaskan-caught fish to be unloaded at

Allied Pacific Packing Ltd., a consortium established by BC's two largest fishing companies, BC Packers and the Canadian Fishing Company. If the fishermen were to be deprived of their catch, the canners should be too.

"We've got to be very careful not to tip them off," cautioned one fisherman.

"Right," answered Darlene. "When we go on air, we'll call it the Safeway caper."

Everyone agreed.

The Ramming of the *Easy Come*

When Eric Taylor and Walter and Barbara Groening returned to their boats at the Rushbrooke floats, they spoke to Kim Olsen aboard his gillnetter, inauspiciously named the *Disrupter*. Olsen agreed to drum up support for the "Safeway caper" on the radiophone and got a surprisingly positive response. Many vessels had already left for the fishing grounds, but he reckoned that at least 50 boats would stay in port to blockade the cannery.[2]

As Olsen was recruiting fishermen, someone called in on the radiophone in broken English. It was a representative of the Vietnamese fleet offering support. These fishermen had become a major part of the gillnet fleet, and in 1989 hundreds of them had caused bad feelings by continuing to fish during the UFAWU's bitter three-week strike against the canners. But now they offered to help barricade the unloading station.

Meanwhile, Arnie Nagy, chief shop steward at the Oceanside cannery, had discreetly informed Olsen that the Alaskan packer *Polar Lady* was due in that evening. Olsen relayed this information to the fishermen out on the grounds, and they organized a sentry network that stretched from Prince Rupert to the Alaska boundary 60 miles away. As support grew, the leaders of the "Safeway caper"—later dubbed the "Safeway Seven" by the media—changed their strategy. Instead of just preventing the packer from unloading at the cannery, they decided to prevent the packer from entering the harbour.

At 5:30 p.m. the airways came alive. A black-hulled packer was entering Prince Rupert harbour through the narrow Metlakatla Pass north of the main entrance. A group of fishing vessels surrounded the packer, and the skipper replied, "Listen, you guys, I understand your problem. I'm a Canadian and my boat is registered in Canada. I'm packing chum salmon from an Alaskan hatchery. I have absolutely no sockeye on board if that's what you're worried about. Just let me drop my anchor in front of the cannery and you can come aboard and inspect my vessel. I'll even let you surround me for a while if it's a media event you're looking for. But after that I expect you to leave me alone so I can unload without further hassles."[3]

In the face of such candour the protestors were disarmed. Some suggested the packer be released immediately. Others insisted the Alaskan fish should be dumped overboard. After much deliberation the vessel was released.

While this was going on, Bob Burkoski, skipper of the gillnetter *B.C. Maid*, was turning his vessel in circles at the entrance to Metlakatla Pass, torn between going fishing to feed his family and listening to the voices on the radio pleading for boats to stay in port. He felt like "a hamster spinning on a wheel," he said later, trapped by declining fish prices, area licensing and Alaskan interceptions.

Then a voice on the radio shouted, "There he is! He's heading in from the Port Edward side. We gotta stop him! It's now or never, boys! Now or never!"

Burkoski realized that it was true—fishermen would have to take action or they would wither and die. He hit the throttle, pulled his vessel out of its circle and headed back to Prince Rupert.

Gary Stewart, skipper of the *Polar Lady*, had no idea what was going on. He had heard talk on the radio about some sort of blockade but didn't think it concerned him. He did wonder, though, why so many Canadian boats were travelling so close to him. Stewart was born in Ketchikan and had worked in the commercial fishery for 35 years, eight of them transporting surplus Alaskan salmon to Prince Rupert for custom processing and, he thought, providing work for a hard-pressed community. Accompanying Stewart were his wife, nephew, son-in-law, two grandchildren, and two other crew.

As the *Polar Lady* neared Prince Rupert, the relay boats alerted those in the harbour, and they formed a phalanx just as the *Polar Lady* reached the entrance. The Canadians had planned simply to stop the skipper and determine the contents of his load. But Stewart, unnerved by the number of vessels swarming about him, refused to co-operate. Later it was suggested that the *Polar Lady* was packing Alaskan pinks and had no sockeye of Canadian origin on board,[4] but the Canadian fishermen did not know this. Stewart slowed down only briefly and made no effort to communicate with the blockaders. Then, when angry voices on the radio shouted, "Yankee go home!" and "Stop stealing our fish!" he panicked. Just as he resumed speed, a 12 m (40 ft) fibreglass gillnetter named *Easy Come* veered in front of the *Polar Lady*'s bow. Stewart threw the 32 m (106 ft) steel packer into reverse, but the two vessels collided violently. The *Easy Come*, owned by Raymond "Beanie" Suzuki of North Delta, keeled over, a trolling pole sheared off and the gunnels and stern damaged.

Hysterical screams burst from the radio, "He's hit Beanie! He's just hit Beanie!" And dozens of boats rushed the *Polar Lady*. The much faster Alaskan vessel sprinted out of the harbour. Those vessels still in hot pursuit called upon the Coast Guard vessel *Point Henry* to arrest the *Polar Lady*, but their pleas were ignored, and the *Point Henry* escorted the Alaskan vessel out of the harbour. By now, however, the entire fishing fleet knew about the incident and hundreds of vessels poured into Prince Rupert, their holds empty, their crews filled with rage.

Kim Olsen lay awake throughout most of the long, rainy night, his mind reeling with the events of the previous day. He thought of poor Beanie Suzuki, whose mangled boat rested on anchor just across the bay and who, well inebriated, was now being protected from prying reporters by a couple of friends. Suzuki's fishing season was now in jeopardy, and no one knew whether he would be compensated for the damage. (In fact, Canadian fishermen later passed the hat and some Prince Rupert businessmen donated to the fund, but neither the owners of the *Polar Lady* or the US government ever assumed any responsibility for the damage, and the Canadian government took no action on Suzuki's behalf.)

As Olsen listened to the radiophone all that night, hearing the continuous chatter of fishermen as they made their way to Prince Rupert to join the protest, he thought about the Canadian Coast Guard escorting the *Polar Lady* back to Alaska, and he thought of Fisheries Minister David Anderson sleeping contentedly in a swank East Coast fishing lodge.

To avenge Alaska's piracy and Beanie Suzuki's loss, Olsen and a group of fishermen decided to target the only symbol of the United States of America that was close at hand: the Alaskan ferry. The plan was simple: circle the ferry when it arrived, then use the media coverage to expose the scandal of Alaskan overfishing, to wake up the bureaucrats in Ottawa and perhaps even to teach the Alaskans a lesson.

According to the British historian Eric Hobsbawm, a deeper under-standing of historical events can be found through "excursions into imaginary or fictional history known as 'counter-factuals'."[5] In other words, studying the "what if" of history can be as revealing as the actual course of events. In this case, had the Alaskan ferry arrived on schedule on the morning of July 19, 1997, the fishermen would likely have sur-rounded it for a few hours and then let it go, just as they did in 1995. However, by some means (the Canadian Coast Guard among them), officials in the Alaskan Ferry Corporation had been informed about the harbour blockade on the previous evening and had shuffled their sched-ule. The MV *Malispina* steamed into Prince Rupert at 6:00 a.m., three hours ahead of schedule.

Canadian fishermen blockade Alaska Ferry MV Malispina *in Prince Rupert harbour, July 1997.*

Tears to a Glass Eye

At 5:45 a.m. Kim Olsen leapt from his bunk as voices on the radiophone screamed, "It's here! The ferry's here and there's only four of us out here. There's no goddamned way we can stop it—it's going too fast!" Olsen awoke as many others as he could, and within minutes, all along the waterfront, sleepy fishermen were stumbling about, cranking their engines and honking their horns. In near pandemonium, dozens of vessels left the dock as fast as they could, but before many of them had traversed the harbour, the *Malispina* was secure at her moorings. Fishing boats bobbed erratically in front of the ferry while angry words were exchanged over the airwaves.

A small group of fishermen organized an impromptu meeting and resolved that the vessels would remain on the scene to symbolically delay the ferry's departure later that afternoon. Then the ad hoc group announced a set of rules to govern the fleet's behaviour: "There will be no violence of any kind. There will be no vandalism. No spray-painting graffiti on the ferry's hull as happened in 1995. There will be no throwing of objects at the ferry, no swearing, and, above all, no harassing the passengers. We have a list of boats delegated to make sure everyone lives by these rules."

Bob Burkoski volunteered to serve on the committee deputized for crowd control. Over the next three days, he and many others were involved in almost non-stop activity: ferrying reporters, attending meetings and controlling the crowd. Kim Olsen tied up in front of the ferry slip to get some sleep. Minutes later, other boats began to arrive one by one, and within half an hour almost a hundred boats had formed a crooked line beneath the towering bow of the ferry. The fishermen had created a barrier considerably more immutable than anyone had planned. It was no easy task to maintain the line in the deep water of the harbour. Their anchors could barely hold as tide and wind whipped the flotilla about. It was with great relief that the gillnetters welcomed Regan Birch, skipper of the seiner *Windswept*, into their ranks. Birch brought a much heavier anchor and a considerable boost in morale. But when a gust of southeast wind shifted everything, Bob Burkoski's *B.C. Maid* became a makeshift tug, towing the anchors of some of the larger boats so that they could stay in the line.

Fishermen hold a press conference during the Prince Rupert ferry blockade, July 1997. Left to right: John Radosevic, Des Nobels (speaking into microphone), Kim Olsen, John Stevens.

A delegation of fishermen went ashore to determine what was inside the reefer trucks that were driving off the *Malispina*. Alaskan ferry officials warned them it was illegal to obstruct the trucks, which carried the US mail. "Why the hell is the US mail being carried in a truck with fish blood and slimy water pouring out of it?" demanded one fisherman. He received no answer.

In Eric Hobsbawm's "counter-factual" theory of history, the question arises: What would have happened if those reefers filled with fish had not been on the *Malispina*? The protest would probably have ended in short order. But to the Canadian fishermen, the stakes had changed: the salmon in the reefers were tantamount to money stolen from their pockets. As Pat Young, Steveston gillnetter, put it, "The blockade must continue because the Alaskans are using the ferry as a big packer."[6]

Soon after this some reporters approached the blockade in a speedboat, and Kim Olsen told them, "We want the Alaskans to quit fishing our salmon. I mean, they're cutting us off. It's like a bloody tap being shut off here!"

"How long do you intend to hold the ferry hostage?" a reporter asked.

"As long as it takes for David Anderson to get up here and do something about the Alaskans!" Olsen answered. "That's how long we'll be in front of that damn ferry!" Bob Rezansoff, president of the Fishing Vessel Owners Association, knew about Beanie Suzuki's boat being hit, and now he knew that the Alaska ferry was surrounded, but he hoped to avoid getting involved in the fracas. For most of the morning of July 19 he ignored all of the people trying to reach him by VHF radio. Finally another member of the Fishing Vessel Owners Association succeeded in reaching him, and asked him what they were going to do about the situation, starting with the low prices.

"What do you want me to do?" Rezansoff replied. "There's a price formula in place. I can't help it if the world markets have gone for a shit."

His colleague commented that at least they should try to stop the Alaskans from taking all the Canadian fish out at Noyes Island.

"That I can certainly agree with," said Rezansoff, "but what do you suggest we do?"

"We could join those guys blocking the ferry in Rupert," another skipper cut in. "We're wastin' our time out here. There's no fish anyway."

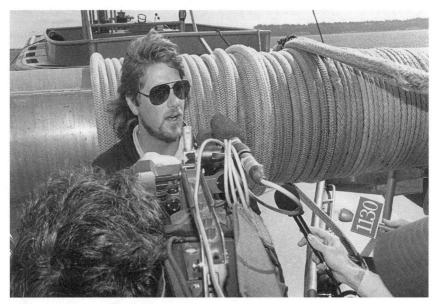

Kim Olsen aboard the seiner Taaska, *speaking to reporters about US overfishing at Point Roberts, August 1997.*

While Rezansoff and several other seine skippers talked, another voice suddenly sliced into their conversation. "Jesus Christ, you guys, I'm fishing up here by the line and a bloody American Coast Guard cutter just circled me! And I'm at least three miles inside Canadian waters! What the hell's going on here!"

This was just too much for the seine skippers. They decided to sail back to Prince Rupert to join the ferry blockade. To Kim Olsen, the sight of the armada of seiners pouring in through Metlakatla Pass, horns blaring and Canadian flags flying, was "enough to bring tears to a glass eye." Later that afternoon, Rezansoff dropped the anchor of his 20 m (66 ft) seiner in front of the 122 m (403 ft) *Malispina* and welcomed the blockade steering committee aboard for a strategy session.

A Fleet Deal, Not a Union Deal

On the morning of July 19, 1997, John Radosevic of the UFAWU–CAW was shocked to learn that the fishermen had surrounded the Alaska ferry. On the previous evening, he and two other officials of the UFAWU–CAW had been amazed to hear about the protest in the harbour and the collision of the *Polar Lady* and the *Easy Come*. They had gone down to the waterfront to offer help, but the fishermen told them it was best if the union did not get involved. Now, as Radosevic approached the ferry terminal, he was overwhelmed by the sight of hundreds of boats, all draped with flags, banners and makeshift signs, massed in front of the ferry. Radosevic also saw the crowd of fishermen refusing to let the reefer trucks pass. And although elated by the display of militancy, he worried about the legal consequences.

The UFAWU has had a long history with *ex parte* injunctions. In 1967 President Steve Stavenes and Secretary-Treasurer Homer Stevens were jailed for a year after refusing to obey a court injunction to lift a picket at the Prince Rupert Fishermen's Co-op. Since then, the union leadership had tried to avoid such legal tangles. But the union leadership had not organized the blockade at Prince Rupert and had no say in the matter. Radosevic could see many UFAWU–CAW members in the crowd, but just as many, perhaps more, non-union fishermen. When he was given an opportunity to speak to the crowd, he praised them for their courage but advised them to use extreme caution to avoid any legal ramifications. A hothead in the crowd shouted, "Butt out! This is a fleet deal, not a union deal."

Kim Olsen, who had emerged as the de facto leader of the blockade, said, "I'm a union member and I want my union involved—which doesn't necessarily make this a 'union deal.' We're all in this together, so for God's sake, let's show some unity."

Later, Radosevic joined Olsen, Rezansoff and others at a steering committee meeting to formulate the protestors' demands: that Fisheries Minister David Anderson meet with them in Prince Rupert, that Allied Pacific Packing refuse to handle any Canadian salmon intercepted by the Alaskans, and that Alaska honour all the provisions of the PST.

After the meeting, Radosevic spotted Rob Morley of Allied Pacific Packing standing just up the hill from the surrounded trucks. Morley was visibly upset, but Radosevic approached him to gauge his reaction to the blockade, assuming that they would at least agree on the need to object to the Alaskan interceptions. Morley, like Mike Hunter of the Fisheries Council of BC, had started his career in the International Affairs Branch of the DFO and thus was well aware of the background to the PST dispute. For several years he and Radosevic had met nose to nose over the bargaining table, and though they were not fond of each other, they had maintained a civil relationship. Now Morley made it clear that the blockade was harmful not only to Allied Pacific Packing but to Canada's PST bargaining position as well, despite Radosevic's suggestion that if the protestors refrained from damaging property and offending the public, the demonstration might be just what Ottawa needed. And Radosevic was left with the impression that Morley thought the UFAWU had organized the blockade. He assured Morley that the union had had nothing to do with the protest, but, he added, "You're damn lucky those fishermen vented their anger on the ferry and not your plant."

The Alaskan Injunction

Meanwhile, Governor Tony Knowles of Alaska hadn't wasted any time responding to the blockade. On Sunday, July 20, his lawyers persuaded a Supreme Court judge in Montreal to issue an *ex parte* injunction ordering the release of the *Malispina*. Three times zones ahead, Judge Max Teitelbaum dispensed his order before most of the exhausted blockaders had risen from their bunks. He ordered that "the defendants, and each of them, and anyone having knowledge of this order, be restrained until further order, from impeding, obstructing or in any way interfering with the navigation of the ships *Malispina*, *Taku*, *Matanuska* or any other public ferry transportation operated by the plaintiffs, at Prince Rupert."[7]

That morning the steering committee informed about 150 fishermen that the injunction had been handed down. The crowd was incensed to learn of the affidavit of Alaska's Attorney General Bruce M. Botelho, which read: "In the absence of a 1997 fishing agreement, the State of Alaska and British Columbia have established management regimes for the various salmon species for the 1997 fishing season. British Columbian fishermen say that Alaskan fishermen are violating the treaty by intercepting excess numbers of sockeye salmon bound for British Columbia streams. The state of Alaska maintains that its management is consistent with general treaty principles and objectives and with conservation and sustained yield goals employed by the State of Alaska."[8]

"That's outright bullshit," declared Bob Rezansoff. "He's stealing fish from these poor guys in Rupert. He's driving this town into poverty."[9]

"If we let it [the ferry] go, we are like our government," Kim Olsen told the defiant crowd, and when the question of obeying the injunction was put to a vote, it was rejected by an overwhelming majority. As for the legal consequences, Wally Nygren, a Parksville gillnetter, shouted, "It's no big deal. If someone gets taken away, there are a hundred people who will take their place."

"In one week I'm finished anyhow," cried Des Nobels. "There's 600 of us here with nowhere to go, with nothing to do, so we may as well spend the little money we have got left fightin' them."[10] "I'm trapped," added John Hird of Cowichan. "The Mifflin plan took away four-fifths of my income potential and now the Americans have taken the last one-fifth away."[11]

The fishermen vowed to hold fast until David Anderson travelled to Prince Rupert to sort out the mess. Meanwhile, in Ottawa, Anderson was telling the press, "The Americans do not respond well to what they regard as pressure or retaliation. I sympathize with the fishermen, but…sometimes you have to realize your tactics have to be tailored to what you are trying to achieve."[12]

On the afternoon of July 20 the steering committee delegated UFAWU–CAW Vice-President Jim Sinclair to negotiate the terms for releasing the ferry with Governor Knowles.[13] Initially, Sinclair demanded that all Alaskan interceptions of BC salmon cease immediately. Bob King, Knowles' press secretary, replied, "We're not going to negotiate fisheries issues when one of our vessels is held hostage."[14] For the next 24 hours Sinclair tried to reach a deal, but during the protracted discussions the steering committee surmised that Knowles wanted to keep the issue alive so that he could launch a multimillion-dollar damage suit against the fishermen. He had no intention of negotiating a settlement, and he suggested that a lawsuit might be stayed if the eight members of the steering committee assumed personal liability for any future blockades. The committee could not assume legal responsibility for acts of mischief beyond their control. In the wee hours of July 21, Sinclair, Radosevic, Rezansoff, Reform MP John Cummins and several others concluded that it was pointless to carry on with the negotiations.

Knowles had stepped up the pressure in the meantime by suspending all ferry service to Prince Rupert from Alaska. The revenue of commercial fishing dwarfs that of tourism in Prince Rupert, but the threat terrorized the local business community. On July 21 the *Vancouver Sun* reported that Prince Rupert Mayor Jack Mussallem estimated BC would lose $10 million in tourist revenue. He had sent a hasty apology to the Alaskans and pledged that there would be "an immediate and enforceable response to any future actions, however unlikely." The national business press then picked up the story. On July 22 the *Ottawa Sun* reported, "We can just imagine how some US senators are relishing the chance to use the Pacific salmon dispute to settle a few trade scores close to their own hearts—whether Canadian grain sales, or softwood lumber, or the Canada–US auto pact, or potatoes, or the huge overall trade imbalance, etc."

Even the canners jumped into the media fray. Rob Morley of Allied Pacific Packing told reporters, "If we don't have that Alaskan fish or access to Alaskan fish on a regular basis, then clearly we don't need this plant. The Alaskan production is based on a relationship with Alaskan fishermen. If they feel we are not reliable and we can't take care of them, they will certainly look elsewhere next year and not come back—so this could have lasting effect."[15] Michelle James of the Fisheries Council of BC said that "less than one percent of the fish being processed is the prized sockeye, and the processors had no way of knowing whether they were fish heading for Canadian waters or American ones."[16] And Doug Souter, president of the Canadian Fishing Company, added, "They [the Alaskans] have always taken Canadian fish. They've just taken less in the past."

However, the blockade had considerable grassroots support. "I'm sympathetic with the fishermen simply because we're talking about their livelihood," said Mavis Brown, a Canadian passenger on the *Malispina*. "…There's a big difference between holidays and livelihoods."[17] "To heck with the tourists," said Kate Johnson of Prince Rupert. "It's the fishermen we're worried about. A lot of people from the surrounding villages also depend on fishing."[18]

On the ferry, confusion reigned. There were 328 passengers on board when the blockade had begun. The *Malispina* was not equipped for overnight accommodation, so officials had scrambled to find hotel rooms for those who needed them. The departure lounge was filled with people demanding refunds or trying to arrange alternate transportation.

In a gesture of goodwill, blockade committee members organized a salmon barbecue for the stranded passengers, but US Customs would not allow the fishermen on board to extend the invitation.

Burning Old Glory

Throughout the standoff the fishermen lived under the intense scrutiny of a battalion of reporters. The media savoured the fishermen's flamboyant rhetoric and the colourful spectacle of their flotilla, and the rank-and-file fishermen relished their brush with fame. It was inevitable that someone—frustrated by the situation, inexperienced in dealing with the media and excited by all the attention—would commit a public relations blunder. Not long after Governor Knowles announced he was suing the protestors for damages, Rod Taylor, a fishermen from Delta, burned an American flag in front of a crowd of reporters. The incident became a major controversy, as the scene played repeatedly on all the major US networks. The public was no longer indifferent to an obscure regional fish flap. America's most sacred icon had been desecrated.

Rod Taylor, who holds dual American–Canadian citizenship, realized his error immediately and tried to apologize for his actions, but the media ignored the anti-climactic apology of an indiscreet hothead, and the incident turned into a diplomatic crisis. The issue of overfishing was buried in the fulminations of US politicians and the grovelling apologies of Canadian diplomats.

More importantly the tide of public opinion turned against the blockaders, who were now referred to as "terrorists," "renegades" and "hijackers." "I think we ought to just roll in a carrier fleet and fly those F-14 Tomcats about ten feet above the water, with supersonic sound," shrieked one caller to an Alaskan open-line radio show. "And let 'em see a couple a' hundred sub periscopes in the bay, and let them think about that."[19] Alaskan Senator Frank Murkowski demanded that President Clinton "do whatever is necessary and appropriate to assure that the government of Canada takes steps to ensure that no future illegal actions against American citizens will be allowed to occur."[20] Washington state Senator Slade Gorton denounced the "lawless Canadian fishermen" for "harassing US citizens."[21] Even Canadian Fisheries Minister David Anderson joined the chorus. "It is quite repugnant to Canada—quite outrageous and unpardonable," he said. "I apologize for the half of him that is Canadian."[22] External Affairs Minister Lloyd Axworthy complained that the blockade was upsetting PST negotiations, though no negotiations had taken place for months.

On Monday, July 21, David Anderson finally travelled to Prince Rupert. "I am not going up there because of the blockade," he told reporters. "I'm going up there because I'm the Minister of Fisheries and I had planned this trip before the blockade. And my purpose in going is to discuss with them what best we can do to achieve the objectives of Canadian fishermen."[23]

On their way to Prince Rupert, Anderson and Defence Minister Art Eggleton met with Premier Glen Clark in Vancouver to discuss the Nanoose issue. Before the meeting Anderson told reporters, "I would like to stress that we have had the threat of closing Nanoose over the heads of the Americans and in the meantime American fishing has redoubled," and Eggleton added that it was not in the interests of BC or Canada for Nanoose to close. Then the two ministers extolled the virtues of "quiet diplomacy" and asserted that Clark's Nanoose threat only encouraged American intransigence.[24]

"Mr. Anderson supported the closure of Nanoose during the election campaign," Premier Clark replied. "All Members of Parliament did, all provincial MLAs, Liberal, Reform, NDP—everybody supported us then—and it's doubly important now that we carry through with that."[25]

Taking the Moral High Ground

In Prince Rupert, John Radosevic spent most of Monday, July 21, with the RCMP, discussing the pending injunction against the blockade and asking for more time to negotiate a solution. Until then, the local police had adopted a wait-and-see policy. "We wish for a peaceful settlement to this matter," Constable Mike Legault told reporters.[26] But after a furious display of rage in the US Congress, Ottawa decided to press the Mounties to get on with the job. David Halton of the CBC reported on July 21 that half an hour after the blockade had begun, Raymond Chretien, Canada's ambassador to the US, had rushed to the State Department to apologize, then demanded that Ottawa hasten the release of the ferry to appease the Americans.

The injunction was officially served, and the members of the steering committee were taken via paddy wagon to the local police station, where they were fingerprinted and put through an intense identification process. At this point the blockade leaders began to comprehend the seriousness of the situation. The local police were sympathetic, but the fishermen had grabbed a tiger by the tail, and it seemed their only hope was David Anderson.

After landing at Prince Rupert's Digby Island airport, Anderson by-passed Prince Rupert and took a helicopter junket over the Alaskan seine fishery in Noyes Island. "It's very clear that they are targeting a run of Canadian fish going to Canadian rivers, and that is against the treaty,"

Anderson told reporters, as though it were news. Later, he and his entourage returned to Prince Rupert for a hasty meeting with the blockade steering committee at the Crest Hotel. A massive press corps waited outside, with reporters from all over North America and Europe.

In the crowded hotel lobby, Kim Olsen and another fisherman were talking about fishing when a young reporter in a tight black dress, accompanied by a full camera crew from a major US network, marched up to Olsen and stuck a microphone in his face. "Mr. Olsen, may I have a word with you?" she demanded. Olsen, dishevelled and exhausted, pushed the microphone back into her face and growled, "Can't you see I'm having a conversation with this guy?"

Just before his meeting with the blockade steering committee, Anderson warned, "The United States is the world's only superpower. No nation on earth can force the United States to do what it does not want to do. We have to show them that their moral position in the world is enhanced. If we do that we have the moral high ground."[27] He then went to the meeting, and John Radosevic was stunned to see Mike Hunter, president of the Fisheries Council, at Anderson's side. At the outset of the ferry blockade, Radosevic had called Hunter to discuss the implications and to propose the UFAWU–CAW and the Fisheries Council communicate throughout the blockade to avoid any misunderstanding. Hunter had seemed receptive to this idea but had not returned any of Radosevic's calls for the next two days. He was the only salmon commissioner invited to join Anderson in Prince Rupert during the crisis, and Radosevic concluded that Hunter must have been in close contact with Anderson all along. During the meeting, while Anderson castigated the fishermen, Hunter said nothing.

The fishermen accused Anderson of failing to enforce the PST and reprimanded him for not retaliating against Alaskans. They suggested he follow Brian Tobin's lead and reintroduce the transit fee. Above all, they condemned Anderson—as the minister responsible for the Coast Guard—for allowing the Alaskan packer that had hit the *Easy Come* to evade justice.

Anderson responded that it was irresponsible to "link" the PST dispute to other trade issues like tourism. "Stick to fish where the Canadian position is unassailable," he said. "We may not like it but that's the way it is."[28]

He also claimed that in angering the Americans with the ferry blockade, the fishermen had undermined Ottawa's efforts to renegotiate the PST.

"We've undermined the negotiations?" Kim Olsen bellowed. "You weren't negotiating! You were on a bloody holiday, sports fishing! I thought you were supposed to be here defending us, but it sounds to me like you're on the Americans' side!"

Aware that their hopes were fading, the committee made a final plea for federal aid to compensate for their lost season. Anderson claimed Ottawa had no money to bail them out, though the federal treasury was as healthy as it has been for decades. The committee then tried to persuade Anderson to allow northern licence holders to participate in the "Canada First" fishing strategy on the South Coast. In theory, this would allow the northern fleet to take the equivalent of the Alaskan interceptions out of Washington state's forecast catch of Fraser River sockeye. Some committee members believed this could be achieved by temporarily lifting the Mifflin area-licensing system. Others—particularly those with more than one licence—refused to go along with that proposal. Finally, the committee asked Anderson to assist them in fighting Governor Knowles' impending lawsuit. Anderson rejected their request but promised to persuade Knowles to drop the lawsuit.

Then, before the meeting adjourned, Anderson told the fishermen to dismantle the blockade. "You want us to end the blockade," Kim Olsen howled, "yet you haven't given us a damn thing!" Anderson did not respond.

The entire fleet was standing by on the radiophones when the committee reported on the meeting. A general chorus of boos greeted the news that Anderson had refused to help in any significant way. The fishermen agreed to assemble later that evening at the ferry terminal.

On July 22 David Anderson told CBC Radio News, "Recently we've blown off collective steam. Now let's get back to the real objective, which is an agreement with our American cousins. I think that we all understand now that this is a time for leadership and not simply showmanship." Ross Howard wrote in the *Globe and Mail*, "Since his arrival on the West Coast, Mr. Anderson repeated that disorderly protest and retaliation against Alaskan overfishing will not work. But he offered no indication of a more successful formula."[29] And according to Barbara Yaffe of the *Vancouver Sun*, Trinity University political scientist John Redekop believed that "Ottawa doesn't feel BC's larger economy is under threat as a result of the salmon dispute. Also, BC isn't a Liberal base of support. In any fish tussle, Ottawa would be more aggressive if Quebec or Atlantic Canada were involved."[30] In Ottawa the next day, Prime Minister Chretien said, "The ferry blockade was out of order...And you know, we have to remain in speaking terms with the states because they have a lot of say into the solution. And for me, we are using the diplomatic way and I think it is the best way."[31]

Later that night, in the pouring rain, the steering committee met with the blockaders to decide their next move. Some individuals argued that the blockade should continue. Others questioned what they had accomplished after so much effort and stress. Then Kim Olsen, who enjoyed everyone's confidence, spoke. "We said we wanted Anderson to come here and he did," Olsen said. "He didn't say what we wanted him to say, but we still made our point. We're losing the public now so we've got to let the ferry go."

After much agonizing, the group voted to let the ferry go. In no time at all the blockade was dismantled and the fishing fleet dispersed. Shortly afterwards, the *Malispina*, with 135 passengers on board, gave three long blasts on its horn, cast off its lines and disappeared into the mist.

Canada First?

In the Canadian–US lexicon all fights were little ones, barely noticed by the United States media and, because of the great assumption of the bilateral relationship, hardly worried about by the average citizen. The great assumption was that because the countries needed one another so much, because they had so much in common, all disputes between them would be necessarily short-lived and the wonderful friendship would be necessarily restored.

—Lawrence Martin, *The Presidents and the Prime Ministers*

After a fine luncheon on August 5, 1997, the Montreal Board of Trade settled back to listen to their guest, William Daley, US secretary of commerce, extol the virtues of the Canada–US Free Trade Agreement. "We have our disputes," Daley conceded. "But if you list those they are a handful and when you compare that with the $1 billion a day in trade between our countries they are minor."[1] He went on to offer as an example the Alaska ferry blockade.

Most of Daley's audience had never heard of Prince Rupert, BC, or thought much about the plight of West Coast fishermen until that moment. And since Quebec is the United States' sixth-largest trading partner, with an annual exchange totalling approximately $50 billion US, they had reason to be pleased with Daley's good-neighbour talk.

William Daley's father, Richard, was the infamous Chicago mayor who ordered police to beat up anti-Vietnam War demonstrators at the 1968 Democratic Party convention. William's own claim to fame was his success in guiding the North American Free Trade Agreement through Congress in 1993. On this day, well aware that the ferry blockade belied the myth of blissful Canada–US relations, he smiled and added magnanimously, "Maybe the activities that have occurred have gotten everyone to the point of a different attitude…I'm not saying those actions were positive and that they should have occurred, but they have jump-started the negotiations."[2]

Daley's remarks caused a ruckus in Ottawa. For almost two weeks, federal Fisheries Minister David Anderson had maintained that the ferry blockade had seriously jeopardized Pacific Salmon Treaty negotiations as well as Canada–US trade relations, and many leading Canadian journalists had parroted his claim. Now, just as the national press had come to accept Anderson's version, here was William Daley, one of the most powerful figures on the US political stage, going "off-message" and saying the blockade had helped restart the talks. The next day, at a luncheon at the US Embassy in Ottawa with Canadian International Trade Minister Sergio Marchi, Daley tried to qualify his remarks. According to Peter O'Neil of the *Vancouver Sun's* Ottawa bureau, "What he meant to say was the blockade drew attention to the dispute." Daley is also quoted as saying, "In no way will illegal actions bring anyone closer to a resolution, or inflammatory comments will spread people apart."[3]

In fact, before the Prince Rupert ferry blockade, Ottawa had been doing nothing to resolve the PST dispute or to stop Alaskan interceptions of Canadian salmon. When West Coast fishermen seized the Alaska ferry, Prime Minister Chretien was in Portugal, Fisheries Minister Anderson was in Labrador[4] and External Affairs Minister Axworthy was in Kuala Lumpur, though on July 18 he had sent the Americans a "strongly worded" diplomatic note protesting Alaskan overfishing. But within three days of the Prince Rupert ferry blockade, Anderson was in Prince Rupert and Axworthy was on his way to Washington, DC, where he met with Strobe Talbot, the top man in the US State Department. On July 24

Axworthy announced that Canadian and US officials had agreed to try to solve the PST crisis through "special envoys," who would be assigned to find out why PST stakeholder negotiations had failed and to recommend ways to resume the talks. They were to report to the president and the prime minister by the end of 1997. David Strangway, former head of the University of BC, was appointed Canada's "special envoy."

Strangway had been chairman of a federal–provincial committee struck to arrange a deal to resolve a lawsuit Alcan had launched against the Crown. In the 1930s Alcan acquired a provincial licence to divert vast amounts of water from the Nechako River to its power station in Kemano, near Kitimat. The Nechako is one of the largest tributaries of the Fraser River, and in 1952 when Alcan built the Kenney Dam, the Nechako's flow was dramatically reduced, endangering its important spawning grounds.

In the early 1980s Alcan demanded the right to complete its project by diverting most of the remaining Nechako water flow. This would put upper Nechako chinook salmon at even greater risk. It would also imperil the sockeye returning to the Stuart River, the Nechako's main tributary and home to dozens of small, fragile sockeye runs. These fish follow a spawning migration route of more than 500 miles, and a delay of even a day or two can threaten their survival, so optimum water flow and passage conditions in the Fraser and Nechako are vital. Therefore, the International Pacific Salmon Commission opposed the further diversion of the Nechako and insisted that Alcan install a special cold water release system at the Kenney Dam.

But in 1987, Tory Fisheries Minister Tom Siddon approved Alcan's application, saying no significant harm to salmon would result. The decision sparked a major controversy, which led to a series of public hearings in 1994, during which three prominent fisheries scientists admitted that both federal and provincial agencies had long been aware of the dam's damaging effects on fish populations. And on May 20, 1994, Glen Bohn of the *Vancouver Sun* reported that even former Prime Minister Brian Mulroney was suspected of trying to force the DFO to approve the deal. Strangway, as chair of the special inter-governmental committee on the Alcan controversy, ruled that there was no evidence of any wrongdoing.

In 1995 the provincial NDP government unilaterally cancelled the Kemano expansion lease, and Alcan sued the province for $535 million in damages. Exactly two years later—on August 6, 1997, the very day that David Anderson and Lloyd Axworthy announced Strangway's appointment as Canada's special envoy in the PST dispute—Glen Clark announced that BC had agreed to provide cheap electricity to Alcan in exchange for Alcan dropping its lawsuit. Instead of being chastised for past destruction of salmon habitat, this multinational corporation would receive 175 megawatts of power at a "special rate," on the condition that it keep its promise to build a new $1.2 billion smelter at Kitimat. The residents of that town enthusiastically embraced the deal, believing that 2,000 full-time jobs would be created. Environmentalists were sceptical, suggesting that with the price of aluminum at an all-time low, Alcan simply wished to cash in on the North American "spot market" for electricity and would never build the smelter. In the event, neither the Kitimat smelter nor the Kenney Dam cold water release facility were ever built. Alcan's long-term financial interests were preserved in large part by the decision of David Strangway, the man now tasked with saving BC's beleaguered salmon. Edgar Birch, a veteran Fraser River gillnetter, spoke for many of the fleet when he told *The Fisherman*:"The only thing we know about him is his role in the Nechako talks when he was ready to give all the fish away to Alcan. If that's who we have holding talks for Canada, what else is he prepared to give away?"[5]

The President's Hired Gun

Meanwhile, the US government had assigned the job of special envoy to William Ruckelshaus. David Anderson hailed Ruckelshaus' appointment, offering it as proof that President Clinton was serious about resolving the PST dispute. Ruckelshaus is a very tall man, with an intimidating political reputation. He was an appointee to the US Federal Environmental Protection Agency during the Nixon era and was reappointed by Ronald Reagan in 1983. According to the American journalist William Greider, Reagan wanted Ruckelshaus to "restore the EPA's tarnished reputation following scandals of non-enforcement." After Ruckelshaus left public office he went into private consulting and played a major role in advising the Superfund Coalition, about which Greider wrote:

> [Its] founding members were the leading culprits in hazardous waste pollution—General Electric, Dow, DuPont, Union Carbide, Monsanto, AT&T, and others. The Superfund Coalition wanted to roll back US federal legislation designed to financially penalize hazardous waste polluters and prevent scandalous industry fixes at the Environmental Protection Agency...To get their campaign off the ground, the Superfund Coalition turned to William Ruckelshaus, now CEO of Browing-Ferris Industries Ltd., one of the largest companies in the hazardous waste disposal business. Ruckleshaus... devised a "select environmentalist outreach program [to review the Superfund legislation]."

After American environmental groups denounced the process, Greider notes, Ruckelshaus decided to "shift the management of the study to the Conservation Foundation [funded by the corporations] and let them run it and throw in some EPA money...If the study was funded by industry, the results would be suspect." In 1988 the EPA launched a $2.5 million study of the Superfund law. "The taxpayers were now picking up the tab for research the polluters had originally envisioned as their political counterattack," Greider writes. "The Superfund law, it is true, wasn't working—partly because the affected corporations were stubbornly refusing their financial liabilities and partly because EPA itself was quite slothful, cleaning up only a handful of hazardous sites each year from the backlog of thousands. Now, the two main delinquents—EPA and the corporations—were teaming up to ask what the problem was."

By 1991 the work of Ruckelshaus and his lobbying team had paid off—the Superfund law was ultimately made to appear "flawed and wasteful." Thus, the fate of the PST was placed in the hands of two men who were described by Rafe Mair as the biggest mismatch since David and Goliath.

The Skunk at the Garden Party

In August 1997 an opinion poll conducted by Environics Research found that 98 percent of British Columbians believed the PST dispute was of critical importance and favoured strong legal action against US fishermen who overfished and violated the international treaty.[6] This seemed to support Premier Clark's hard-line position. The same poll found that only 8 percent strongly approved of David Anderson's performance. But Clark went further, criticizing the new special envoys process, claiming it was nothing more than "talks about talks," and on August 4, 1997, he told *Maclean's* magazine, "The eminent persons will have no mandate to negotiate, no power to recommend a resolution and no deadline for completing their work." When asked if this was not a good time to drop the Nanoose threat, Clark replied, "Not until, and unless, the eminent persons have a real mandate to end the dispute."

Fisheries Minister Anderson and Defence Minister Art Eggleton condemned Clark. Eggleton threatened to expropriate the provincially owned seabed at the Nanoose testing range and Anderson took pains to exclude Clark from a special salmon summit meeting with US governors in Seattle. Eggleton's threat brought criticism from unexpected quarters. On August 2, Allan Fotheringham declared in the *Financial Post*, "Anderson has, as they say in BC, been 'Ottawa-ized.' He no longer represents BC interests, he represents what Ottawa thinks is good for BC." Fotheringham, no fan of the NDP, then added, "Glen Clark is now the Brian Tobin of the Pacific, not invited to the garden party where he would be the skunk. And it has reassured his re-election. Congratulations, Ottawa."

But Clark did not cash in his political chips at that point. He was furious that Anderson and Eggleton had told the press that he was looking for a way to back down from his Nanoose threat and that he had said so in their presence. On August 8, Clark told the *Province*, "Clearly this is unacceptable behaviour—treasonous behaviour—on the part of the federal government…This may well be the first time—certainly in my memory—that the Canadian government doesn't stand on the side of Canadians."

Fishermen Barbecue the Anderson Plan

The Strangway–Ruckelshaus process notwithstanding, the DFO still had to get through the remainder of the 1997 season. North Coast gillnetters, whose season had been disrupted by the Alaskans, faced stringent domestic conservation measures to protect endangered steelhead and coho. Local recreational fishing lobbyists insisted that the gillnet fleet had a high bycatch of coho and steelhead during Skeena River pink and sockeye fisheries, and the gillnet fishery was closed in early August. The DFO allowed a "selective" seine fishery to continue for two weeks at the mouth of the Skeena because the seine fleet could harvest sockeye and pinks, while releasing all coho and steelhead alive. The gillnetters asked to participate in the fishery, but the DFO refused, and about 25 vessels held a six-hour protest fishery on August 5, 1997, to prove that gillnetters could fish selectively. The protest was organized by the Native Brotherhood of BC, the UFAWU–CAW, the Northern Gillnetters Association and the Metlakatla and Port Simpson band councils. As a DFO patrol helicopter buzzed overhead, Des Nobels told a *Nanaimo Daily News* reporter, "It's a good catch. We got some very big and beautiful sockeye. We wanted to show DFO that we can manage this fishery and we did that today…There was no coho out there today and most of the pink salmon or steelhead that were caught were released."[7] The sockeye caught in the protest fishery were given away to hundreds of people at a public barbecue in Prince Rupert to thank residents for their support during the ferry blockade. Response to this gesture was mixed. The editors of the *Prince Rupert Daily News* lauded the event as "a wonderful goodwill gesture," but Gord Brooks, a local businessman, said, "a lot of people think it's just a way to suck up to the community because they know they've done some harm."

Then, as if the gillnetters' season had not already been bad enough, the DFO brought charges against the protestors. Only four coho had been inadvertently killed, but DFO local manager Dave Einarson told CHTK radio that the fishermen were "poachers" who "have no concern for coho and steelhead," and said, "Who knows? Who knows how many coho were caught?" And the following day Jim Culp of the Sports Fishing Advisory Board said, "It's hogwash for commercial fishermen to claim their protest fishery could selectively harvest sockeye…This is no longer a game, this is real serious business."

Nevertheless, the DFO later agreed to allow a small group of gillnetters to experiment with selective fishing techniques, including the use of very short sets, in a daylight-only fishery. Some 70 percent of the very small bycatch of coho survived, proving the Sports Fishing Advisory Board lobbyists wrong. The gillnetters also reasoned that if they knew where the coho congregated in abundance, they could design sockeye fisheries that avoided these "hotspots," so the program was designed to map out those areas. Such an approach in the latter part of the 1997 season could have allowed the harvesting of what was left of the surplus sockeye and pink stocks and salvaged some income for the fishermen, but the DFO ruled that the data from the test fishery was too sketchy to apply to the entire gillnet fleet. The $8,000 earned from the sale of the sockeye caught during the experimental gillnet fishery was donated to Prince Rupert charities.

Tracking Each and Every One Down

As the debate raged over the four coho taken in the protest fishery, a total of 1,923,000 coho were taken in southeast Alaskan fisheries during 1997. As much as 30 percent of this catch was of Canadian origin, including many endangered upper Skeena stocks.[8] On July 28, Attorney General Bruce Botelho of Alaska had pushed his way through a crowd of protestors outside the courthouse in Vancouver and triumphantly announced that the court had granted a sweeping injunction to prevent BC fishermen from blockading Alaskan ferries in future. He also said that Alaska was suing the government of Canada and Canadian fishermen for $2 million in damages. Canadian reporters asked whether the ferry service to Prince Rupert would now resume, and Botelho declined to give a straight answer. Just a few days earlier, a delegation from the Prince Rupert city council had gone to Juneau, Alaska, and learned that the cancellation of the ferry was as hard on Alaskan communities as on Prince Rupert. And on August 1, the *Vancouver Sun* reported that according to an Alaskan government memo, regardless of the blockade, the MV *Malispina* had been scheduled for suspension from service because the Alaskan Marine Highway Service had failed to maintain the vessel to international safety standards. Botelho reacted angrily when reporters asked whether

proceeds of the lawsuit would go toward the *Malispina*'s refit, and in the *Anchorage Weekly Press* of August 6 he vowed to take whatever steps necessary to seize the vessels of the protesting fishermen. "We intend to track down each and every one of them," he said.

Meanwhile, those same BC fishermen had succumbed to financial ruin. The gross income of the 800 northern salmon licence holders had plunged to an average of only $8,000 for the entire season, and the Community Fisheries Development Centre in Prince Rupert estimated that at least half of the northern fleet would be bankrupt before the end of the year. At the Oceanside cannery, only

Alaska Attorney General Bruce Botelho is confronted by protestors after securing a court order from a BC court to end the Prince Rupert ferry blockade, August 1997.

800 of the 1,700 shoreworkers on the seniority list worked in 1997, and of that group only 250 earned enough weeks to qualify for Employment Insurance benefits. In a press release on August 15, Reform MP John Duncan said:"Anderson is saying that the fishing plan is working. He is painting a picture to have us believe the 1997 Canadian fishery is a success. This is just more smoke and mirrors from the Minister of Inaction. Anderson is painting rosy pictures of happy fishermen while northern BC fishing communities are struggling to survive and are in desperate financial circumstances."On September 5 the *Kodiak Daily Mirror* reported that Anderson had refused to provide any legal support to the 200 fishermen named in the Alaskan lawsuit. "We are not going to support them financially for illegal acts of civil disobedience," said Anderson. "You can't do it for this group and not for others." Premier Glen Clark,

however, stepped in and hired a Vancouver law firm to represent the destitute fishermen free of charge. He was roundly criticized by the press for wasting taxpayers' dollars on the unruly fishermen while the DFO spent considerably more for highly paid consultants, special assistants, political navigators and special envoys to resolve the PST crisis—to no avail.

Fish Don't Take Trains

On the morning of August 7, 1997, the Canadian seiner *Taaska* headed south through the choppy waters of the Gulf of Georgia. Upon reaching the beacon marking the international boundary near Point Roberts, skipper Bob Rezansoff cut the engine and allowed the vessel to wallow silently in the swells. On deck a number of fishermen and reporters braced themselves against the salt spray and watched dozens of American seiners furiously setting their deep black nets a short distance away.

Kim Olsen, the leader of the Prince Rupert ferry blockade, shook his head in amazement. "Look at that," he said. "This is like the bloody Alaskan fishery all over again. At the very least the whole Canadian fleet should be fishing off the west coast to stop all the fish going into US nets. But we're not doing anything. Where's the Canada First Fishing Strategy? Where the hell is David Anderson?"[9] John Sutcliffe, the Fraser Valley organizer for the UFAWU–CAW, explained to reporters that an industry advisory panel had developed the "Canada First" fishing strategy to restrict the American catch. The DFO had never released the report, because, according to a "source" close to Minister Anderson eight out of the 13 recommendations posed a risk to conservation.[10] "If the US is allowed to intercept as many fish as they want, why should they bother to negotiate a treaty?" Sutcliffe pointed out. And Bob Rezansoff added, "If you look at this historically, the only time the US has come to the table is when we've kicked the shit out of the fish."[11]

All this time the Canadian fishermen knew that deep in the murky waters of the strait, millions of sockeye were swimming toward the mouth of the Fraser River, only a few miles away, and that the Americans planned to take a minimum of 21 percent of the Total Allowable Catch (TAC) of that Fraser run. The "Canada First" fishing plan, had it been implemented, would have limited them to 17 percent, the last offer tabled by Yves Fortier before the stakeholder talks had collapsed in May.

Now, on August 7, the Americans had already been fishing for more than two weeks, but the Canadian commercial fishery had yet to open. Paul Sprout, the DFO's operations director, explained, "By pinpointing the [Canadian] fishery and allowing it to occur a bit later, when the maximum number of sockeye are entering the area, we can minimize the incidental catch of coho."[12] John Radosevic of the UFAWU countered, "It is not a conservation issue. We just need to put some backbone into Canadian politicians." Athana Mentzelopoulos, Anderson's press secretary, mocked Radosevic. "This is like the rooster crowing at the dawn and then taking credit for the day. There is no undue delay. Fish don't take trains and it doesn't make sense to put out a strategy when you don't know where the fish are going to be."

Meanwhile, both the Americans at Point Roberts and the in-river aboriginal fishery were targeting the early Stuart and early summer sockeye, the first runs to enter the Fraser system each year. The DFO had predicted that at least 800,000 early summer-run sockeye would reach the spawning grounds, but on August 8 the Pacific Salmon Commission reported that warm ocean temperatures had delayed the Fraser run as a whole, and trollers off the west coast were reporting an abundance of exotic warm-water species such as sunfish, mackerel and tuna. This did not bode well for the salmon, which can thrive only in cool water. Worse yet, some salmon were showing signs of sexual maturity in the ocean environment, something never before witnessed.

In the Fraser canyon the situation was even more alarming as a combination of warm temperatures and high water flows were wreaking havoc with the early runs struggling up the river. Dr. Jim Woodey of the PSC reported that the swift current and river turbidity were so extreme the snouts of the migrating sockeye appeared to have been sand-blasted.[13] Dr. Steve MacDonald, an expert in sockeye migration behaviour, told the Fraser panel of the PSC that the unusual passage conditions were delaying the sockeye, increasing the likelihood of pre-spawn mortality. Many sockeye tried to spawn in non-natal streams in the Fraser Canyon area, and whole stocks were lost.

Playing Russian Roulette with the Resource

On August 9, when the DFO allowed the Musqueam and Sto:lo Native bands to conduct an AFS pilot sales fishery in the canyon, 200 members of the BC Fisheries Survival Coalition conducted a protest fishery in the lower river. DFO arrested three of the "ringleaders" of the protest, and chained their vessels to the dock in Steveston, and DFO Fraser River manager Dick Carson told the *Vancouver Sun*: "When you start disrupting the management of the fishery in this way, it's effectively playing Russian Roulette with the resource. And that's one thing we won't take lightly. We can't."

The next day David Anderson announced that the Survival Coalition's protest had harmed the stocks and undermined Canada's bargaining position with the US. "These are fish that the Americans let through," he complained. The fact that the run was endangered and that no fishing on that segment of it should have occurred in late July had not fazed the Americans, who could point to the AFS pilot sales fishery in justifying their own fishery.

By mid-August the water in the Fraser Canyon had cooled somewhat, and the Fraser sockeye run was just starting to peak. This run had been forecast at 18.2 million sockeye and 11.3 million pinks, with most of the sockeye in the mid-timed summer-run stock. After deducting an escapement of 4 million sockeye and 6 million pinks, the total catch (TAC)—despite a weak early Stuart run—was expected to be 19 million salmon. In theory, such a potential catch would be more than enough to satisfy all the fishermen with South Coast licences. Moreover, if the "Canada First" strategy was successful in limiting the American catch to 17 percent, a significant incremental catch would fall to Canada. In the opinion of some industry representatives, including me, this bonus catch could give the impoverished North Coast licence holders a one-time opportunity to fish in the South Coast licence area and thus contribute to the "Canada First" fishing effort, if South Coast licence holders agreed to temporarily suspend the Mifflin area-licensing system.

Premier Clark put me to work on a provincial strategy paper that would lay out the details of such a plan. At the same time, as a PSC commissioner, I served on a 14-person committee set up by the DFO to advise on the "Canada First" strategy. While the plan was being debated in these two forums, a group of northern fishermen wrote an open letter to southern fishermen requesting their support:

> Most of the northern fleet has tied up to add strength to Canada's position in the Pacific Salmon Treaty. People in the north are extremely frustrated because the Alaskans are intercepting a large portion of our northern TAC...[but] we want you to understand that we do not advocate taking one scale of southern allocations...The northern fleet is not tied up to attack the Minister or change DFO licensing. However, we have been feeling frustrated because Minister Anderson won't return any calls or talk to us. We have been sensitive to worries of southern fishermen and we have designed our position so that it won't upset your allocation. It can only help us all if in the process we can get a treaty. We need your support.[14]

Then, just before the Fraser fishery opened, I attended a meeting of southern licence holders at the Sunbury Hall in North Delta to discuss how to help the northern fishermen. I was stunned when my patriotic appeal on behalf of the northern fishermen was met by an icy response. Virtually no one, including several UFAWU–CAW stalwarts, wanted to allow North Coast fishermen into the South Coast area. The Mifflin area-licensing scheme had created such divisions within the Canadian fleet that even the presence of a common enemy could not overcome them.

West Coast Trollers Betrayed

Because of warm water in the north Pacific during the summer of 1997, more than 80 percent of the sockeye approached the Fraser River through Johnstone Strait instead of the Strait of Juan de Fuca—just as they had done during the legendary run of 1958. In pre-Mifflin Plan days, this would have been of great benefit to Canada in the fish war with the Americans. But with area licensing, the high sockeye diversion rate prevented the 450 trollers restricted to the west coast of Vancouver Island (Area G) from making their pre-season target of 1.6 million sockeye. At the peak of the run in mid-August, they crowded into the tip of Area G, hoping to catch a portion of the diversion, but few sockeye were present.

When area licensing was first introduced, many fishermen believed that the DFO would allow those boats that failed to catch their share—due to unforeseen natural circumstances—to move to another area. In fact, the "Three Amigos" had recommended such flexibility in emergency situations. But now, DFO officials asserted that like it or not, any area group that failed to catch its share in its licensed area was out of luck, and Canadian fishermen began fighting each other instead of the Americans. On August 12, some 200 Area G trollers left the fishing grounds and sailed into Port Hardy to discuss what to do about their shortfall. Dan Edwards, a Ucluelet troller, told the press:"This rigid plan is bankrupting the fleet. Mr. Anderson committed himself to improve the Mifflin Plan by providing this flexibility. He's now backtracking on his commitment, which is devastating the small-boat fishermen. The situation is becoming volatile."[15]

When interviewed by CKNW's Rafe Mair, Cathy Scarfo of the Area G Trollers Association said: "Here we are internationally saying the Alaskans don't share when we're not sharing domestically. This is supposedly Canada First, which we're refusing to call Canada First because basically it's just a big canning company first, and to hell with the rest of us Canadians..."

David Anderson happened to be visiting a salmon enhancement project near Port Hardy that day, and the next morning the *Province* reported that he had reluctantly agreed to meet with the Area G trollers in a local hotel. He gave them 25 minutes and claimed to sympathize with the fishermen, but he offered no relief. When they threatened to fish in defiance of the area boundaries, he said, "If I responded to every threat in this fishery, there would be chaos." But a day later, the DFO did extend the Area G troll boundary by a few miles—little help to the trollers as the bulk of the sockeye run was already well south of that line, but it did confirm that DFO could make changes to the area-licensing system without dire results.

On August 14 Anderson flew to Campbell River, where he told the press that the "Canada First" fishing strategy was a great success, with Canadian fishermen landing 3.5 to 4 million sockeye, compared to only 300,000 by US fishermen. He did not mention that most of the Canadian catch had been taken by the seine fleet, dominated by the canning companies, who wanted no adjustments to the area-licensing system.

A War Based on Greed

As part of the "Canada First" fishing strategy the DFO opened the Strait of Juan de Fuca net fishery off the southern end of Vancouver Island, ostensibly to restrict the flow of sockeye entering Washington state waters through the southern approach. Very few sockeye passed through that strait, so the move had little effect on the Americans. But there was reaction in other quarters. Ron McLeod, a former regional director of the DFO, told Rafe Mair on August 14 that the department had put BC coho stocks at risk by opening the fishery. But McLeod, who is greatly respected throughout the industry, chose his words carefully and did not condemn the idea of taking strong action against American violations of the PST. He did not think that the entire commercial fishery should be closed to protect coho, he said, "but the Juan de Fuca fishery is not necessary to harvest the available stocks of Horsefly [sockeye]." And he added, "They can be harvested in Johnstone Strait and by the gillnet fishery in the Fraser and be subject to only two fisheries." Yet the DFO was trying—as in 1994—to redirect as much fishing effort as possible to the Strait of Juan de Fuca and to restrict fishing in Johnstone Strait and the Fraser River.

The next day McLeod's subtle criticism of the DFO was amplified into a shrill tirade by a coalition of environmental groups that included Greenpeace, the Sierra Club, the Western Canada Wilderness Committee, the Steelhead Society of BC, the Speak for the Salmon Society and the Fraser River Coalition. On August 15, Judith Lavoie of the *Victoria Times Colonist* reported that David Ellis, spokesperson for the coalition and a former commercial fisherman, had said that "63,000 coho will die during the fishery, even with brailing—dip-netting the fish onto boats and releasing coho, chinook and steelhead." In fact, the death toll Ellis referred to was DFO's maximum projected bycatch of coho for all net fisheries on the entire South Coast for the entire 1997 season. And the ceiling was a mere fraction of the historic commercial South Coast coho catch of more than 2 million per year. These details were never reported, and the environmental coalition condemned the "Canada First" strategy as being "completely based on greed."[16]

The Trollers Fight Back

On the morning of August 28, 1997, about 75 Area G trollers mustered at Beaver Cove at the northern entrance to Johnstone Strait and prepared for action. Poor catches had forced them to abandon the area they were legally allowed to fish, about 50 miles away. Now, staring at their fish finders, the fishermen could see the fish very clearly. To the untrained eye, they were just irregular patches of colour moving slowly across the screen, but to the fishermen, they were millions of Horsefly sockeye swimming deep in the dark waters of the strait. The coloured patterns on the screen also symbolized bank payments, operating expenses, income to feed a family. So close yet still out of reach, thanks to the Mifflin area-licensing scheme.

The trollers dropped their lines—without hooks—into the waters of the strait, and moments later, a host of armed DFO enforcement officers leapt into their inflatable speedboats. Charging that the hookless lines were a "hazard to navigation," the DFO patrols boarded several trollers and ordered the fishermen to cease and desist.[17] Eventually the DFO succeeded in laying charges against several trollers, despite the fact that not a single salmon was caught during the protest.

The day after the Area G troll protest, two women met in the Vancouver office of DFO to discuss the trollers' plight. It was an interesting match, given the macho image of the fishing industry. Donna Petrachenko, regional director and recent successor to Louis Tousignant, had agreed to meet with Cathy Scarfo, a spokesperson for the Area G trollers. After a 90-minute discussion, Petrachenko told reporters an understanding had been reached. The next day the *Vancouver Sun* reported that Area G fishermen would be given no special permission to harvest their uncaught share closer to the Fraser. "Has the position of the Minister softened?"

said Athana Mentzelopoulos, Anderson's press secretary. "The answer is no!…They asked to fish in another area and were told they couldn't—that decision stands." The trollers had to settle for a vague promise that if they failed to reach their quota in their licence area in 1997, the DFO would consider a catch-up system the following year.

The department continued to defend the Mifflin Plan, saying that special arrangements for Area G fishermen would be unfair to those in other areas, especially trollers in the Gulf of Georgia, even though most of the other groups, including the Gulf Trollers, were achieving their share. "It's unfortunate," Anderson told Stewart Bell of the *Vancouver Sun*. "It's not that I don't sympathize with them. I do. But I'm not put in this job to make simple answers or simply give in to pressure."[18]

Traditionally, the minister of fisheries is obliged to ensure that any given group of licence holders has a reasonable chance to harvest any surplus for which they are licensed to fish. Given the abundant Fraser sockeye run, the DFO could have made a temporary adjustment in the area-licence boundaries to help the trollers. Anderson's colleague Brian Tobin had done that very thing during the 1994 fish war. But ever since the East Coast cod disaster, the DFO had been accused of putting the interests of "industrial fishing" above conservation. And John Fraser had raised the spectre of disaster being 12 hours away. There could be no political advantage to Anderson if he helped the Area G trollers.

Not long after the trollers' protest, the 1997 sockeye season and the "Canada First" fishing strategy came to an end. In its annual review of the season, the Pacific Salmon Commission reported: "Based on preliminary estimates of catch…the return was 17,246,000 sockeye and 13,000,000 pink salmon. This return was the third largest on the 1997 cycle, exceeded by returns in 1989 and 1993. Preliminary estimates of the Fraser River sockeye catch totalled 11,688,000 fish: 8,737,000 in Canadian commercial fisheries [not including aboriginal pilot sales], 1,338,000 in US Treaty and non-Indian fisheries in Washington state, 240,000 in Alaska, and 1,191,000 in Canadian aboriginal fisheries."

Washington state fishermen had been held to only 13 percent of the Fraser sockeye catch, compared to the "Canada First" objective of 17 percent, but this Canadian victory in the South Coast salmon war was a pyrrhic victory. The nasty allocation disputes between trollers and net fishermen had marred the season, as had tensions between the recreational, environmental, aboriginal and commercial sectors. The public was confused by all the squabbling. But the fish war with the Americans was over, and now Ottawa could concentrate on its power struggle with the premier of BC.

A Leaky Ship of State

Early on the morning of August 22, 1997, Mike Emes had spotted an official-looking document tacked to the galley door of his gillnetter, the *Ocean's Best*. The notice, prepared by a Vancouver law firm on behalf of the State of Alaska, read:

> The blockade of the *Malispina* caused financial losses to our client exceeding US $2,800,000 in principal and we have commenced an action in the Federal Court of Canada against the blockading vessels and their owners to recover the losses. Your vessel is one of the defendants.

Mike Emes displays a notice from the State of Alaska that his gillnetter Ocean's Best *was about to be arrested because of his participation in the Prince Rupert ferry blockade, August 1997.*

> Our client has instructed us not to arrest your vessel
> until September 15, 1997, to avoid interfering with the
> British Columbia salmon fishery. We are, however, in-
> structed to arrest your vessel after September 15, 1997,
> unless security in an amount and form satisfactory to
> the Federal Court of Canada is provided prior to that
> time.[19]

UFAWU–CAW President John Radosevic asked, "Where is David
Anderson? BC fishermen are facing the seizure of their boats and the
piracy of their salmon in Alaska, but the federal government doesn't
utter a peep."[20]

The Alaskan lawsuit followed closely on the heels of a strongly worded letter from US President Bill Clinton, threatening harsh countermea-
sures if there was "any recurrence of illegal and inexcusable actions"
such as the Prince Rupert blockade. Alaska Governor Tony Knowles had
announced that the ferry service to Prince Rupert would not be restored
unless Premier Clark wrote him a personal apology. And Prince Rupert
Mayor Jack Mussallem had William Smith, Prince Rupert's city clerk,
write a letter to Clark on behalf of himself and his council urging him to
"respond positively to Governor Knowles' letter."[21] The *Vancouver Sun*'s
editorial board, which seldom sided with Clark and his NDP government, labelled Mussallem "Alaska's messenger" and added, "Knowles is
bent on playing the noble and aggrieved party here and on milking the
ferry incident for opportunities to take a swipe at Mr. Clark, his political
antagonist."[22]

On September 9, 1997, Premier Clark announced that he had
launched a $325 million lawsuit against the US for stealing millions of
BC salmon. On the same day, the *Sun* ran a story by Peter O'Neil about
a "leaked" federal memo, issued by the Department of Foreign Affairs
and International Trade (DFAIT), which rejected the idea of suing the
Americans in their own court system. "It is the second time that Ottawa
has released information that has undermined BC's fish war strategy,"
observed O'Neil. "Early last month the federal government revealed a
private conversation Clark had had with two federal ministers over the
issue of cancelling the seabed lease at Nanoose. The timing of the leak

provides more evidence that Ottawa and Victoria are deeply at odds over how to resolve the bitter fishing dispute."

As a Canadian salmon commissioner, I knew that the DFO had been contemplating such a legal action for many years, but the DFAIT and members of the federal cabinet had resisted the idea for fear of upsetting trade relations with the US. Clark, after repeatedly calling upon Ottawa to jointly sponsor a lawsuit, had finally given up and proceeded on his own.

David Anderson, highly critical of Clark's action, had told the *Kodiak Daily Mirror* on September 5, "I don't want to suddenly have that superseded by people saying 'Hell, if you're going to court, that's the end of any attempt to deal with this through the Ruckelshaus-Strangway process'." American reaction to the lawsuit was mixed. David Benton, salmon commissioner for Alaska, told the *Province* on September 9 that Clark was "more interested in creating media events than...workable compromises that everybody can live with." Curt Smitch, special advisor to Washington state Governor Locke, said, "I don't want to say we welcome people filing lawsuits against us, but this sends a message to our federal leaders that we need leadership."[23]

Throughout the PST dispute the media had consistently criticized Clark for his "radical" approach. But now even the *Vancouver Sun* editors had to concede, on September 10, "Since quiet diplomacy hasn't achieved a salmon treaty, Clark is right to go to court." David Anderson, BC's senior representative in the federal Liberal government, still could not acknowledge that Glen Clark could do anything to help him solve the PST dispute.

On September 11, 1997, Bob Wright, the man the *Vancouver Province* had dubbed the "czar" of BC's sports fishery, and known to the fishing industry as "Mad-Dog Wright," resigned from the Pacific Salmon Commission. He had no choice, he said, because the "Canada First" fishing strategy had put BC salmon stocks at risk.

Back in 1962, with $600 in his pocket and a "dream," Robert H. Wright had begun building his sports fishing business empire, the Oak Bay Marine Group, which now has 19 divisions in three countries, including sports fishing resorts, tourist attractions, restaurants and marinas. Wright had a favourite saying about publicity: "I don't do windows, and I don't do interviews!" But after his resignation in 1997, he did not hesitate to be interviewed repeatedly.

Wright had sat on the commission for 12 years but now stated that the Pacific Salmon Treaty had been unworkable from its inception. On September 12 he told the *Vancouver Province*, "It was a bare-bones document, with no agreement on simple concepts. It was rushed…doomed from the day it was signed…Although it was supposed to be a treaty between two nations…Canada is, in fact, forced to satisfy the demands of four different parties in the US. It's a terrible deal for Canada." Commenting on the "special envoys" process on September 11, he told the *Globe and Mail*, "The Queen and the Pope are pretty eminent persons, too, but they wouldn't be able to solve the salmon issue either if they had to work with this treaty." He then declared that Clark's "ill-conceived" lawsuit in the US court system was the "last straw" for him.

Meanwhile, on the CBC's *Dayside* radio show, David Anderson said, "I want to pay tribute to the work Mr. Wright has done over the years. Mr. Wright has been extremely successful in building up a multimillion-dollar empire and I congratulate him for the tremendous work he's done in the sports fishing sector. But I think it is important to recognize that yes, the orientation of the Department of Fisheries in the old days was towards the commercial fishery…And Mr. Wright developed, along with a few others, a much more valuable fishery per fish, which is, of course, the sports commercial fishery, the guided lodges…" Anderson went on to pledge his support for the sports fishery, whose value "is equivalent to that of the traditional commercial fishery, and in addition you have 400,000 British Columbians who take out sports fishing licences who want the opportunity of catching fish."

CHAPTER 11

Please, Prime Minister

*Governments are becoming increasingly irrelevant.
They can no longer...defend their currency, or the jobs
of their citizens. And they have failed to create a shield
against the environmental degradation and vast cultural changes now sweeping unhindered across their
borders.*

—Frank Ogden, *Ogden's Third Law*

In the fall of 1997, "special envoys" Strangway and Ruckelshaus heard testimony from dozens of industry experts, including the two chief negotiators, Yves Fortier of Canada and James Pipkin of the US. In his submission to them on September 29, Fortier said, "The treaty did not take shape overnight. Nor was it, as Ambassador Pipkin suggests, merely one of a long list of attempts to 'temporarily settle' the issue. The PST was negotiated with a view to settling once and for all questions regarding the basis on which the parties' salmon fisheries were to be conducted... This lack of agreement [on the annexes], however, does not mean, as the US argues, that the equity principle is unworkable or irrelevant, or should be ignored."

Fortier also noted that conservation would prove impossible in the absence of an equitable long-term catch-sharing arrangement: "Simply put, 'equity' provides the necessary incentive to invest in conservation, enhancement and general environmental initiatives by guaranteeing that the country which does so will receive the benefits of such investments [the carrot]. Implementation of the principle also entails the obligation for each country to co-operate with the other in ensuring that benefits are returned to the country of origin, failing which a country is required to correct any imbalance [the stick]."

Fortier said he believed the PST dispute could be solved through good faith bargaining, but not through the stakeholder process. The only solution, he said, was "to secure the firm commitment of the US federal government to demonstrate increased political will in dealing with a disagreement relating to a treaty which it, not the states or tribes, negotiated and signed."[1]

James Pipkin submitted a brief to the envoys that was virtually the same presentation he made to the US House of Representatives Committee on Resources on September 12, 1997. I had attended that meeting in Washington, DC, on behalf of the premier and had watched in amazement as Pipkin suggested the PST was merely one of many attempts to "temporarily settle" the century-long conflict over Pacific salmon, and quoted Bob Wright, Canadian Commissioner and owner of a multimillion-dollar sports fishing business, to support this claim. As for the matter of equity, he stated, "Treaty negotiators left it to the Pacific Salmon Commission to work out how the principles should be applied, and that has not often proved possible. Each country has its own interpretation of how the principles should be implemented, and each believes strongly that the other country's interpretation is wrong."

In Pipkin's opinion the Canadian interpretation of equity was nothing more than "theology," and therefore totally unrealistic. And, he said, "It is not fair to penalize fishermen in Washington state for what happens in Alaska and vice versa." Ambassador Christopher Beeby had addressed this concern in 1996 by proposing an equity formula calculated on a panel area basis. Pipkin said that Beeby had withdrawn because "the two countries were simply too far apart" for the mediation process to work,[2] but in fact Pipkin had flatly rejected Beeby's comprehensive settlement proposal, although Yves Fortier had accepted it for Canada.

I approached committee chairman Senator James Saxton for permission to speak. He agreed, but later his staff told me that Ottawa would not allow me to testify, and Canadian embassy bureaucrats said that they considered the Senate hearing little more than a "venting session," unworthy of an official response. They also said that challenging the US testimony would only push the two sides further apart. The special envoys had everything under control, they assured me, and a diplomatic solution to the PST dispute was near.

After the congressional committee hearing, I told a group of reporters that the testimony of the American officials was "ill-informed and over-blown." Before I had finished speaking, Alaskan commissioner David Benton accosted me to charge that I had misrepresented the facts. And Brian Kennedy, the Canadian Press Washington bureau correspondent, reported:

> [A]n impromptu debate broke out between a close advisor to Premier Clark and an official from Alaska. Dennis Brown, Clark's special adviser, was being scrummed by print and TV journalists when the Alaskan official, David Benton, moved in, shook Brown's hand and proceeded to give his views on the dispute. Progress was being stymied "because of political rhetoric coming out of British Columbia inciting people to ferry blockades," said Benton...
>
> Benton suggested all politicians back out and leave the talks to fishermen and other stakeholders directly involved in the issue. Brown suggested to Benton that both sides go to binding arbitration to resolve the dispute. When the Alaskan demurred... "I would suggest to you that your fear of third party arbitration suggests a weakness," Brown told Benton. "What have you to hide? What have you to fear?"

Making a Separatist Out of a Nice Lady Like Me

Throughout the 1997 fishing season the federal government was pre-occupied with two issues that have shaped Canadian life over the past 30 years: the relationship of the US and Canadian economies, and the question of the constitution, particularly as it related to Quebec's separatist sentiments. Because of his high-profile intervention in the PST dispute, BC Premier Glen Clark landed in the middle of both issues like the proverbial cat among the pigeons.

That September the 10 premiers met in Calgary to hammer out a new eight-point "national unity" pact, ostensibly to replace the failed Charlottetown Accord. At this meeting even the prairie premiers agreed to an arrangement, known as the Calgary Declaration, that would give Quebec special status within Canada. Behind all this was the careful manoeuvring of an improbable alliance, led by the federal Liberals and fronted by Mike Harris of Ontario and Ralph Klein of Alberta. They gambled that BC's premier would want to be part of the "national consensus," but when the vote was taken, the lone opponent was Glen Clark. "I won't be part of it," he told the *Vancouver Sun* on September 12. "Anything I do in Calgary I will be bringing back to BC for further discussion."

There were many reasons for Clark to challenge Ottawa, but the PST dispute symbolized most pointedly the growing rift between the two governments. The crisis came to a head when Ottawa took legal action to block the province's attempt to cancel the Nanoose lease. Clark accused Ottawa of treason, and Fisheries Minister David Anderson remarked that the injunction had "saved Clark from being road-kill on Nanoose."[3] Tory Senator Pat Carney suggested that BC should consider separating from Canada, and on September 25 she told the *Vancouver Sun*, "The lesson of the salmon war is that BC does not count. That's a fact. I think we have to rethink what we want from Confederation because the current arrangement is not meeting our needs and the fish war proves that." And in a speech to the National Press Club in Ottawa, entitled "How the Central Canadian Media made a Separatist out of a Nice Lady like Me," Carney declared, "It is as if we had no regional identity, no national vision beyond Quebec. We are not viewed as Canadians in our own right. Here they are in Ottawa talking about the fiscal dividend and the surplus and everything else like that and they are categorically denying British Columbia, across the board, all its priorities...If they can write off coastal communities...who are they going to write off next?"[4]

Although Carney later said her "separatist" comments had been taken out of context, she also reported a massive outpouring of public support.

At the height of this controversy, Prime Minister Chretien granted Barbara Yaffe of the *Vancouver Sun* a special interview. He said he really did care about BC, and that he had visited the West Coast more than any other prime minister. BC had prospered within confederation, he said. He acknowledged that the PST issue was troublesome and "very complex." When Yaffe suggested that Glen Clark might be the cause of the PST impasse, Chretien readily agreed. "Yes, he is," he said. "But it's for the people of BC to judge him. I'm not voting here." And he dismissed Senator Carney's BC separation campaign as "easy politics."

From Featherweight to Heavyweight

On October 11, Peter O'Neil, the *Vancouver Sun*'s Ottawa correspondent, reported that Liberal Party chieftains feared that the PST imbroglio might threaten their tiny toehold of six federal seats in BC. Ross Fitzpatrick, a powerful BC Liberal insider, said that the Prime Minister's Office was going to great lengths to transform David Anderson from a "featherweight" into a "heavyweight." According to O'Neil, "In the summer of 1997, Chretien's office launched a new rescue operation, making Randy Pettipas—Chretien's western advisor—Anderson's executive assistant. Brian Bohunicky, who recently took over from Pettipas, has become Anderson's press secretary." It was now Bohunicky's job, along with ex-sports-fishing lobbyist Velma McColl, to pull out all the stops to defend Anderson on the issue of his greatest vulnerability: the PST. It was not ideal for a federal cabinet minister to be so at odds with the premier of his home province, but Anderson continued to insist that "deals here and there will never end BC's yelping."

Meanwhile, an anonymous DFO official had complained to the media that Clark "can do all this feel-good stuff, all this posturing [on the PST], without really considering whether his tactics will help us or hurt us." But David Mitchell, a BC historian and former Liberal MLA, argued that Clark "is popular, I believe, because he has been willing to stand up to the Americans who are clearly overfishing and poaching a Canadian resource." As for claims that Clark's PST intervention was political opportunism, Mitchell said, "It's surprisingly well thought out. It doesn't simply seem to be an ad hoc action by some tin pot autocrat on the west coast spouting off without thinking things through."

Finally the staff at the PMO began to sense that something had to be done about the PST problem. Unchecked, this issue could ignite even broader discontent in BC and perhaps elsewhere, and, as Peter White of the Council for Canadian Unity warned, should Ottawa stumble, BC could become "the natural leader of western Canada."[5]

The PMO took steps to quell the discontent. After months of inaction, Human Resources Development Canada (HRDC) hinted that new social support programs for West Coast fishermen were forthcoming, and even that Ottawa was willing to drop plans to de-staff more lighthouses in BC. Finance Minister Paul Martin travelled to Vancouver to release his economic outlook statement—the first time it had not been tabled in the House of Commons. In addition, Stephane Dion, minister for national unity, was dispatched to the West Coast to give a pep talk on federalism. Dion claimed to "understand BC's feelings," but on October 18 he told the *Vancouver Sun*, "I repeat, there are no issues in any province that justify secession or even the threat of secession."

Dion may have been concerned that Clark's actions might spark renewed anti-federal feelings in Quebec, where support for separation had recently dipped to 39 percent, the lowest level in years. As well, Gilles Duceppe, leader of the Bloc Quebecois, had begun to take an unexpected interest in the Pacific Salmon Treaty. He even took a road trip to the West Coast, where he said, "I would say they [British Columbians] have a certain resentment against Ottawa and the bureaucracy in Ottawa. They have a sentiment that Ottawa is making decisions for them, not good decisions for BC."[6] The national media accused Duceppe of mischief but clearly Clark's PST stand had swung the compass of the national unity debate far to the west.

Yankee Doodle David

Meanwhile, Ottawa was poised to announce its first surplus budget in 28 years—a fiscal "miracle" credited to Finance Minister Paul Martin. Establishment pundits rejoiced when Martin declared that closer economic ties with the US would lead to a "new golden age" for Canada.

Gillnetter A.S. "Snuffy" Ladret, dressed as Uncle Sam, at a rally in Vancouver to protest "Yankee Doodle David" Anderson's PST leadership.

Many average Canadians were less enthusiastic about this achievement since Ottawa had carved more than $7 billion annually out of education, welfare and health care programs since 1996, and provincial treasuries had had to make up much of the difference. Reduced federal transfers, along with the massive reduction of federal departments, had compounded the recession in BC, and now Martin offered the provinces a meagre $148 million from his record budget surplus. Of that amount, BC, suffering the most serious effects of the Southeast Asian recession as well as major structural change in the primary resource industries, received $18 million.

In BC, however, the local press was still blaming the province's economic woes on the "tax and spend/anti-business" proclivities of the NDP government, especially after the BC Liberal Party accused Clark of lying about budget forecasts during the 1996 election. Although a Provincial Court judge later ruled that such charges were unfounded, Clark and the NDP government never overcame this allegation. Ironically, the NDP government was as committed as Paul Martin and most other governments to neo-conservative fiscal policies dominating the global economy. Clark was repeatedly reviled as "socialist," but did not implement any alternative economic agenda. One of the few attacks that Clark actually mounted on the power structure implicit in the "new global order" was his action on the PST front, and it was one of the few issues in which he enjoyed popular support. Perhaps this was because he was striking a blow at the myth of harmonious Canada–US relations.

A week before the start of the Asia Pacific Economic Co-operation (APEC) Summit, a meeting of 16 powerful world leaders, in Vancouver in November 1997, the UFAWU—which had recently merged with the Canadian Auto Workers Union (CAW)—held a protest outside the federal cabinet offices in Vancouver. The rally was held to pressure Prime Minister Chretien into doing something about the Alaskan threat to seize BC fish boats. Snuffy Ladret, a gillnetter, dressed in an Uncle Sam costume and sang a tune titled "Yankee Doodle David," and the protestors raised a noise so loud that UFAWU–CAW President John Radosevic told the press, "Ottawa may not be able to see us over the Rockies, but they're bloody well going to hear us."[7]

The fishermen were also concerned that Raymond Chretien, Canada's ambassador to the US, might endorse a bilateral salmon enhancement fund as a way out of the PST dispute. Speaking in Washington, DC, Chretien had said,"The negotiations have fallen on the whole business of equity the last couple of years, and they're [the Americans] prepared to address it also through funding."[8]

Premier Clark responded, "[A fund] is not acceptable to me because it would be trading fish for money and it means the livelihood of people here would be jeopardized. And frankly, any money that's invested in conservation won't survive very long if we're growing fish for other people to catch."[9] John Radosevic added, "We have families in trouble, people losing their homes, people moving out of coastal communities, losing their boats…We expect them [Ottawa] to stand up for us, and now we find they'll take money."[10]

In Ottawa, when reporters pressed External Affairs Minister Lloyd Axworthy about whether the prime minister and the US president would meet about the PST during APEC, he replied, "We're not going to drive the process to suit a timetable of an APEC meeting which is to discuss the whole question of Pacific Rim trade liberalization and other matters...Their mandate was to report by the end of the year, not by November 24."[11]

As Prime Minister Chretien, US President Bill Clinton and other luminaries travelled around Vancouver streets in their motorcades, and the Canadian media reported enthusiastically on globalization, Canada was not enjoying much success protecting its economic interests at the APEC conference. Our country had chosen to go along with "free trade" policies rather than protecting its domestic industries, yet it was plagued by foreign tariffs instituted by its APEC partners—particularly the Americans. Besides fighting US tariffs on BC softwood lumber exports, Trade Minister Sergio Marchi was dealing with trade restrictions against Canadian fish exports in the APEC zone. As a result, Mike Hunter of the Fisheries Council of BC, a strong advocate of free trade, was complaining that $300 million in semi-processed fish and value-added products was at risk.

Please, Prime Minister!

The shy 13-year-old took a deep breath, anxiously licked her braces, then read from her prepared script, "Hello. My name is Julie Nygren. I live in Qualicum. My dad's a fisherman. But it's hard for him to earn a living these days because Americans are catching too many Canadian salmon. It's not fair. Please, Prime Minister Chretien, we need your help. Tell President Clinton it's wrong to take our salmon. Stand up to the Americans before it's too late."

Julie Nygren's 30-second radio "announcement" had been paid for by the Salmon for Canada Committee, a group established to assist the Prince Rupert ferry blockaders who were being sued by the state of Alaska. The committee could only afford to air the announcement a few times on a few radio stations, so they decided to release it in Vancouver on November 21, the opening day of the APEC summit, when both Prime Minister Chretien and President Clinton would be arriving in town. Julie had gone to the recording session with her mother Joan and Sheila Fruman, a communications consultant with the premier's office. Fruman, who had written the text of the ad, then sent out a notice to tell

Julie Nygren, a teenaged girl, speaking to the national convention of the Canadian Auto Workers in Toronto, on how the Mifflin Plan has hurt her family, 1997.

the media to expect it. To journalists, the teenager's heartfelt plea about her family's distress was an irresistible human interest story. Fruman's low-budget radio ad campaign mushroomed into a front-page national news story.

So, in the midst of the opening ceremonies of the APEC conference, Prime Minister Chretien found himself being pestered by reporters about the Pacific Salmon Treaty. He was ill-prepared to comment on it and he appeared awkward and confused when asked about it.

For Joan Nygren, none of this was a mere publicity stunt. On November 21 she told Chris Montgomery of the *Vancouver Province*, "Our house is up for sale. We've been getting by with the help of friends. We're holding on for now. But this can't go on forever." She said that her husband Wally, a second-generation gillnet fisherman, had opted for a northern licence when the Mifflin Plan was imposed in 1996. However, he could not make ends meet by fishing a single area, particularly after the huge increase of Skeena sockeye intercepted by the Alaskans in 1997. Although in principle they opposed licence stacking, the Nygrens had applied for a loan to buy a second licence the previous season but were turned down by the banks. "We used to make a good living," she said. "We could pay our mortgage. And without stress. But now you spend

$7,000 to $8,000 before you even leave the dock, more for seiners. And there's no money when it's over...We've been married 20 years and we were happy. But we're fighting now, we're at each other." She spoke of suicides and divorces in her community, and said, "I'd like Mr. Anderson to spend a while in our shoes, to know what it's like not to have enough money to pay your bills. He says he has services in place to help us. That's a load of crap. I know. I've looked. It's like the funnel of a hurricane. People are just hanging on. They desperately want to fish, and they have a right to fish. I want the Prime Minister to respond to the fishing people of this coast, to speak to President Clinton about the serious matter of the interception of our fish. I want him to put the salmon treaty back in place."

Senior federal officials thought it highly inappropriate that the matter had been taken to Chretien at all, and they reminded the press that the PST issue had been referred to the special envoys. No one pointed out that Strangway and Ruckelshaus had not been heard from for almost six months, or that Canadian issues get much more attention in Washington, DC, when the prime minister intervenes. As Allan Gotlieb, Canada's former ambassador to the US, notes, "It is a sign of staggering ignorance for Canadians to think that personal relations between the president and prime minister are not of unique importance. If a matter is on the president's personal agenda, there is a far better chance of a favourable outcome...The Canadian who is best placed by far to get an item on the president's personal agenda is our prime minister...Without the prime minister in play, the president will not be in play."[12]

He Came, He Golfed, He Went

On the blustery evening of November 23, 1997, the APEC conference delegates, including Jean Chretien and Bill Clinton, gathered for a gala dinner under the cavernous dome of BC Place stadium in Vancouver. The menu featured BC smoked salmon on a bed of mesclun greens and sea asparagus with fresh tarragon dressing. But wild salmon—BC's cultural icon—was not available that evening. The dignitaries were served Atlantic salmon dispensed from a local fish farm. Indeed, in 1997 for the first time BC's aquaculture sector had out-produced the wild sector with a production total of 49,000 metric tonnes to the fleet's catch of 37,000 metric tonnes. At the same time the DFO had been scaling back the traditional wild fishery, it had been promoting aquaculture, with the support of the bureaucrats in the provincial Ministry of Agriculture, Fisheries and Food (MAFF). In Alaska, state officials have banned fish farms, believing them to be anathema to the well-being of wild stocks.

On the evening of November 23, the APEC diners were preoccupied with wild salmon, not because of the food on their plates but because of the media stir caused by the 13-year-old Julie Nygren. In President Clinton's statement at a pre-dinner media briefing, he said, "I think this issue [the PST dispute] has gone on too long. It's caused too much friction between our people. I want to reaffirm to you publicly that I believe this process [the Strangway–Ruckelshaus special envoy process] can produce an agreement in good faith and I will do my part to implement it in good faith."[13]

The day after the APEC conference, Chretien and Clinton discussed the PST over breakfast, though they refused to reveal the details of their conversation. As John Radosevic put it later, "At least Clinton said something at APEC. Chretien said nothing. He came, he golfed, he went."

Julie Nygren's father, Wally, was one of the hundreds of fishermen named in the Alaskan ferry blockade lawsuit. Like many other BC coast fishermen, he was scrambling to prevent his boat from being seized. His main hope lay in the secret plan developed by members of the UFAWU–CAW.

On November 1, John Stevens, a Ladner fisherman, told the *Vancouver Sun*, "We will do what we have to do to stop them, including civil disobedience, if it comes to that." Stevens's gillnetter, the *Wishing Well*, was one of the nine vessels to be taken in the first round of seizures. "We have to guess, to anticipate, and pre-empt," said Lorne Iverson, owner of the troller *Autumn Venture*. And in Campbell River, Rick Frey, a gillnetter also on the list, warned, "As soon as they say that they're ready to come looking for the boats, then I guess we'll have to go into our plan. I can't tell you, but we're not going to roll over and let them scratch our bellies."[14]

First, however, the fishermen decided to appeal the Canadian Federal Court ruling that had granted the Alaskans the right of seizure. Emerging from a 90-minute closed session between over 100 fishermen and their lawyers on November 13, UFAWU–CAW President Radosevic told the *Vancouver Province* that the fishermen intended to launch a countersuit. "Alaska basically stole the first part of our season by stealing our fish," he said. "Now they're stealing our boats! How can the perpetrator of a crime take advantage of his crime by suing people who protested the crime?"

The Ferry Comes and Goes

On December 1, 1997, Governor Tony Knowles of Alaska cancelled plans at the last minute to restore the ferry service to Prince Rupert, blaming a secret plot by UFAWU–CAW members to block the ferry a second time. Knowles was in the middle of an election campaign, and he had vocal critics like Mike Doogan, an *Anchorage Daily News* columnist who on October 3, 1997, had written: "Gov. Tony Knowles has written another shameful chapter in the salmon war with Canada. Without so much as an apology from the band of criminals who held one of our ferries hostage for three days last summer, Knowles has restored ferry service in Prince Rupert, the very city where our noble state flag was dishonoured... Let's be honest here. Canadians only understand one thing: force. Don't let their reputation for being clean and polite fool you. It's all an act."

UFAWU–CAW members were aghast. They had made it plain they would defend their vessels, but they had never considered another blockade. Bob King, Knowles's press secretary, admitted that the threat of another blockade was "vague," but he said, "We don't want to be put in a position where we have a boat going down and there's even the remotest chance of it happening again."

Finally, on the morning of December 3, Tony Knowles relented, and for the first time in 20 weeks, the Alaskan ferry MV *Aurora* returned to Prince Rupert. Local community officials had been planning to celebrate the event for weeks. Inside the ferry terminal an official welcoming party of politicians, city staff, business people and sports fishing charter operators (nearly outnumbered by out-of-town reporters) greeted the Americans. Mayors Jack Mussallem of Prince Rupert and Bob Weinstein of Ketchikan shook hands and embraced in a gesture of neighbourly goodwill.

Outside the ferry terminal, in the pouring rain, an unofficial "welcoming committee" of local commercial fishermen handed out leaflets entitled "Canadian fish for Canadian fishermen—stop the piracy!" Gillnetter Des Nobels, interviewed there by the *Prince Rupert Daily News*, said, "I'm happy the ferry's back and that, perhaps, our starving merchant community will have a good Christmas. But I'm also here to keep in the forefront the real reason it all happened, and how we have to get back to work and get our fish back." Nearby, two of Nobels's colleagues, Rusty Doane and Paul Paulsen, waved signs advising passengers that gas was cheaper in nearby Terrace. Paulsen was particularly incensed that city officials were so concerned about local business and so indifferent to the plight of fishermen, and he claimed that Prince Rupert businesses charged excessively for goods and services.

One Prince Rupert businessman in attendance accused Paulsen of being a "terrorist," and Paulsen retaliated by accusing community officials of "kissing Alaska's ass."

Moving Fish to Canada

On January 12, 1998, while the ice storm in Montreal dominated the news, the special envoys released their long-awaited report. At a press conference in Seattle, they ordered that the stakeholder process be cancelled, and in a special report submitted to the prime minister and president, they wrote: "Despite some major efforts and some progress, the stakeholders, in both the North and the South, simply could not close the substantial gap posed by the dispute over sharing. The breakdown again focused on the differences in the expectations of the two sides regarding how the sharing provisions of the Treaty were to be used in crafting fishing arrangements. The bridging of such differences is further complicated by the added difficulty of the stakeholders being viewed as representative of local constituencies."[15]

The special envoys concluded that the job of allocating the catch between the fishermen should be left to the two federal governments, and they warned that strong "political will" would be required to not only solve the dispute but to withstand the inevitable criticism. To this end, they recommended:

1) The governments [states, tribes and federal government on the US side; federal and provincial governments on the Canadian side] should cause to be adopted interim fishing arrangements for all relevant species of salmon for up to two years. The development of these arrangements should be led by the fish managers supported by the fishers and fish scientists but the arrangements must be made and the governments must ensure that they are.

2) During this two-year period, governments from both sides should develop a practical framework for implementing Article III leading to the establishment of longer term fishing arrangements.

The special envoys also wrote, "If an agreement was to be reached for the term of the agreement, it would necessarily involve a compromise in the form of movement of fish to Canada and a willingness on the part of Canada to agree that not all the fish they deemed to be theirs would be returned." This statement seemed to validate the Canadian position that long-term fishing arrangements should lead to balance in interceptions. Although the special envoys were unclear about what "moving fish to Canada" really meant, everyone on the Canadian side expected that the amount of fish "moved to Canada" would be substantial. But after the release of their report, the special envoys did virtually nothing to ensure that the American interception of Canada's salmon was equitable.

Ottawa's position had apparently been vindicated, but the federal government downplayed the envoys' report. On January 12, 1998, David Anderson told CFTK news, "What we have received from Dr. Strangway and Mr. Ruckelshaus is the blueprint, not the building." He praised the conservation recommendations in the report but was evasive on the matter of equity. And when Julian Beltrame of the *Montreal Gazette* asked him on January 13 whether equity would be achieved through government-to-government talks, Anderson replied, "Clearly we cannot continue to simply repeat as a mantra equity, equity. Equity means this, means this, means this! We have to remember that we've stuck with a hard position and seen the Americans take more and more

Canadian-bound fish. This suggests to me that sticking to the hard position is better 'PR' than management." When Ross Howard of the *Globe and Mail* suggested this was a major shift in Canada's policy, Anderson replied, "What alternative is there?"

Stormy Weather

During a blinding snowstorm on January 13, 1998, the Pacific Salmon Commission met in Seattle for the first time since the release of the special envoys' report. The Canadian national section was as frustrated during that session as the motorists outside spinning their wheels in the snowbound streets. Canadian stakeholders gained no momentum from the envoys' decree that there be "a movement of fish to Canada."

Taking advantage of the envoys' recommendation that interim fishing plans for the next two years be worked out in advance of long-term equity, US chief negotiator James Pipkin insisted that the parties focus on short-term fishing arrangements, with everything to be worked out at the fish managers' level (that is, the Chinook Working Group and the Northern Boundary Coho Technical Committee). He suggested that such arrangements, once complete, would address Canada's long-term equity concerns as well. Given the ongoing emphasis on conservation, this plan of action appeared to be logical and responsible—the involvement of fish managers and biologists was critical to the development of fishing plans that would address certain conservation issues. Neither fish managers nor biologists have the political mandate or the expertise to address the thorny issue of equity, but Pipkin seemed convinced that any interim arrangements could somehow be embellished and become a solution to the equity issue.

He was particularly keen on getting a quick agreement on chinook salmon. Several Washington state stocks were about to be listed as endangered under the US federal Endangered Species Act (ESA), a move that would affect virtually every industry in the Pacific Northwest. A renewed PST agreement would be Washington Governor Gary Locke's only easy way out of the ESA noose: he could claim that reduced Canadian interceptions under a new long-term salmon interception treaty would sufficiently protect Washington state salmon.

Counterbalancing Washington state's urgent need for a treaty was Alaska's determination to stall negotiations. In complete defiance of the special envoys' report, David Benton insisted that future negotiations could only occur at the stakeholder level.

Intense debate took place in the Canadian national section about the best way to proceed. Most delegates were reluctant to negotiate interim fishing arrangements without firm guarantees on long-term equity already in place. They also feared that short-term concessions, especially those driven by short-term conservation concerns, would permanently prejudice Canada's long-term equity position. Yet, throughout the debate, Assistant Deputy Minister Pat Chamut seemed impatient with the delegation's refusal to concede on equity, and warned the delegates that the current situation "was not business as usual." He declared that Canada's immediate priority was the conservation of Vancouver Island chinook, upper Skeena coho and Thompson River coho, and he expressed doubt that Canada could withstand another fish war if the negotiations failed.

No one in the national section argued against protecting endangered stocks, but they could not allow the talks to be confined to conservation problems, especially since short-term deals always worked out to the advantage of the Americans. Indeed, the Canadian national section believed Canada could still build on the momentum of the envoys' report if Prime Minister Chretien would appeal directly to President Clinton to get the equity issue referred to binding arbitration. In the end, all of this was academic. The Americans refused to make any commitments, and the Seattle meetings ended without any progress having been made.

Shortly after this, David Strangway told Premier Clark that he and Ruckelshaus were contemplating a new negotiating format in which senior-level bureaucrats would report directly to the key politicians on each side. Strangway also intimated that it might be necessary to appoint new chief negotiators as the Americans considered Fortier an impediment to progress. Officially, the Americans said that further negotiations under the direction of Fortier and Pipkin would simply prolong the stalemate, but it is likely that they recognized Fortier would hold firm on the equity issue. Strangway claimed to support the BC government having a role in the talks, and suggested that Doug McArthur, Clark's deputy, should represent the province on the Canadian team, yet he admonished the premier for demanding equal status with Ottawa. He explained that Ottawa wished to avoid setting a precedent that Quebec might make use of in other international matters.

In the last week of January 1998, the federal Parliamentary Standing Committee on Fisheries made a rare appearance in coastal BC. Its purpose was to review some important West Coast issues—including the Pacific Salmon Treaty, the Mifflin Plan and the AFS pilot sales program—during a week-long tour of coastal communities. But just before the hearings were scheduled to start, committee members learned that senior DFO officials in Ottawa had ordered that all personnel who intended to testify at the standing committee's hearings must report to head office. The directive discouraged most DFO staff and seriously hampered the committee's ability to gather important information on West Coast fishing policies.[16]

When David Anderson testified before the committee that the Mifflin Plan was paying off because it had "raised the income of the average fisherman," a chorus of hoots and jeers rose from the audience of more than 200 fishermen squeezed into a room in the Steveston Buddhist temple. "Remember you're in a church," one fisherman called out in exasperation.[17] Corky Evans, BC minister for agriculture, fisheries and food, then told the visiting MPs: "The committee needs to know that something is broken in BC in the fishery. Some economists said that we should leave everything to the marketplace, but the result of that has been the GATT rules and the Mifflin Plan, which eliminated marginal producers, heaped huge costs on those remaining in the fishery, and reduced the number of jobs and communities."

Throughout the week, the overwhelming majority of witnesses appearing before the parliamentary committee were critical of the Mifflin Plan. Anderson needed a "good news" story, and he got it. On January 22 he announced that he had made a deal with Governor Knowles to settle the Alaskan lawsuit against BC fishermen. The deal was a public relations coup for both politicians, albeit an expensive one for Ottawa: Anderson had agreed to spend $1.25 million for a campaign to promote tourism to northern BC, the Yukon and Alaska, another $215,000 to encourage tourism in Prince Rupert and $1.26 million to give the Alaskan ferry a 50 percent reduction in its Prince Rupert docking fees. Despite these costs and the continuing interception of BC salmon by Alaska, Anderson said, "I regard this as a win-win. I'm sure there are some Canadians who will take offence to this deal... But they don't understand the complexity of the problems."[18]

Governor Knowles now described the ferry blockade as a "footnote in history," but Anderson pronounced it a "black eye for the region," and he refused to help the fishermen in their countersuit against Alaskan overfishing. "The Federal government is not party to these court proceedings and is not involving itself in the litigation," he said in a press statement on January 22. "...The decisions and legal steps required to end the lawsuit must be taken by the fishermen themselves, and they must be transacted between Alaska and these defendants."

The editors of the *Vancouver Province*, who had criticized Anderson's handling of the PST affair, described the new deal as a "healing process" and applauded his "diplomatic approach." Many BC fishermen did not agree, they feared that the Alaskans would obtain a blanket injunction against not only ferry blockades, but any protest against Alaskan overfishing.

Coincidentally, on February 3, 1998, three days before BC fishermen were to vote on Anderson's deal to settle the Alaska ferry dispute, the results of another fishermen's vote were released. The DFO announced that of 2,700 fishermen, 73 percent had voted to retain the policy of stacking salmon licences—which, it claimed, vindicated the Mifflin fleet-restructuring plan. The UFAWU–CAW noted that almost 1,000 licence holders had not voted. As well, the vote had taken place a full year after licence stacking had been introduced, and those who had had to stack their licences in order to make a living would naturally vote to keep stacking. Even those single-licence holders who opposed the stacking system were compelled to vote in favour, to preserve their chances of catching up with those who had more than one licence. On February 5, BC fishermen voted overwhelmingly to accept Anderson's deal with Alaska after ensuring that their right to legal protest had not been obstructed. But John Stevens, UFAWU–CAW small boat vice-president, spoke for many of them when he said, "This is a good news–bad news settlement. Anderson said nothing about Alaskan overfishing in this agreement."

The Courts Rule

The fishermen's vote on licence stacking and acceptance of the Alaskan settlement could not have come at a better time for David Anderson, who could now claim to be a peacemaker. Until that point, Alaska had been suing BC's fishermen, who were countersuing the Alaskans, BC was suing the US for overfishing and Ottawa was suing BC for threatening to close the Nanoose Bay torpedo-testing range.

Then Justice Howard Thomas convicted Reform MP John Cummins of being part of a 1996 protest fishery against the Aboriginal Fishing Strategy (AFS), though he gave Cummins an absolute discharge. In his written decision, Judge Thomas declared, "I therefore conclude that the purported opening of the aboriginal commercial fishery from October 26 to October 28, 1996, by either the Aboriginal Communal Licence or by variation order was a nullity. The result, in my view, is that the fishery was not lawfully open to anyone except aboriginals exercising their right to take fish for food, social, or ceremonial purposes, and was otherwise closed." The judgement was a legal bombshell—it rendered the DFO's AFS Pilot Sales program unlawful.

Anderson claimed that despite the ruling, as minister he still had the right to authorize the Native-only commercial fishery. But the repercussions of the judgement continue to this day. On July 28, 2003, for example, when Provincial Judge W.J. Kitchen ruled on the case of nine commercial fishermen charged with fishing illegally during a 1998 protest fishery against the AFS pilot sales program, he completely rejected the legal underpinnings of the program. He acknowledged the rights of the Native people to fish for food, social and ceremonial purposes (as per Sparrow) but he said that in fulfilling its fiduciary obligation to them, the Crown must not discriminate against non-Native citizens:

> Racial discrimination in our society takes on many guises. Any racial group may be the victim. The aboriginal people in Canada have obviously been the victims of racial dynamics and discrimination that have disadvantaged them in many ways...Ameliorative programs are necessary to remedy this, but they must be carefully crafted to balance the interests of all members of society.

The pilot sales program has not met this standard...

If the Department perceived that aboriginals are at a disadvantage in their abilities to enter the commercial fishery and exercise the general public right to access the fishery, I find this not to be the case...since prior to the pilot sales programs there have been preferential government entry programs, lower licence fees, buy-back programs, and tax-free income as incentives to aboriginals not available to the rest of society. This has put aboriginals at an advantage.

I conclude that the pilot sales fishery draws a distinction and defines two groups on the basis of whether or not individuals have a bloodline connection to the Musqueam, Burrard or Tsawwassen bands. This is analogous to a racial discrimination. The group without the bloodline connection is subjected to differential treatment by having a benefit withheld—their right to participate as equals in the public commercial fishery. This has the effect of promoting the view that these individuals are less capable, less worthy of recognition, and less valuable as members of Canadian society...

Although probably well-intentioned, the program was misconceived, illogical, and ineffective in any way in dealing with any disadvantages the three bands may experience. The pilot sales program therefore offends the provisions of Section 15 of the Charter of Rights and Freedoms and violates the rights of the accused thereunder.[19]

Justice Kitchen's verdict was appealed, and Judge Donald Brenner of the BC Supreme Court ruled on July 15, 2004, that Kitchen had erred in equating the chaos created by the AFS pilot sales program with government-sponsored racial discrimination. But the Brenner decision was not an affirmation of the program per se, and shortly after it was handed down, the Native Brotherhood of British Columbia publicly denounced the program as harmful to the interests of First Nations along the coast.

At the end of 2004 the matter was still in the courts, and the bitterness and confusion engendered by the AFS continued.

Just one week after Judge Thomas's ruling on the AFS in 1998, the Supreme Court handed down its landmark decision on the Delgamuukw case. In 1990 the Gitksan Tribal Council had made claim to a massive territory in northwestern BC, and on March 8, 1991, Chief Justice Allan McEachern had ruled that their claim of hereditary ownership had been extinguished by the Royal Proclamation of 1871. The Appeal Court overturned McEachern's decision on June 26, 1993, ruling that oral evidence provided by the Gitksan Wet'suwet'en had been unfairly rejected. The Crown, without the support of BC Premier Mike Harcourt's NDP government, had appealed, and now, in 1998, they lost. Native leaders reacted by claiming total ownership of all BC lands and resources, and on February 11, 1998, a "leaked" memo from the attorney general to the premier suggested that virtually every act of government would now be subject to "First Nation consent prior to decisions being made." The Delgamuukw decision precipitated a huge crisis for bureaucrats, resource managers and politicians, and tensions grew between aboriginal communities and so-called third parties. In an op-ed piece in the *Vancouver Sun* on February 24, Ernie Crey of the Lower Fraser Fishing Authority declared that the Delgamuukw case had trumped Thomas's ruling on the AFS program, and that BC Fisheries Survival Coalition members were "in a fight they cannot win."

On January 30, 1998, US District Court Judge John Coughnour threw BC's lawsuit against the US for overfishing out of court. I represented the province in the Seattle courtroom that day and listened while a battalion of attorneys representing the US Department of Justice, Alaska and Washington state argued for immediate dismissal of the case. The gist of their argument was that the PST dispute was not a matter that the court could resolve and was best left to the bargaining table, despite the fact that no substantive progress had been made at the bargaining table for more than five years. They also argued that it was improper for BC to ask an American court to dictate the terms of an international treaty to the US executive, given that the government of Canada (the party that had signed the treaty) was not involved in the lawsuit. Moreover, they claimed the equity provision, upon which

BC based its case, was not part of the treaty but was instead merely "a broad generality."

Gerry Scowcroft, BC's attorney in Seattle, argued that the PST was a "self-executing" document that the US executive must honour. He asked Judge Coughnour to order the US parties to submit to a technical dispute resolution panel as provided under Article XII of the PST, exactly as Canada's chief negotiator Yves Fortier had tried to do on several occasions.

Judge Coughnour questioned how he could order a technical dispute panel when "one half of the parties to the treaty [the Canadian federal government] is not here." A few hours later he issued a written judgement dismissing BC's case not because of BC's legal argument but because the province lacked "standing" in US Federal Court. Those involved in this lawsuit did not expect to win in the first round, placing their hopes instead on the appeal process, which would have considered the case in much greater detail. But David Anderson's quarrel with Glen Clark precluded any hope of the federal government joining the province in an appeal. On February 24, Clark told *The Fisherman*, "We lost the first round. But I want you to know that we instructed our lawyers in Seattle, Washington, to file a motion of reconsideration of that decision. Because this fight is not over yet."

Fortier Resigns

On January 30, 1998, the same day Judge Coughnour dismissed BC's case, Yves Fortier resigned as Canada's chief negotiator for the Pacific Salmon Treaty. In a letter to ministers Anderson and Axworthy, he wrote:

> Representing my government and its many constituents in the matter of the Pacific Salmon Treaty has been a high honour. I am extremely disappointed that I was unable to negotiate a deal. However, it is evident that, for many reasons…there was never any deal to be had with the US. In view of my long association with this file and the opinion which I hold concerning the likely

outcome of negotiations at this stage, I believe that Canada's interest will be better defended and advanced by someone else as its chief negotiator.

Officially, Fortier explained that he no longer had time to devote to the PST file because he was "working 22 hours per day" preparing the federal government's case in the impending Supreme Court decision regarding Quebec's right to separate from Canada. However, his letter made it clear he was fed up with the American antics at the bargaining table. The task of realizing equity had proved impossible, he said, because:

> [I]n the end, Canada ran into the very obstacles that had caused the impasse in the first place: greed and fear. Greed on the part of US regional interests who, being in what the MOU refers to as the "advantaged" position and feeling immune to any meaningful pressure, had little or no incentive to reduce their harvests of Canadian fish. Fear on the part of a US Federal Administration reluctant to exercise the political will necessary to challenge those regional interests so as to satisfy its national obligations toward Canada under the Treaty.

Above all, Fortier had lost all patience with US claims that the stakeholder process was the only way to settle the dispute. He noted that although the Americans had made a commitment "to resolve, by means of negotiations at the government-to-government level, all issues left unresolved by the stakeholders," but "in all the political, diplomatic, and media events surrounding the failure of the government-to-government negotiations in June 1997, not once did the US, its negotiators, officials or diplomats see fit to recall that the agreed process called for anything more than a 'good try' by stakeholders."

In effect, Fortier was making it clear that US Secretary of State Madeleine Albright, US Chief Negotiator James Pipkin and Alaskan Salmon Commissioner David Benton had violated the original understanding regarding the stakeholder process. Fortier also commented that the US would never agree to the steps recommended by the special envoys,

Strangway and Ruckelshaus. And he predicted that "in the end it is the nature and scope of the compromise which Canada is ready to accept that will be the determining factor in the outcome of future negotiations with the US."[20]

Fisheries Minister Anderson tried to deny that Fortier's resignation was a major setback. He told the *Vancouver Sun* on February 7 that he still had faith that William Ruckelshaus would find a solution to the dispute. Reform MP Gary Lunn (Saanich–Gulf Islands) asked the House of Commons, "If Canada's ambassador does not believe in government's process, how can British Columbian fishermen believe in this government?"

On February 6, 1998, Lloyd Axworthy, Canada's minister of foreign affairs and international trade, sent Yves Fortier a curt three-sentence letter, accepting his resignation. The federal cabinet took no steps to persuade Fortier to stay on, and ignored his suggestion that the issue be sent to international binding arbitration, although in 1992 he had successfully solved Canada's dispute with France over fishing near the islands of St. Pierre and Miquelon, and Canada and the US had agreed to send the Georges Bank boundary dispute (between Nova Scotia and Maine) to the International Court of Justice in 1984.[21] The Georges Bank case belies the US claim, made repeatedly throughout the PST dispute—and parroted by David Anderson—that the US never submits to third-party arbitration.

Meanwhile, Pat Chamut of the DFO confirmed that Ottawa had been searching for a new chief negotiator for quite some time, and that Ottawa had not necessarily intended to replace Fortier but had hoped to put him in a new role as part of a new negotiating team. But when the National Section of the PSC asked whether Fortier could be persuaded to return, Stephen Drymer, his assistant, said cryptically, "What the prime minister wants, the prime minister gets."[22]

In a last-ditch attempt to bring Fortier back, more than 30 members of the national section signed a letter to Anderson and Axworthy that read:

> The undersigned members of the Canadian National
> Section of the Pacific Salmon Commission…do not

believe that Mr. Fortier's efforts on Canada's behalf have ever been an obstacle to success, as some on the US side may have suggested. Indeed, this sort of criticism is eloquent testimony to his ability to articulate and defend the Canadian position…We ask that you make a personal effort to impress upon him that this is not the time to leave and attempt to persuade him to reconsider his decision.[23]

The letter was ignored, and Yves Fortier, who had done a valiant job in defending the principles of the treaty, was quickly replaced by a negotiator acceptable to the Americans.

Coping with the Coho Crisis

The ecological crisis is not a crisis of carrying capacity which requires increased efficiency and the internalization of costs, so much as it is a social crisis requiring a challenge to appropriation and domination.

—Raymond A. Rogers, *Solving History*

At a crowded news conference in Seattle on February 26, 1998, Will Stelle, regional director of the US National Marine Fisheries Service (NMFS), dropped a bombshell that shook the entire political establishment of the Pacific Northwest. He announced that 13 salmon stocks, ranging from San Francisco to the Canadian border, were about to be listed as endangered, in what was to be the most ambitious application of the federal Endangered Species Act (ESA) in its 20-year history. In his announcement Stelle declared, "Extinction is not an option...With the ESA proposals today, we face an opportunity to get it right one last time. We do not have a lot of time, and we do not have a lot of choices. We either face this responsibility and take it upon ourselves to meet this challenge or we run the risk of having these stocks go extinct."[1]

Stelle said that the NMFS would schedule a series of public hearings to discuss the implications of the proposed listings, and that the Service would suspend the listings if various state, local and tribal governments could implement a comprehensive stock recovery plan within a year. Failing that, the NMFS had the power to penalize any industry or development that threatened the salmon. The April 1998 edition of *The Alaskan Fishermen's Journal* said: "The spotted owl controversy [that plagued the Pacific Northwest lumber industry] was mosquito-like compared to the spectre cast by the proposed listing of Pacific Northwest salmon stocks." And Washington state Governor Gary Locke declared, "This is like being told that Mt. Rainier may disappear from our skyline, or that Puget Sound is going dry. Now we face not just one, but two threats. The first, of course, is the imminent danger of compromising our salmon into extinction. The second is that if we don't act now...the federal government will step in and make decisions for us on how we use our water and our land, and therefore we would lose control of our own destiny."

Throughout Washington state an intense and at times acrimonious debate took place between citizens and political interest groups. On March 25, the *Olympian* reported that Billy Frank, Jr., chair of the Northwest Indian Fisheries Commission, a group supportive of the ESA listings and critical of uncontrolled industrial growth, had warned, "You can't recover salmon without population growth control." His view was echoed by many environmentalists. Kathy Fletcher, executive director of a pro-development group called People for Puget Sound, defended big business, saying it was increasingly sensitive to "green values," and she told the *Olympian*, "There's a huge difference between growing smart and growing dumb. For years, we have been growing dumb." But with the new "smart" business strategies, Fletcher said, corporations and governments could now promote economic growth while caring for the environment and wild species.

In his book *Mountains in the Clouds*, Bruce Brown describes how industrial development in Washington state affected salmon during the twentieth century. Regarding the hydroelectric dams on the Columbia River, he writes:

> Eight unladdered dams were built on Columbia tributaries from the Tieton River to Salmon Creek. On the Yakima River, the bureau's dams wiped out the sockeye that had been the single largest run in the river and

played a major role in reducing the salmon population from 600,000 to 9,000 fish. During the 1930s, the bureau decided to dam the Columbia itself near an immense glacial outwash known as Grand Coulee. Hailed as the greatest engineering feat ever undertaken by man, Grand Coulee dam was also the single most destructive human act toward salmon in all time. When this unladdered colossus was completed in 1942, it closed more than 1,000 miles of spawning rivers and streams in the upper Columbia.[2]

The American biologist Jim Lichatowich, in his book *Salmon Without Rivers*, also traces the decline of Pacific Northwest salmon. Lichatowich explains that the Salmonidae go back more than 100 million years, yet within less than 150 years of European contact, several species of salmon in North America were facing extinction. Lichatowich describes the fur trade, which exterminated the beaver populations that were vital to juvenile salmon rearing ponds; placer mining, which devoured huge amounts of gravel from spawning beds; logging, which destroyed hundreds of watersheds through flooding and siltation; ranching, which destroyed riparian vegetation; farming, which diverted vast quantities of water for irrigation; and a network of hydroelectric dams, which ultimately blocked the Columbia River system to the migration of the world's largest salmon population. Lichatowich offers convincing evidence that environmental degradation, not overfishing, caused the collapse of the Columbia's salmon runs. In contrast, he says, the focussed authority of the International Pacific Salmon Fisheries Commission (IPSFC) managed to save Fraser salmon runs from the disaster that befell the Columbia:

> From 1930 to 1980, the Canadians and later the IPSFC certainly sought out and accepted the findings of science more readily than the Americans. The Canadians closed all their hatcheries in British Columbia in 1936…This decision removed the option of mitigating for dams with hatcheries, an option that seems to have been so

readily and unjustifiably accepted by the Americans. Even when faced with the threat of the Moran Dam in the 1950s, the Canadians still relied on science and did not allow the hatcheries' promise of a quick fix lure them into trading away the Fraser's mainstem."[3]

Lichatowich also points out that from 1937 to 1985, the US has spent some $3 billion on restoration, and another $1.5 billion is needed, whereas the International PSC spent $21.3 million on the Fraser.[4]

The Key to Locke's Door

It was in this context of several centuries of destruction that Washington Governor Gary Locke faced the task of persuading local government, tribal groups, environmentalists, hydroelectric authorities, real estate developers and industrialists to accept his scheme to restore habitat and rebuild wild salmon runs. It was still hard for them to accept any explanation besides "overfishing," and none of them would agree to the Locke plan unless there was a guarantee that the endangered stocks would make it back to the spawning grounds.

On the other hand, although Canada had repeatedly offered to curtail its interception of Pacific Northwest coho and chinook stocks if the Americans would reciprocate, the offer had been continually rejected. But now Governor Locke had to protect these endangered stocks or jeopardize his state's expanding economic growth, and he knew he could not evade the ESA listings without Canada's full co-operation in passing endangered US stocks through Canadian waters. The price of Canada's co-operation was a renewed PST agreement. And for the first time in a long while Canada, in principle, had the upper hand in negotiations.

Having known since he became Washington's governor in 1996 that an ESA listing was looming for salmon stocks, Gary Locke had appointed Curt Smitch to the job of Special Assistant for Natural Resources Policy early in 1997. Smitch's mandate was to ensure that environmental issues did not threaten the burgeoning Pacific Northwest economy, so one of his key assignments was to develop an emergency salmon recovery plan for Washington state to delay the NMFS endangered species legislation. Near the end of 1997 Smitch was appointed to the PSC as the commissioner for Washington state, and at the January 1998 meeting he suggested to me that we consider ways of improving relations between Premier Clark and Governor Locke. Shortly after this, Ottawa announced its intention to marginalize BC's role in the PST talks. However, Smitch agreed with me that a potential settlement would require the involvement of the provincial government. He also expressed his frustration with Alaskan overfishing, which had contributed to conservation problems, and he hinted that Locke had called upon President Clinton to whip Alaska into line. But Clinton would not intervene, he said, if Canadian officials—particularly Glen Clark—continued to attack the Alaskans in public. He suggested that a more low-key approach by the Canadian side would allow the Americans to be less defensive and more amenable to compromise.

On March 10, 1998, two weeks after Will Stelle's announcement of the pending ESA ruling, Premier Clark, Deputy Minister Doug McArthur and I met Governor Locke and Curt Smith in the governor's mansion in Olympia. Following a brief and cordial in-camera discussion, the two politicians held a joint news conference in which Governor Locke announced he would support the BC government being given a seat at the PST bargaining table. "I fully understand it's up to Canada to create its own negotiating protocol strategy," Locke announced. "However, we have a much higher likelihood of success if the province is part of the process."[5] In exchange, Clark suspended the provincial lawsuit against US overfishing, changing his role from aggressor to peacemaker.

New Negotiators

On the same day that Clark and Locke met, Ottawa announced the appointment of Don McRae as Canada's new chief negotiator for the PST. McRae, the head of the Department of Business and Trade Law at the University of Ottawa, had also served as chair of Canada's first Free Trade Agreement dispute panel. He was barely familiar with the West Coast fishery.

The link between the PST imbroglio and NAFTA had been considered by Thomas Walkom, national affairs writer for the *Toronto Star*, on

Premier Glen Clark tells a press conference that his government will sue the US for overfishing BC salmon, False Creek fishermen's wharf, Vancouver, 1997.

December 21, 1997. "Is it possible for Canada to win anything in a face-to-face disagreement with its nearest and most powerful neighbour? Is it even worth trying?" he had asked "...These questions are not new. In one form or another, they have plagued Canada since the first United Empire Loyalists trekked north in 1783 to escape the American revolution. But as Fisheries Minister David Anderson acknowledges, they have become particularly relevant since the Free Trade agreement of 1989, when Canada tied its economic future even more inextricably to that of the US."

Walkom reminded readers that when the federal Liberals were campaigning for the 1993 election, they had promised to end the "buddy-buddy days of the Brian Mulroney era" insofar as Canada–U.S. relations were concerned. After they took office they had changed their tune, and Walkom observed, "The reasons for Ottawa's increased timidity have much to do with the free trade pact and its successor, the 1994 North American Free Trade Agreement. Both altered dramatically the nature of the Canadian economy...The net result has been a greater unwillingness to do or say anything that might discomfit the United States. In this sense, Ottawa's passive stance in the BC salmon fight fits a pattern."

Shortly after McRae's appointment, Roberts Owen, a Boston-born State Department legal adviser and troubleshooter, was named the new

American PST negotiator. Owen was listed in the *Who's Who of America* for many diplomatic assignments, such as producing the Dayton Peace Accord for Bosnia and sorting out the American hostage crisis in Iran in 1980–81. The Canadian media celebrated his appointment, considering it evidence that the White House finally intended to settle the dispute. However, they had greeted the appointment of James Pipkin, who delivered no results during the four years he was on the job, in much the same way.

Owen's reputation as a "heavy hitter" caused the *Vancouver Sun* to question whether a mismatch might be in the making, but an Ottawa official was quick to point out that McRae had "a formidable intellectual presence along with the easy-going personal skills needed to win over BC fishermen." And, he added, "He is substantively stronger on trade law issues than the flamboyant and charming Fortier who occasionally coasted on his reputation."[6]

Doug McArthur, Premier Clark's deputy minister, was one of six Canadians who accompanied Don McRae to his first PST negotiating session in Washington, DC, on March 30, 1998. However, there were other more pressing things on McArthur's mind as he listened to McRae and Owen exchanging polite pleasantries across the bargaining table. It was highly unusual for someone of McArthur's rank to be directly involved in such complex and time-consuming negotiations, but Clark's high-profile stand on the Mifflin Plan had helped the NDP to win the provincial election of 1996, so McArthur stayed informed and launched several fisheries-related programs, including the establishment of a new provincial fisheries ministry and negotiating a Canada–BC Fisheries Agreement with Ottawa.

These initiatives were conceived as part of Clark's populist, anti-Ottawa "fish campaign," but with the new ministry (MoF), under the direction of Fisheries Minister Dennis Streifel, came new responsibilities. For example, the province now had to define its role. Would it share fisheries management with Ottawa, as envisioned in the Canada–BC Fisheries Agreement, or would it seek total provincial control? It soon became apparent that the senior bureaucrats in the new ministry were content to remain a junior partner to the DFO. The MoF sponsored a comprehensive strategic planning process for the recreational fishery in

1998, *BC Tidal Anadromous Sports Fishery: a Joint Government and Sector Initiative,* but not for the commercial sector.

McArthur, in the meantime, appeared to be unable to change the polarized and acrimonious nature of fisheries politics in the post-Mifflin era. The process was complicated and time-consuming, and the stakeholders seldom reached consensus on anything meaningful. Above all else, the threat to cancel the provincial lease at Nanoose, which had been intended to push Ottawa on the PST front, was very troublesome.

As well, McArthur had other worries. The NDP government was mired at a dismal 24 percent approval rating in the polls, with more than two years of its mandate already gone. And the new provincial budget was causing pandemonium in the press. On March 31, Finance Minister Joy McPhail announced that the government would spend $1 billion on improving roads, hospitals and schools, despite a deficit of $95 million the previous fiscal year. The budget was completely out of sync with those of most other provinces. Although BC's accumulated debt of $31 billion had begun in the early 1980s, the pundits placed all the blame on the NDP.

McArthur passed the PST file on to Bill Valentine, deputy minister in the MoF. Meanwhile, as PST talks dragged on, provincial Fisheries Minister Streifel tried to pressure Ottawa for more financial support for hard-pressed BC fishing communities, particularly because of the apparent favouritism of the federal government toward the East Coast fishery.

Enough to Bury US

June 19, 1998, was a gruelling day for David Anderson, and his gaunt features, framed by his ashen beard, gave him an even more haggard look than usual as he addressed a crowded press conference at the Pan Pacific Hotel in Vancouver. The day had begun 12 hours earlier at another press conference 4,000 miles away in St. John's, Newfoundland. There, he and Pierre Pettigrew, the federal minister of human resources, announced a federal scheme to "revitalize" Canada's commercial fishing industry: $400 million would be spent in the Pacific region, and $750 million in Atlantic Canada.

The East Coast funds were on top of the $1.9 billion already spent on The Atlantic Groundfish Subsidy (TAGS), the second largest expenditure made by the Chretien government after the National Infrastructure Program.[7] Although Newfoundland Fisheries, Food and Allied Workers Union–Canadian Auto Workers (NFFAWU–CAW) President Earle McCurdy had criticized Ottawa for the way it administered the TAGS program, claiming that large amounts of money had been squandered through bureaucratic ineptitude, the public had got the message that a welfare scam of epic proportions had occurred in Newfoundland outports. And although some West Coast critics accused Ottawa of favouritism toward the Atlantic provinces, East Coast fishing workers did not share this view. In the middle of the St. John's press conference, 51-year-old Elsie Reid of Harbour Grace had torn up Anderson's press release and thrown it in his face. According to Southam News, Reid, who had worked in the fishing industry for 31 years, was furious to learn that she was too young to qualify for Ottawa's proposed early retirement plan. Instead, she was facing unemployment with nothing more than a one-time taxable payment of $10,000. "It's enough to bury us," Reid declared. "There's enough to go down to the funeral home and give it to them."

"My family came to Petty Harbour in 1760," said Lawrence Kieley, a fisherman. "They fished in the harbour since. If I take the licence buy-out now, that is the last for the Kieley family fishing in the harbour. And that's very disappointing after they survived for nearly 250 years."

After the bitter reception by East Coast fishermen, Anderson's handlers made sure that security was extremely tight when he faced the press in Vancouver. Consequently, a minor row broke out when a group of fishermen were barred entry by a battalion of undercover police and security guards. This heavy-handed approach further alienated working people in coastal BC from the DFO.

Anderson announced the details of his long-awaited coho recovery plan. He then introduced a radical new approach to fisheries management that would later be dubbed the Anderson Plan. He explained that $200 million of the $400 million aid package was earmarked for another licence buyback, $100 million would go to habitat restoration programs and the final $100 million would go to economic adjustment programs. He emphasized that his Coho Recovery Plan and the 1998

Salmon Management Plan would result in permanent changes to the West Coast fishery. He had rejected advice from some scientists, he said, to shut down the salmon fishery entirely in 1998 to save the endangered coho, but "That would be giving up on the fishery and its future. I am not going to do that. Addressing conservation does not mean no fishing. It means fishing in a new way."

Anderson was proposing to replace the traditional system of aggregate stock management with a new system of "weak" stock management, based on so-called selective fishing in "terminal" areas. In fact, this new scheme was the brainchild of lobbyists who belonged to the Sports Fishing Institute of BC (SFI). In a report titled *Creative Solutions for the New Millennium* by Brent McCallum, the SFI had laid out all of the fundamental elements of the Anderson Plan. Among other things, their report called for an end to all mixed-stock "gauntlet-style" commercial fisheries; the elimination of the commercial bycatch of "weak" stocks such as coho, chinook and steelhead; the elimination of commercial trolling off the west coast of Vancouver Island; and DFO enhancement of fishing opportunities for the recreational sector.

There would be no fishing, Anderson said, in a series of so-called "red zones" where any mortalities of the critical upper Skeena or Thompson River coho stocks might occur. He also announced that sports fishing would be allowed in a series of "yellow zones" when there was minimal risk of coho mortality. To most reporters Anderson's plan seemed a model of pragmatism. Not only was he protecting endangered species, he was also being sensitive to the needs of fishermen.

After some fierce lobbying by the sports lodge operators and over the objection of DFO's regional staff,[8] senior officials in Ottawa decided to change certain "red" zones near Langara Island, just off the Queen Charlotte Islands, to "yellow" status. This allowed the clients of sports fishing lodges to continue fishing as usual, as long as they released any coho. The commercial fleet would have loved the same opportunity to release its bycatch of coho, but DFO did not allow it. On April 29, 1998, the *Vancouver Sun* reported that Paul Sprout, the DFO's Director of Pacific Operations, had said that zero mortality "means that anywhere you could have a bycatch of coho, you wouldn't have a fishery. There would be no fishing anywhere coho could be harvested." Anderson's policies had made it next to impossible to harvest any other species of salmon, regardless of their level of abundance.

That is why Anderson, fully aware that his coho policy would devastate the commercial sector, had apportioned half of his $400 million aid package to a licence buyback fund. On June 16, just two days before the announcement of the Anderson Plan, an anonymous DFO official had told Barbara Yaffe of the *Vancouver Sun* that the department expected a huge backlash after the announcement of Ottawa's fisheries restructuring plan, but that Ottawa anticipated an easier "sell" on the West Coast, where licence buy-outs were more readily accepted than in Atlantic Canada. The federal Liberals stood to gain few votes by giving BC fishermen the sort of income support programs in place in Atlantic Canada, but many votes by emphasizing concern for the environment. Yaffe wrote, "Unfortunately for fishery workers, taxpayers have reached a point where they want the fishery to pay for itself. And Ottawa has come around to their point of view."

But this time Anderson—unlike his predecessor Fred Mifflin—found many fewer voices in the commercial sector in support of fleet reduction. The pro-Mifflin sector, who had supported reduced competition on the fishing grounds through a forced licence buyback in 1996 were a chastened lot. The expected payoffs from the Mifflin Plan had been offset by falling dockside prices, American interceptions and DFO "conservation" measures.

On June 29 *The Fisherman* reported that the economist Gordon Gislason had recommended that 900 to 1,900 commercial vessels be retired. With only 3,000 salmon licences left in the fleet after the Mifflin Plan, this proposal posed a serious threat to coastal communities. Furthermore, such a huge buyback could seriously erode the traditional sharing arrangements between the small boat fleet and the canning company-dominated seine sector. UFAWU–CAW small boat organizer John Sutcliffe told the paper, "Fishermen accept that there has to be fleet reduction. But without any consultation with fishermen to design a balanced fleet and without any plan to rebuild the industry, fleet reduction in numbers like that is going to lead to the decimation of the small boat fleet."

If the public was going to support the Anderson Plan, the coho crisis would have to be presented as dramatically as possible. In a press statement issued on June 19, 1998, Anderson said:

> Salmon help define who we are and where we live. We share the land and the water with the salmon. From today forward, we will do it more respectfully...The future of coho salmon—indeed the future of all salmon—depends on their habitat. I have lived on this coast all my life and have fished in these waters for most of those years. I have seen change upon change, development upon development, clear-cut upon clear-cut, strip the life away from streams and rivers that are home to salmon. When we build houses, roads, and culverts, when we plow and fill, when we log and dam, when we spray, ditch, and drain—we are lengthening the odds against our fish. It's time to take a long, hard look, as a society, at our relationship with the salmon.

Anderson's remarks were accurate—fish habitat was being lost at an alarming rate all over the province. But the question remained: what would he and the federal Liberal Party do to reverse this onslaught against the salmon? Would they simply resort to Band-aid solutions and continue to make scapegoats out of commercial fishermen?

Something Has Gone Very Badly Wrong

Oncorhynchus kitsutch, known as coho salmon, are a special breed. They range from California to Alaska and, of the five species of Pacific salmon, they have the shortest life cycle after pinks. The American Fisheries Society counts 2,594 individual stocks of coho in BC and the Yukon alone. Yet overall coho populations have been in decline since the late 1960s.

Historically, BC fishermen have harvested approximately 70 percent of the available returns of coho, theoretically leaving the remaining 30 percent to spawn. This harvest rate seemed sustainable for decades, but it proved calamitous when ocean survival conditions suddenly worsened following the El Niño events of 1992 and 1993. At the commencement of the Mifflin Plan, the DFO had reduced the coho harvest rate to only 30 percent, but even this proved insufficient, as escapements continued to dwindle. Commercial overfishing was generally thought to be the culprit, but BC coho stocks remained in jeopardy well after most commercial harvests had been eliminated.

Of the three main threats to coho—poor ocean survival conditions, fresh-water habitat destruction and overfishing—scientists have speculated that indeterminate climatic variations in the ocean environment have had the major effect on Pacific coho. The DFO's chief coho coordinator, Ron Kadowaki, said that the survival rate of coho during the 1980s was about 14 percent of the fry, and by the late 1990s that figure had dropped to only 4 percent. The DFO could not explain why. But according to Carl Walters, a UBC fisheries biologist:

> Coho are not the only species to have suffered severe declines in marine survival rates since the mid-1980s. Similar trends have been observed in steelhead populations from Oregon through BC, in many spring-type chinook salmon from interior streams, and even in Atlantic salmon stocks off eastern Canada. There is scientific concern that these large-scale correlations may not be accidental, and that there may in fact be something going very badly wrong with freshwater or coastal rearing habitats throughout North America...Since these declines in survival rates have been observed mainly in species that rear in freshwater for a year, it has been suggested that some factor like ultraviolet radiation is impacting the fish while they are in freshwater. The implication is that this impact does not kill them immediately, but instead makes them vulnerable to mortality during the stressful period of early ocean life.[9]

The Pacific Fisheries Resource Conservation Council describes these dramatic changes in the ocean environment as "regime shifts," or change in some or all patterns of "atmospheric pressure, sea-surface temperatures, population dynamics of various fish species and density of plankton and other forage species that provide vital food for various fish species."[10]

Scientific understanding of how the marine environment functions is sketchy at best, and recent cuts to the DFO's budget have undermined vital research in this field. Ottawa came up with the money to underwrite marketing campaigns for the recreational lodge operators and to advertise the Anderson Plan on TV, but it did not secure funds to study the effects of changing ocean environment on Pacific salmon.

The ocean environment and much of the precious fresh-water habitat on which salmon depend are severely compromised. Coho are especially susceptible to these threats because most individual stocks spend their first vulnerable year in small streams, many of which are only a few feet wide. A 1977 DFO study under the auspices of the Fraser River Action Plan found that: "Of 779 streams from Hope to the Strait of Georgia, 117, or a full 15 percent, were considered to have been lost as a result of culverting, paving, draining, or filling over. Furthermore, another 375 [48 percent] were classified as endangered, 181 [23 percent] ranked as threatened, and only 106 or 16 percent of the streams were considered to be wild."[11]

Another DFO study conducted in the early 1970s found that 70 percent of the original tidal lands in the Fraser River estuary had been altered as a result of human activity, and more than 50 percent of the actual fish habitat in the area had been lost since 1880.[12] And an independent study conducted by the American Fisheries Society found that out of a total of 9,662 salmon stocks in BC, 230 were of special concern, 78 were at moderate risk, 624 were at high risk and 142 had been extirpated within the last century. Of the 2,594 individual coho stocks in BC and the Yukon, it was reported that 16 percent were at risk of extinction. Most of the documented extinctions were the result of habitat destruction caused by logging, hydro power and urbanization.[13]

The infamous "no net loss" habitat policy, combined with severe cuts to the DFO's enforcement budget, had resulted in a further alarming loss of salmon habitat. The Canadian auditor general's 1997 audit of the DFO concluded that the department's habitat-monitoring programs were woefully insufficient. In the forest industry, for example, there was disturbing evidence that the Coastal Fisheries/Forestry Guidelines were being routinely ignored, and a Sierra Legal Defence Fund report in February 1997 showed that 83 percent of all streams were clear-cut to the banks, 89 percent of all field-checked cut-blocks had non-identified or misclassified streams, 82 percent of all streams checked in the field were felled and yarded across and only 43 percent of the streams that should have been classified as fish streams under the code were properly classified as fish streams. As well, the auditor general found that the referral process designed to control urban development in five different watersheds between 1985 to 1995 had been a disaster; only 28 percent of all projects audited were in full compliance with regulations.

Sadly, in spite of all the conservation rhetoric that came with the announcement of the $400 million Anderson Plan, very little was done to reverse any of the abuses of fish habitat. Out of the $100 million Anderson said he had earmarked for restoring salmon, only $20 million was assigned to the Salmon Enhancement Program (SEP), and it came nowhere near to making up for the years of debilitating cuts under the Tories and then the Liberals. The $30 million set aside for a Salmon Endowment Fund seemed impressive, but only the annual interest from that fund could be spent. The remainder of the $100 million earmarked for salmon enhancement was spent on hiring habitat stewardship coordinators and funding various volunteer streamkeeper projects. These programs no doubt had great merit, but they were designed to repair habitat that was already lost rather than to prevent further loss from occurring. And although these expenditures were of indirect benefit to commercial fishermen, they can scarcely be compared to the direct-income support programs offered to East Coast fishermen and their families.

The Ballad of Parzival Copes

Long before David Anderson's coho conservation plan was announced in June 1998, I had suggested that the provincial fisheries ministry (MoF) initiate a public inquiry into the coho crisis, to explore ways to protect endangered coho and ensure that commercial fisheries continue for other stronger stocks of salmon. Bill Valentine, the provincial deputy minister of fisheries, agreed, and Dr. Parzival Copes, Emeritus

Professor of Economics and Fisheries Analysis at Simon Fraser University, was commissioned in April 1998.

The son of Dutch immigrants, Copes was born on a fruit farm near the tiny BC interior town of Nakusp. His family later moved to Vancouver, where his father worked as an accountant. In 1933, during the Depression, the family moved back to Holland, where Copes was active in the underground resistance.[14] He ended up doing hard labour in a Nazi concentration camp, and near the end of the war he joined the Canadian army.

Copes then returned to Canada to pursue a degree in economics at UBC, which he financed by commercial salmon fishing with his brother in the summer months. After completing a doctorate at the London School of Economics, he became a professor of economics at Memorial University in St. John's, Newfoundland, and began doing research for the troubled East Coast fishing industry. Although he returned to Vancouver in 1965 as the charter head of economics and commerce at the newly established Simon Fraser University, he continued to research the Newfoundland fisheries. In 1972 he published a highly critical report, *The Resettlement of Fishing Communities in Newfoundland*,[15] demonstrating that government failure to deal with chronic high unemployment had caused people to use the inshore fishery as the "employer of last resort." Enormous subsidies were needed, and the industry put excessive pressure on fish stocks. Copes predicted that, failing a reversal of government policy, the fishery would become increasingly non-viable. He also criticized the government's policy of moving people from smaller coastal communities to the supposed "industrial growth centres" because there were few alternate employment opportunities for the many displaced fishermen. The real alternative, Copes said, was to use federal subsidies to help Newfoundlanders find jobs in mainland Canada. Neither the fishermen nor the Newfoundland government agreed, and a derisive song called "The Ballad of Parzival Copes" became popular in many outports. Yet by 1992, when the northern cod stocks finally collapsed, many of Copes's predictions had come to pass.

In his study of the West Coast fishery, Copes favoured modest reductions in the fleet but opposed the massive restructuring brought about by the Mifflin Plan and recommended instead that Ottawa explore ways to ensure the survival of BC's small boat fleet. This advice seemed to contradict his prescription for the East Coast fishery, but it did not. Simply put, he believed that all fisheries management is based on a simple harmonic triad—biological conservation, economic efficiency and social equity—and that any management system that allowed them to get out of balance was doomed. In his report to the Coastal Community Network in 1999, he wrote, "Following the narrow advice from different single-discipline experts, the focus of Canadian fisheries policy has often jumped around from one set of issues to another, concentrating in turn on social affairs, economic profitability and conservation, without adequate attention to the cross-over effects among policy areas. The results of such 'uni-dimensional' policy applications, concentrating entirely or primarily on a single policy area, may turn out to be disastrous."[16]

In Copes's report to the provincial government regarding the coho crisis, released on April 29, 1998, he warned, "Top priority must go to immediate measures for the protection and restoration of threatened stocks. There is, however, a serious danger if that priority is pursued with excessive zeal, for instance, by shutting down all salmon fisheries in an attempt to make sure that not a single fish from a weak stock is taken. That would devastate fishing communities, turning fishermen and their families into an 'endangered species.'"[17]

Copes rejected the notion prevalent within DFO circles that "short-term cut-backs in harvesting" to meet conservation objectives justified "long-run capacity reduction and industry restructuring." He disagreed with Peter Pearse and others who argued that privatization would automatically result in more sustainable fishing practices, saying that such ideas "rest on serious misconceptions regarding the nature of the marine environment."[18]

Copes pointed out that recent experiments with individual transferable quotas (ITQs) in fisheries around the world had led to serious conservation problems—even to total stock collapse—because of quota-busting, high-grading, and overfishing undertaken by fishermen who were overcapitalized. The legal underpinning of Copes's analysis was drawn from the United Nations Convention on the Law of the Sea

(UNCLOS), whose "abstention" principle says that where a fish stock is fully utilized, no other additional groups should claim admission to the fishery; and whose "adjacency" principle says that resident populations have first claim on available local stocks. Copes wrote, "Because resident populations are most often the first to make substantial use of local fish stocks, the adjacency principle may often combine with the abstention principle to establish a strong claim by coastal or river communities for continuing priority access rights to local stocks."[19]

Copes was striking at two major problems threatening the West Coast salmon fishery: American overfishing and the DFO's controversial licensing policies. At the same time, he was exposing the fundamental flaws of the Anderson Plan. First, David Anderson made no apparent use of the Law of the Sea Accord or the International Court of Justice to counter American interceptions of endangered BC coho. If the Americans refused to submit the issue to arbitration, as Anderson claimed, Canada might have embarrassed them on the international stage—particularly because the US had solicited international support to stop the interception of Alaskan salmon by high-seas driftnets from Asia. Second, Copes declared that the DFO's reliance on market-driven rationalization devices such as licence buybacks and licence staking put small fishing-dependent communities unnecessarily at risk:

> A retiring fisherman of modest means living in a small community is unlikely to forgo the opportunity to sell his licence to the highest bidder, even if it means that his access share of a community resource [which he may have received free of charge at the inception of transferable licensing] is being alienated from that community. The stacking provisions of the Mifflin plan apparently have now started a similar process of alienating from coastal communities their access to local fish resources. The question needs to be asked whether this outcome is federal government policy or the unwanted result of a misunderstood process. If it is the former the public should be told so in clear terms. If it is the latter the process should be put in reverse.[20]

In the context of the UNCLOS adjacency principle, Copes maintained that coastal communities would be the best stewards of the resource as their local economies are dependant on the long-term viability of the stocks. As an alternative, Copes recommended that all salmon licences be based on an owner-operator provision (similar to Don Cruickshank's 1991 Fleet Rationalization Report), which would prevent corporate concentration of salmon licences and ensure the continued survival of small-boat fishermen in small communities. He also expanded on an idea—first sketched out by the UFAWU in 1991—calling upon the two governments to jointly establish a licence bank, so that coastal communities, independent fishermen and First Nations could acquire licences at affordable costs. During years of low salmon abundance, he said, governments could buy up excess licences to reduce pressure on the stocks. But instead of being permanently extinguished, the licences could be held in trust until stocks were rebuilt, then leased back to fishermen. Immediate conservation concerns could be addressed through voluntary reduction of fleet, and over the long term governments could use the licence bank to stimulate local employment and enjoy a permanent source of revenue through leasing of licences.

As well, Copes offered some practical ways to overcome the "mixed stock" management dilemma precipitated by the coho crisis, including a ban on fishing coho in "hotspots" and at peak times, and the use of special gear.

Most of Parzival Copes's advice on selective harvest techniques was, in one way or another, adopted by the DFO. But his appeal to empower coastal communities and save independent owner-operators fell on deaf ears.

Minister Streifel's executive assistant Chloe Burgess and I persuaded Fisheries Renewal BC (FsRBC) to fund a study on Copes's licence bank concept, and Dr. Robert Brown of Simon Fraser University was given the job. Brown produced a report titled *Community Fisheries Licence Banking Trust: A Proposal for Community-Based Fisheries* and released on April 17, 2000. Unfortunately, the NDP provincial government did not act on the report, and the DFO ignored it.

Copes's report sparked a wave of criticism and debate, and the most hostile response came from people in the commercial fishing sector.

Mike Hunter, president of the Fisheries Council of BC—and formerly a graduate student in the SFU Economics Department, which was chaired by Copes—was the most vigorous critic of the report. On April 30, 1998, he told the *Vancouver Province*, "It's all political. It's not about fish at all. It's an attempt to do some social engineering on the backs of the fish." He scorned the idea of trying to maintain coastal communities through a government licence bank and suggested people were leaving coastal communities because of the changing nature of the modern fishery.

In fact, it was not only working people who were abandoning coastal BC, but also the canning companies, who had begun to concentrate their operations in urban centres.

The Full Mifflin and the Full Retreat

When you're up against powerful interests, you've got to be smarter not stupider.

—Fisheries Minister David Anderson, *Vancouver Sun*, September 18, 1997

It was a classic case of life imitating art. On May 14, 1998, as loudspeakers blasted out the bump and grind soundtrack of Twisted Sister's "We're Not Gonna Take It," five fishermen leapt onto a flatbed truck that was parked opposite the provincial legislature and began a striptease. Their protest mimicked the hit movie *The Full Monty*, in which unemployed British millworkers do a strip show to make a living. The fishermen's striptease was dubbed the "Full Mifflin." Hats, raincoats and gumboots flew into the crowd of more than 200 bystanders, who shrieked with delight as one man twirled a fishnet stocking over his head, then tossed it into the crowd. As the grand finale, the dancers wiggled and turned in unison to reveal an unflattering portrait of Fisheries Minister David Anderson emblazoned on their undershorts.

The Full Mifflin protestors said they would accept nothing less than what was provided to displaced East Coast fishing families.

After the show, the crowd marched to the minister's constituency office in Victoria, intending to present his staff with their shirts, which

Fishermen protest against the Anderson Plan by performing the "Full Mifflin" in front of the BC legislature in Victoria, May 1998.

read: "DFO has taken the shirts off our backs." Anderson's office door was locked, however, so they draped their shirts on the door handle. "We've been stripped of our dignity and stripped of our livelihoods," Kim Olsen told the crowd. "The naked truth is that Ottawa's secret agenda is to strip us of our salmon resource!"

Minister Anderson was taking credit for spending $400 million on aid programs, but on April 27, 1998, *The Fisherman* had reported that no more than $22.5 million had actually been spent to support fishermen and their families. Moreover, a good portion of the "$400 million" came with strings attached. For example, the much publicized $15 million Fisher's Early Retirement Program was dependent on a $7.7-million matching contribution from the BC government, which had been allowed almost no input into the Mifflin Plan. Victoria had balked and Ottawa had quietly cancelled the program, leaving a large number of older unemployed fishermen, who were not yet eligible for Canada Pension, without any financial relief. And when fishermen demanded that the DFO provide income support to get them through another poor season, they got no sympathy from Mike Hunter, president of the Fisheries Council of BC, who told Mark Hume of the *Vancouver Sun*, "The world has changed and there's no going back. What we need is a program that gets people out of the business, not something that gets them through 1998."

The Full Mifflin protest captured the attention of the international press, but the next day Minister Anderson told the *Vancouver Sun* that although he sympathized with fishermen and their families, a certain amount of pain was necessary if the industry was to adapt to the demands of the future.

During the week of the protest, I attended the next round of the PST negotiations in Portland, Oregon. On the eve of the talks, another "leaked" Ottawa memo suggested Canadian negotiators were prepared to accept much less than full equity to reach a long-term settlement. According to the *Vancouver Sun* on May 12, the memo said: "It is not realistic to expect the US to adjust its fisheries to even come close to balancing the amount caught by each country...The issues are sensitive and complex and encompass questions that have proven to be largely unanswerable in the past. To insist on addressing them now, in the expectation that we can reach an agreement in six short weeks, would likely lead to failure." In other words, no one should expect Washington and Oregon to pressure Alaska to make major concessions in 1998 because the strict conservation policies to be imposed on Canadian fishermen—the Anderson Plan—would provide major "pass-through" benefits to the northwest states, thus solving most of their conservation problems. The memo went on to note that Governor Gary Locke did not want to antagonize Alaska senators Stevens and Murkowski just before a critical vote in the US Senate on salmon enhancement project funding.

Premier Glen Clark told CBC Radio that the memo was "really shocking and a betrayal of British Columbia, because it almost surrenders before we go into formal discussions."

Leaving Portland

All during the week of May 12, 1998, the national sections of both Canada and the US bided their time in a sprawling Portland hotel complex while a small team of mid-level fish managers negotiated behind closed doors. Canada's chief negotiator, Don McRae, had earlier put the long-term equity talks on hold and assigned these DFO officials to secure short-term fishing arrangements. Assistant Deputy Minister Pat Chamut, who headed the Canadian team, was anxious to reach a deal at any cost, as a recent report by the Pacific Stock Assessment Review Committee (PSARC) indicated that coho stocks were in worse condition than feared. The committee was calling for a strict zero mortality in all fisheries, and said that coho stocks on Vancouver Island's west coast and in Georgia Strait "are not expected to achieve three females per kilometre [of spawning beds], even in the absence of fishing mortality."

Meanwhile, Senator Pat Carney, the former minister of international trade, chose that week to take another swing at her Liberal Party adversaries. In a guest editorial in the *Vancouver Sun* on May 13, she wrote:

> I am concerned that Canada will allow the Americans to split the equity issue off from other treaty issues and deal with it on a stand-alone basis. This separate-table approach would doom the Pacific Salmon Treaty, in my view, because my experience...showed that an issue on a separate table never gets resolved. Canada must maintain the position that all treaty elements, including equity and conservation, are on the negotiating table and that all elements are addressed...The separate-table approach would threaten the resource itself because Ottawa would be unlikely to fund new conservation and habitat-renewal measures aimed at growing fish if Canada did not reap the economic reward. Why should Canadian taxpayers raise fish for US fishermen?

The Americans, however, were still not prepared to address coho conservation concerns or move fish to Canada. The Alaskans, who had been stunned by the Strangway–Ruckelshaus Report six months earlier, now rejected Canada's demands. The Washington state delegation was fully aware that the Anderson Plan would stop Canadian interception of their stocks, and they refused to make any significant concessions on Fraser River sockeye. In fact, they demanded a substantial increase in their percentage of the total allowable catch. Nonetheless, Don McRae was reluctant to publicly criticize the American intransigence. Concerned that Ottawa was squandering the momentum generated by the Strangway–Ruckelshaus Report, and selling out, I called Victoria on the morning of May 16. Clark's deputy minister, Doug McArthur, was away, so I spoke with Geoff Meggs, Clark's director of communications. We concluded that it would be necessary to blow the lid on the talks, and that Bill Valentine and I must go to Victoria to brief the premier, then rush back to Portland.

The quick trip proved impossible because it took us several hours to get a flight out of Portland. Thanks to the delay, the press jumped on us for pulling out of the talks after making such a big fuss about getting a seat at the table. Anderson was quoted in the *Province* as saying, "Damage has been done to the Canadian fishermen because of the disunity displayed. You wouldn't expect the Americans to roll over and play dead. Americans are among the world's toughest negotiators, and the Alaskans are the toughest of the Americans…We obviously threw away the advantage given by the first-ever admission by a top-ranking American that Canada is due fish."

Saying that negotiations were still underway, however, Anderson refused to comment on their progress. I then attempted to inform the public by telling the *Vancouver Sun*, "We're going backwards on Alaska and the interceptions. We're making no progress on the US south. At what point does quiet diplomacy end and standing up for your country begin? If there was something happening at these talks we wouldn't be walking from the table and reviewing our position."

Here We Go Again

On May 16, Premier Glen Clark held a press conference in the rose garden at the legislature, where he told the press, "Ottawa is taking positions which are completely antithetical to British Columbia's position almost on all counts. If there is any resolution, it will be one which is profoundly to BC's disadvantage…They are prepared to sacrifice the fish in BC for bigger political reasons to keep the relationship with the US, not rock the boat, things like the auto pact and others, and they really don't care."

Some journalists charged that his "anti-Americanism" was damaging BC's reputation; others maintained that a marginal "sunset industry" was not worth all the hullabaloo. Above all, Anderson's coho conservation stand served to trump Clark's nationalist rhetoric. The press did not sort through the complicated matter of balancing interceptions and establishing equity. In simple terms, their story was that Clark was standing up for the narrow interests of commercial fishermen, whereas Anderson was saving endangered salmon. *Vancouver Sun* columnist Vaughn Palmer wrote, "[Clark] told reporters: 'The stakeholders were feeling that they were just spinning their wheels, things were going badly. The stakeholders now understand that BC is not complicit in this agreement.' Yes, the stakeholders—mainly the fishermen and especially the unionized ones. Mr. Clark disrupted the Canadian position to re-cement his relationship with groups that have no more incentive to compromise than he does."

Palmer had no way of knowing what was going on behind the scenes in Portland, nor any appreciation of the long history of intransigence on the US side, and until then he had paid little attention to the PST situation. "The Portland talks were being monitored by negotiator Bill Valentine and fisheries advisor Dennis Brown," he went on. "Both know the issue, but neither is as diplomatic or patient as Mr. McArthur and they may well have given up prematurely."

Valentine and I returned to Portland the next day to a very frosty reception from DFO officials and learned that the talks were just about to adjourn. No progress had been made.

However, on May 22 Anderson told the *Seattle Post-Intelligencer*, "Coho are being exploited by fishermen in Alaska, British Columbia, Washington, and Oregon. In Canada, we will take the necessary conservation measures. Our American neighbours have a moral obligation to do the same...I have promised Governor Locke I will do everything I can to preserve [American] stocks. The extinction of a coho salmon stock in Washington state would be a tragedy to both our nations, as would be the extinction of a coho stock in the upper Thompson River." Cathy Scarfo, head of the West Coast Trollers Association, commented, "Sounds like you are going to have a zero exploitation rate for Canadians and 50 to 60 percent for Americans," and Anderson snapped, "The American fishery is in American waters. We have absolutely no control over it...We cannot say to our grandchildren, 'We sat around and waited for the other guy to go first.'"[1]

After the collapse of the Portland negotiations, Don McRae reassured the media that all was not lost and that negotiations would resume within six weeks. But in Alaska, David Benton was publicly denouncing Canada for not bargaining in good faith and insinuating that Canada had summarily rejected Alaska's offer to make major reductions in its catch. On May 16 he told the *Yakima Herald Republic*, "At this point Alaska has offered to reduce its sockeye take by 75 percent over last year. That's still on the table."

In fact, the Alaskans had only offered to abide by the terms of the expired annex, which limited the Noyes Island seine fishery to 120,000 sockeye before week 31 of each year. In claiming this was a major concession, Benton did not mention that Alaskan seiners had illegally landed four times the treaty limit in the previous season.

Alaskan managers also suggested that the absence of an agreement for 1998 posed no threat to the endangered stocks. On May 19, Bob Clasby, director of commercial fisheries management for the Alaska Department of Fish and Game, told the *Juneau Empire*, "We always work with them [Canada] informally in season, particularly if either one of us has conservation problems with our stocks. Typically we've pretty much maintained the spirit of the last agreement, with any adjustments based on abundance."

The truth is that the Alaskans not only violated the sockeye annex in 1997, they had intercepted alarming numbers of BC's endangered coho. In 1997, the coho harvest of southeast Alaska had been 1,900,000 pieces, compared to only 162,286 in all of BC. And DFO officials estimated that 570,000 of those 1.9 million coho were of BC origin.

While the Americans were blithely overriding the Strangway–Ruckelshaus Report, David Strangway was the guest speaker at a $75-per-plate dinner at the Four Seasons Hotel in Vancouver, sponsored by the Environmental Managers Association. He spoke about protecting Pacific salmon, discreetly avoiding any mention of American impudence.[2]

The countdown to the 1998 salmon season was well underway when the media began complaining that the protracted PST dispute had become a staged routine for politicians seeking headlines. On May 20 a *Victoria Times Colonist* editorial announced, "Get ready, because here we go again. It's getting warmer, the salmon season is almost upon us, and finger pointing is underway."

History, Hogwash and Hokey Science

On May 26 David Anderson announced that he would send a smaller group of negotiators to the next round of negotiations in Juneau to try to reach a deal. The growing willingness of the Alaskans to "communicate, coordinate, and co-operate"—and the smaller Canadian negotiating team, he said, augured well for a settlement: "We want to make sure we proceed, and large and unwieldy delegations don't seem to be as quick in deliberations as smaller groups." In fact, Anderson never called the Canadian national section together again before the 1998 season, much to their dismay, and later that fall he removed me from the commission.

Anderson maintained that his conservation stance would eventually embarrass the Americans into making concessions. Until the introduction of zero mortality policy for coho, he told Peter O'Neil of the *Vancouver Sun* on May 26, "They couldn't be sure we're serious. Now there's no question in anyone's mind we're serious."

Curt Smitch, Governor Locke's special assistant, told the *Olympian* on May 26 that he was delighted that Anderson had "put conservation first and allocation second."

Thus, when the negotiations finally resumed in Juneau on May 28, David Anderson was in for an unpleasant surprise: the Alaskans dismissed his "moral lead" on conservation. Jeff Koenings of the Alaska Fish and Game Department declared that the decline of Skeena River coho stocks, which had precipitated the Anderson Plan, had been caused by Canadian mismanagement, not Alaskan interceptions. Anderson had obviously not been listening on May 16, when Koenings had told CHTK radio in Prince Rupert that Canada had underestimated its own take of coho on the upper Skeena River and then tried to pin the difference on Alaska. The take of endangered upper Skeena coho in Alaskan fisheries was less than a quarter of one percent of the total catch, Koenings said, and "to forgo the harvest of two to three million coho for 25 percent of the catch is just not something we're willing to consider." Bob Thorstenson, the spokesperson for Alaska's South East Seiners Association, told CBC radio on May 28, "For Canadian officials to come out and blast Alaska and complain and say that this is a new problem caused by Alaska trends and overfishing—and evidence of overfishing—is hogwash!" In response, Assistant Deputy Minister Pat Chamut told CBC radio, "We are absolutely convinced that the science that we've got with respect to the problem with coho is one that demands the sort of action that we are taking. So we're not doing this on the basis of some hokey science."

But the Juneau talks ended without a deal mere days before the start of the 1998 salmon season. The Alaskan negotiators were quick to report that once again the two sides had come close to reaching a deal but at the last minute Canada walked away from the table. "Aside from dealing with coho issues, we were there," Bob Thorstenson told the *Juneau Empire*. Don McRae retorted that the two sides were never even close to a deal.

At this point the media became sceptical about Anderson's strategy. An editorial in the *Victoria Times Colonist* on May 30 said, "It doesn't look like anyone is prepared to rein in Alaska...So far Ottawa has been tough on BC but lapsed into its usual obsequious toady routine with the Americans."

Clark told the *Nanaimo Daily News*, "Alaska has been insulting to say the least, questioning even our science, questioning whether or not we have a coho or conservation crisis...Renegade states like Alaska can't scuttle international treaties between Canada and the US." However, Mike Hunter of the Fisheries Council declared, "I'm very pleased Mr. Anderson has taken the bit between the teeth...We witnessed the collapse of the cod fishery in Atlantic Canada and we know what happens to a struggling fishery when the affected parties don't take the long view."[3] And Mark Hume of the *Vancouver Sun* praised Anderson for his conservation stance and condemned Clark for his fed-bashing.

Meanwhile, David Anderson was spending large sums of the DFO's money on newspaper and television ads for his coho conservation crusade. Brian Bohunicky, Anderson's aide, said the ads were necessary to change BC's "attitude" toward the PST dispute. Patrick Gossage, Pierre Trudeau's former press secretary, commented to the *Vancouver Sun*, "In Trudeau's era it was believed something was wrong if an ad was necessary for a government to get its message out."

On June 3, 1998, Don McRae and Roberts Owen met at the Seattle airport to discuss ways to salvage the PST negotiations, but they refused to talk to reporters after their closed-door meeting. Alaska had not changed its stand on coho conservation. BC fishermen, bitterly disappointed, threatened to "create an international incident" by blockading

Alaskan cruise ships. "If [Anderson] doesn't do something very quickly, we're going to embarrass the hell out of him," warned Kim Olsen.

Officials of the UFAWU did not endorse blocking cruise ships, but they did understand the fishermen's frustration. "I don't think it's a question of us leading that kind of stuff," said UFAWU–CAW President John Radosevic, "but if people feel forced to the wall, we're going to be right with them." Glen Clark told the *Nanaimo Daily News*, "I think it would be a mistake for fishermen to take illegal action which would cause serious disruption to the economy of British Columbia. But I do think that we can't ask fishermen to look in the eyes of their children and say they have no money, that their community is dying and that the government isn't going to help them."

The provincial opposition did not share his concern. "Tourism is a $200 million-a-year industry that employs thousands of people," Liberal Gary Farrell-Collins complained, "many of them in just as difficult straits as are the fishermen. And for us to take the problems going on in one industry and visit them on another industry...is ridiculous."[4]

John Radosevic met with the BC Council of Tourism and promised that the cruise ships would not be impeded, and the tourism sector made some vague statements in support of the fishermen's cause. Nevertheless, the negative publicity surrounding the blockade threat was never overcome.

Nonsense and Outright Lies

By late June, rumours that Anderson was about to conclude a conservation pact with Washington's Governor Locke were rampant. Bill Valentine, BC's representative at the PST talks, sent a confidential memo to Deputy Minister Doug McArthur, warning that Anderson had "personally hijacked" the negotiating process and was preparing to make major concessions on equity. He wrote that Don McRae, Canada's chief negotiator, was "almost completely marginalized" and that US negotiator James Pipkin was "both delighted and smug" at "the supplicant approach" of David Anderson's team. The federal negotiating team, he went on, believed "a bad deal is better than no deal" and they were "under considerable pressure to get a deal."

Valentine's memo, however, was leaked, and on June 25 the *Globe and Mail* reported its contents. The next day Brian Bohunicky, responded that "[Valentine's comments] are outright lies written by people with an obvious political interest in failure to reach an agreement with the US so they can continue to bash both [the Canadian and US] governments."[5] Don McRae sent an angry note to Valentine, which he also released to the media. Valentine, who had played no part in the leak, was mortified by the affair and concerned about falling out of favour with McRae and the rest of the DFO team.

Then, in an about-face, Anderson's political staff acknowledged that the minister had met privately for four hours with Governor Locke in Olympia. No deals had been made, an aide told the *Vancouver Sun* on June 27, but "We're more positive about how it is going."[6] Joy Thorkelson, the UFAWU–CAW representative on the PSC northern panel, received a tip from someone in the DFO that Anderson was willing to offer the US 25 percent of the Fraser River sockeye TAC, more than the 17 percent the Americans had asked for the previous year. But when Thorkelson made this public, Brian Bohunicky called her accusations "nonsense."

Finally, on June 26 in Seattle, Anderson and Locke jointly announced that they had agreed to a "landmark" conservation accord. Washington state agreed to reduce its catch of coho by 22 percent in exchange for a 50 percent reduction in BC's interception of Washington state chinooks. The issue of Fraser River sockeye catches remained unresolved. Governor Locke told CBC radio, "This is a breakthrough because we are committing the State of Washington to working with Canada on conservation of our salmon and recognizing that our salmon travel through each other's waters. But if we are true to conservation each side must make sacrifices, each side must step forward with tough decisions to save the icon of the Pacific Northwest."

Later that afternoon Anderson and Locke travelled to a second press conference in Richmond, BC, where they were met by a crowd of protesting fishermen. CKNW reported that one angry fisherman stood on a railing outside, banged his fist on the window and yelled, "Talk to the people who are going to lose their jobs!" Anderson, with Governor Locke at his side, responded, "My arguments are not being heard by these people…[The agreement is] an opportunity to leave behind the stalemate over who gets to catch the last few fish."

Anderson had reduced Canada's century-long struggle to gain sovereignty over its West Coast salmon resource to a matter of conserving stocks at all costs. No one in the industry who championed the equity cause had ever advocated fishing to the "last few fish," as Anderson implied. Indeed, the whole point of the equity struggle was to avoid such a dire prospect. And in negotiating his pact with Locke, Anderson had completely marginalized the advice of the Canadian national section. The deal was cobbled together by Velma McColl, Don McRae, Patrick Chamut and Anderson himself for Canada, and by Smitch, Ron Allen of the Northwest Tribes, Roberts Owen and Locke for the US. Worse, Anderson and his coterie of political advisors had set a precedent by making a deal with a US subnational government. The deal contradicted the essence of the Pacific Salmon Treaty, an international agreement reached by two sovereign nations. By making a separate deal, Anderson dispensed with the traditional Canadian strategy of forcing the northwest states to put pressure on Alaska, and he relieved the US federal government of having to reign in Alaska, as well as to uphold the equity principle. Furthermore, the Vienna Convention on the Law of Treaties establishes that signatories to an international agreement may not use domestic legislation as a pretext for violating a treaty.[7] Thus the perennial American argument that US enabling legislation gave sub-national governments such as the state of Alaska a veto over the provisions of the PST is invalid in international law. The Canadian government, fearing a negative American response, never pressed this issue in any international legal forum.

The details of the Anderson–Locke agreement were as dubious as the process of negotiation itself. BC's 50 percent reduction on interception of Washington state chinooks would allow an additional 14,000 chinook salmon (4,000 wild and 10,000 hatchery stock) to return to the state.[8] In return, Washington had agreed to curtail its harvest of coho by 22 percent, a dramatic contrast to the 100 percent restriction imposed by Anderson on BC fishermen.

While Anderson and Locke were still in Seattle at their first press conference, I consulted quickly with DFO officials to determine precisely how many endangered Thompson River coho—the focus of Minister

Anderson's environmental *cause célèbre*—would be saved by this strategy. I was told that the projected 1998 catch of coho in Washington waters was about 142,300, of which 31,085 to 66,135 would be intercepted Canadian stock. Locke's commitment to reduce the Washington coho harvest by 22 percent would therefore result in approximately 7,000 more coho being passed through to Canada. Of that number, only 264 to 440 would be from the endangered Thompson River stocks.

Obviously, the trade-off of 7,000 coho for 14,000 chinooks did not balance either numerically or financially. And the sacrifice made by Anderson was even greater by far, because the DFO's domestic coho conservation regime nullified Canada's entitlement of 360,000 chinooks and 1.8 million coho under the expired annexes of the PST. Had Canada fished in 1998 to these theoretical entitlements off the west coast of Vancouver Island, it could have seriously threatened Washington chinook and coho. Locke knew this wouldn't occur because of Anderson's coho conservation measures, yet Washington state never made an equivalent sacrifice on Fraser River sockeye. The accumulated benefits to Locke and his constituents were enormous, and the benefits to Canada were almost nil.

Before Anderson and Locke wound up their Seattle press conference, I got in touch with Mike Clark, a reporter for CKNW, who then asked Anderson exactly how many endangered Thompson River coho would be saved by the deal. Anderson had to turn to DFO officials for help. After some dithering they acknowledged that Anderson's "landmark" conservation accord protected 440 Thompson coho at most.

I briefed Premier Clark, and he convened a separate press conference in Vancouver and declared the agreement to be "a half a deal at great cost to Canada and BC. And we still don't know the worst part of it. We have essentially given away all the leverage we had." He pointed out that Washington state had gained what it needed and BC had got almost nothing. "[Anderson] has essentially bargained away 10,000 more chinook—Canadian chinook—to pass through to the US in exchange for 400 endangered coho."

Anderson told CKNW that every Thompson coho was important: "Four hundred fish may be just what you need," he said. On June 27 he told Sandra Bullock of the *Victoria Times Colonist*, "I care about the people of tomorrow, next year, five years hence, our kids. Their parents who have made a professional job out of opposing this agreement simply don't understand that the kids coming along will see this as a turning point."

Bullock noted that more than just "professional protestors" had objected to the deal. She quoted Russ Hellberg, mayor of Port Hardy and chair of the Coastal Community Network, as saying, "Anderson has literally given away the farm for not a damn thing. It's just disbelief over here." And John Young of the BC Sustainable Fisheries Group pointed out that had Washington state's chinook stocks been put on the ESA list, there would have been no need for Anderson to give away BC fish: the Americans "wouldn't be allowed to catch our coho because the coho intermingle with the chinook."

The Facts (Plus a Lot of Sockeye) on the Table

The day after Anderson's announcement, Glen Clark vowed to kill the deal and accused the federal government of treason. Ottawa officials announced that it was time "to put some facts on the table," and on Sunday, June 28, Ross Howard of the *Globe and Mail* reported that a team of anonymous federal officials had held a highly unusual emergency media briefing. They said Clark's criticism could jeopardize the remaining two days of talks scheduled before the July 1 deadline, and one high-ranking DFO official, who refused to be named, declared that for Clark "to characterize these talks as treasonous is either grossly misinformed or deliberately dishonest." No DFO staff could or would provide an example of where Clark was wrong, but the headline of the *Vancouver Province* on Monday, June 29, screamed: "Clark blasted by Feds."

When the press questioned why there was only a 22 percent reduction in the Washington state coho catch but a zero mortality regime was imposed on Canadians, an anonymous official replied, "We had to do zero percent in Canada in any event to save our coho. It [the 22 percent harvest reduction in Washington] is a small step, but it's an important one we can build on."

The officials then admitted that Canada had proposed a limit of 25 percent on the Washington state harvest of sockeye. Yet only a few days earlier, Anderson's staff had dismissed as "nonsense"—Joy Thorkelson's suggestion that Canada was about to make further concessions on sockeye. The DFO took great pain to rationalize this decision, explaining that the Americans had demanded 30 percent of the catch in 1998.

Premier Clark lambasted Ottawa for even considering a figure higher than Fortier's last offer of 17 percent of the Fraser catch in June 1997, and the DFO said the 1998 Fraser sockeye run was forecast to be much lower than 1997, so a 25 percent ceiling for Washington state would result in a catch of only 1.25 million fish, 100,000 less than in 1997—or just a bigger share of a smaller pie. Numerically, they said, it was still a good deal for Canada. In fact, the American catch of Fraser sockeye for the previous three cycle years of the 1998 run had been 22.6 percent in 1986, 13.9 percent in 1990 and 14.1 percent in 1994, an average of 16.86 percent. During those years Canada had enjoyed annual harvests of several hundred thousand US-bound coho and chinook, which offset the interception balance. In 1998, thanks to the Anderson Plan, those harvests were reduced to zero.

On July 4, I attended a large press conference on the sockeye "deal" in which Anderson appeared by video hookup from Ottawa. I did my best to refute Anderson's claim that the sockeye deal was consistent with the Strangway–Ruckelshaus directive to move fish to Canada, but Strangway himself declared by speakerphone, "William Ruckelshaus and I discussed the deal and we're pleased conservation came first."[9] Any hope that the Strangway–Ruckelshaus process would balance the catch between the two countries was gone.

By the Canada Day holiday, the negotiating deadline set by Don McRae and Roberts Owen had passed and no comprehensive interim fishing plan, as ordered by the special envoys six months before, had been reached. On July 2 the *Victoria Times Colonist* reported that Minister Anderson had extended the deadline. "If they need more time, they obviously have something to talk about," he said hopefully. But he had little to show for all his "diplomatic" efforts. His coho conservation deal had foundered in the face of severe criticism, and he still had no interim agreement for Fraser sockeye. Above all, there was no movement at all from the state of Alaska.

CHAPTER 14

The Blockade of Seymour Narrows

Appeasers believe that if you keep on throwing steaks to a tiger, the tiger will turn vegetarian.

—Heywood Broun, American journalist and novelist

In 1998 for the fifth consecutive year, the commercial fishery in British Columbia commenced without the terms of the Pacific Salmon Treaty in full effect. Despite all the fanfare accompanying the Locke–Anderson conservation accord, the problem of Alaskan overfishing remained unresolved. The recently announced Anderson Plan had wreaked havoc on the commercial fishery in BC in the name of coho conservation: hundreds of thousands of Skeena coho were being slaughtered just across the border. In fact, by the end of the 1998 season, no fewer than 2.9 million coho—870,000 of which were estimated to be from BC rivers—were landed in southeast Alaska.[1] This disparity was an embarrassment even to Fisheries Minister David Anderson, and his political team worked feverishly behind the scenes, well past the negotiating deadline of July 1, to strike a deal with the Alaskans.

DFO issued a special operations command order on July 2, 1998: "As a result of the 1998 salmon management plan [the Anderson Plan], and the need to protect Skeena River coho stocks, Canada will not be conducting commercial salmon fisheries in the disputed area in

Dixon Entrance. Following discussions between the Canadian and US Pacific Salmon Treaty negotiators, Alaska has advised that there will be no US commercial salmon fishing within the disputed area in Dixon Entrance."[2]

According to Anderson's staff, the state of Alaska had, for the first time since the inception of the PST, engaged in substantive and productive talks with the government of Canada. On July 3 Anderson's aide Brian Bohunicky acknowledged to the *Vancouver Sun* that "eliminating" Alaskan fisheries in Dixon Entrance was only a small step, but he suggested further "significant" progress was likely in the near future.[3] The press heralded the agreement as another diplomatic coup for Anderson, although it was Alaska, not Canada, that had achieved the long-sought historic breakthrough.

A Nuclear Submarine Highway

Dixon Entrance is a wild place. Fierce tide rips swirl over the western edge of the Learmonth bank and clash with the huge swells rolling in from the north Pacific. To the south lies Graham Island, the largest of the Queen Charlotte Islands, and to the east the rugged Dundas and Zayas islands. On a clear day, from the middle of Dixon Entrance one can see Dall Island, Prince of Wales Island and Cape Fox, floating surrealistically above the horizon at the southern end of the Alaskan panhandle. Dixon Entrance teems with marine life and is therefore a favourite haunt of Canadian salmon trollers, halibut longliners and trawlers. More important, it is a strategic access route for American vessels, especially nuclear submarines, bound for panhandle military bases, which are otherwise surrounded by a labyrinth of reefs and islands to the west.

The political history of these waters is long and disputatious, beginning with the Alaska purchase in 1867 and continuing with the establishment of a boundary by a tribunal of six men. "By their award of October 20, 1903, Cape Muzon became the point of commencement of the boundary, and the islands lying off Portland Channel were divided by the two nations. By a majority decision a continuous fringe of coast not exceeding ten marine leagues in width, was to separate the British possession from the seacoast between the 65th parallel and Cross Sound."[4]

Nevertheless, in the years that followed, the Canadian government refused even to acknowledge, much less discuss—at least in public—the American claim. Canada maintained its sovereignty over Dixon Entrance with a large fleet of trollers, who traditionally fished along the "A–B" line. Occasionally the trollers were harassed by the US Coast Guard, even though they were operating on the Canadian side, and American vessels were routinely spotted operating in Canadian waters. Twice during the 1981 season US vessels were arrested for fishing in the middle of Dixon Entrance. Canadian fishermen responded with a blockade of Prince Rupert harbour for four hours on June 26, 1981, and more than 100 trollers commemorated Canada Day by staging a six-hour "fish-in" along the A–B line. Tom Perry, the DFO's acting northern manager said, "The government feels that such actions would jeopardize our present fairly shaky international position if we get too defiant."[5]

Eight years later, on July 7, 1989, two Canadian trollers—the *Viscount* and the *Fonzie*—were forcefully boarded by armed US Coast Guard personnel. Bruce Devereaux, skipper of the *Viscount*, was physically assaulted while attempting to resist arrest. Both vessels were made to travel to Ketchikan, where their catch was confiscated. Before surrendering, the Canadian skippers contacted DFO officials, who counselled them not to resist and offered vague assurances of political protection. But they failed to defend the two Canadian fishermen, who eventually lost their catch and faced heavy fines before being released.

These boundary skirmishes aside, the A–B line remained an indisputable symbol of Canadian sovereignty—until David Anderson and his political advisors tacitly accepted the Alaskan claim to half of Dixon Entrance in return for some cheap publicity. American designs on Dixon Entrance were not limited to the requirements of the Alaskan fishing fleet. Indeed, the crux of the Dixon Entrance dispute relates directly to the US military. In October 1991, then NDP MP Jim Fulton (Skeena) released a secret federal cabinet memo by the Mulroney Tories that authorized the unrestricted passage of US nuclear submarines through Dixon Entrance, "to protect Canada's legal position [in the Dixon Entrance dispute]...And to offer support to the objective of improving the effectiveness of the US submarine-based nuclear deterrent." The memo also acknowledged that British Columbians would oppose the decision, so the announcement, planned for September 3, 1991, was postponed indefinitely. When Fulton warned the House of Commons that Dixon Entrance was about to become a "nuclear submarine highway," Tory Environment Minister Jean Charest replied, "I'm glad to see the honourable member probably found the de-coder ring in his cereal box."[6]

The Americans appear to believe it is their God-given right to sail military vessels through Dixon Entrance or anywhere else on earth, and Ottawa appears to believe that this is not a problem. The US went along with the pretence of Canadian sovereignty in Dixon Entrance as long as its military interests were not compromised. By acknowledging without protest that the Alaskans "might" have fished in Dixon Entrance, Anderson participated in validating their long-standing claim to its waters. And the ostensible purpose of the deal he had struck—the protection of endangered coho—was meaningless: the Americans' interceptions of BC coho continued unabated. In a press release, the Alaska Fish and Game Department said, "The countries have been unable to agree on the status of coho salmon stocks in the Northern Boundary area. In recognition of this uncertainty and with respect to the claims of each country of the waters of the Dixon Entrance District, these waters will be closed."[7] In response to those who questioned whether the "closure" in Dixon Entrance was really a concession to Canada, Bob King, Governor Knowles' press secretary, insisted, "We regularly fish there."

Some senior DFO officials in the Pacific Region privately expressed embarrassment over Anderson's Dixon Entrance "deal," but not one of them spoke out in public. And one mid-level manager in the Prince Rupert office of the DFO told the *Vancouver Sun* on October 3 that the Dixon Entrance agreement was worthwhile because "in its absence the Alaskans might have fished in Dixon Entrance, even though they had never done so before...For once we have an agreement."

Not a Disaster After All

After the Dixon Entrance announcement, Anderson's staff tried to extract further concessions from the Alaskans. On July 10, however, the minister admitted that efforts to obtain a comprehensive conservation agreement with Alaska for the 1998 season had been abandoned. The Upper Skeena coho crisis warranted draconian cuts in Canada's domestic fishery, Anderson insisted, but he discounted the effect of an unregulated Alaskan fishery on those same stocks. "This is not a disaster. It would have been better, preferable to have an agreement," he said, "but what was on the table was unacceptable. I said earlier I wouldn't sign a bad deal and I mean it." He told the press that he was confident the Alaskans would "fish responsibly" in 1998.[8]

John Radosevic, president of the UFAWU–CAW, responded, "The [conservation] sacrifice we're making is therefore irrelevant and wasted." Only a few days before, Radosevic had threatened that fishermen would anchor their vessels in the middle of the Nanoose Bay testing range as part of a symbolic "picnic" should Anderson fail to deliver a deal. The *Anchorage Daily News* reported that Bob King had replied, "We don't respond well to threats. Our focus is on Skeena River fish rather than torpedo ranges." And Anderson dismissed the UFAWU's threat: "The union and the province have a love affair with illegal activity. I would strongly advise against it... [I]t's very, very difficult for that union, which has been for years one of the most radical left-wing unions and it's had a leadership which has been so radical, to adjust to new conditions. I can understand the problems of Mr. Radosevic. He's got a lot of hard-liners who just want to do it in the old way..."[9]

As for endangered Skeena River coho, on July 10 Alaska's Fish and Game Commissioner Frank Rue told the *Victoria Times Colonist*, "We don't think we're talking about biological extinction [of coho]." And Dale Kelley, executive director of the Alaska Trollers Association, added, "This is our bread and butter... You're getting mismanagement from Ottawa." The Alaskans claimed that the lack of a new treaty annex was irrelevant since they could unilaterally monitor and control the bycatch of Canadian coho.

In the meantime, Premier Clark, called the collapse of the talks "a full-blown crisis" and called upon Anderson to reintroduce the transit fee on vessels travelling to and from Alaska. "There has to be retaliation," Clark told Justine Hunter of the *Vancouver Sun* on July 10, "which tries to convince these Americans that a rogue state like Alaska, with 400,000 people, can't stand up to a respected nation like Canada and can't destroy the future of the salmon for our children." Washington Governor Gary

Locke said, "It comes down to the Alaskans. They have to stop catching so many fish from Canada as well as from Washington and Oregon."

But former Washington State governor Mike Lowry—himself a Democrat—pointed out that the Republican sweep of both Congressional houses in 1995 had greatly stiffened Alaskan intransigence: "It's not Knowles' [Democratic governor of Alaska] fault this is happening. It's Stevens and Murkowski [Republican senators]. For a while it looked like the Clinton administration was going to step in, but Stevens, Murkowski and Young [Alaska congressman] got their way."[10] Both Stevens and Murkowski chaired important Congressional committees—Appropriations and Natural Resources—which allowed them to exert powerful influence over Locke, Knowles and even the White House.

Tossing West Coast Fishermen to the Wolves

The collapse of the talks with Alaska was a cruel blow to North Coast fishermen, who were already reeling from the effects of Anderson's zero mortality coho policy. On July 12, CBC Radio's *Summer Daybreak* interviewed a number of Prince Rupert fishermen about their plight. "We're dead," said one unidentified fisherman bitterly. "Over! Done! Our own government is conspiring against us…We're not being supported by our federal fisheries. They've abandoned us. They've tossed us to the wolves. They don't care." Another fisherman added, "Because the DFO allows over-escapement of the Skeena [sockeye] because of the sports fishing sector up the Skeena here, the Alaskans decided…that there's no reason why a million extra fish should go up the Skeena and rot on the spawning banks. They're taking this extra million fish—which has happened now for seven or eight years of over-escapement, even though they're really fishing hard. We conserve because of steelhead concerns, because of spring [chinook] concerns, because of coho concerns, and they take the fish."

The urban-based media were still favourably impressed with Anderson. On July 4, 1998, Stephen Hume wrote in the *Vancouver Sun*: "For once we have a politician with backbone instead of bluster who's prepared to do what must be done before it's too late. For this he endures the abuse of fools. If you care about coho survival, tell Anderson to stand in there, that you're on his side, not Jurassic Clark's." Hume's colleague Barbara Yaffe added, "[Anderson] knows that you can only push the Yankee behemoth so far. He's done what he's had to do ... But also, he has in mind the fact that Canada's overall bilateral trade relationship with the United States is worth $1.5 billion, billion with a 'B,' per day, versus the fact the BC salmon fishery is worth just $400 million annually."

On the other hand, wrote Kevin Potvin in the *Vancouver Echo* on July 22, "What Anderson is expected by the Liberal party executives to do is not save the fish, per se, but to contain the fishery crisis and keep it a purely regional problem ... With Anderson as bagboy, Ottawa has traded the livelihood of coastal communities and the future of fish stocks in British Columbia for concessions on other matters more dear to constituents in Liberal ridings in Ontario ... "

But the public was convinced that BC fishermen were to blame for the coho conservation crisis, and Premier Clark could not manoeuvre on the PST issue as effectively as he had. Like a king on a chessboard, he was put in check by the combined pressure of the Americans, Ottawa bureaucrats, the tourist industry, the sports fishing lobby, the press and the environmentalists. On July 14 he tried to break the impasse by chartering a plane and taking a group of reporters to the A–B line to witness an Alaskan gillnet fishery target Canadian sockeye. I went along to offer technical details and some history on the Dixon Entrance boundary dispute. The reporters seemed offended by a hundred or so Alaskan gillnetters clustered at Tree Point, at the extreme southwest of the panhandle, when the Canadian fishery was closed. Yet all of us, including Clark, were amused when some of the Alaskan crews pulled down their pants and bared their buttocks in defiance. Later we travelled to Port Simpson, a BC Native village just 20 km (12 miles) from the A–B line, where the entire population turned out in ceremonial dress to greet the premier.

Lax Kw'Alaams Chief Gary Reece explained how the Alaskan interceptions had affected his community. "It's taken a lot of our salmon away," he told the reporters. "...It makes me quite angry to see they are fishing four or five days out of the week whereas our fishermen are getting 15 hours an opening."[11]

The story of the A–B line fishery occupied the media's attention for only a day. Even Premier Clark had to turn his attention to other pressing issues for the rest of the summer. In the meantime, with the Alaskan fishery operating at full capacity, BC commercial fishermen were thrust into the maelstrom of the 1998 salmon season.

Protest Activities in the Area

Of all the treacherous waters along the BC coast, few command as much respect from mariners as Seymour Narrows, just north of Campbell River. Here the powerful currents of Johnstone Strait, the Gulf of Georgia and several mainland inlets meet in an awesome tidal vector, forced twice daily through a gap only 600 metres (1980 ft) wide. Vessels can be capsized suddenly by the gaping whirlpools and tide rips that swirl through the channel during the peak of the ebb and flood. Between 1875 and 1958, Seymour Narrows claimed 114 lives and sank 119 vessels, the first of which was the USS *Saranac*, an American sidewheel steamer bound for Alaska in 1875. The rapids were calmed somewhat in 1958 when Ripple Rock, a treacherous reef in the centre of the narrows, was dynamited in the world's largest non-nuclear explosion.

Fortunately, Seymour Narrows also serves as the gateway to the sheltered waters of BC's fabled Inside Passage, and the task of keeping the narrows safe for marine traffic has been a prime occupation of the Pacific regional Coast Guard. It was a shock, therefore, when on the morning of August 27, 1998, a large fleet of commercial fish boats steamed toward Seymour Narrows with the firm intention of barring passage through it.

As the first cool breath of autumn floated in with the tide from Johnstone Strait, two traditional Native war canoes, each with a crew of 14 men paddling in synchronized rhythm, skimmed the sunlit waters just south of the narrows. Immediately behind them was a flotilla of more than 50 seine boats, most of them crewed by members of the local Campbell River and Cape Mudge Indian bands. Over the VHF marine radios of the seiners came the Coast Guard's warning that all mariners avoid Seymour Narrows because of protest activities in the area. A large contingent of reporters buzzed about in airplanes and speedboats, as did armed RCMP and DFO officials. On shore in Campbell River a throng of supporters and bystanders had assembled. Two toddlers in the crowd,

Fishermen and First Nations protesters blockade Seymour Narrows, August 1998.

Bradlee Dick and Shelby Ordano, held signs: "We need food, shelter, and clothes" and "All I wish is that my Daddy could fish!"

Two days before the blockade, I had represented the premier's office at a meeting of Native and non-Native commercial fishermen at the Thunderbird Hall in Campbell River. The organizers had invited the DFO to come and explain why the South Coast (Area B) seine fleet had only fished for 15 hours during the entire 1998 season, despite the large numbers of Fraser River sockeye pouring through Johnstone Strait, but Donna Petrachenko, the Pacific Region director, had declined. Eventually the Campbell River protest forced Petrachenko to fly to Campbell River with a police escort. Once there, however, she announced that she would only meet with a delegation of six fishermen, instead of attending a public rally held on the day she arrived. The protestors had vowed to meet with DFO representatives en masse or not at all, and Chief John Henderson told the overflow crowd that the DFO and in particular Minister Anderson had insulted his people by refusing to meet with them. "Empty promises, lies, and press releases do not meet the needs of fish," said Henderson. "There will be a fight if he refuses to meet with us." Gerry Roberts, one of the more militant seine skippers in the crowd, said, "Anderson lied to us for three weeks with the hope of an opening. Let's go out and show 'em we mean business." Charles McKee, a troller, claimed that Anderson and his department had violated section 119 of the Criminal Code by refusing to open the fishery. "He's robbed us of our livelihood," said McKee. "the RCMP should arrest him, not us."[12]

It was shortly after this stormy exchange that the group made the decision to blockade Seymour Narrows.

The Long Hot Summer of '98

The 1998 fishing season had been a disaster for South Coast commercial fishermen right from the start. The Pacific Salmon Commission had forecast that 11.2 million sockeye, including the famous Adams River run, would return to the Fraser River. Such a run would once have been considered a bonanza, but with the DFO's new risk–averse management approach, an escapement goal of 6 million sockeye was established— three times the spawners the department had traditionally required on this cycle. This left a total catch of only 5.3 million to be taken in all fisheries that year.

To make matters worse, David Anderson's deal with Governor Locke had guaranteed the Americans 24.9 percent of the catch right off the top. DFO biologists had advised Anderson that the run would return to the river via the Strait of Juan de Fuca. They feared that without an agreement the Americans would take 60 percent or more of the run, so they convinced Anderson—and later the press—that an American share of 24.9 percent, though well above the cycle average catch of 18 percent was a very good deal for Canada.

The biologists were wrong. Ninety percent of the run returned through Johnstone Strait. Few sockeye migrated through US waters, and the department had an extremely difficult job delivering the Americans their 24.9 percent, a share that was mandatory because of the Anderson–Locke agreement, which stated that the Canadian fisheries were to be managed "in a manner that anticipates and accommodates catches in the US fisheries."[13] Anderson insisted that the DFO do all in its power to live up to the agreement's terms, even if it meant closing the Canadian fishery in Johnstone Strait at the peak of the run.

On August 11, with most of southern BC blanketed in forest fire smoke, the Fraser panel of the PSC met to discuss the early summer run, which at that point was struggling through the Fraser Canyon. So far, it was the hottest summer on record, with an average temperature of 16.5°C (61°F), 0.7 degrees hotter than normal. Locally, Kamloops had recorded a temperature of 39.9°C (104°F), and the town of Salmon Arm, not far from the Adams River spawning beds, was threatened by a 5,000-hectare blaze in the nearby hills. Steve MacDonald of DFO warned the panel that high temperatures in the Fraser could kill 40 percent of the sockeye run.

Wayne Saito, the chair of the Canadian section of the panel, recommended that Canada increase the sockeye escapement goal by reducing the harvest rate of the fishery by a further 40 percent. This would halt commercial fishing for the balance of the season, and the panel debated it hotly. DFO officials knew it would be nearly impossible to impose a similar closure on the Native sector because the Aboriginal Fishing Strategy pilot sales fishery had been a problem all season long. In early July the Musqueam Band had threatened to defy DFO closures, and on July 13 Sam Douglas, a former chief of the Cheam Band, had organized a Native protest fishery on the severely depressed early Stuart sockeye run. When his armed protestors were approached by DFO officers, they had refused to cease fishing. Terry Tebb, a high-ranking DFO official, was dispatched to the Cheam reserve to quell the protest, but instead of charging the protestors, Tebb compromised and allowed them to continue fishing. That same summer Douglas was involved in a violent altercation with US customs officials at the Canada–US border. Although the Cheam Band had not signed a pilot sales agreement with the DFO, Douglas had been caught carrying 11,250 kg (25,000 lbs) of sockeye worth $16,000 (US) across the border.[14]

It was in this supercharged atmosphere that the DFO announced that thousands of Fraser sockeye were dying because of high water temperatures in the canyon. Then on August 10 Saito tried to persuade his American counterpart, Dennis Austin, to reduce the American commercial harvests of Fraser sockeye by at least 40 percent. Austin refused, saying that American fishermen were at least 120,000 pieces short of their 24.9 percent allocation. It was Canada, he said, not the United States, that was in the "conservation box."[15]

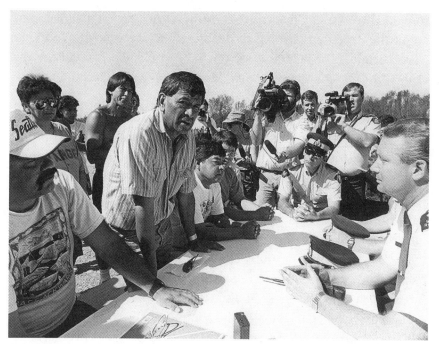

Sam Douglas, a leader of the Sto:lo Nation, blocks the CN Railway near Chilliwack to protest DFO closure of Aboriginal Fishing Strategy pilot sales program, July 1998.

On the morning of August 13, 1998, Clark's deputy, Doug McArthur, instructed me to accompany a BCTV film crew in a helicopter flight over the Point Roberts fishery. There we saw about 50 US seiners hauling their nets a stone's throw from the BC Ferries Tsawwassen terminal. Two days earlier, on the west coast of Vancouver Island, the 15-day fishery for the BC troll fleet had been halted after only eight days. With the fish passing rapidly through their licence area, they were told that every remaining fish was needed for escapement. Now, in light of what was happening off Point Roberts, Cathy Scarfo of the Area G Trollers Association told the *Vancouver Sun*: "It's clear the Americans have a priority over conservation. The DFO has jeopardized the livelihood of coastal BC in exchange for a bad deal with the Americans." Wayne Saito of the DFO replied, "We would prefer the US not fish, but the terms of the [Anderson–Locke] agreement stipulate a number of options for them."

Outraged, Premier Clark demanded that the Americans stop fishing immediately, and he announced that he would reactivate BC's $375 million lawsuit over US overfishing. Minister Anderson remained silent about the Americans fishing in defiance, but was quick to condemn Clark's action. "The BC court case might be won and be a totally pyrrhic victory," he told the *Vancouver Sun*, "even assuming that it could be won, which is highly unlikely."

"These are excuses," snapped Clark. "If he doesn't like our court case, what action is he contemplating? The answer is none." And Christopher Harvey, a Vancouver marine lawyer, wrote, "By allowing increased interceptions, the Alaskan authorities are themselves in breach of their own fisheries law."[16]

By the time the Point Roberts fishery ended on August 15, the Americans had taken another 100,000 sockeye, bringing them very close to their 24.9 percent allocation. That controversy had hardly subsided before problems erupted in the Native fishery in the Fraser Canyon. On August 17 the BC Fisheries Survival Coalition threatened a protest fishery because the DFO had closed the commercial fishery on the grounds that stocks were at risk yet authorized a Native fishery. On August 17, Phil Eidsvik of the BCFSC told the *Vancouver Sun* that "The DFO is carrying on an illegal fishery that unfairly divides fishermen."

Dave Wheeler of Fort Langley added, "There's documented evidence that [the catch] is being sold. One way or the other the government's got to address this issue, or it's only going to get worse." The DFO would never admit that it had bowed to pressure from the coalition, but the next day it cancelled the AFS fishery, bringing the 1998 salmon season to an abrupt close.

Blocking the Narrows

As the flotilla of protest vessels massed at the entrance to Seymour Narrows on August 27, the fishermen insisted on a meeting with Anderson and Chamut, Saito and Sprout of the DFO. They demanded that the minister provide immediate compensation for the mismanagement of the 1998 Fraser sockeye run. They also called for an independent review of the management of the Fraser sockeye fishery in 1998, the restructuring of the DFO for local control of Johnstone Strait rather than by the Pacific Salmon Commission, and the assurance of equitable allocation for all user groups. As well they demanded guaranteed traditional commercial catch levels for the Cape Scott to Cape Mudge area and immediate funding for their own observers to monitor Fraser River escapements. Finally they wanted the minister to explain how the US had acquired a priority over Canadian fisheries.

David Anderson refused to respond to the protestors. He issued a press statement saying that he would never meet with them in response to "threats of illegal activity. To do so would only encourage similar actions by others." This caused Reform MP John Reynolds (West Vancouver–Sunshine Coast) to issue his own press statement: "The minister can defuse a threatened blockade of Seymour Narrows by simply granting these frightened and frustrated fishermen an hour of his time. The last time we had a blockade, the minister was nowhere to be found and I suggest this time he saves the country any further embarrassment and gets to Campbell River. A blockade can be avoided if the minister can lose his pretence for a moment, ignore his spin-doctors and media hacks and give these fishermen a chance to state their case."

The lack of fish, Anderson insisted, had made closure of the fishery necessary. His statement flew in the face of the facts: the test fishery had shown the run was exceptionally strong, and the test catch in Johnstone Strait for the four days prior to the blockade—26,000, 11,366, 24,661 and 15,268—proved that there were large numbers of sockeye in the area. The weaker late run and the stronger summer run had unexpectedly overlapped, making it difficult to separate them for harvest purposes, so Anderson, committed to risk–averse management, was determined to forbid commercial fishing in Johnstone Strait, regardless of the traditional assessment methodology espoused by the Pacific Salmon Commission. In a report in 1995 to the Fraser Sockeye Review Panel, PSC staff had written:

> Historically, regression of run size on peak week catch and CPUE for purse seine fisheries in Juan de Fuca and Johnstone straits was the major source of run-size information. In Area 20 and Areas 12 and 13, fish are confined to relatively narrow migration routes and are highly vulnerable to purse seine fisheries. These fisheries harvest

sockeye which are from four to eight days' migration distance from the Strait of Georgia. Catch information from fisheries early in the week normally provide estimates for Friday panel meetings and allow for the development of fishing plans in Panel Area and non-Area fisheries for the following week. These models require accurate estimates of total purse seine catch and gear count by area and information on the duration of each fishery and area restrictions...Purse seine catch models are, therefore, particularly important for assessing late-run sockeye abundance because they provide run-size estimates early enough to adjust outside fisheries to meet escapement and catch allocation goals.[17]

Fraser panel chair Wayne Saito, though claiming to be sympathetic to fishermen, took no steps to see if the fleet could selectively crop the strong summer-run stock and avoid the late run. Instead, he told the press, commercial seine licence holders had been given the option before the season started of receiving a one-time cash payment of $10,500 rather than fishing. Those who had chosen to stay in the fishery had to accept that they had gambled and lost. Saito did not mention that $10,500 would scarcely cover a vessel owner's moorage and basic maintenance costs.

In the late afternoon of August 27 the blockade was temporarily suspended, and the flotilla returned to Campbell River to discuss further action. The next day Premier Clark abandoned his holiday and flew to Campbell River to meet with the protestors. They were preparing to block the narrows a second time, and Clark, often accused of being too confrontational, assumed the role of peacemaker. He promised a provincial inquiry into the management of the 1998 salmon season if the fishermen would forsake further blockades, and they agreed. Former Newfoundland Premier Brian Peckford, now a BC resident, was appointed to the job and was given a month to prepare an interim report on what had gone wrong. Brian Bohunicky dismissed the inquiry as "an empty gesture. Mr. Clark doesn't need an inquiry. He needs a briefing on how salmon conservation decisions are made...The problem is a lack of fish. And all the fed-bashing in the world won't change that."[18]

Anderson did not allow DFO staff to appear before the Peckford Inquiry, which he told the *Vancouver Sun* was "inappropriate and politically motivated." This posed a serious problem for Peckford, who needed DFO expertise to complete his work. His old rival, John Crosbie, the former Tory fisheries minister who had presided over the East Coast cod collapse, declared that Peckford's main function "is to criticize what the federal government does and try to blame it for everything." Six years earlier Crosbie had threatened to quit Brian Mulroney's cabinet if massive public funding were not made available for the Atlantic Groundfish Subsidy. Similar support programs for the West Coast might have reduced the pressure on both the DFO and fishermen during the 1998 season and might even have allowed Anderson to advance his conservation agenda. Ottawa certainly had the money, including a $19 billion surplus in the Employment Insurance fund, partly because of a policy that made it difficult for seasonal workers such as commercial fishermen to qualify for benefits.

On September 6, a day after the Peckford Inquiry began, the Pacific Salmon Commission announced that the preliminary estimate of the 1998 Fraser sockeye run was only 9.1 million, about 2 million short of the original forecast of 11.2 million. As well, the late run, which was bound for the Adams River, was only 1.7 million instead of the 3 million forecast. Anderson seemed vindicated in his zealous conservation stand. At the same time, however, thanks to the Anderson–Locke agreement, American fishermen had enjoyed a much better season than their Canadian counterparts. The total commercial catch for Canada had been 1,256,000, with most of the commercial licence areas far below their target shares; the US catch was 708,000, or 21.5 percent of the total catch—just below the targeted 24.9 percent but well above the cycle share of 14.8 percent in 1994 and 14.4 percent in 1990. The Canadian sports catch was 18,000 and the aboriginal catch a healthy 844,000 pieces, not including a further 99,000 taken in a surplus-to-spawning escapement fishery.

However, several months later the PSC released its final report on the 1998 sockeye return, quietly showing the run size as 10,850,000—just

3 percent below the pre-season forecast.[19] An astounding escapement of 4.6 million fish had been ushered past the commercial fleet, and so history had repeated itself. As in the cycle year of 1994—the year of the Fraser Inquiry—the public had been led to believe that the Fraser River run was at the brink of disaster, but the spawning escapement had been more than adequate. And once again, commercial fishermen had been cast in the role of irresponsible villains.

CHAPTER 15

A Question of Balance

Licence retirement will significantly improve the finan- cial viability of those who remain in the commercial fishery... The commercial sector is expected to be substantially better off following the current Licence Retirement Program... The remaining commercial fleet will be the primary beneficiary of these increased har- vest levels.

—DFO New Directions Policy Paper, 1998

On September 28, 1998, after hearing from more than 500 people and attending 10 public meetings, Brian Peckford released his interim report, which he titled *A Question of Balance*. In the preface, he wrote, "There is an emergency on the Pacific Coast, and the federal gov- ernment must give fishermen and their families the same attention and resources that they provided fishermen and their families on the East Coast when government actions created similar hardship for citizens of Canada."

He said that the DFO had botched the 1998 season by adopting "an over-zealous 'preservationist' policy" that undermined "a prudent management system with reasonable conservation and harvest factors": "From late June until late September this year, 10.9 million sockeye returned to our waters, 2,981,000 sockeye were caught and 7,836,200 passed Mission. This was the biggest escapement and 2nd smallest catch this cycle since 1950...From Prince Rupert to Chilliwack, people asked me to investigate why—given the large number of sockeye they could see migrating towards the Gulf of Georgia—they were not given more opportunity to fish what was to their eyes, a very big run."

Peckford said that Fisheries Minister David Anderson's deal with Washington state Governor Gary Locke on July 2 had been "unprecedented, and a step backwards from previous positions, and [it] failed to recognize the full potential of the Strangway & Ruckelshaus recommendations in January 1998."[1]

A legal opinion by Robin Junger, a Victoria lawyer, was appended to the report. Junger wrote, "by negotiating directly with individual US states Canada may have diminished its ability to demand acceptable and comprehensive national positions from the US in future negotiations, which are essential to long-term cooperation and conservation."[2]

Peckford's report was critical of the DFO but contained none of the gratuitous rhetoric that David Anderson and former Fisheries Minister John Crosbie had predicted. The report included a list of recommendations designed to improve the management of the fishery, and a call for financial assistance to West Coast fishing families.

A Tiresome Little Charade

The Peckford Inquiry may have been doomed to fail right from the start. The original "media roll-out" for August 28, 1998—the day the Seymour Narrows protestors agreed to end their blockade—had been intended as the occasion for the premier to announce the inquiry. But Clark had gone further before the cheering crowd in Campbell River: he had accused David Anderson and the DFO of mismanaging the fishery. Whatever truth there was in this claim, Clark appeared to be prejudging the inquiry's outcome before it had even started. This left him vulnerable to charges that the whole exercise was a propaganda stunt at the taxpayer's expense, and those charges were made.

In the fall of 1998, with a provincial election imminent, the local media paid little attention to the crisis facing the West Coast fishery or the content of Peckford's report. On August 29, an editorial in the

Vancouver Sun cynically dismissed Peckford as "Clark's stenographer." As for the fishermen's protests that had led to the Peckford Inquiry, the editors wrote, "This is a tiresome little charade whose rituals, as all participants know well, are as formalized as kabuki theatre."

The media were not alone in attacking the Peckford Inquiry. Two days before the Peckford Report was to be released, the David Suzuki Foundation released a report by Terry Glavin, a former newspaper reporter, titled *Last Call: The Will to Save Pacific Salmon*. Glavin declared that the commercial fishery had to be radically restructured to ensure the biodiversity and sustainability of salmon stocks: "It's time to face the fact that the 'industry,' as we know it, is over and must be replaced by something new...The Pacific Salmon fishery will never return to 'the good old days'." The fishery needed to become more "selective" in its harvest methods, Glavin wrote, and "mixed stock" fisheries like that in Johnstone Strait had to be eliminated. However, unlike the Copes Report of May 1998, *Last Call* provided no details on how fishing methods might be improved. And few people in the commercial fishing industry were nostalgic for the "good old days." For working people the industry has always been a place of alienation and struggle, whose conditions are set by forces far beyond their control or liking. Fishermen, too, were in favour of "something new" as long as they were included in the process of change. The Mifflin and Anderson plans—both of which Glavin enthusiastically supported—offered little such hope to working people in the fishery.

Glavin then offered a personal assessment of the economic viability of the industry. Even if there was no conservation crisis, he wrote, the commercial fishery would have to be downsized because of declining salmon prices. In an argument almost indistinguishable from that of the big canners, he declared that the excess capacity of the harvesting sector had to be reduced if the fishery was to be viable. He did not mention the wide discrepancy between prices received by working fishermen and those paid by consumers. In 1988 fishermen got only a dollar per pound of sockeye, and the processors were charging up to three times that amount in the marketplace. Glavin also echoed the DFO's economists in complaining about "too many fishermen chasing too few fish," but did not mention that the canners were showing little interest in investing in new value-added products or exploring new markets. After the 1994 provincial inquiry into the fishery, the BC Seafood Sector Council had been established, co-chaired by former UFAWU President Jack Nichol and Don Millerd, a processor. Under the leadership of Joe Weiler, a UBC law professor, this council had tried to develop innovative processes to increase the industry's economic output and allow independent owner-operators to remain viable.[3] Neither Ottawa nor Victoria was prepared to make a long-term investment in this work. The council's effectiveness gradually withered, and the canners reorganized the processing sector around cheap salmon imported from Alaska.

A central theme of Glavin's report was the failure of the Pacific Salmon Treaty to achieve its objectives, "which were to avoid harvest-share disputes between Canada and the United States. Instead it has caused significant strains in relations between Canada and the US, and even between Canada and the province of British Columbia." He called for a new treaty, "informed by the importance of maintaining biological diversity in salmon populations, rather than by only short-term industrial purposes," but offered no strategy for negotiating such a treaty, given 100 years of US intransigence. In Glavin's view it was a mistake to mount a strong nationalist defence of Canada's equity interests at the PST table. "Such disputes are a luxury the salmon, and the public, can no longer afford," he wrote. "… The current disputes between Canada and the US, and the governments of BC and Canada, are detracting from the far more critical and historic dialogue about the future of Pacific salmon, period."[4]

On October 19 *The Fisherman* carried a review of *Last Call* by David Lane, executive director of the T. Buck Suzuki Foundation, an environmental organization named after the late Tatsuro Suzuki, a commercial fisherman (and a relative of David Suzuki). The foundation strives to build alliances between environmentalists and people in the industry. Lane said that Glavin had "pointedly under-played" the significance of habitat protection and renewal and made no recommendations for improvement. On the subject of the Pacific Salmon Treaty, Lane wrote:

> Since he doesn't offer a strategy for moving Canada towards a new salmon treaty, Glavin doesn't give us any

practical tools for building an alliance of forces capable of achieving what we want...This summer [1998] with a severe crisis on upper Skeena and upper Thompson coho stocks, neither Washington or Alaska were willing to adopt conservation measures similar to those taken by BC fishermen...A new "conservation-minded treaty" will never come about unless there is strong political leadership of all governments involved, and a unified grassroots campaign launched by conservation and fishing groups on both sides of the border. The direction for that is not found in Glavin's report, nor is it clear how such a treaty would look.

Reaching Out: The Final Peckford Report

Peckford's interim report, released in September, had emphasized the need to provide fishermen and their families with emergency relief and had sparked an outcry from the mainstream press. In his final report, released on December 5, he replies to his critics: "Is it forgotten that this country protected Quebec's textile industry [not a common property resource] through a favourable tariff policy, the Ontario motor vehicle industry [hardly a common property resource] through the Auto-Pact, the agricultural industry of the West through favourable transportation support, the energy and pulp and paper industries through the whole of Canada and special support of mining ventures in many provinces of Canada?"[5]

He recognized that BC as a whole was better off financially than the Atlantic provinces, but "a salmon-dependent family in Alert Bay, British Columbia, is in the same empty boat as a cod fishing-dependent family in Jo Batts Arm, Newfoundland." He then offered a new vision of how the West Coast fishery might be managed. Inspired by a proposal made in January 1991 by Aidan Maloney to Newfoundland Premier Clyde Wells, Peckford called for a new agency to "replace the existing functions of the Department of Fisheries and Oceans and the newly created provincial Ministry of Fisheries."[6] The new agency was to be located in BC, funded equally by the federal and provincial governments and administered by a board of 10 people (three federal, three provincial, three First Nations and a neutral chairperson). The mandate of the agency would include a commitment to biodiversity of all marine stocks, a watershed planning approach, community-based management, selective fishing techniques, a comprehensive program to restore fisheries habitat, an expanded salmon enhancement program, an improved consultative process and a voluntary fleet reduction/early retirement program.

Peckford also listed recommendations on the ecological problems facing the fishery. He implored both levels of government to make more effort to address the impact of global climate change, industrialization and population growth. He also recommended selective fishing methods and other policies to reduce fishing pressure.

Peckford's approach differed dramatically from that of the DFO in calling for working people in the industry to be included in the process of change. "The real 'trick' for societies the world over is how to effectively manage…change," he wrote, "and make it work for the betterment of that society. A large part of the answer to how is, I believe, through engagement and involvement of those affected by the change."

In spite of accusations that he was a propagandist for Glen Clark, Peckford did not endorse Clark's call for exclusive provincial control over the West Coast fishery. The strength of Peckford's recommendation lay in the fact that both levels of government would have a stake in the fishery, and a permanent checks-and-balances system would be created. Yet neither Ottawa nor Victoria heeded Peckford's advice.

Unanswered Questions

On December 4, the day before the release of Peckford's final report, DFO officials held a major press conference to announce that the management of the 1998 salmon season had been a success. They also took credit for having had the foresight to flood the spawning grounds with record escapements, since approximately 3.3 million sockeye had died before they spawned. The DFO had set an optimum escapement goal of 97,000 for the early Stuart sockeye run, but 159,000 of them had actually migrated past the PSC hydro-acoustic grid at Mission. However, of these 159,000 a mere 31,000 had spawned. The escapement goal for the early summer sockeye had been 400,000 and the number to swim past Mission was 536,000, but the spawn was only 230,700. On the summer run, the goal had been 2,660,000, the number past Mission 3,677,700 and the spawn only 2,359,900. On the late run the goal had been 3,609,000, the number past Mission 3,554,000 and the spawn 1,839,000.[7] As in 1962, 1992 and 1994, the DFO could not explain the catastrophe, but one thing was certain: this time it could not be blamed on overfishing by the commercial fleet.

Many veteran fishermen suspected that the DFO's radical risk–averse management policy, adopted after the Fraser Report of 1994, had been a contributing factor: the excessive numbers of spawners swimming up the river had encountered a traffic jam in the narrowest sections of the Fraser Canyon, and the swift current and high water temperatures had killed the fish as they waited in the calmer water of the back eddies. In addition, the BC Fisheries Survival Coalition suggested, the millions of salmon stalled in the back eddies had been vulnerable to rampant poaching under the cover of the AFS pilot sales program.

The members of the old International Pacific Salmon Fisheries Commission (IPSFC) had long ago expressed the fear that over-escapements were almost as big a threat as under-escapements. Excess spawners, they suggested, especially those at the tail end of a run, tended not only to disturb the spawn in the gravel but to cause difficult passage conditions for other salmon moving upstream. This theory has been rejected by some environmentalists, who say there is no such thing as an over-escapement. Yet the DFO has never provided proof that the "optimum escapement goals" that they have tried so hard to attain since the Fraser Report are practical or desirable. What is known is that according to records kept since the late 1880s, the current optimum escapement goals have rarely been achieved. Salmon runs—not to mention the commercial fishery—survived and even flourished for more than a century at escapement levels far below those deemed necessary today. In fact, the large increase in escapement targets in recent years—sometimes double the historic averages—is little more than a grand experiment to test the reproductive capacity of the various watersheds. In the long range, such an endeavour is no doubt useful, but to "rebuild" runs to "optimum" levels almost overnight without adequate social support for fishermen and their communities transcends the principles of good resource stewardship. The old IPSFC managers envisioned the rebuilding of stocks as a step-by-step process, and they appear to have had a better track record than contemporary "experts." As John Sutcliffe, a UFAWU–CAW organizer, told *The Fisherman* on December 18, 1998, "We've got more than three million missing sockeye, most of them from the late group, when the water was cooler. That's a huge loss—and DFO should be trying to find out why it happened on such a large scale. Those fish shouldn't be just written off."

Given David Anderson's boycott of the Peckford Inquiry and the DFO's refusal to hold a review process of its own, the answers to many important questions were not forthcoming.

Minister Anderson ignored Peckford's recommendation to establish a new fisheries agency and instead created the Pacific Fisheries Resource Conservation Council to serve as a watchdog over DFO managers. The idea of such a council had first been proposed by John Fraser in his 1994 report, and the top job went to him. Despite crushing cuts to DFO staff and programming, the new council was outfitted with an annual budget of almost $1 million. The council went on to sponsor a variety of conferences on such general subjects as climatic change in the ocean environment, and to publish some glossy reports on the status of BC salmon stocks, but it is not at all certain that the council has made any difference to the salmon.

Perhaps because of all the bad press he had received, Glen Clark avoided dealing with the Peckford Report from the time the inquiry was launched. BC Fisheries Minister Dennis Streifel acknowledged that the report provided "a new perspective on the complexity of fisheries management," then turned it over to his senior bureaucrats, who essentially left the commercial salmon fishery to the DFO. Moreover, they had no wish to carry on Glen Clark's political feud with the DFO, and thus when Streifel was dragged into a diversionary debate with the media about taxpayer support for fishing families, he appeared awkward and uncomfortable. The press was alert to any possible repeat of the huge cost overruns in the multibillion-dollar East Coast TAGS program. Streifel said that less than $50 million would be needed to do the job on the West Coast, but that his own tiny ministry had no resources to commit to the task.

Although Peckford's report received strong support from Newfoundland Premier Brian Tobin, who believed that a new fisheries agency was long overdue, Dennis Streifel's senior bureaucrats insisted that restoring "normal" relations with Ottawa was far more important. Streifel, therefore, declined to join in common cause with Tobin, arguing that a new fisheries agency would require that Ottawa agree to surrender its exclusive jurisdiction.[8] No one was prepared to be its political champion, so the Peckford Report—along with the high hopes of the Seymour Narrows protestors—faded into oblivion.

McArthur Moves On

The reason why the premier's office withdrew from the fisheries front at the time of the Peckford Report may have had to do with the imminent departure of Doug McArthur, Clark's deputy minister. McArthur had closely supervised the provincial fisheries strategy ever since the Mifflin fight and had conceived the "On Your Side" slogan that had played so well during the 1996 provincial election. In addition, he had masterminded the use of the Nanoose Bay torpedo-testing range as a bargaining chip in the PST campaign. But by the summer of 1998, McArthur was totally preoccupied with shoring up the shaky political fortunes of the NDP.

McArthur hailed from Saskatchewan, where he had served as minister of education in the NDP government from 1978 to 1982. After the defeat of the NDP, he taught at the University of Saskatchewan, then worked for Yukon Premier Tony Penikett negotiating an important Native land claims settlement, then served as deputy minister of aboriginal affairs in BC Premier Mike Harcourt's NDP government. McArthur then vaulted to the most powerful position in the BC civil service. In that post he was supposedly politically neutral, but McArthur had a penchant for the cut and thrust of partisan politics, and during Harcourt's regime his power within the bureaucracy was unrivalled. However, after the 1996 election victory, Clark appointed Adrian Dix and Tom Gunton to equally powerful positions, and according to Vaughan Palmer of the *Vancouver Sun*, the rivalry between the three senior officials undermined the effectiveness of Clark's government.[9]

In Clark's government McArthur was responsible for several key political files, including the Pacific Salmon Treaty, the Nisga'a treaty negotiations, the revamping of the provincial welfare system, the Jobs and Timber Accord and the Forest Practices Code, but by the spring of 1998 he was showing signs of fatigue and disenchantment. This may explain his unexpected absence during the critical phase of the PST negotiations in May, by which time the premier's PST crusade, along with its "standing up for BC" refrain, was losing some of its shine. And by mid-November 1998 it was clear that Anderson's "conservation" message had eclipsed Clark's patriotic stance: in a federal government poll, 63 percent of those surveyed believed Glen Clark's intervention in West Coast fisheries was motivated by political opportunism, and only 11 percent believed that Clark cared about conserving BC salmon.

To complicate matters, McArthur was also faced with a showdown over the Nanoose Bay seabed. This issue had ignited a political powder keg. Not only was the threat to cancel the Nanoose lease an affront to American military dominance, it also struck hard at the nexus of federal–provincial power relations. By the summer of 1998, the press was vilifying Clark for being anti-American as well as confrontational.

The Nanoose controversy had flared up again at the first ministers' conference held in Saskatoon in August 1998. With the massive federal surplus, the premiers hoped to reclaim some of the $6.2 billion previously cut from annual provincial transfer payments, so most of them were in an unusually conciliatory frame of mind. All eyes were on Clark, who adopted a more co-operative style during the conference but did not refrain from what his critics called "Ottawa-bashing." When asked on August 5, 1998, by Jim Beatty of the *Vancouver Sun* how he viewed his role in Canadian federalism, Clark replied, "This day in this country, the deal-maker's deal-maker. Think Nisga'a...Think national and international drum roll coverage. But our man's differences with the federal government are the stuff around which front pages are built. Think fishermen's friend."

Clark's bravado was too much for Premier Roy Romanow of Saskatchewan, who condemned his threat to cancel the Nanoose lease.

Premiers, he declared, should not infringe on Ottawa's foreign policy mandate, particularly when it involved military relations with the US. The media made much of the spat between the two NDP premiers. Their disdain for Clark's Nanoose threat was fed by Romanow's attack, and according to former BC MLA Judi Tyabji Wilson, a number of people within the NDP were already plotting against Clark during this period.[10]

Neither Clark nor McArthur had expected the fisheries feud with Ottawa to drag on so long. At first they had believed that the memorandum of understanding (MOU) on fisheries signed with Ottawa would provide a gracious exit strategy from the chaos engendered by the Mifflin Plan. And they had assumed that the renegotiation of the salmon treaty was a straightforward task that would not require them to follow through on the Nanoose threat. Yet conflict in coastal BC did not subside after the signing of the MOU, and neither did the tension between Ottawa and Victoria over the PST. In fact, these conflicts seemed to intensify, poisoning virtually all relations between the two levels of government and making McArthur far less keen to stoke the PST fires again.

McArthur shifted his focus to the Nisga'a treaty. On this issue, he and the rest of Clark's brain trust calculated that the federal Liberals would align with the provincial NDP government rather than with Gordon Campbell's right-wing provincial Liberal Party, because Campbell had opposed the deal ever since the framework agreement had been initialed in 1996. As well, the federal Liberals were anxious to resolve the matter: former Prime Minister Brian Mulroney had promised to settle all land claims before 2000, and few agreements had been signed. Ottawa needed BC, and Doug McArthur was gambling that an accord on the Nisga'a issue would help repair federal–provincial relations, improve NDP electoral fortunes and possibly even prevent Ottawa from expropriating Nanoose.

Hence, in the late spring of 1998, McArthur left his office next to the premier's in the legislature, set himself up in another office and gathered a special issues team drawn from various provincial ministries. This team was to speed up the negotiations and prepare a $5 million public relations campaign to sell the Nisga'a deal to the public.

The Nisga'a Treaty

As he climbed the red-carpeted stairs and passed through the imposing front gates of the legislature, Chief Joe Gosnell of the Nisga'a completed an epic journey begun by his people 111 years earlier. In 1887 a delegation of Nisga'a had paddled more than 1,000 km (600 miles) from their home in the Nass Valley to request that Premier William Smith settle their land claim. Smith had refused to meet them, and the Nisga'a were left to endure a century of hardship and despair. Now, on the afternoon of November 30, 1998, another flotilla of Nisga'a canoes approached the provincial legislature, only this time they were greeted with pomp and pageantry. The Nisga'a delegation beached their canoes and stepped forth, calling out the names of all the original land claim petitioners.

Waiting for Gosnell at the top of the legislature steps was Premier Glen Clark and his deputy, Doug McArthur. In an article on December 10, 1998, *Vancouver Sun* columnist Vaughan Palmer described the scene. "Although even the most powerful civil servants are supposed to remain in the background and let the politicians reap exclusive glory at such events, a beaming Doug McArthur turned up on the front steps of the legislature alongside Premier Clark as the Nisga'a procession approached Monday afternoon. Only at the last minute did he think better of his position, and move to the sidelines, leaving the premier standing solo at the center of the legislature steps to greet the Nisga'a." In a symbolic gesture of conciliation, the premier shook Gosnell's hand and said, "I want to thank all the Nisga'a people, whose struggle for 111 years has been characterized by integrity, perseverance, dignity, and above all enormous patience... [Your] patience, I hope, is about to be rewarded today."

The BC legislature had been recalled for a rare fall sitting to debate the proposed Nisga'a settlement, and in keeping with the historic nature of the event, Gosnell was given the rare privilege of addressing the legislative assembly. For Doug McArthur it was a grand moment, as he was the man responsible for concluding the deal in time for the provincial election. However, for the citizens of BC it was just the beginning of a rancorous debate about the nature of the special rights held by Native people.

As a former member of the BC Treaty Negotiations Advisory Committee (TNAC), I had once had grave misgivings about the Nisga'a deal, not so much because of the actual salmon catch Ottawa had offered the Nisga'a—a fixed percentage of the overall annual harvest, therefore much preferable to the absolute number guaranteed, regardless of run size, in the AFS pilot sales fishery—but because of the precedent it might set. The Nisga'a fishery sub-agreement is confined to the relatively isolated Nass River salmon stocks, with few implications for the conduct of fisheries elsewhere on the coast, and most of those who have traditionally participated in the Nass River fishery are Nisga'a fishermen. However, if the same per capita harvest entitlement was applied across the board to all the other Native groups along the coast, there would be no harvest left for non-Native fishermen. This is especially true for Fraser River runs, which are harvested by Native fishermen from the Alaska boundary in the north to the headwaters in the BC interior.

On several occasions the fishing industry reps on the TNAC—Jack Nichol, Ron Fowler, Paddy Greene, Mike Hunter and myself—questioned treaty negotiators about such implications. The negotiators did not dispute our calculations, but they assured us that in theory, in future settlements with southern bands the amount of fish offered would decline proportionally. To us this implies that Ottawa had a coast-wide limit on the amount of fish to be alienated as part of the claims process. The federal negotiators never confirmed that, but they expected TNAC representatives to accept their assurances in good faith. Before the Nisga'a treaty was ratified, the UFAWU–CAW annual convention, in a demonstration of goodwill, voted to support it.

Meanwhile, the public's response to the Nisga'a deal was not quite as favourable as Doug McArthur and Glen Clark had hoped. On October 22, 1998, the *Vancouver Sun* reported that only 51 percent of those polled by the Angus Reid Group believed the Nisga'a treaty was a "step in the right direction." Clark went ahead and reconvened the legislature on March 22, 1999, in order to debate the Nisga'a land claim settlement. The opposition accused the NDP of using the debate to divert attention from BC's deficit, projected to be $890 million. This, combined with the revelation that the new fast ferries project was at least $57 million over budget, destroyed any NDP hopes that the fall legislative sitting could be devoted to the Nisga'a debate. On April 24, with Clark at an all-time low in the polls, the NDP brought the session to a halt by using its slim majority to endorse the Nisga'a deal—only to be delayed further when Ottawa refused to comply with Clark's timetable. Federal Minister of Indian Affairs Jane Stewart seemed suddenly concerned that the treaty was being rushed and declared that BC had taken so long in endorsing its portion of the deal that Ottawa would not be able to respond for several months. It is likely that the federal Liberals—particularly David Anderson—wanted to distance themselves from Glen Clark and to let him take most of the advance political flak for the Nisga'a treaty, even though Ottawa was jurisdictionally responsible for most of its provisions. Thus the issue over which Glen Clark had been prepared to fight the coming election started to slip from his grasp.

The Beginning of the End

When Glen Clark's wife Dale opened her front door on the evening of March 2, 1999, she was shocked to see two RCMP crime investigators standing in the floodlights of a BCTV news crew. The Mounties claimed that Premier Clark had surreptitiously intervened in a neighbour's casino licence application in exchange for renovations to his east Vancouver home. It was the start of three and a half years of hell for Clark and his family, and it was the end of the NDP provincial government.

Clark was forced to resign on August 23, 1999, after BC Attorney General Ujjal Dosanjh announced that Clark was subject to a criminal investigation.

Because provincial fisheries policy between 1996 and 1998 had been so closely tied to Glen Clark, his departure signalled the end of a brief yet exceptional era in the West Coast fishing industry—an era that owed more to Clark's personal volition than to any well-considered public policy initiative. Yet Clark's intervention had been so intensely partisan, striking at the very foundations of the Canadian power structure, that no one else in the NDP government would touch the file after his fall. Dennis Streifel and his senior Ministry of Fisheries officials were soon bogged down in a long series of bureaucratic meetings to define the roles and responsibilities of Ottawa and Victoria under the BC–Canada Fisheries memorandum. Dan Miller, who succeeded Clark as caretaker premier, barely touched fisheries issues, even though he represented the fishery-dependent community of Prince Rupert. And in February 2000, Miller embarked on a junket to Alaska ostensibly to "mend fences."

Corky Evans, who as fisheries minister had stood behind Clark during the apogee of the Mifflin–PST feud with Ottawa, now had to adopt a more low-key approach, concentrating on programs sponsored by the Fisheries Renewal Crown corporation. Andrew Petter took responsibility for the Nanoose file during Clark's last days, but he redefined it as an anti-nuclear issue, severing it entirely from the PST.

One of the most interesting aspects of Glen Clark's fall is that just before the RCMP raided his house, it appeared that his feud with Ottawa was about to pay off. On January 15, 1999, Ottawa discreetly abandoned the Calgary Declaration which had proposed that Quebec's "unique character" be recognized within Canadian federalism— vindicating Clark's opposition to that accord. And shortly after this, the federal government indicated that it was willing to reconsider its threat to expropriate the Nanoose Bay testing range, and possibly to swap the federally owned Royal Roads military college property for the Nanoose Bay seabed.

As well, Clark seemed finally to have made an impact on Ottawa in regard to its discriminatory transfer payments to BC when federal Finance Minister Paul Martin promised to put an additional $350 million into the provincial coffers over the next three years. Martin also delivered a whopping $1.9 billion to BC for health-care payments over the next five years, finally bringing this province into line with Newfoundland and Quebec.

Then, just a short while before the police raid and Clark's rejection of the offer to swap the Royal Roads land, Ottawa offered the province $125 million in cash over 30 years in exchange for the Nanoose lease. Again Clark turned it down. "They were trying to give us money to solve it," he said. "That's never been the issue for us...We couldn't get the federal government to understand this is about fishing communities and families and livelihoods..."[11]

But after the police raid, Ottawa abruptly changed course and launched the first hostile expropriation of provincial land in Canadian history. And on May 15 federal Defence Minister Art Eggleton told the *Vancouver Sun*, "Holding Canada's critical defence needs hostage to unrelated interests was not appropriate." Clark said that the federal action demonstrated "contempt for BC," and Anderson responded, "It's a political thing. Sometimes when you're in trouble at home you find an enemy somewhere else."[12]

The Nanoose Bay test range, which Ottawa leased from BC for one dollar per year, employed only 70 people, not all of whom were military personnel. Most equipment and facilities were provided by the US, and its operations were overseen by the US Naval Underwater War Centre in Key Port, Washington. In 35 years of operation, 31,000 torpedoes had been fired at the 24 km (14 mile) test range. It is not clear how the activities at this testing range protect Canadian citizens, as Eggleton had suggested. Jim Fulton of the David Suzuki Foundation believes the presence of nuclear weapons there actually poses a security risk to the BC populace, as he wrote in the *Vancouver Sun* on May 14: "Should there be a serious accident it would be like a mini-Chernobyl in the air or water in the midst of three million people."

When questioned on this safety issue, the federal cabinet—including David Anderson, who was so admired for his environmental concerns—was mum. Ottawa's standard reply was that no one knew whether there were nuclear weapons on board the ships, as the US military does not divulge such information.

When Clark had first threatened to cancel the Nanoose lease to back up his PST campaign, both the provincial Liberals and the federal Reform Party had endorsed the idea. But now that Clark was under a cloud of suspicion, the opposition parties reversed their position. Gary Lunn, who at one time had noted that Ottawa's threat to expropriate Nanoose would aggravate "western alienation," now accused Clark of playing with politics, and Lunn's colleague Keith Martin pronounced the Nanoose action a threat to Canadian servicemen.[13]

One of the few prominent political figures opposed to the Nanoose expropriation was federal Tory leader Joe Clark, and on May 25 he told the *Vancouver Sun*, "Ottawa is exploiting Premier Clark's low popularity to justify expropriating the Nanoose Bay testing site. Were the Liberals dealing with any premier other than a premier as unpopular as Glen

Clark there would be a much stronger national reaction against the principle of the federal government moving so quickly toward expropriation of provincial land."

By December 1999 Ottawa had completed the process of expropriating the Nanoose Bay seabed and granting the Americans a 10-year extension on their lease.

But Glen Clark was vulnerable now, and Ottawa did not stop with the Nanoose expropriation. On June 4, 1999, David Anderson and his advisors, in the absence of strong political opposition from BC, concluded an agreement with the US that forever altered the spirit and intent of the original Pacific Salmon Treaty. Anderson agreed to a 10-year deal that dispensed entirely with the traditional concept of equity. The centrepiece of the deal was a $140 million "endowment fund" allegedly designed to restore and enhance salmon runs in both countries. This fund was to be held in trust, with annual interest to be spent at the discretion of a bilateral committee.

Anderson also claimed that the deal would reduce American interception of Fraser River sockeye. In 1999, the US would be entitled to 22.4 percent of the Fraser sockeye catch and 25.7 percent of the pinks. In 2000 the US share would drop to 20.4 percent; and in 2001 to 18.4 percent. For the following 10 years (2002–2010), the Americans would be "limited" to 16.5 per cent of the Fraser sockeye catch. In addition, the coho chapter of the original treaty was amended and the Canadian catch ceiling of 1.8 million coho was surrendered. The two parties agreed to establish a bilateral coho working group to develop a new abundance-based management regime and a new stock-assessment system. Canada's one significant leverage against the US was gone. "It will be a poor year," Anderson announced. "But for coastal communities this agreement is indeed a very important step towards a prosperous future."[14]

Anderson's deal took harsh criticism from many quarters. In fact, a fracas broke out between security guards and industry representatives when Anderson's staff restricted access to the news conference explaining the new deal. "The people who are going to be impacted by this treaty should have been allowed in," cried Doug Walker, executive director of the BC Wildlife Federation. "This is an abysmal process!"[15] However, Tom Bird, a representative of the Sports Fishing Institute of

BC and a former DFO employee, told the press, "Anything that sees an improvement, particularly on the part of the Alaskan element, will put us further ahead than we were yesterday." He was probably referring to a clause saying that Alaska would, at its own discretion, close a slender strip along the A–B line if there were conservation concerns. The vast majority of Alaskan fisheries would remain entirely unaffected by the agreement.

The strongest praise for Anderson came from the American side. John Kitzhaber, the governor of Oregon, said, "Mr. Anderson, whose courage and whose persistence and whose steadfast belief that a solution was possible, was critical in bringing us to this moment,"[16] and Washington Governor Gary Locke proclaimed "an end to the US–Canada salmon wars."

On June 5 Peter O'Neil of the *Vancouver Sun* reported that insiders had indicated that Anderson had encouraged Locke to follow "his lead" in "marginalizing once powerful commercial fishermen" and thus end "the annual salmon wars ritual." He also noted that Anderson's exclusion of the Canadian national section from the talks had been the "final contributing factor" in concluding a deal. Bill Woolf, advisor to Alaskan Senator Frank Murkowski, was able to declare, "Mr. Anderson was able to streamline the process on the Canadian side and that helped." O'Neil also noted that "Governor Locke complied in large part because major corporate players in Washington state's economic and political life are facing major new costs to comply with Endangered Species Act requirements."

Hubert Haldane, a Canadian PSC commissioner, did not congratulate Anderson. He told the *Vancouver Province* he was "very angry" with the way Anderson had brokered the deal: not only had he given in on the equity question, but also he had compromised the rights of Native people by excluding them from the talks. Paddy Greene, a former salmon commissioner, told the *Globe and Mail* on June 5, "I don't think Ottawa gives a damn about BC. There's a minimal understanding of the problems faced in coastal communities…They have done just about everything they could to ruin the salmon industry." And Glen Clark was irate. On June 4 he told the *Victoria Times Colonist*, "We've become a fish farm for the Americans to harvest…This year BC will not catch any endangered coho. The Alaskans will catch endangered BC coho next year, the year after that, and every year for the next ten years. The Anderson deal entrenches within the treaty the right of Alaskans to do this."

It took almost a month for the full implications of the deal to be made public. Bud Graham, provincisl assistant deputy minister of fisheries and formerly a key PST expert for the DFO, provided a detailed critique of the accord at a BC-sponsored media briefing session on July 4. "Under the new rules," he said, "Canada held Alaska to a much lower conservation standard than it has set for itself. In short, under the new rules Canada will continue to pass through Washington and Oregon-bound salmon while the US will be entitled to a larger share of Fraser River sockeye." He also pointed out that the US had intercepted an estimated 870,000 endangered BC coho in 1998 and was likely to do so again in 1999.

Pat Chamut, Graham's old boss, was outraged. He told the *Vancouver Sun* on July 5 that Graham was "using correct statistics in a misleading way to deliberately distort the truth for political reasons," and that "only a few thousand or far less than one percent" of the coho caught by Alaskan fishermen had been "endangered upper Skeena coho." His argument was a carbon copy of that used by the Alaskans, and he did not mention the damage to BC's own commercial fishery for the sake of a similarly small bycatch of coho.

At the July 4 briefing Graham also pointed out that Anderson's offer to the US of 16.5 percent of the Fraser sockeye in 2002–2010 was an increase in their traditional share. Washington state's average annual take of Fraser sockeye had only been 15.6 percent before the four-year 7-million cap in 1989.[17] Chamut could not deny that this was technically true, but he argued that those catch levels were impossible to replicate because "Canada can no longer afford aggressive fish wars as a result of conservation concerns."

Some important figures in the environmental community were also unimpressed with the new agreement. "The Americans won big-time on conservation issues here," warned Jim Fulton of the David Suzuki Foundation. "They gave up very little of their commercial, sport and aboriginal catch effort for conservation in BC and in Canada, but we gave up enormously on all our fisheries to give them more fish for conservation… It's quite clear that if this agreement were put on a scale of 10, the Americans would get a 10 and Canadians get a 1."[18]

David Anderson's deal put an end to a Canadian struggle that had begun in 1882 with the first efforts to study the life cycle and behaviour of Fraser sockeye, and that had produced the first tentative joint salmon regulations in 1908 and the formation of the International Pacific Salmon Fisheries Commission in 1936. This period was marked by intense rivalry between the two countries, including diplomatic chicanery and betrayal, but also by important scientific findings and engineering feats. Throughout the process, Canadian negotiators had been determined to minimize or reduce US interceptions, and to provide Canada with harvests or benefits equivalent to its salmonid production. Now, in one fell swoop, Anderson had dramatically set back Canada's longstanding goal of realizing "benefits equivalent to the production of salmon originating in its waters" (Article III, PST).

A Time of Hunger

Power takes as ingratitude the writhing of its victims.

—Sir Rabindranath Tagore, *Stray Birds*

*I*n summer 1999, hundreds of vacationing tourists thronged the beaches and enjoyed the sparkling waters of 30,000 ha (75,000 acre) Shuswap Lake. Few of them knew that just eight months earlier, in the labyrinth of rivers that intertwine the Shuswap watershed, the legendary Adams River sockeye had laid their eggs. For about two months, as the eggs lay beneath a carapace of winter ice, they were covered only by a sheer membrane that absorbed oxygen and protected the proteins, fats and salts of the embryos from the shifting gravel.

First, disproportionately large globular eyes appeared. Next, a backbone became apparent. Then, when conditions were just right, each embryo secreted a chemical that dissolved the shell, and a tiny alevin, 2.5 cm (one inch) long, wriggled free. The creature had an eel-like shape and a bulging yolk sac that would feed it for several more weeks while it lived beneath the gravel. Now the creature, called a fry, emerged into the world under cover of night. During their first days out of the gravel, the fry hovered under the sheltering banks of their natal streams to avoid the many predators—large insects, cutthroat trout and waterfowl. In some years as few as 10 percent of the eggs survive the fry stage, and many of those succumb to predation later in their lives. They in turn prey on smaller insects, plankton and parasites.

Massive schools of Adams River sockeye fry swam downstream to Little Shuswap Lake, where they joined the progeny of other streams. Then they headed back upstream to Greater Shuswap Lake, where they would reside for the first year of their lives, grazing on immense pastures of phytoplankton.

Salmon Go Missing—Again

Despite the seemingly endless controversy in their industry, BC commercial fishermen spent the spring of 1999 preparing for the coming salmon season. Then, on July 6, the DFO forecast that the 1999 Fraser River sockeye run would be 8,248,000, made up of 318,000 early Stuart, 477,000 early summer-run, 5,328,000 summer-run and 2,125,000 late-run sockeye. After allowing for escapement and the American percentage of the catch, there was still a potential Canadian catch of 4,146,000, which would be divided between the commercial fleet (2,936,000), the sports fishermen (50,000) and the AFS (1,160,000).

On July 21 the DFO announced its pre-season management plan for the Fraser River fishery. In theory, the 2,507 eligible salmon licence holders of the commercial fleet would be entitled to catch those 2,936,000 sockeye, under a catch-sharing formula that would allocate 42 percent to seiners, 29 percent to gillnetters and 29 percent to trollers. With an estimated landed value of $50 million, this catch would give a much-needed financial boost to those fishermen who had waited out the Mifflin and Anderson restructuring processes.

Both the Fraser and Skeena runs were expected to be good, but fishermen feared that the DFO would sacrifice most of the sockeye harvest to limit the bycatch of coho. The UFAWU–CAW, Community Fisheries Development Centre and Coastal Community Network called upon Ottawa to hire unemployed fishermen to restore damaged salmon habitat and perform other conservation tasks. Fisheries Minister David Anderson refused. He had, he stated, already provided $400 million in aid to fishermen.

As the 1999 season got underway during the week of July 30, some limited commercial fishing took place in both Canadian and American waters. Almost immediately the Pacific Salmon Commission, taking note of the extremely poor landings, was forced to lower the in-season run estimate to a mere 3,100,000 fish, less than half of what had been forecast, and on August 6 the commission recommended that all commercial sockeye fishing be closed for the balance of the season. Of the catch of 387,000 pieces to that date, 333,000 had been taken in the Native fishery and only 54,000 by commercial fishermen. For the first time in a century, no significant commercial fishery for Fraser River sockeye occurred in British Columbia. It was a crushing blow, but the commercial fleet supported the sockeye closure. Some aboriginal leaders, however, insisted they had a special right to continue fishing regardless of the low return. A day after the PSC decision, Sto:lo leader June Quipp declared, "We do not have conservation concerns. We'll look at the numbers that should be returning, then decide."[1]

And, despite David Anderson's 1998 PST deal, Alaskan interceptions continued unabated. In fact, that year the Alaskans took 40 percent of the 1999 return of endangered Upper Skeena coho stock during DFO's total ban on the take of coho by BC commercial fishermen. Alaskan gillnetters at Tree Point caught 160,028 Canadian sockeye (50,000 over treaty limits), and Alaskan seiners at Noyes Island intercepted 160,000, for a total of 320,028; BC fishermen confined to the North Coast licence area caught only 316,000 Skeena sockeye during the entire season. In other words, the Alaskans caught almost as much Canadian sockeye (320,028) that season as did the entire BC commercial fleet in all areas of the coast (370,000).

On September 20, long after the season was over, the PSC upgraded the 1999 Fraser sockeye estimate to 3,580,000. All of these fish had been safely ushered onto the spawning grounds, so the DFO could claim that it had successfully managed the resource.[2] For many commercial fishermen, the only positive note was that this time the DFO did concede that the unexpectedly low returns in 1999 were not the result of past overfishing by the BC fleet. Although no one could say for sure what had happened to the run, the cause was generally understood to be poor ocean survival conditions. Some scientists suspected that large numbers of cycle-year smolts had died from malnutrition because of unusually meagre plankton blooms in the Gulf of Georgia during the spring of 1996; others thought severe temperature fluctuations in the mid-Pacific, caused by El Niño, had wreaked havoc on the run.

During the autumn of 1999 the Adams River sockeye fry extended their range, foraging through the five major arms of Shuswap Lake. Here they formed huge schools, some more than two or three km (a mile or two) long and 20 m (6 feet) deep. These schools clustered along the banks of the lake during the day and spread out at night. The fry were now much larger and more resilient. With the coming of the dark winter months, the plankton blooms upon which they were feeding would fade. Then they would enter a state of near suspended animation, subsisting on what food they could find until the following spring. Yet even then survival would be uncertain. Some years there is not enough food. During the 1970s the IPSFC feared that the fry of the large sub-dominant years of 1967 and 1971—which were similar in size to the dominant Adams River runs of 1966 and 1970—were affecting the food supply of the fry produced by the dominant-year escapements.[3] Subsequent studies seemed to refute this theory, but no one can explain why the famous Adams River run declined so precipitously in the years after the record run of 1958. This question remains unanswered about runs in other parts of the BC coast as well—Rivers and Smith inlets, the Skeena, and the Fraser—all places where the DFO made dramatic efforts to increase escapements, yet production declined suddenly. In any case, for the tiny salmon in Shuswap Lake, winter is a grim struggle for survival, a time of hunger.

A Time of Hunger

Dan Edwards sat alone in the dark, staring out the wheelhouse window. Heavy raindrops whipped by the cold December wind pounded the glass, each drop coloured by the bright lights of Granville Island. The cluster of shops, boutiques and restaurants was just a hundred yards from the fish boat Edwards was staying on at the False Creek fishermen's wharf, yet it was a universe away. As the evening crowd parked their cars and entered the bistros and restaurants, he prepared his daily broth of lemon juice, maple syrup and strained vegetable juice. He was on a hunger strike to protest the DFO's mismanagement of the West Coast fishery, and for Dan Edwards, a third-generation commercial fisherman from Ucluelet, it was a struggle for his life.[4]

Edwards had been fasting for 58 days, and the next day, December 22, 1999, he would be meeting with federal Fisheries Minister Herb Dhaliwal, who had recently replaced David Anderson. For several weeks senior DFO officials had refused to grant Edwards a meeting, accusing him of pressuring the department with "emotional terrorism." But finally, in a sort of Dickensian twist, Dhaliwal's department had agreed to a meeting three days before Christmas.

Edwards's protest had begun when the DFO had summarily closed the commercial sockeye fishery in August. Shortly afterwards, Edwards and Russ Hellberg, chair of the Coastal Community Network, had sponsored a meeting in Richmond to discuss the sockeye crisis. I had attended on behalf of the BC government, though the senior bureaucrats were less than enthusiastic about the issue. The meeting was also attended by representatives from the commercial fishing sector, First Nations and coastal communities, who later called themselves the Fraser River Sockeye Crisis Committee. This committee agreed that the closure was necessary to protect the sockeye and also agreed with the DFO that natural factors, not mismanagement, had caused the fiasco. Thus, in their view Ottawa was obliged to provide disaster relief to all fishermen affected by the unexpected closure.

There was plenty of data on the effects of the crisis. In his report for the DFO, *Fishing for Direction*, the economist Gordon Gislason estimated that BC's 2,400 commercial fishermen had incurred a loss of $47.5 million in earnings as a result of the closure. The BC economy had also suffered $114–133 million in lost revenue. Gislason feared that the collapse of the run would diminish the presence of BC canners in the world market as well. Even as he was making this prediction, the canners were delivering their own bad news to the beleaguered industry. The Weston corporation, owner of BC Packers Ltd., the province's largest fishing company, had decided to pull out of the West Coast fishery, severing connections that dated back to the earliest days of the industry. It sold the BC Packers seine fleet and the Oceanside cannery in Prince Rupert to the billionaire Jimmy Pattison. Later Weston reaped a huge real estate windfall by converting the site of Steveston's historic Imperial Cannery into a sprawling housing development. For a further princely sum they sold the lucrative Cloverleaf brand, a symbol of premium-quality Canadian canned salmon, to International Home Foods Ltd. A short time later, this giant American conglomerate allowed foreign salmon, processed by lower-paid workers in Korea, to bear the venerable Cloverleaf label.

The Weston corporation abandoned the BC wild salmon industry but retained control of more than a dozen fish farms on the BC coast through a subsidiary, Heritage Aquaculture Ltd. They also had substantial interests in the burgeoning aquaculture industry in Chile, where the average wage is $169 (US) per month. Thus, while BC Packers executives repeatedly claimed that they had to lower prices to fishermen in order to remain competitive with fish farms, their superiors at the Weston head office were busy investing in the aquaculture sector.

In 1999, in spite of such pressures on the price of most species of wild salmon, a recent downturn in the world supply of sockeye—which cannot be raised in netpens—had seemed to imply that the dockside price for sockeye would be substantially higher. This fact, combined with the DFO's favourable pre-season catch forecast, had raised fishermen's hopes. Many of them had invested heavily in vessel preparations, gear, licences and fuel. The DFO had collected more than $3 million in vessel licence fees and $360,000 in personal registration fees from the commercial fleet before a single scale was landed.

Unfortunately, in 1999 the South Coast fleet had little to count on besides Fraser River sockeye, what with closures on both chinook and coho fisheries plus poor sockeye returns to Rivers and Smith inlets and Barkley Sound. For those fishermen confined to South Coast areas by area licensing, the Fraser sockeye catch represented 92 percent of their earning potential.[5] So when the run failed and the fishery was cancelled, they saw themselves as victims of a natural disaster. But the federal government refused to provide them with financial relief, once again harking back to that $400 million they had already spent to help West Coast fishing families. Who had been helped by this money? As the Coastal Community Network pointed out, "These funds have all been allocated to existing programs—stewardship initiatives, habitat restoration, sustainable fishing techniques and fleet reduction." The CCN also quoted Gordon Gislason's report, commissioned by the DFO, which was "highly critical of these programs, particularly in the areas of information and coordination, red tape, and regulatory inertia…" Gislason had warned, "Many commercial and sports fishing operators are struggling under a backlog of bills and high debt load. They are in dire need of low-interest loans, extended EI benefits and other support to stay afloat."[6]

The Fraser River Sockeye Crisis Committee presented these facts and more to provincial Fisheries Minister Dennis Streifel, Attorney General

Ujjal Dosanjh and DFO regional director Donna Petrachenko, but no help was forthcoming. The political fallout from the Fraser Report in 1994 had not yet faded from memory, and both levels of government were speaking as positively as they could. The DFO's communications strategy had focussed on the fact that large numbers of spawners had made it to the spawning grounds, which had convinced the public that all was well, despite the grumbling of a few die-hard fishermen. If either level of government had declared the situation a natural disaster, they could be accused of mismanaging the resource. And haunted by the spectre of The Atlantic Groundfish Subsidy (TAGS) on the East Coast, they knew that an aid package of any kind for fishermen could provoke public outrage. To do nothing was the safest course.

Thinking Globally, Acting Locally

That fall, BC commercial fishermen as a group were so demoralized that they could scarcely muster the energy to protest, but a small group of activists vowed to keep up the fight. After much deliberation, they decided a hunger strike would best dramatize their plight, and in early October Dan Edwards, a sturdy, determined troller from Ucluelet, volunteered for the task. His 23-year-old daughter, Danielle, decided to join him. To keep the story in front of the Vancouver news media, they would stay in a trailer in Steveston.

The media were less than accommodating. On October 12 Pete Mc-Martin of the *Vancouver Sun* questioned why a bunch of "finger-pointing fishers" should ever be given financial assistance. "No one comes to the help of other beleaguered workers," he wrote. "Why does a fisherman think his work is any more deserving of government assistance than, say, the sales woman behind the [Eaton's] counter selling Chanel?"

In a way McMartin was right—the federal government had done little to help workers who lost their jobs because of industrial restructuring. But this was not true of corporations. At a time when both West Coast fishermen and Eaton's workers were being cast adrift, Ottawa provided one-half of Canada's 100 most profitable corporations—including the five chartered banks—with Human Resources Development (HRDC) grants to tide them over "difficult times." Molson Breweries, with a profit

Dan Edwards, a Ucluelet troller, with his daughter Danielle during his first hunger strike, Steveston, BC, October 1999.

of $111 million in 1998, received an HRDC grant of $313,188; Loblaws, with a profit of $260 million, got $299,158; Union Gas got $263,473.[7]

After the first week of Dan Edwards's hunger strike, Herb Dhaliwal's political assistant, Lenore Copeland, phoned him to ask him to end his strike before the Thanksgiving holiday. In exchange, Copeland promised to meet and discuss the Sockeye Crisis Committee's concerns. Shortly thereafter, Edwards and Copeland met twice. At the same time, however, Copeland met with a number of "fishing industry representatives" who opposed the Sockeye Crisis Committee's demands. One of these groups recommended that only vessel owners who had invested in licences, gear and other pre-season preparations should be eligible for assistance. The Sockeye Crisis Committee maintained that all affected parties, including crews, First Nations fishers and fishing communities, should be eligible. Once again the divisions within the industry had reared up and prevented a united campaign. The canners, meanwhile, completely rejected the idea of compensation for fishermen, which they said would damage the industry's reputation. Citing a divergence of views, Minister Dhaliwal and his staff took no action at all.

At the time of his hunger strike, Dan Edwards was also locked in a struggle with senior DFO officials over the issue of community-based fisheries management. He felt that BC's primary industries were being destroyed by policies that gave large corporations control over the province's natural resources. In the forest industry, for example, multinational corporations were granted timber-harvesting rights without having to maintain secondary processing and manufacturing jobs in forest industry-dependent communities. This arrangement had begun in the heyday of the old 1950s–'60s Social Credit Party regime, when Premier W.A.C. Bennett had granted the forest companies an abundant supply of cheap wood in exchange for good-paying jobs. The formula worked for some time, but by the 1980s, with the province running out of cheap, accessible timber and the lumber market growing increasingly competitive, the Socred paradigm had begun to unravel. Thousands of good jobs in the hinterland disappeared forever. But rather than intervene, government officials allowed even more corporate control over public forests, and signed the NAFTA and Softwood Lumber Agreements with the US.

At the same time, citizens' groups were calling for community-based forest licences, to gain control over local resources and to create secure jobs in rural communities. In the late 1990s the provincial NDP made some sporadic attempts to create such licences, but it was too little and too late. (In early 2005, the provincial Liberal government was in the process of changing the Forest Act to allow private corporations to control all aspects of BC's forests. Meanwhile, more than 50 organizations, united as the Coalition for Sustainable Forest Solutions, had drafted a private member's bill on community forest tenures for BC.[8])

Dan Edwards, whose wife Bonnie had been dismissed by MacMillan Bloedel after an extended illness, saw a direct parallel between the crises in the forest and fishing industries. He believed that workers in both industries were doomed to marginalization and unemployment unless they could have a say in the use of BC's natural resources. Expanding on the community forest tenure idea, Edwards and several allies in the Clayoquot Sound Regional District proposed a Regional Aquatic Management Society (RAMS) to oversee all fisheries management on the west coast of Vancouver Island. They also proposed a community licence bank, which would reserve part of the fishery in any given area of the coast for the benefit of adjacent communities. In 1997 this idea had inspired then provincial Fisheries Minister Corky Evans, backed by the UFAWU, to order the International Hake Consortium to land a portion of its catch in Ucluelet to protect the jobs of local shoreworkers. However, nothing quite so ambitious had ever been tried in the salmon fishery.

Edwards's mission to give coastal communities a greater say in the fishery did not receive a warm welcome from all elements of the commercial sector. In fact, Mike Hunter of the Fisheries Council of BC and others in the industry maintained that the dispersal of fishing privileges was the sole prerogative of the "free market" and that community licences were a dangerous form of "social engineering." Some individuals insinuated that Edwards was part of a conspiracy to carve out special fishing rights for Natives at the expense of existing commercial fishing licence holders.

Edwards, a former director of the Pacific Trollers Association, had helped organize the BC Fisheries Survival Coalition in 1992 in response to the AFS pilot sales program. But he also maintained, as he had for years, that the AFS wasn't the only threat to commercial fishermen. He had observed that more and more precious fish habitat was being sacrificed to logging and other land development on the west coast of Vancouver Island, and that it was increasingly difficult for West Coast trollers to catch their quotas of coho and chinook salmon as laid out in the Pacific Salmon Treaty. So Edwards had joined Dave Christensen, Bill Irving, Nelson Keitlah, Cliff Atleo and several other local people to form the West Coast Sustainability Association (WCSA). Their mandate was to rebuild fish stocks through an ambitious program to enhance the region's natural habitat, while striving to give communities a voice in local fisheries management.

To attend his first WCSA meeting, Edwards had to cross the half-mile stretch of inlet between Ucluelet and the local Native reserve. He had lived in Ucluelet for more than 40 years, yet this was his first trip to the reserve—and his life changed forever. Members of the Nuu-chah-nulth Band knew that he was a member of the BC Fisheries Survival Coalition, which they abhorred, but they respected him for his efforts to defend his livelihood. As the new group took hold, its members came to recognize that it was not the competing interests of stakeholders or even the *sui generis* rights of Natives that jeopardized their future as much as the decisions made in government offices and corporate boardrooms thousands of miles away. After that first meeting at the reserve, Edwards urged his fishing partners—especially Survival Coalition members—to forge links with Native commercial fishermen and to repair the rift between Natives and non-Natives that left them both vulnerable to the actions of the federal government. Whether or not the DFO was deliberately feeding the AFS controversy by portraying commercial fishermen as obdurate racists, the fishermen were being divided and conquered, and Edwards feared that the independent small-boat fleet was doomed.

Then, one night just before Christmas 1992, Edwards received a call from an old colleague who wanted to organize a meeting of the Survival Coalition in Ucluelet to protest the AFS pilot sales program. When Edwards protested that such a meeting would cause serious tension in the village and possibly split the WCSA, the caller denounced him as a traitor to the commercial fleet. Later, Edwards attended a Coalition meeting in Parksville, where he explained that the WCSA's strategy of aligning with Native people was not tantamount to accepting the AFS or to undermining the interests of commercial licence holders. But the Survival Coalition's guest speaker that evening was Mel Smith, a former deputy minister and constitutional advisor to the defunct Social Credit Party. His recently published book, *Oh Canada: Our Home or Native Land?*, was extremely critical of the AFS and the entire Native land claims process. Smith acknowledged that it was good to build better relations between commercial fishermen and the Native community, but most Coalition members in attendance rejected Edwards's proposal for unity.

Edwards was unshaken in his belief that Native and non-Native people had much in common and that they were injured by the same forces of economic injustice, but he knew that he could not realize his dream of a common front against policies of the DFO. With a heavy heart he severed ties with many friends in the Survival Coalition.

After leaving the coalition and participating in the struggle against the Mifflin Plan, Edwards decided that a grassroots alternative to corporate ownership of resources was necessary. Without it, Natives, other workers and natural resources would be mere grist to the corporate mill. He began devoting his energy to building a Regional Aquatic Management Society (RAMS) in the Port Alberni–Clayoquot region. Some middle-ranking bureaucrats in the federal and provincial governments liked the concept of decentralizing fisheries management, but senior DFO officials resisted the idea. Ever since the Pearse Plan of 1983, they had favoured the privatization of Canada's fisheries—to cut costs and to offload the burden of management.

The Economists' Fig Leaf

Dan Edwards was not alone in his work on community-based fisheries management. The world-renowned cultural anthropologist James R. McGoodwin, for example, believes that overfishing can best be avoided by encouraging "indigenous management" practices rather than privatizing fishing rights. In a modern context, "indigenous management" requires a careful analysis of the customs and practices of traditional fishing societies. This is a difficult task—there is almost no written record of such practices—but McGoodwin points to new research that is providing important insights. He also argues that the rubric of "indigenous management" includes the myriad ways that contemporary small-scale fishermen and fisheries-dependent communities go about regulating common-property resources. Even more important, McGoodwin dispels the myth popularized by Garrett Hardin's "tragedy of the commons" thesis that all "common-property" fisheries are destined to collapse from overfishing. McGoodwin asserts that common-property fisheries are often mistakenly confused with the notion of "open access," which implies unregulated fishing activity. From time immemorial, he says, fishing societies controlled fishing activity through social protocol—"informal" regulations that include etiquette for the use of favoured fishing spots and the sharing and hiding of information.

McGoodwin does not suggest that indigenous management practices are infallible or that modern fisheries management should be discarded. But he argues that when fishermen are directly involved in management, the resource is more sustainable, and that fish managers must learn to appreciate the social objectives of the fishery: "The concept of MSY [Maximum Sustained Yield] has nothing to say about the allocation of access to the resource, while MEY [Maximum Economic Yield] as a concept provides no guidance regarding how resource rents should be distributed through society...These [economic] concepts have the appearance of rationality...whereas in reality they provide a convenient fig leaf of objectivity to cover what is in essence a highly political process...The scope of a fishery manager's goal will be too narrowly defined if it merely emphasizes the maximization of the net economic return because for many people the net economic return may be less important than some other more desirable goal—full employment, for instance." Government policy making, he says, tends to favour economic theory over social theory because the former appears more "scientific." He points out, "A recurring problem inherent in many of the formal models economists employ is the implicit assumption...that all economic behaviour is motivated by a basic necessity in all societies to allocate scarce means...in the most efficient manner possible." The ideology of a great deal of modern economic theory, McGoodwin says, exacerbates rather than solves the dilemma of overfishing: "It seems that intense and increasing competition—particularly that posed by participation in modern market systems—more than any inherent flaw in the character of fishers themselves compels the behaviour associated with the tragedy of the commons."[9]

The University of BC sociologist Ralph Matthews, in his book *Controlling Common Property: Regulating Canada's East Coast Fishery*, writes: "There is a strong historical and practical basis for allocating the regulation of fishery property rights to the local fishing community." Such community-managed fisheries are preferable, he says, if they can limit the number of eligible participants, specify the rights and duties of participants, allocate resource units proportionally, develop monitoring arrangements, create a governance system that gives most members an active voice in determining the rules to be used, devise conflict-resolution mechanisms, and develop regularized procedures for changing rules when necessary.[10]

Matthews' colleague Evelyn Pinkerton, editor of *Co-Operative Management of Local Fisheries*, asserts that most contemporary fish management systems undervalue the knowledge of working fishermen, particularly First Nations fishermen, and that economic prescriptions flowing from the "tragedy of the commons" thesis are flawed because they focus on ownership rights. Community-based management is more than a simple "anthropological curiosity," she says; it offers the "means of moving beyond the question of right to the question of how to find solutions to management problems."[11]

These academic theories lent credence to Dan Edwards's proposals, but few people in positions of power would even consider such an alternative. Edwards carried on his crusade to pioneer this new approach to fisheries management, but at the same time he was fighting a rearguard battle for his own economic survival against powerful adversaries. He would only succeed, he concluded, by taking the WCSA's quest for a Regional Aquatic Management Board beyond Ucluelet to fishermen elsewhere on the coast. He decided that the Sockeye Crisis Committee's campaign might serve as a launching point for a coast-wide discussion about regionally based, democratic resource management.

Not long after he ended his hunger strike, Dan Edwards found that his phone calls were no longer being returned by Minister Dhaliwal's staff or senior DFO officials. But he decided to carry on the fight, and on October 25, 1999, he again stopped taking solid food.

This time, despite the physical demands of the fast, Edwards resolved to take his crusade as far afield as possible and to build enough public support to embarrass the government into acting. He helped organize a rally of Canadian and US fishermen at the Peace Arch border crossing near Blaine, Washington, to emphasize that the same problems threatened the livelihoods of commercial fishermen on both sides of the border. Then he went to Ottawa to appear before the Parliamentary Standing Committee on Fisheries. Unfortunately, BC Fisheries Minister Dennis Streifel also appeared there, and on the advice of his staff, declared that the sockeye crisis of 1999, although serious, could not be called a disaster. Streifel did request $30–50 million in special support programs, but he made it plain that his own ministry would take no financial responsibility for the Fraser sockeye crisis. Once again, in the wake of Glen Clark's resignation, the NDP government showed little interest in the West Coast fisheries.

Dan Edwards at the end of his second 58-day hunger strike, December 1999.

Daniel in the Lions' Den

Edwards returned to BC from Ottawa in an exhausted state, but continued his hunger strike aboard David Emes's gillnetter, *Silver Spray*, moored at False Creek in Vancouver. It was there, on December 21, the 58th day of his hunger strike, that Dhaliwal's office called to propose a meeting. The two men met in the federal cabinet offices adjacent to the Vancouver Public Library—a replica of the famous coliseum in Rome and an appropriate setting for this modern-day Daniel entering the lions' den. Dhaliwal literally held Edwards's fate in his hands. The minister began by listing the many good things his government had done for the West Coast fishery, and Edwards replied, "But where are you getting your advice from for your policies? It sure as hell isn't from people in coastal communities. Even the auditor general of Canada has said your consultative process is a mess." It seemed to Edwards that Dhaliwal was caught off guard. He paused for an awkward moment, then cheerfully continued his oration. Finally, wishing to end Edwards's hunger strike before Christmas, he promised that he would personally oversee a review of the DFO's consultative arrangements. Now on the brink of serious physical harm, Edwards had little choice but to trust Dhaliwal.

The two men held a joint press conference to describe the nature of their "understanding," and on December 23, the *Vancouver Sun* quoted Edwards as saying, "The main reason I went on the hunger strike was specifically process issues. I'm willing to work with the Minister and the Ministry here to get that process back on track." Dhaliwal smiled into the TV cameras and said, "I'm very happy, and I'm sure his family and friends will also be happy, that he's called off his hunger strike." He then made it clear that his deal with Edwards implied no financial obligations: "The government has made a huge commitment in the $400 million." When asked about the response of the BC government, Edwards replied, "We've sent a letter to the attorney general again, asking for them to review that process [disaster relief]. They have to formally ask the federal government for help."

Edwards then returned home to his family in Ucluelet and, in an attempt to restore some measure of joy and normality in his life, indulged in a few drinks and a Christmas feast; afterwards he was seized with a fit of violent nausea.

Signing Treaties and Burning Boats

While Dan Edwards was recovering from his hunger strike, another critical issue was thrust to centre stage. In a surprising reversal of form (and at a point when Glen Clark could no longer take credit for it), the federal Liberals invoked closure in the House of Commons and passed the Nisga'a Treaty. Another aboriginal issue—Native fishing rights—flared up in another context: the Supreme Court of Canada ruled that Donald Marshall, a Micmac activist in Atlantic Canada, had been wrongly charged with fishing illegally for eels. Citing a treaty signed in the 1770s, the court ruled that Native persons in Canada had a right to derive a "modest income" from fishing. The decision provoked a political maelstrom. Within days, aboriginal activists on both coasts laid claim to the entire fishery, non-aboriginal fishermen reacted ferociously and Natives and non-Natives clashed violently over the lucrative East Coast lobster fishery. The confrontation reached its climax in the village of Burnt Church, near Miramichi Bay, New Brunswick, where some Native fishing vessels were rammed or set on fire. Mike Belliveau, executive director of the Maritime Fishermen's Union, told the press:

> The Maritime Fishermen's Union will not support, organize or encourage any direct actions in the water that takes enforcement into our own hands, but we will use all peaceful means at our disposal to ensure basic enforcement of our members and their communities' livelihoods is done...everything about the history of the MFU tells you that we were formed to organize the underdog, the inshore fishermen who were years ago scheduled to disappear...We are absolutely in solidarity with Native peoples' efforts to break years of poverty and injustice, but solidarity is not a one-sided proposition and we refuse to give credence to a dead-end declaration of sovereignty that will inevitably isolate small bands of people and mislead them into thinking they are not interdependent with the rest of us.[12]

Belliveau's union was faced with the same dilemma that had plagued the UFAWU following the introduction of the Aboriginal Fishing Strategy: how can a democratic union defend the livelihoods of its members while embracing principles of racial equality and justice? The question will not be answered so long as we uphold an economic system that promotes competition that rewards a wealthy elite, while Native and non-Native workers take turns in the welfare lines.

The Supreme Court of Canada rarely issues clarifications of decisions, but they did so in the Marshall case. In a 30-page document, the judges explained that although Ottawa has a fiduciary duty to uphold Native fishing rights, it must also limit and regulate those rights to protect the interests of society as a whole.

Once again, litigation rather than negotiation had driven Natives and non-Natives further apart.

Waiting in Vain

In early February 2000, the DFO announced that the West Coast salmon licence buyback was complete. They had reduced the fleet to less than half its size before the introduction of the Mifflin and Anderson plans. There were now only 271 seine licences on 198 eligible seine boats, 1,348 gillnet licences on 1,190 eligible gillnetters and 527 troll licences on 494 eligible trollers. Over three rounds, 1,409 licences (216 seine, 731 gillnet, 462 troll) had been bought back at a cost of $275 million. In the meantime, the prospect of future licence-stacking threatened to reduce the fleet even further.

Later that month, Corky Evans lost to Ujjal Dosanjh in his bid to replace Glen Clark as leader of the provincial NDP and premier of BC. Some political commentators suggested that Dosanjh had close ties to the federal Liberal Party[13] (and in the 2004 federal election, Dosanjh was elected as a Liberal MP). Whatever the reason, it was clear that Dosanjh did not want to upset the Ottawa establishment on fisheries issues or any others. He fired Dennis Streifel, a Clark loyalist, from cabinet and shuffled the short-lived Ministry of Fisheries back into a revived Ministry of Agriculture and Food (MAFF). Then he reappointed Corky Evans to head up MAFF. Then in the spring of 2000, Dosanjh ordered Evans to terminate the province's lawsuit against the US for overfishing, in favour of a "more co-operative" approach. The decision was the death knell for the province's short-lived confrontation with the US over the Pacific Salmon Treaty. The federal government moved quickly to complete the expropriation of Nanoose Bay and renew the US Navy's multi-year lease on it.

Meanwhile, Dan Edwards had waited in vain for Herb Dhaliwal to keep his promise of December 1999 to review DFO consultative processes. At last, on February 4, 2000, Edwards met with Dhaliwal again, along with Edward John, Grand Chief of the First Nations Summit, and John Henderson, Chief of the Campbell River Band. They presented Dhaliwal with five recommendations adopted by a conference of First Nations organizations in Port Hardy on January 9, 2000: to establish an independent review of the DFO consultative process; to implement a disaster relief program for coastal communities; to develop a comprehensive policy forum for the BC fishery; to start immediately on the consultative review to ensure timely delivery of disaster relief and proper consultation on future policy changes; and to ensure that the BC government declared the fishery situation of 1999 a natural disaster.

On May 16 Minister Dhaliwal appointed Stephen Owen, former BC ombudsman, to conduct the independent review of the DFO's consultative process. However, Owen was not to begin his work until the fall of 2000, and the question of disaster relief for 1999 fell between the cracks. Edwards also expressed the fear that the DFO would make major policy decisions—including licensing changes and cuts to the salmon enhancement program—before Owen began his review.

It Was All Lies!

I want to see the fishing lifestyle retained. I don't want to see it destroyed because of some grand plan that some economist has devised to manage the resource easier. I am not particularly concerned about how easy the resource is to manage or how easy it is for the DFO. DFO managers are being paid to do a job. If there are changes, it should not be to make the managers' lives easier, it should be for the benefit of fishermen.

—Don Cruickshank, March 1991

*W*hen spring arrived in the Shuswap Valley in 2000, the year-old sockeye fry began feeding on the burgeoning blooms of plankton. Then, as if obeying some grand cosmic clock, they migrated en masse from Shuswap Lake. Now known as smolts, they were ready to undertake the perilous 483 km (290 mile) journey down the Thompson and Fraser rivers. When they passed through the turbulent Hells Gate in the Fraser Canyon, they swam backwards against the current to maintain their equilibrium. Eventually they arrived at the broad intertidal marshlands at the mouth of the Fraser, where they delayed just long enough to adjust to the salt water. Here they were confronted with a multitude of threats posed by human activity. Only 30 percent of the original Fraser River marshlands—which are vital to the rearing of juvenile salmon—

remain, so the young sockeye had to survive a deluge of sewage waste and toxic contaminants before they reached the sea.

By late April the tiny fish were massing in the miles-long plume of muddy water that extends from the mouth of the Fraser into Georgia Strait. The water was less salty here, and young sockeye found abundant food. Then, in late May, they drifted westward to graze on the shoals adjacent to the Gulf Islands and eastern Vancouver Island. In late June or early July, the massive school split in two. One group of smolts headed south to the open ocean through the Strait of Juan de Fuca; the other was swept north through Johnstone Strait by the huge tides of early summer. Eventually the two schools of young Adams River sockeye gathered again in Queen Charlotte Sound and travelled, at 2–3 km/h (1–2 mph), through BC's Inside Passage to the waters off Alaska.

In July 2000, as the Adams River sockeye smolts headed out to sea, they crossed paths with hundreds of different races of adult salmon returning home to spawn, including an unexpectedly strong run of Skeena River sockeye. The DFO had predicted that this run would be very poor, and this, along with conservation concerns for upper Skeena coho, had convinced them to close all fishing on the Skeena by July 18.

Early on, however, Skeena gillnetters enjoyed unexpectedly good fishing and by July 18 had caught an unprecedented 1.2 million sockeye—more than the entire expected catch plus escapement.

The cumulative bycatch of coho was well below the 10 percent limit that DFO biologists had deemed acceptable,[1] and the sockeye run had yet to peak. Commercial fishermen began to fear a repeat of 1994 and 1995, when the preservationist policies of the Skeena Watershed Committee had led to a massive over-escapement of sockeye. The spawning grounds had been so crowded that the fungal disease Ichthyophthirius (ICH) had broken out, and returns in 1998 and 1999 were very poor. To prevent such a calamity in 2000, the UFAWU–CAW, Native Brotherhood of BC and other northern commercial fishing groups united to lobby the DFO and Prince Rupert City Council for more opportunity to crop the excess escapement. Their cause was supported by an experimental test fishery conducted by Skeena River gillnetters, showing that 85 percent of the small coho bycatch could be released alive. According to this data, the gillnetters should have been allowed to fish for another eight days,

Gillnetters hauling their nets while fishing for sockeye.

said UFAWU–CAW Vice-President John Sutcliffe. But the DFO refused to reconsider. "They insisted on holding to the same position they took pre-season," said Sutcliffe, "despite what science is saying and despite what's happened in some past years where there has been a huge over-escapement." He estimated that for each day's fishing that was lost to the DFO's risk–averse management plan, $6 million in potential earnings for fishermen was sacrificed. Joy Thorkelson, northern representative of the UFAWU–CAW, added: "If they were caught in the net fishery and processed, they could have brought millions to the Prince Rupert economy and helped hundreds of fishermen to get back on their feet after three bad years."[2]

On July 23 a large group of fishermen circled Prince Rupert harbour in a scene reminiscent of the 1997 ferry blockade. They honked their horns and waved signs that said: "Welcome to Canada. We can afford to waste $90 million—contact DFO for details." Despite the protest and the huge waste of sockeye, the DFO didn't budge. Meanwhile, thanks to David Anderson's deal with Locke, nothing could be done about the hundreds of thousands of Canadian coho that were being taken in southeast Alaska.

Later, the DFO reported that more than 2,551,432 sockeye had arrived on the spawning beds—two and a half times the optimum escapement goal of 1,010,877. In a last-ditch effort to avoid another over-spawn and outbreak of ICH disease, they authorized three Native bands to harvest more than 750,000 sockeye in an escapement surplus fishery—a clean-up catch almost as large as the entire commercial catch. But the fish were in very poor condition by this time, worth only a fraction of the price they would have commanded had they been caught in the regular commercial fishery. The sole purchaser of the catch was the Black Fishing Company, unknown to commercial fishermen. It was never publicly revealed where the fish were processed or how much the company paid for them, and the DFO refuses to divulge the information.

The waste of a valuable resource was only part of the problem for commercial fishermen in 2000. They also faced drastic cuts to the dockside price of salmon. By July 31 the retail price for sockeye fillets in Lower Mainland stores had climbed to $5.85 per kg ($12.99/lb). BC fishermen received the lowest down payment since the new price formula had been introduced in 1994, partly because non-unionized fishermen in Alaska had accepted prices as low as 50 cents per pound. But the fishing time on the South Coast was so short, fishermen did not take any action.

The 2000 season marked the centenary of the historic Fraser River fishermen's strike for higher dockside prices and the beginning of trade unionism in the BC fishery. In 1900, to secure a price of 25 cents for each sockeye, white, Native and Japanese fishermen had joined forces to fight the canners with a three-week strike. Outraged, the canners tried every trick in the book to break the fishermen's will, then finally enlisted the support of the Duke of Connaught's Own Rifles—dubbed the "Sockeye Fusiliers" by the strikers. The fishermen settled for 19 cents per fish.

On the Loose

In 2000 an unprecedented number of escaped Atlantic farm salmon were caught in commercial nets, despite government assurances that the number of such escapees was negligible. Officials from the Ministry of Agriculture, Food and Fisheries (MAFF) had previously announced a new regulatory policy to prevent the escapes, and the problem might never have become known had there not been an unexpected gillnet fishery in Johnstone Strait on August 22. There, in one 24-hour opening, 10,400 Atlantic salmon were landed. According to *The Fisherman*, a loaded Stolt Sea Farms Ltd. fish packer had lost approximately 4,500 pieces en route to a processing plant on Vancouver Island. Five days later, a fish pen in Sergeaunt Passage lost another 77,000 Atlantic salmon. "What if we hadn't had a commercial fishery?" asked Rick Frey, a Campbell River gillnetter. "How long would this have gone unreported?" He and many other fishermen were very concerned that the escaped Atlantic salmon would infect the wild stocks with disease.

The MAFF bureaucracy finally admitted that the number of escapees was much larger than they had thought, but they reassured the public that the Atlantic salmon posed no threat to wild fish and would likely die of starvation. The Simoom Sound environmentalist Alexandra Morton quickly demolished this myth by demonstrating that the Atlantic salmon turning up in commercial nets had needlefish, herring and krill in their stomachs.[3]

(In March 2001, the Dosanjh government lifted the moratorium on the expansion of salmon farming. Minister Evans tried to minimize the political fallout by encouraging the aquaculture industry to move to "closed containment" pens to prevent escapes and disease epidemics, and his successor Ed Conroy approved a pilot project by Agrimarine Industries Ltd. of Campbell River to test the new closed containment technology. In exchange, Agrimarine was given additional net-pen sites to raise Atlantic salmon near Kyuqout on Vancouver Island. But in April 2001 a MAFF report revealed that 27 out of 124 farms monitored did not provide the required information, 70 percent of the farms were using toxic copper-based anti-fouling paint on their nets, and more than half the farms were discharging disinfectant solutions directly into the marine environment.)

Inappropriate Commissioner

On August 28, 2000, I was unceremoniously dumped from my position as one of the two Canadians on the Pacific Salmon Commission representing the commercial sector. The new appointees were Ron Fowler of the Northern Trollers Association, Christine Hunt and Hubert Haldane of the Native Brotherhood, the DFO's Donna Petrachenko and Paul Sprout, Gerry Kristianson of the Sports Fishing Institute, Gibby Jacobs of the Squamish Indian Band and Rich Chapple for the sports fishing sector. Later, when Bill Valentine, deputy minister of MAFF, voluntarily stepped down as the provincial commissioner, I hoped that I would be re-appointed by the province. But Corky Evans chose Christine Hunt of the Native Brotherhood, because—as one senior government official told me—it would have been "inappropriate" to appoint me. It seems likely that my high-profile association with Glen Clark's PST strategy was a major factor in this decision.

Transfers to the Rich

By mid-fall 2000 the Adams River sockeye smolts had travelled more than 3,000 km (1,800 miles) from the Fraser River, though they were still hugging the shoreline of the Alaskan panhandle. By early winter, they were pulled to sea by the Alaska gyre—a gargantuan counter-clockwise current rotating out in the mid-Pacific. Once in the open sea they followed the same migratory course as hundreds of other races of salmon that emerged from the labyrinth of streams and rivers along the coast, but in the vastness of the north Pacific, the various races seldom mingled.

In the fall of 2000, Prime Minister Jean Chretien called an election for November 27. It was a lacklustre campaign, memorable mainly for Stockwell Day, leader of the newly named Canadian Alliance, who stumbled from one faux pas to the next. The Liberals made vague promises of continued fiscal responsibility balanced with a "social conscience," although Canada's average annual unemployment level had climbed from about 4 percent during the 1950s to 9.5 per cent during the 1990s.

The Liberals also eroded Canada's social safety net. As the Canadian author Mel Hurtig noted, "Where in the late 1980s well over 80 percent of the unemployed in Canada received benefits, by 2000 that number was down to only 36 percent. In the last few years the Employment

Insurance surplus passed $36.5 billion and was headed for $44 billion..."
Chretien's Liberals said they could no longer afford such "lavish" social
benefits because of "tight fiscal times." Yet Canada's corporate sector
had never had it so good: annual corporate profits, which had averaged
$152.1 billion in the 1970s, skyrocketed to $694.6 billion in the 1990s.
Provincial budgets had also been hit hard. "From the time Chretien and
Paul Martin took over to last year [2001]," Hurtig wrote, "Ottawa's total
transfers to other governments and persons have fallen by a huge $62
billion."[4]

In BC the federal election campaign of 2000, unlike that of 1997, featured no vitriol about BC separation, no obstreperous BC premier beating
the anti-Ottawa drum, no squabbles over naval bases, no flamboyant talk
about seizing control of West Coast fisheries—just the occasional mention by Premier Ujjal Dosanjh of federal–provincial co-operation.

The Liberals achieved a comfortable majority but made no gains in
BC. David Anderson and Herb Dhaliwal retained their seats, and Liberal
strategists were relieved that Stephen Owen was elected in Vancouver
Quadra, a seat formerly held by Ted McWhinney. But Owen's victory
spelled disappointment for Dan Edwards and many West Coast fishermen, because he had barely begun the so-called independent review of
the DFO's Pacific region consultative process when he had entered the
federal race. The review was passed on to the University of Victoria Institute for Dispute Resolution. The UVic team conducted an extensive
investigation into the DFO's process of policy making in the Pacific region. Their report called for improved DFO decision-making standards,
a more transparent consultative process, an integrated planning process,
a policy advisory committee to oversee DFO decision making, greater
involvement of First Nations in the fishery, greater involvement of
communities in DFO decision making, and a tiered approach to consultation with First Nations given priority.[5]

The report was thorough, but the UVic Institute for Dispute Resolution lacked the political clout of Stephen Owen. This may have been one
of the reasons why the DFO never directly responded to the report, nor
did it amend its consultation process. Another two years would pass before they made changes to their consultative system, and those changes
countermanded everything in UVic's report.

End of the NDP Run

When spring 2001 arrived, the Adams River smolts were far out in the mid-Pacific. It had been assumed at one time that North American salmon smolts did not venture past the International Date Line in the mid-Pacific. However, tagging studies by the IPSFC in 1955 revealed otherwise. The salmon apparently follow the shrimp-like crustaceans known as krill. Current, salinity, sunlight and upwellings of cold, nutrient-rich water all play a vital part in the blooming of the phytoplankton that support the entire food chain of the ocean. Many scientists fear that global climate change caused by greenhouse gas emissions may be destroying this delicate web of marine life, turning the world's oceans into watery deserts. During the Mifflin Plan years, these increasingly adverse ocean conditions had a more devastating impact on West Coast salmon than commercial fishing ever did.

By the end of their first year at sea, in late April 2001, the Adams River sockeye were somewhere south of Kodiak Island, following the galactic sweep of the Alaskan gyre. The demands of constant swimming were taking a toll on their metabolism, yet slowly the sockeye were growing. During their second oceanic winter they again swerved to the north and repeated the vast circuit until they reached their maximum size of 2.73 kg (6 lbs) the following year.

On May 16, 2001, Ujjal Dosanjh led the provincial NDP to its worst electoral defeat in history. With 21.62 percent of the popular vote, they secured only two seats in the legislature. Gordon Campbell's Liberals won the other 77 seats. According to pundits and Liberal spin doctors, there was really only one issue in the election: the need to rid BC of all traces of Glen Clark. The RCMP investigation into Clark's activities was still in process, making it impossible for Clark to clear his name and for the NDP to escape a catastrophic political backlash.

As I cleared out my office after the election, Mike Hunter, former president of the Fisheries Council of BC, was settling into his new role as a Liberal backbencher. But on June 5, when Campbell announced his cabinet, it was not Hunter who got the Agriculture, Fisheries and Food portfolio but John van Dongen, a dairy farmer and the MLA for Abbotsford. He had kept a very low profile as fisheries critic during the NDP regime, and although he had spoken in favour of greater provincial control over West Coast fisheries, his top priority was the expansion of the fish farming industry.

Yet Another Disastrous Season

In the spring of 2001, after five unmerciful years, BC's commercial salmon fishermen looked to the coming season with desperate hope. The 2001 sockeye run would consist of the progeny of the brood of 1997, the year of the Prince Rupert ferry blockade and the "Canada First" fish war. That year the Fraser River sockeye escapement had been the third highest in 50 years. The 2001 Fraser sockeye return was expected to be as high as 12.85 million, and the forecast for the Skeena run was 2 million. It looked as if 2001 would be a very good year.

Then, just prior to the season, North Coast fishermen were dismayed to learn that coho conservation concerns and depressed sockeye returns to the Nanika River, a tributary of the Skeena, might prevent any fishing on the Skeena. Commercial fishermen and the Wet'suwet'en Fisheries Commission, in whose territory the Nanika lies, took matters into their own hands. After some discussion, the commercial gillnet fleet donated 8,000 sockeye from other stock groups to meet the winter food requirements of the Wet'suwet'en in exchange for their agreement not to take endangered Nanika sockeye within their traditional territory.

Meanwhile, the DFO's coho fishery cut-off date of July 18 still posed a problem for the North Coast fleet. The Alaskans continued to take upper Skeena coho while the DFO maintained a 10 percent bycatch limit on BC commercial fishermen in all sockeye fisheries. So the UFAWU–CAW helped organize a new management plan. The gillnet fleet cut their nets to half the normal 220 fathoms and limited their sets to 20 minutes, so that most of the coho bycatch could be released alive. As a result, despite nine extra days of good sockeye fishing after the July 18 cutoff, the coho mortality rate on the North Coast was held to only six percent and 1,188 sockeye were caught for every coho that was accidentally killed.

Both the Nanika agreement and the selective gillnet fishing initiative proved that working fishermen could resolve most of the DFO's weak-stock management concerns through practical problem solving rather than harsh restrictions. The DFO's risk–averse approach—especially after the Anderson Plan—had cost coastal communities incalculable amounts of income, and at the same time Anderson's much-celebrated conservation plan had caused over-escapements that imperilled some cycles of Skeena River sockeye. As James McGoodwin pointed out, conservation-oriented management is best realized with the direct involvement of commercial fishermen.

On the South Coast, commercial fishermen did not fare as well. Despite the return of 26 million sockeye, pinks and chums to the Fraser in 2001, the DFO limited the seine fleet in the Strait of Juan de Fuca to two days of fishing, seiners in Johnstone Strait to two days, gillnetters in Johnstone Strait to five days and Fraser River zero, trollers on the west coast of Vancouver Island to 19 days and those in the Gulf of Georgia nine days.

As in every year since the introduction of the Anderson Plan, the DFO was prepared to sacrifice the harvest of millions of surplus salmon to protect a very small number of coho. To complicate matters, in the absence of reliable catch data from regularly scheduled commercial openings, the Pacific Salmon Commission once again underestimated the incoming 2001 runs until it was too late for them to be harvested. At season's end the DFO reported that the return of Fraser sockeye had been 6.4 million pieces—similar in size to that of the cycle-year catch of 7.7 million in 1987. But in 1987 there had been 10,000 gillnet/boat-days of fishing effort in the Fraser River, and in 2001 there was none. The entire South Coast commercial sockeye catch in 2001 was 295,000 pieces, compared to 3,232,000 in 1987. Meanwhile, the AFS harvest leapt from 508,000 in 1987 to 831,000 in 2001.[6]

We Should Go Fishing Anyway

Early in 2002 the Adams River sockeye, which had begun their life cycle in 1998, embarked on their final journey, travelling thousands of miles to return to the exact site of their birth. Celestial alignment, polarized light, magnetic and electrical fields, salinity gradients, pheromone attraction—no one knows how the salmon accomplish this amazing feat. In the final stages of their homeward journey, the sockeye stop feeding and rely on their reserves of body fat. The extra energy they expend at this stage of the migration can be taxing—a sockeye loses two percent of its weight for every 160 km (100 miles) it travels. In years when the Pacific Ocean is warmer, salmon migrate farther north, seeking cooler temperatures. This makes their journey back to their natal stream much longer, and consequently they arrive in much poorer condition.

As the Adams River sockeye turned homeward in early March 2002, representatives of various commercial fishing organizations gathered at the Maritime Labour Centre in Vancouver to develop an alternative to the DFO's risk–averse management system. This ad hoc committee agreed that intra-gear issues should be set aside and that each licence area would develop plans to harvest its share of the TAC. They also agreed that there would be no priority for AFS pilot sales fisheries and that fishing plans would include acceptable bycatch mortality. For in-season stock assessment and data gathering, all fisheries would be full-fleet fisheries, and any necessary controls must not exclude eligible licence holders. (The latter point was a critical one, because DFO, following the Anderson Plan, commissioned a number of so-called special assessment fisheries to determine stock abundance and to experiment with selective fishing techniques. These fisheries often involved small groups of fishermen who many in the industry believed had close ties with DFO managers. Naturally, these privileged individuals would reap great financial rewards while the vast majority of the fleet remained tied to the dock.) Finally, they decided that future escapement targets would be realistic and based on a sliding scale.

Before the season opened, the DFO announced that for conservation reasons, it would limit the South Coast bycatch of Thompson River coho to a mere three percent and the bycatch of steelhead to 10–20 percent, and that there would be no fishing on the early Stuart and early summer sockeye components. In addition, extensive "no fishing" zones might be imposed throughout the South Coast to protect rockfish populations. The DFO also announced its pre-season forecast for Fraser River sockeye: between 7.9 and 15 million. The wide margin came from the department's use, since the 1994 Fraser Report, of two different forecasting methods. One was an ultra-conservative approach—the DFO assumed a 75 percent probability of being accurate. The other, much closer to traditional management practice, assumed an accuracy of 50 percent. It was a confusing system that allowed the DFO to hedge its bets. If it understated the forecast by using the 75 percent probability factor, the run was more likely to be much larger than predicted, and the DFO's management performance would look better. For fishermen, this numbers game made it even harder to plan for the coming season.

But the commercial fishing representatives on the Fraser panel of the PSC agreed to the risk–averse management scheme, as long as the DFO agreed to practice management flexibility if any of the identified conservation problems could be avoided. In its pre-season Integrated Fisheries Management Plan for 2002, the DFO promised, "If stock assessment indicates that the late-run sockeye are delaying in the Strait of Georgia similar to historical migration patterns, then a more flexible management option [than the 15 percent bycatch limit] may be considered." The DFO also pledged that once the late-run escapement was confirmed as between 2,095,000 and 5,087,000, it would allow a harvest of 15 to 65 percent of the remaining late run.[7]

On April 30 the ad hoc fishermen's committee held a rally in Nanaimo to build support for the alternative management principles they had developed in March. Paul MacGillivray, the DFO's director of operations, attended the rally and said, "Ten years ago our emphasis was on producing and catching as many fish as we could. We put $40 million a year into salmon enhancement to meet that goal. And our management focus was on catching as much of the surplus as possible. We used to harvest 70 percent of all coho stocks. But now we only take 3 percent, as DFO's primary objective today is meeting conservation. If we're gonna make a mistake it will be on the side of conservation." He reminded the crowd that the industry roundtable had agreed to this course of action back in 1996. "We had to implement area licensing, single gear licensing, licence stacking and licence buybacks to deal with the problem of lower salmon returns and declining prices," he said. This brought forth a chorus of exasperated groans. "Sure did us a lot of good, didn't it?" shouted one fisherman from the back of the hall. MacGillivray answered that the DFO had never promised "economic viability." "The round-table had to decide whether there was enough money to go around in a fleet of 4,400," he said. "The fleet decided to reduce itself. But there were no guarantees." About the issue of weak-stock management of coho and late-run sockeye in 2002, he said that the DFO would be as flexible as possible within the parameters of risk–averse management. "Your objective is to get on the water and make money," he said. "But there are restraints. We can't move away from our conservation agenda. My key message is: we have policies we must maintain, but we want to work with you."

At that point, Calvin Siider, a gillnetter from Sointula, leapt to his feet and challenged MacGillivray:

> How many fish were wasted on the Fraser last year? Fifty million dollars swam past us for the sake of a handful of coho. Your test fisheries are all at the wrong places. There has to be some flexibility. For 80 years each season we started fishing, and if there were fish, we got extensions. If there were no fish, we went home. The DFO will never get any meaningful information about runs unless we get it for them. We should open the whole coast on an agreed day every week. If the department agrees, fine. If it doesn't, we should go fishing anyway!

This inspired a wild outburst of applause from the audience.

Before the meeting adjourned, Jack Jantzen, a gillnetter from Nanaimo, addressed the crowd. "You know," he said, "I quit going to these kind of meetings because they are a waste of time. The DFO never listens to us." Then he turned to the DFO officials at the head table and asked, "Are you going to allow AFS pilot sales fisheries?"

Ed Lochbaum, a veteran DFO South Coast manager, replied, "No one has officially notified me of that, but I suspect that's likely."

Jantzen replied, "In the past I never participated in protest fisheries against the AFS pilot sales. But this time I will and so will all the guys who never did before. And it won't just be protest fisheries against the AFS. Guys will do it if we're closed like we have been for the past five or six years…There are solutions: be fair in your allocations, be flexible, set realistic escapement goals. But if you guys don't change, there will be consequences."[8]

The Gulf Trollers Fight Back

Swimming as far as 45 km (27 miles) per day, the first of the Adams River sockeye made landfall in early August 2002. But this year, although the water off the west coast of Vancouver Island was not unusually warm, the vast majority of the sockeye ignored the predictions of DFO scientists and migrated north, through Johnstone Strait, as their ancestors had done in the legendary run of 1958. They appeared at the mouth of the Fraser River, delaying in the Gulf of Georgia until the bulk of the run arrived in mid- to late August. Then the entire run migrated upstream in mid- to late September. Thus, although a few Adams River sockeye entered the river early, causing concern about pre-spawn mortality—as in the cycle year and in 2001—millions more Adams River sockeye were still on their way back from their ocean odyssey.

Just after noon on August 14, 2002, Guy Johnston steered his troller, the *Michelle Rose*, through the tricky stretch of water known as the Yuculta Rapids. In a few more hours he would reach Johnstone Strait, where he planned to fish. He and his deckhand Peter Moskovicz, a former troller who had sold his licence to the Mifflin buyback, had been tying a bunch of new hootchies and flashers since leaving Powell River at 6:30 that morning, so they'd have enough gear. They didn't expect to get rich, but they hoped to put a few dollars in their pockets.

And then they heard the news over the radiophone—the troll opening for sockeye in lower Johnstone Strait, scheduled for August 17, was cancelled. Guy Johnston was dumbfounded. It was the second time that season that he'd made the long, costly trip north to the strait, only to leave empty-handed.

For the past three seasons, Johnston had fished prawns instead of dealing with the stress and politics of the salmon fishery. He was very fortunate to have acquired his prawn licence years before all the problems beset the salmon fishery, and prawn fishermen had enjoyed good catches and prices for three seasons. However, in 2002 the price had dropped and Johnston had decided to turn to salmon to make ends meet. Now, despite excellent test fishing in Johnstone Strait the previous week, the PSC Fraser panel had cancelled all commercial fisheries. And the panel was not scheduled to meet again until September 6, well after the sockeye run was over.

The 2002 Fraser River sockeye run was now estimated to be at least 14,383,000, well above the pre-season forecast of 13.3 million—one of the best returns in modern history. Yet the Fraser panel worried about the status of the late-run sockeye bound for the Adams River and the rest of the Shuswap Lake system. The late run was estimated to be at least

5.8 million, but the PSC believed that up to 90 percent of the fish would die before spawning. For several years the late-run stock had entered the river a month earlier than "normal" and had died of a gill disease that afflicts sockeye when they delay too long in fresh water. Therefore, the DFO had already ordered that during the harvest of the 2002 summer run, the bycatch of late-run sockeye could not exceed 15 percent—down from 17 percent the previous year.

Normally the summer and late-run stocks arrive two weeks apart, allowing the summer run to be safely cropped. As it turned out, the late run started pouring through Johnstone Strait in early August, almost a month ahead of schedule, mixing with the summer-run group of Chilko, Quesnel, late Stuart and Stellako sockeye. By August 16 the PSC was estimating that the peak of the summer run was five days late, and the peak of the late run was eight days early. As far as the management of the commercial fisheries was concerned, this was the worst-case scenario.

By late August the total catch of Fraser sockeye by US fishermen was 442,000, and the Canadian catch—including a Native catch of 740,220 and 72,600 taken in controversial experimental fisheries—stood at 2,862,000. And the recruitment of summer-run spawners past the Mission hydro-acoustic sounder was looking extremely good at 200,000 per day for over a week. In fact, the summer-run escapement had already surpassed 3.5 million, well above the target of 2.9 million. More important, the late run was far larger than anyone had dreamed. The DFO managers, however, made no adjustment to the 15 percent bycatch limit for late-run stock. When the fishermen demanded that the DFO honour its pre-season pledge to reconsider the limit, the DFO said that it needed as many late-run spawners as possible to offset the threat of pre-spawn mortality—even though the late-run sockeye that had already migrated up the river were showing no signs of stress. Some 818,000 late-run sockeye had moved up the river during August, and an estimated 2.5 million spawners were still delaying, as was normal in the Gulf of Georgia. According to a test fishery in Johnstone Strait, millions more late-run sockeye had yet to arrive. But there was another factor involved for the DFO: prior to the season, it had promised the US to maintain that 15 percent late-run harvest limit unless the US agreed to an in-season adjustment. At the time, Canadian negotiators had been so convinced that the late-run sockeye were in danger that they had failed to even consider a backup plan.

When Guy Johnston phoned his fishing partner, John Hird, about the bad news, he learned that a number of Gulf of Georgia trollers had headed to Campbell River to discuss a possible protest fishery in defiance of the closure. Johnston wanted to attend the meeting, but years before he had promised his wife Michelle that he'd cut down on his involvement in fish politics. With a family to support, he had to think twice about risking his boat and licence, and he was also reluctant to raise the hopes of other fishermen, only to have them crushed. After a certain point you couldn't continue to beat your head against a brick wall. Too often, a friend or neighbour would ask, "Are you still trying to be a commercial fisherman? I thought you guys had already caught the last fish!"

Johnston took a long time to work up the nerve to call his wife. He was embarrassed that he had not yet earned a penny after spending so much money getting the boat ready. He also felt bad for his poor deckhand, who had been taken on a wild goose chase. When at last he talked to Michelle, she told him that he had no choice but to make a stand, even if it seemed like a hopeless cause. There was more than money to consider—their dignity was on the line.

Johnston tied his boat up at Denman Island, where his family was staying for the summer, and drove to the meeting in Campbell River. There he was pleasantly surprised to see that most of the fleet had sailed into port, and crowds of fishermen were gathered in spirited discussions on the docks. At the meeting, Mike Griswold, the Area G troll representative on the PSC's Fraser panel, told them that as a member of the panel he could not participate in a protest fishery. Then he tried to explain the DFO's rationale for the closure and reported that an emergency meeting of the panel had been called for Monday, August 19. Wayne Saito, the chair of the panel, was considering changes to the fishing schedule. Many of the fishermen found this unacceptable, but in the end they agreed to wait until the panel had met again.

The next day Johnston went back for his troller and sailed her up to Campbell River. A strong spirit of unity still prevailed on the docks and almost everyone talked about the need for action, regardless of the legal consequences. But not everyone was in favour of a protest fishery.

Some fishermen felt such a move would alienate the public and be tantamount to poaching. Johnston's impression was that most of those who shared this view had quotas to fish other species or had salmon licences for other areas, so they could survive the salmon closure. Some of them might even be calculating that the closure would force many single-licence trollers out of the business, leaving more fish for them in the future. But most of the fishermen expressed a determination that went far beyond the routine complaining that went on in bars and coffee shops after the season. For once, fishermen had gathered at the peak of the season and had something meaningful to fight for.

On August 19 Mike Griswold reported that the Fraser panel had decided to continue the closure, ostensibly to protect the late-run Fraser sockeye. The trollers left Campbell River en masse to catch the tide in Seymour Narrows, where exactly four years earlier the seine fleet had mounted its blockade to protest similar policies. Then they proceeded north to Otter Cove near Chatham Point and anchored for the night, vowing to fish in defiance of the DFO the following day.

All night long, Guy Johnston tossed and turned in his bunk. Would the fleet still be there in the morning? Would he have to urge the fishermen to risk their boats and licences to mount the protest? But when he rose at dawn on August 20, several trollers were already getting ready to set their gear. They had agreed that their objective was to make a political point, not to catch a lot of fish, and that to gain public sympathy they would donate a number of the fish taken to the food bank in Nanaimo. Not long after the protest began, a DFO patrol vessel came alongside the *Michelle Rose* and charged Johnston with fishing illegally. Within a few hours, several other fishermen were charged. Eventually the fleet ended the protest and returned to port. Not long afterwards, the Gulf Trollers Association mounted a legal campaign to defend those who had been charged.

Of the 60 sockeye Guy Johnston caught, some he canned and the rest went to his neighbours in Cowichan Bay.

The Sinking of the *Cap Rouge II*

Just before the Gulf trollers launched their protest fishery on August 20, the South Coast seine fleet had been given a short opportunity to crop some of the tail end of the summer-run sockeye in the Strait of Juan de Fuca, as they had not come close to taking their pre-season allocation. Following that opening, on August 13 the salmon seiner *Cap Rouge II* headed to Vancouver to unload its catch of 3,000 sockeye. The boat was travelling with a light load but was also top-heavy because the seine skiff was stowed on deck and the heavy purse-seine net was wrapped around the large aluminum drum, instead of being stashed on the deck for better stability. The skipper was well aware of the danger, but like many fishermen, he took such chances in order to save time. The wind was gusting at 17–25 knots, which could be dangerous in the shallow stretch of water at the mouth of the Fraser. In the choppy waters the skipper decided to transfer water from one tank to another in preparation for unloading. Seconds later the *Cap Rouge II* flipped, and five people, including a nine-year-old boy and an 11-year-old girl, were trapped inside. When the Richmond-based Search and Rescue hovercraft appeared on the scene, Coast Guard commanders told divers on board the 33-year-old vessel that they were not authorized to attempt a rescue. As well, according to Bob Rezansoff, skipper of the seiner *Taaska*, who arrived on the scene shortly after the *Cap Rouge II* rolled over, the Coast Guard divers did not have sufficient air in their tanks.[9] They were ordered to stand by the *Cap Rouge II* and wait for a military rescue team based in Comox, 90 minutes away. The military diving crew arrived far too late to save any of the victims.

This gruesome event sent a host of federal politicians and bureaucrats scrambling for cover. Robert Thibault, federal minister of fisheries and minister responsible for the Coast Guard, offered his sympathies to the families of the victims. Two weeks later he told the *Vancouver Sun* that the Coast Guard divers might have been able to enter the overturned hull after all.

Coast Guard personnel gave an entirely different account of the incident. According to the *Vancouver Province*, the rescue team was "overwhelmed by the afternoon's demands, either because they were understaffed or because regular staffing levels were insufficient." It was later revealed that Herb Dhaliwal had axed the funding for the diving team while he was still minister of fisheries.

UFAWU–CAW President John Radosevic cried, "There's going to be another death, another tragedy, because the Department of Fisheries is making cuts without regard to public safety. Anyone who rides on a ferry, anyone who rides on an airplane, anyone who works on the water in tugboats...needs to be concerned." He pointed out that by October 2002 the DFO was planning to decommission one of the two rescue hovercraft stationed in Richmond, and that cuts to the budget of the Kitsilano Coast Guard base had limited staff to an eight-hour day with a 30-minute emergency callout provision.

Even as this tragedy was unfolding, Finance Minister Paul Martin was using his reputation as the slayer of the federal deficit in his bid to replace Jean Chretien as leader of the federal Liberal Party. And Chretien, preoccupied by the politics within the Liberal caucus, had almost nothing to say about the incident.

The Fishermen's Fishing Plan

On August 22, the day after the Gulf trollers staged their protest fishery, Garth Mirau, vice-president of the UFAWU–CAW, Bill Duncan, executive director of the Native Brotherhood, and I organized a coast-wide conference call for fishermen to discuss the situation. They reported in from all over the coast, and we listened as Guy Johnston and other trollers explained how the protest fishery in Johnstone Strait had come to take place. Before long, dozens of gillnetters and seiners were demanding that a much larger protest be launched the next day.

Garth Mirau, a former seine skipper himself, facilitated the discussion in a low-key manner, dispensing no fiery rhetoric or advice as the fishermen decided what they wanted to do. When the majority of the fleet called for another protest fishery, Mirau outlined the serious legal implications of such an action. He said that the UFAWU–CAW could not advise them to break the law or guarantee legal representation for anyone who was arrested. However, he promised that the union would do all in its power politically to defend the fishermen if they defied the DFO closure.

The fleet agreed to hold another conference call after the Fraser panel meeting the following morning, August 23. At that meeting the panel decided to extend the closure, saying that the late-run sockeye conservation crisis was greater than ever, but scheduled another panel meeting for the next day to provide further information on the status of the late run.

During the conference call that evening, the fleet overwhelmingly endorsed the idea of a mass protest fishery involving all gear types. The more militant fishermen suggested that the fleet begin fishing immediately, but Mirau proposed that they first present an alternative risk–averse fishing plan to the DFO. He also suggested that the fleet carefully plan the protest fishery to maintain public support and to refute any notion that they were acting irresponsibly. The fishermen agreed that a volunteer strategy committee would meet in the UFAWU–CAW hall on the morning of Saturday, August 24. I worked with that committee in developing an alternative "fisherman's fishing plan," designed to maximize the harvest of the huge surplus of summer-run sockeye while avoiding the late-run stock as much as possible.

Later that afternoon, Don Sananin, a veteran seine fishermen, read the committee's proposed alternative fishing plan over the airwaves. It recommended that the DFO merely revise its bycatch limit on late-run sockeye from 15 to 25 percent. This cap would permit the harvest of the surplus of summer-run sockeye still arriving in Johnstone Strait and also ensure that 75 percent of the late-run sockeye remained untouched. Given the current estimate of the late run, 5.8 million, a 25 percent bycatch would still produce twice as many Adams River spawners than the DFO had predicted at the start of the season. Contrary to what some critics had charged, at no time did the fishermen propose a wide-open fishing effort. They simply proposed taking approximately 500,000 more sockeye: 237, 725 fish for Johnstone Strait seiners and 177,625 for Johnstone Strait gillnetters, 51,400 for Outside trollers, and 67,200 for Gulf of Georgia trollers. This was not enough to make a decent season for anyone, but it would pay a few bills and feed a few families.

The fishermen agreed to keep the fleet informed through a series of coast-wide conference calls each day, and more and more fishermen participated in each successive call. They agreed that the fleet would muster on the fishing grounds in Johnstone Strait at 8:00 on Monday morning, August 26, unless the Fraser panel authorized a "legal" fishery before that time. Meanwhile, Mirau tried desperately to reach Fisheries Minister Thibault in Ottawa to present him with the fishermen's alternative plan, but Thibault was in a Liberal Party caucus meeting. Later, when questioned in the House of Commons, he said, "It would be the first time I am asked for anything probably because there's too much fish. The Pacific coast salmon is a difficult species to manage because it intermingles with other species. There was a high rate of mortality in season spawning. I'm very happy to see that didn't happen this year. Mr. Speaker, I cannot take responsibility for this. The Minister of Environment [David Anderson] is to blame. It is under his direction as Minister of Fisheries that he took the difficult decision in '98. That means there are so many fish today."[10] Mirau retorted, "If these fish were headed up the St. Lawrence and fishermen in Quebec were facing a similar plight, you can be damn sure Thibault would return calls."

Finally, on Sunday, August 25, the Fraser panel reported that all commercial fishing for Fraser River sockeye would close for the balance of the season to protect the Adams River run. In fact, even though the late run was clearly much larger than expected, the Americans had refused to allow the 15 percent bycatch limit to be increased, even though they would have got a greater share as well. They knew that the vast majority of the 2002 Adams River sockeye were migrating through Johnstone Strait and they would have a hard time catching their share, so they were content to make use of a "catch-up–make-up" clause in the PST that allowed them to carry unharvested shares into the following year. As the 2003 run was already forecast to be poor, they calculated that any carry-over from the 2002 run would be to their benefit. This was yet another legacy of the failure of the federal government to defend the Pacific Salmon Treaty and preserve Canada's sovereignty over its salmon stocks.[11]

During the fishermen's conference call that evening, Mirau took a roll call to estimate the potential support for a protest fishery the next day. In a truly inspiring display of grit, more than 100 vessels radioed in that they were ready to fish regardless of the legal consequences. Mirau told the press, "Fishermen are very, very angry...No one wants to harm the run. All fishermen want to do is prove that there are a lot of fish out there."[12] Wayne Saito, the man in charge at the DFO, responded, "Our allowance to ensure that our conservation objectives could be met was taken in prior fisheries. There was no remaining balance that would allow us to conduct fisheries and still stay within those objectives."[13]

Prior to the season, however, the DFO had announced that an escapement of 1.6 million late-run spawners would have been more than adequate. Indeed, all during the 1950s, '60s and '70s the average spawning count for the dominant cycle of the Adams River run had been approximately 1.4 million. DFO managers fretted about conservation concerns, but they were well aware—based on abundant information from fishermen—that millions of Adams River sockeye were holding in the Gulf of Georgia. More importantly, there was no evidence that most of those fish were in a stressed condition, or likely to succumb to the same pre-spawn mortality rates as had occurred in the cycle year of 1998.

In any event, the commercial fishermen had never proposed to take any of the fish already in the Gulf of Georgia. They simply wanted to crop the tail end of the surplus summer-run sockeye still approaching through Johnstone Strait, 320 km (200 miles) to the north. They needed only a 10 percent adjustment in the bycatch limit on the late run. Yet the DFO refused to grant even this modest request, perhaps afraid of an orgy of finger-pointing as had occurred after the release of John Fraser's report in 1994.

The Johnstone Strait Protest Fishery

At 8:00 a.m. on Monday, August 26, the fishermen embarked on a four-hour protest fishery in Johnstone Strait. Before starting, they listened as UFAWU–CAW Vice-President Garth Mirau said over their radios, "I spent all night thinking about how serious this action could potentially be. I thought of a lot of legal reasons why you should not fish. But I can't think of a single moral reason why you should not. Fishermen can't stand by forever and allow DFO to waste these fish. Everyone would prefer that this be done the right way and the fisheries be legally sanctioned. But if not—we have no choice but to act."

Minutes later, gear was going into the water. Lorne Thames dropped the lines from his troller *Avante* at Chatham Point just north of Campbell River, but because he had been charged for participating in the first protest fishery on August 20, he set his lines without hooks. On August 27, he told the *Vancouver Sun*, "People have to protest because this is a huge run and we've had very little access to them. Before the fishing season started, they come up with this fishing plan which sounds all great and we'll get quite a bit of fishing time, and they're telling us that we're going to have so many fish. And all of a sudden, things changed and they said, 'No there's no fishing.'" After more than six years of disappointment and frustration, Thames, a veteran of 30 years' fishing, had had enough. He had once enjoyed an annual income of more than $50,000 by fishing salmon each season. In 2002 he'd had seven days' fishing.

Steve Ordano, a gillnetter from Campbell River, said, "It doesn't seem to matter how many fish there is now, you don't get to fish. It doesn't matter if there's 10 million, 20 million, 100 million. There's always some excuse. Well, most of us after six years have realized it's over. There will never be a salmon fishery again. It was all lies."

Meanwhile, far away in Sabine Channel, Guy Johnston was also taking part in the protest fishery. At about 10:00 a.m., just before he dropped his lines in the water, a DFO patrol vessel approached the *Michelle Rose*. Johnston knew that the patrolman was not keen on laying charges, so he engaged him in conversation long enough for the rest of the trollers in Sabine Channel to haul in their lines and disperse. "If I were you," Johnston told him, "I'd just go around the point and have a coffee and let the guys do their thing. They won't be fishing that long." The officer nodded stoically and made his way slowly up Sabine Channel. By noon, as agreed, all of the fishermen had pulled their lines from the water.

After the protest, the DFO claimed that 133 vessels, scattered between Campbell River and Port McNeill, near the northern end of Johnstone Strait, had taken part. A department spokesman said that only 18 vessels had been observed actually fishing, and just 11 fishermen had been charged. The DFO estimated the protest catch at about 5,000 sockeye. Garth Mirau told the press, "The first thing I want to do is reassure Canadians that the resource is not at risk. Second, I want to thank everybody for their support. The whole industry owes a debt of gratitude to those who had the courage to defy the DFO today."[14]

The DFO Finally Sees the Fish

Deep in the murky waters of the Gulf of Georgia, millions of Adams River sockeye continued to accumulate at the end of August 2002 until a gigantic ribbon of fish stretched from the Sandheads at the muddy mouth of the Fraser to the distant blue waters of Johnstone Strait. Schools of sockeye crept along the shore of Bowen Island and the Sunshine Coast. Other schools swam through the deep sub-marine trench that extends from Sabine Channel, near Texada Island, to Campbell River. In Seymour Narrows, hundreds of thousands more sockeye raced through on each flood tide, and there were still fish all the way to the northern tip of Vancouver Island. Meanwhile, large numbers of sockeye were also arriving through the southern approach route of the Strait of Juan de Fuca and the San Juan archipelago.

Two days after the protest fishery, a test fishery in Johnstone Strait showed that the number of late-run sockeye in the area was still very large, and the DFO did a remarkable about-face and opened Johnstone Strait for commercial fishing on August 29. The majority of the fleet was still on the grounds considering a further protest fishery when the announcement was made. But Wayne Saito of the DFO vehemently denied that the protest fishery had influenced his decision to open the fishery.

From the fishermen's point of view, the statistics for the 2002 Fraser River sockeye run were grim. The total run was almost 16 million pieces—more than twice the pre-season forecast of 7.9 million—but the commercial fleet had harvested only 2.2 million, a fraction of the traditional commercial harvest rate on such a large run. The aboriginal fishery, however, including the commercial pilot sales program, landed 1,021,500, far above the pre-season expectation. The recreational sector took 127,500 sockeye, also above the pre-season expectation.

The only fishermen who had a good season in 2002 were those of the Fraser River gillnet fleet. After three seasons of almost no fishing, they were finally able to catch 934,700 summer-run sockeye in just two 12-hour openings. Yet even this bit of good fortune had almost been missed—mere hours before the Fraser panel opened the river on August 12, the DFO's cumbersome integrated management team had been dithering over whether the summer-run stock could sustain a commercial gillnet fishery in the river. The DFO "experts" were wrong. The gillnetters landed the biggest catch in a 12-hour opening on the Fraser in the entire history of the industry. Despite this record-breaking catch, millions of extra summer-run spawners flooded the spawning grounds. With its long-term risk–averse stock-rebuilding program, the DFO had hoped for a total escapement of 8.3 million, well above the average escapement of 2.9 million on this particular cycle, but an unbelievable 11.2 million sockeye spawners had flooded the grounds. The most dramatic excess occurred on the summer-run stock grouping: 4,740,900 spawners, when the pre-season goal was 2,448,000. Assuming a 75 percent probability, DFO forecast a late run of 2.1 million. If the bycatch had been 15 percent, approximately 142,000 late-run spawners would have failed to reach the grounds (factoring in DFO's 90 percent mortality rate). In contrast, had the bycatch been 25 percent, theoretically 179,000 spawners would have made it to the grounds. Thus, to save 37,000 spawners, DFO was prepared to sacrifice the harvest of 1.2 million surplus summer-run sockeye. These figures are conjectural—the mortality rate for the late run in 2002 was minimal, and the final return twice as large as forecast—but commercial fishermen were outraged. They could have harvested at least 1.2 million fish, worth $12–24 million, had the DFO accepted their advice to adjust the late-run bycatch limit from 15 to 25 percent, and only 37,000 fewer late-run spawners would have reached the spawning grounds. An abundant harvest, with no harm to the resource, had been sacrificed.

Returning to the Adams River

History can't tell us what will happen, only what problems we will have to solve.

—Eric Hobsbawm, *On History*

In late September 2002, the sockeye entered the Fraser River. Travelling up to 5 km/h (8 mph), they surged on the tide past the erstwhile fishing village of Steveston, past the fashionable houses and condominiums built by the Weston Corporation on the site of the ancient cannery bunkhouses and net lofts, then past Vancouver's suburban sprawl and industrial wastes. Two or three days later they had cleared the meandering stretch of the Fraser Valley. Then, at the village of Yale, where the river makes a great swing to the north, they entered the maelstrom of the Fraser Canyon. After another day's travel, they struggled through the fury of Hells Gate and into the peaceful waters of the Thompson River. Finally, in mid-October, they navigated for the last time through Shuswap Lake to arrive, exhausted, at the exact place of their birth.

On August 29, 2002, the same day South Coast fishermen were finally permitted to fish legally in Johnstone Strait, Glen Clark sat nervously waiting in a Vancouver courtroom. After nearly two hours of deliberation, Justice Elizabeth Bennett announced that he was absolved of all criminal charges regarding his alleged involvement in a casino licence application, and the crowded courtroom erupted in wild cheers. One of the ugliest chapters in BC's highly partisan political history was finally over. Millions of taxpayers' dollars had been spent, the legislative system had been paralyzed for more than two years, a political party had been almost destroyed, yet in the end the former premier had been vindicated.

By then the Ministry of Fisheries, through which Clark had tried to wrest control of West Coast fisheries from Ottawa, was long gone. Senior officials sympathetic to Clark's vision had been fired or transferred to other jobs. Fisheries Renewal BC, the Crown corporation Clark had established to rebuild the fishery, had been dismantled. The struggle for equity under the PST was just a memory, Canadian salmon were still being loaded into the holds of Alaskan fish boats, and torpedoes were still being tested at Nanoose Bay.

Was it coincidental that Glen Clark took such a tumultuous fall from power? Or was he targeted because he challenged the myth of American neighbourliness and fought against the rationalization agenda of the large canning companies? Whatever the case, after almost two decades of industrial restructuring and the fact that thousands of people have lost their jobs, just as much wealth, if not more, is being extracted from the BC fishery as a whole.

In a May 2004 report, commissioned by DFO and the provincial Liberal government, Peter Pearse once again urged that BC marine resources be privatized—because, he declared, the West Coast fishing industry is economically unstable. It can be argued that no other individual can take more credit for this circumstance than Pearse himself. His ideas have shaped every major restructuring initiative undertaken by the DFO since 1969.

One of the worst effects of the restructuring of the West Coast fishing industry has been overcapitalization. Bob Grant of the Community Fisheries Development Centre, who contributed to a national fisheries sector study report prepared by the Praxis Research group and sponsored by Human Resources Development Canada and the Canadian Council of Professional Fish Harvesters, estimated that the West Coast industry had to support a capital burden of $2.3 billion in 2004. This load consists almost entirely of the "paper" value of licences and quotas.

Worse, half of the landed value from the fishery is now dissipated in an economic rent collected by "armchair fishermen" who lease quotas and licences.

Grant reports that the original "A" salmon licence category, which once carried the right to harvest virtually all species on the coast, now represents only $272 million out of the total. This means that privileges to fish black cod, halibut, shrimp, prawns, geoducks, crabs, rockfish, sea cucumbers, herring, etc. are now worth about $2 billion. Most of the limited-entry licences for these species did not even exist until after the release of the DFO's *Vision 2000* document in 1990. Those fortunate enough to qualify for such licences and quotas—and who, in most cases, paid nothing for them—naturally support the current licensing system, and the thousands of individuals who have been forced out of the industry have no say on the DFO's current policies. But the question is: when the current crop of licence holders retire or leave the industry, who will buy them out? Ordinary people from coastal communities or fishing-industry families will not be able to do so. The resource will inevitably fall into the hands of large corporations through quota systems unless a radically different solution is found. Meanwhile, the problem is compounded by the fact that ex-DFO bureaucrats, including Michelle James, Lloyd Webb, Ed Zyblut and Bruce Turris—many of whom helped engineer the individual transferable quota (ITQ) system while still on the government payroll—landed new jobs as representatives of various quota and gear associations that make up the BC Seafood Alliance, which replaced the Fisheries Council of BC.

Proponents of privatization invoke New Zealand as a success story, but in 2004 Catherine Wallace of Victoria University in Wellington released a study that contradicts this view. In "New Zealand Fisheries Quota Management: Theory and Experience," which describes the decline of orange roughy stocks after the introduction of the ITQ system, Wallace notes, "[Private] property rights [in the fishery] do not remove the incentive to 'mine' a resource and to use the proceeds elsewhere." As for the assertion by Peter Pearse and others that privatized fishing rights lead to better conservation and management, Wallace says, "The outcome [of ITQs] is that 'fishing down' stocks will be done co-operatively [by quota holders] and more efficiently from a financial point of view." She also reports that New Zealand's experience with ITQs has concentrated quotas in the hands of large companies, financially benefited the few fishermen lucky enough to get quotas in the first round, economically harmed small owner-operators and their communities, and reduced stocks. She concludes that ITQs have "allowed quota owners to invest uncaptured resource rentals into influencing officials and politicians, and... into engineering the evolution of institutions to further enhance their power and control and marginalize other interests."[1]

By early 2005 there were no ITQs in the BC salmon fishery because fisheries managers had conceded that the unpredictable nature of salmon returns made it difficult to allocate guaranteed harvest quotas. But salmon ITQs may soon become a reality in BC. The DFO will try to convince the public that such a policy change will ensure better resource management.

If the government does move in this direction, it will be violating the Fisheries Act, according to a legal opinion obtained by the Canadian Council of Professional Fish Harvesters. This opinion says that the granting of ITQs would contravene section 16 of the Act, which states:

> 1) A document [fishing licence or quota] is the property of the Crown and is not transferable.

> 2) The issuance of a document of any type to any person does not imply or confer any future right or privilege for that person to be issued a document of the same type or any other type.[2]

As the New Zealand experience demonstrates, fish stocks can be overfished in a private quota fishery just as easily as in a fishery based on the principle of common property access. Nor does the market-driven model result automatically in the best social use of the resource. Both of these overriding imperatives will be realized only by a new consensus between fish harvesters, government regulatory agencies and the public. The well-being of the fish must be the first consideration, but the survival of small-scale fish harvesters and their communities must be a close second. Ways must also be found to extricate fishermen from the tyranny of debt, overcapitalization and market insecurity—an unlikely outcome if our marine resources fall into the hands of a select few.

Are these ideas utopian or unrealistic? If we can put a man on the moon, surely we can design a commercial fishery that can sustain fish stocks, feed the world and allow working fishermen to make a decent living.

The Real Return

It was a scene that Tom Thomson, one of Canada's greatest landscape painters, would have loved. The bright blue autumn sky lit the waters of Shuswap Lake with sparkling hues of mother of pearl, and brilliant groves of aspen rose like frigid yellow flames against the dark green of the surrounding Shuswap hills. From a dense jungle of tangled stumps, shifting gravel bars and brooding cottonwood groves came the incessant roar of the Adams River, its icy waters teeming with vast schools of alizarin crimson sockeye.

The lake boiled, blood red, for as far as the eye could see, as millions of sockeye salmon jostled near the surface of the water. After more than four years of perpetual motion, the great schools of sockeye were stalled at the mouth of the river where they were born. Try as they might, they could not enter. Immense columns of fish had already filled the river, making further passage almost impossible. The fish were packed together so tightly that some were thrust out of the water, their bodies slapping awkwardly on top of the roiling mass, and the fish had trouble taking water through their gills. Thousands of snouts protruded from the water, and the salmon's mouths opened and closed erratically, as if the fish were uttering silent screams.

In late October 2002, I stood watching as John Radosevic, president of the UFAWU–CAW, and Garth Mirau, vice-president, surveyed the spectacular scene on the rocky flats where the Adams River enters Shuswap Lake. Next to them stood three veteran fishermen, Edgar Birch, Nick Carr and Joe Smith, and farther along the shore Dan Edwards and his wife Bonnie took photos. Few words were exchanged. All of them were lost in thought, for no one can fail to be moved by the sight of so many spawning salmon—one of the wonders of the world. But these fishermen were also bitter that they had not been given the opportunity to take part in the harvest of such a bounty after so many years of hardship and sacrifice.

The DFO is not sure how many spawners returned to the Adams River in 2002. Some estimates are as high as 4 million, far more than in the legendary run of 1958, when the International Pacific Salmon Fisheries Commission (IPSFC) built an electric fence to prevent the excess fish from disturbing the 1.7 million prime-quality spawners recruited from the peak of the run. Yet despite that huge return in 1958, only four years later, in 1962, the return was a near disaster. The IPSFC had wondered whether the mass of phytoplankton in Shuswap Lake was sufficient to support the progeny of such a large run. On February 5, 2002, then UFAWU–CAW Vice-President John Sutcliffe echoed this concern as he testified before the Parliamentary Standing Committee on Fisheries: "There's a high correlation between over-escapement and poor returns, particularly for sockeye. Every major over-escapement event since 1958 has resulted in a near collapse in the Skeena, in Rivers Inlet and the Fraser River. But our managers go on dumping more and more fish on the spawning grounds."

When those fishermen stood on the banks of the Adams River after the season had ended in 2002, all they knew for sure was that the DFO had been wrong in predicting that 90 percent of the Adams River run would die before spawning. The fish had arrived on the spawning grounds in robust condition and in record numbers. The race of salmon that the commercial fishing fleet had been accused of "wrecking" during the fish war of 1994 had surpassed all previous known spawning records. Yet for the fifth year in a row, commercial salmon fishermen had been given virtually no opportunity to make a living.

Meanwhile, about a mile away in a large clearing in Roderick Haig-Brown Park, the official Salute to the Sockeye ceremonies were getting underway. Crowds of people gathered around a cluster of information booths, teepees and food stands. Convoys of yellow buses discharged throngs of schoolchildren, who ran and shouted, oblivious to the solemn public officials assembled on a stage at one end of the field. One by one, the dignitaries took the microphone and uttered clichés about the mystique of the salmon. Eventually John Fraser, the official spokesman for the Pacific Fisheries Resource Conservation Council (PFRCC), told the crowd, "The council is delighted in the good news regarding the number of sockeye spawners this year, especially as in recent years mortality rates of the late-run sockeye have reached astounding heights—as high as 90 percent!" Then, almost as an afterthought, he added, "We would hope that perhaps the ability to forecast could be improved, if that is possible. Because we're also concerned about the fact a good many of the people who fish for a living did not get as much out of this much larger run as they would have hoped. So we do emphasize the fact that in fairness one has to keep in mind the last couple of years which were serious indeed."[3] Fraser then officially released the 2001–2002 Annual Report of the PFRCC—the first time, he said, that the public had been presented with a transparent and comprehensive overview of the status of southern BC salmon stocks. "A rich diversity and abundance of Pacific salmon populations continue to exist in many locations," the report said. "More favourable ocean conditions have recently contributed to improved salmon production, and conservation measures implemented have also been crucial factors in recovery, particularly for southern BC coho."

A sombre warning followed quickly:

> The Council believes that there can be a viable and productive future for Pacific salmon in southern BC…but attention must be paid to protecting habitat and ensuring an empirical basis for stock assessment, management, and enforcement decisions. A broad fisheries resource base remains, but despite recent improvements in spawning escapement, levels of production in most cases continue to be substantially below those of the past. These recent improvements cannot give rise to complacency about future conditions. Habitat restoration and stock conservation measures will continue to be required.[4]

Fraser spoke in a much less bombastic manner than he had in 1994, when he had accused commercial fishermen of fishing the Adams River run to the brink of disaster. In 2002 they had scarcely been permitted to fish, while the multitude of threats to Pacific salmon, especially global climate change, remained unchecked. All Fraser could offer was a series of muted denunciations of the DFO for its diminished capacity to protect salmon habitat.

In fact, after more than a decade of federal budget cuts, the DFO was functionally in ruins. Thousands of employees had been laid off or given early retirement, and critical programs such as scientific research, stock assessment, salmon enhancement, catch monitoring, enforcement and in-season management were starved for funds.

Not Enough But Plenty

At the same time, Ottawa was wallowing in a multibillion-dollar surplus, and millions of dollars were being spent on decentralizing the DFO. Under the direction of former Regional Director Donna Petrachenko, the Pacific Region had been balkanized into a network of disjointed regional offices. The new system, designed to encourage enhanced "regional management," only created more inertia and interdepartmental confusion. For example, as part of the new risk–averse management paradigm, a 41-person integrated management team that had been dispersed across the entire province was now required to be involved in all South Coast fisheries management decisions. This group could barely communicate with one another in a timely way, much less make critical management decisions that must often be made within hours. To make matters worse, by early 2005 the provincial Liberal government had chopped 2,678 full-time staff from the Natural Resources Ministry.[5]

The PFRCC Annual Report identified dozens of examples of how cutbacks by both the federal and provincial governments have put certain salmon stocks at risk. Yet no alarm has been sounded by the media, and we have seen no attempts to apply risk–averse principles to logging, fish farms, road building, urban sprawl, sewage and industrial effluent treatment, water diversion schemes, dredging, diking, paving and so on.

Neither has there been a push to restore the millions of dollars slashed from the DFO's budget.

In 2002, $41 million was cut from salmon restoration programs funded by both levels of government. The provincial Liberals cut $11 million from salmon restoration when they shut down Fisheries Renewal BC, $18 million when they closed Forest Renewal BC and $2 million when they cancelled the Urban Salmon Habitat Program. The federal government chopped $7 million from the Habitat Restoration program and Salmon Enhancement Program (SEP) and $3 million from the Habitat Conservation Stewardship program. Another $3.5 million in cuts to the SEP were proposed for 2003. All of this prompted biologist Otto Langer, formerly with the DFO and now with the David Suzuki Foundation, to say, "We're seeing ethical bankruptcy on the part of government willingness to protect fish and fish habitat. We're slipping backwards from the 1980s and 1990s in terms of terrible leadership and budget cuts."[6] Yet virtually nothing about any of this is reported by journalists.

To make matters worse, the Pacific Salmon Endowment Fund, negotiated by David Anderson in 1999, turned out to be a bust. At the time, Anderson and Don McRae had implied that Canada had won a $140 million (US) salmon enhancement fund in lieu of securing a long-term equity deal. Even if this had been true, it would not have been an impressive negotiating feat, given that millions of dollars' worth of Canadian salmon are intercepted by the Americans every year, and the fact that Canada has never been compensated for decades' worth of American interceptions—a loss to the economy of hundreds of millions of dollars. Anderson never obtained the results for which the media gave him credit. Instead, the Americans had insisted that "the [southern/northern transboundary] Fund shall be held by the Pacific Salmon Commission bylaws and invested in accordance with the terms of a "Trust Agreement" to be drawn upon by the parties... Expenditures shall not exceed the earnings from the Fund. The cost of administering the... Fund shall be drawn from the income of the Fund."[7] In other words, Anderson had only secured the right for Canada to share in the expenditure of a portion of whatever annual interest accrued to the Pacific Salmon Endowment Fund. Worse, the 1999 deal specified that when the agreement expired—or if either country served notice of cancellation—the remaining principal (and interest) would revert to the US government. And to top off Anderson's non-accomplishment, The Pacific Salmon Endowment Fund was invested in the stock market. At the time he cut the deal, both Canada and the United States were in the throes of the longest running "bull" market since the crash of 1929. This was the period immediately before the American stock market spectacularly collapsed and the NASDAQ index fell 73 percent. The seed money for the Pacific Salmon Endowment Fund had been left to the tender mercies of a subsequent "bear" market, and no surplus earnings whatsoever were forthcoming.

In fact, six years passed before any money from the Endowment Fund was actually spent to enhance any salmon runs anywhere. On July 6, 2004, the Pacific Salmon Commission announced that $3.9 million (US) would be spent on 63 different salmon enhancement projects in British Columbia, Washington, Oregon and Alaska. But at least half of this money was to be spent on enhancement projects in the US, so Anderson had surrendered the equity principle of the PST for just a couple of million dollars. Nonetheless, in their press release DFO officials celebrated the Pacific Salmon Endowment Fund expenditures as though it were good news. "The northern and southern funds allow and require the bilateral co-operation that is so necessary given the interdependence of both Canada and the United States on the free swimming resource," said John Lubar, Canadian co-chair of the Northern Fund. Such a statement would have been inconceivable in an earlier era, when Canadian negotiators vowed that Canada's top priority was to reduce the $60 million annual US interception. Ron Kadowaki, Canadian co-chair of the Southern Fund, added, "Canada views these Funds as increasingly important given the growing challenge to maintain healthy salmon stocks." Kadowaki made no reference to the fact that Ottawa had slashed the DFO's salmon enhancement budget by an amount far in excess of anything forthcoming from the Endowment Fund for years to come.

The height of denial, however, was reached by the Pacific Salmon Commission in its official press release of July 6, 2004: "The Treaty fell on hard times through much of the 1990s when disagreements between Canada and the US over sharing of the catch and management of fisheries resulted in expiration of many of the original fishing regimes. Since the 1999 agreement, the Treaty had operated much more smoothly, in part because of the establishment of the two endowment funds." If things have operated "smoothly" over the past six years, it is because politicians like David Anderson gutted the spirit and intent of the original 1985 treaty and refused to admit it.

When all was said and done, the establishment of the Pacific Salmon Endowment Fund marked a return to the old continentalist approach to salmon enhancement, once symbolized by the Hells Gate fishways. For a pathetically small amount of money, the door would again be open to American claims to enhanced Canadian production. In other words, Canada would continue to grow the fish and the Americans would continue to intercept them. The issue of lost Canadian sovereignty is a moot point with many political interest groups, such as environmentalists who intone that their interest in fisheries transcends political boundaries—even when some of the players are violating the most elementary conservation principles. And, in this era of globalized "free" trade, the canning companies are less interested in the source of Pacific salmon than in the price of the fish and of the labour to process it.

In Anderson's 1999 dealings, he had also agreed to hand over $500,000 as Canada's "contribution" to the Pacific Salmon Enhancement Fund, which was heralded as a means of compensating Canada for US overfishing. This payment amounted to a refund of the transit fee Brian Tobin had imposed on Alaskan seiners during the 1994 fish war. Not only did Anderson surrender Canadian equity claims, he also annulled the one occasion in recent history when Ottawa had stood up to the Americans on the issue of overfishing.

In winter 2002 the vast Shuswap watershed was still blanketed in winter snow, but deep beneath the gravel and ice lay billions of sockeye salmon eggs. Soon they would emerge and start their epic journey into Shuswap Lake, and the life cycle would begin again.

As he packed his gear off the *Michelle Rose* in the fall of 2002, Guy Johnston reflected on the past season. He hadn't made much money on salmon and he would have to fish prawns in the winter to support his family. Despite that, and the fact that he was facing a day in court, the protest fishery had been an experience he'd never forget. He had got a glimpse of old-fashioned virtues like solidarity and professional pride, he'd seen Native and non-Native fishermen work together without rancour, and he'd witnessed seiners, gillnetters and trollers casting aside their differences and fishing alongside one another in a common cause. Above all he had been astounded that the press had not reported the story of the protest in a cynical way and that some environmentalists had even supported the fishermen's protest.

Johnston would have loved to catch a few more sockeye, but mostly—like all commercial fishermen—he was relieved that the fish had survived and glad to have seen what Jack Lloyd, a veteran gillnetter, had once called a "triumph of nature over the fisheries department."

It would be hard to survive as an independent owner-operator, especially because fishermen would have to fight to maintain government funding for salmon enhancement programs and the protection of salmon habitat as well as fishing for a living. And they would have to keep alive the belief that the salmon produced in Canadian rivers should remain the common birthright of all Canadians. Johnston figured that he and the other fishermen he knew were up for it. Yeah, he thought, if the judge doesn't throw me in jail or take away my licence, maybe I'll hang in there—'til the last dog is hung, as the old-timers used to say.

The Administration of Justice

Guy Johnston never went to jail. On June 17, 2003, Judge Brian Saunderson threw out the DFO's case against the 40 Gulf trollers charged with fishing illegally during the protest of August 2002. In his ruling the judge noted that although the DFO had closed the commercial fishery at the time, it had still permitted Native fisheries to continue, despite alleged conservation concerns. He wrote:

> The issue here is whether acts of civil disobedience should be punished when the civil authority, through

its own policies, action and inaction, has lost the right to demand the respect of the public. This is not a matter requiring proof of a direct causal link between the Aboriginal Fishing Strategy and the fishing closure in question. Nor is it a matter of people who fish illegally avoiding punishment if they can show, after the fact, that the DFO could have opened the fishery without harm to the fish stocks. Such is not a proper decision for the court. At the end of the day, it comes down to a matter of fairness and the perception of fairness. Unquestionably on the facts of the case, the DFO has not acted in an even-handed way toward all commercial sockeye fishermen. It cannot now be heard to seek the punishment of these accused men. Nor would the public interest be served by doing so. Indeed, the administration of justice would be brought into disrepute by convicting the defendants as that would make the court complicit with the DFO.[8]

In 2003 the DFO set up a new and highly controversial consultative system based on a series of "area management boards" that would include elected "industry representatives." However, only those holding licences in a given area were eligible to vote, and the area boards were dominated by the groups spawned after the introduction of the Mifflin area-licensing system, and others who were outright proponents of privatization. The new "consultative" arrangements effectively disenfranchised thousands of people who lived in coastal communities if they no longer held—or could no longer afford to hold—commercial fishing privileges. In December 2003 hundreds of salmon fishermen wrote letters of protest to Fisheries Minister Thibault, claiming that the new consultative system had been designed behind their backs and expanded the influence of the big companies. Their protests were ignored by senior DFO bureaucrats, and the new, inclusive approach to consultation that Herb Dhaliwal had promised to end Dan Edwards' hunger strike never came to pass.

Winners and Losers

My father Al Brown sold his salmon licence to the final DFO buyback in 2000 and has since retired from fishing. His boat, the *Sea Deuce*, sits tied to the dock in False Creek. But my father's story is the same as that of thousands of other ex-fishermen up and down the coast. All they have left are memories of the great industry that once supported them and their families. Many more of the poignant stories of BC's commercial fishermen have yet to be told. They are the stories of the winners, the losers and those who managed—for the time being, at least—simply to survive.

But what has happened to the rest of the players in this story?

Aerial view of Alert Bay in the halcyon days before the Mifflin Plan, after which the economy of this community and dozens of others like it were devastated.

Following the 2004 election, former Fisheries Minister David Anderson was dropped from the federal cabinet, but because of his fine reputation as an environmentalist, he is being touted for a Senate seat.

Former fisheries ministers Tom Siddon, John Crosbie and Fred Mifflin have exited the political stage to retire with comfortable pensions. This is true also of Bruce Rawson, Art May, Louis Tousignant, Wayne Shinners, Patrick Chamut and other senior DFO bureaucrats. Their slightly younger cohort, Brian Tobin, has faded into political obscurity. Former Premier Glen Clark now works for the billionaire Jimmy Pattison, running a publishing company. Pattison also owns the Canadian Fishing Company Ltd., which operates the last two major salmon canneries on the coast and benefits from imports of cheap salmon from Alaska. In 2003, citing conservation concerns, the DFO allowed the harvest of only 480,000 Fraser River pink salmon out of a run of 25 million. Pink salmon were once the mainstay of the canning industry, and the silence of the Canadian Fishing Company in the face of such lost opportunity was deafening.

In 2004 Dan Edwards agreed, against his will, to the introduction of an ITQ system in the dogfish fishery. It had been one of the last species—other than salmon—that was still based on the common property model. Edwards had to accept ITQs or abandon his link to an industry in which his family had participated for three generations.

Des Nobels is no longer a gillnetter. He still works part-time for the T. Buck Suzuki Foundation, trying to protect North Coast fish habitat. Cathy Scarfo, Kim Olsen, Bob Burkoski, Darlene and Bob Wulff, John Stevens, Mike Emes, Glen Arkko, Terry Lubzinski and hundreds of others just like them are still trying to hang on in the salmon fishery. Within the ranks of the Native Brotherhood, Hubert Haldane, Chris Cook, Edwin Newman, Josh Duncan, Jerry Roberts, Greg Wadhams and many other Native fishermen are locked in the same struggle to defend their livelihoods. Having barely survived the fiasco known as stackable area licensing, they now face the prospect of ITQs. If they do not accept them, the DFO may close the fishery entirely.

Fishermen in Alaska and Washington state, however, have had a different experience. In 2004 their government paid them up to $10,000 each in subsidies from the Trade Adjustment Assistance program of the

US Department of Agriculture, to offset the drastic drop in the dockside price of salmon following a worldwide expansion of fish farming.[9] In Canada, this same decline in salmon prices was one of the government's main justifications for the Mifflin Plan, which gutted the fleet. The United States—the most laissez-faire, pro-free trade nation on earth— still sees fit to support its fishing fleet financially during difficult times. Meanwhile, fish farms proliferate in BC, promoted by provincial Liberal Fisheries Minister John van Dongen as symbols of a bright new future, even as unemployment in coastal BC continues to rise.

Once again, in 2004, 1,874,686 Fraser sockeye went "missing" between the mouth of the Fraser River and the spawning grounds. And once again the DFO had the answer: warm water in the Fraser Canyon caused unusually high levels of pre-spawn mortality. Yet the DFO has never proven that this was the cause of the missing fish in 1992, 1994 or 1998, let alone 2004. Every year the DFO declares that there are too many fish on the spawning grounds, or there are too few. And after a decade of turmoil, after the displacement of thousands of commercial fishermen, after devastating cuts to the commercial fishing effort and after a long series of unsuccessful economic prescriptions, the resource is still imperilled.

Faced with this continuing crisis, the public is understandably dismayed, as wild salmon stocks are an important indicator of the well-being of our natural environment. History tells us that we will not solve the problem by resorting to simplistic solutions, such as the elimination of commercial fishermen. What can be done?

To start with, we must use our rights as citizens to insist that our elected officials devote the necessary resources—money, time, and political will—to protect the salmon resource. On the Pacific Salmon Treaty front, we must continue to stand up to the Americans on the key issues of conservation and equity, as we prepare for the next round of negotiations, which will take place in 2008. As part of this process we must draw attention to the ongoing overfishing of Canadian stocks by Alaskan fishermen.

But our pressure on the US should not be limited to renegotiating the annexes of the Pacific Salmon Treaty. The survival of wild salmon—and, indeed, all life—depends on how we deal in future with "big-picture" environmental issues such as global climate change and nuclear testing, for which the American policy-makers bear a preponderant responsibility. Changes in the ocean environment, much of which is apparently caused by global pollution, may be damaging our salmon stocks more than any other factor, so we need to impel the US not only to sign an equitable salmon treaty, but also to sign the Kyoto Accord, designed to reduce global greenhouse gas emissions. Meanwhile, here at home, we must put a stop to reckless forest-industry practices, fish farms, offshore oil exploration, urban sprawl and other practices that have destroyed fish habitat. We must also restore funding for the salmon enhancement program and the many volunteer streamkeeping programs.

From a socioeconomic perspective, governments must enact laws and policies to keep control of our natural resources at the local level. In the commercial fishery this would entail a completely different approach to licensing based on the owner-operator principle, and a strategy to promote value-added harvesting, processing and marketing techniques. In other words, if fishermen, shoreworkers and communities could realize greater financial returns from each fish landed, there would be less need for the industry to exploit the biomass as a whole. As well, if coastal communities are to look forward to a brighter future, governments must resolve the outstanding issue of aboriginal land claims, in a way that ensures justice for Native people and fair treatment for non-Native citizens. The AFS pilot sales program may have to be scrapped.

These and other potential solutions require major changes in the way we have been managing our salmon resource. They will take time and they may seem unrealistic or impossible to achieve. But we do not have to start over—we have a vast body of knowledge and expertise to guide us in future. The vision, ideas and strategies provided by experts such as Don Cruickshank, Dan MacInnes, Christopher Beeby, Patricia Marchak, Robert Brown, Brain Peckford, Parzival Copes—to mention only a few—are there to build on. So is the legacy left by the efforts of thousands of working people, who have devoted their lives, most of them anonymously, to ensuring that the wild salmon will endure forever.

Endnotes

Preface

1. E.P. Thompson, *The Making of the English Working Class* (London: Penguin Books, 1980), p. 12.

Chapter 1

1. The source of all information pertaining to the 1958 strike is *The Fisherman*, Aug. 15 to Nov. 14, 1958, and Aug. 24 to Dec. 14, 1962.
2. According to *The Fisherman* (Nov. 19, 1990), p. 8, the number of commercial licences leapt from 10,800 in 1956 to 14,300 in 1958.
3. *The Fisherman* (Oct. 17, 1958), p. 2.
4. Interview with Dr. Jim Woodey (Feb. 7, 2002).
5. Pacific Salmon Commission (Oct. 25, 2004).
6. James R. McGoodwin, *Crisis in the World's Fisheries: People, Problems, and Policies* (Palo Alto CA: Stanford University Press, 1990), p. 20.

Chapter 2

1. Eric Hobsbawm, *The Age of Capital 1848–1875* (London: Abacus, 1975), p. 49.
2. George North and Hal Griffin, *A Ripple, A Wave* (Vancouver: Fishermen Publishing Society, 1974), p. 1.
3. Gordon W. Hewes, *Northwest Anthropological Research Notes* (Vol. 7, No. 2, 1973), pp. 133–55.
4. Martin W. Lewis, *Green Delusions: An Environmental Critique of Radical Environmentalism* (Durham NC: Duke University Press, 1992).
5. McGoodwin, p. 58.
6. Hewes, p. 148.
7. M. Shepard and W.A. Argue, *The Commercial Harvest of Salmon in British Columbia, 1820–1877* (Ottawa: Dept. of Fisheries and Oceans, Aug. 1989), p. 6.
8. Philip Gilhousen, *Estimations of Fraser River Sockeye Escapements from Commercial Harvest Data, 1892–1944* (IPSFC, 1992), p. 102.
9. *Ibid.*, p. 102.
10. North and Griffin, *A Ripple*, p. 2.
11. John Roos, *Restoring Fraser River Salmon: A History of the International Pacific Salmon Fisheries Commission 1937–1985* (Vancouver: Pacific Salmon Commission), p. 11.
12. L.S. Parsons, *Management of Marine Fisheries in Canada* (Ottawa: National Research Council of Canada, 1993), p. 337.
13. Roos, *Restoring*, p. 24.
14. *Ibid.*, p. 29.
15. *Ibid.*, p. 44.
16. *Ibid.*, p. 47.
17. Jim Lichatowich, *Salmon Without Rivers: A History of the Pacific Salmon Crisis* (Washington DC: Island Press, 1999).

18. Roos, *Restoring*, p. 63.
19. *Ibid.*, p. 63.
20. *Ibid.*, p. 64.
21. Lichatowich, *Salmon Without Rivers*, p. 201.
22. Parsons, *Management*, p. 598.
23. "Meet Denounces Treaty Sell-out," *The Fisherman* (Dec. 14, 1962), p. 6.
24. North and Griffin, *A Ripple*, p. 54.
25. Roos, *Restoring*, p. 132.
26. North and Griffin, *A Ripple*, p. 45.
27. Record of Agreement, United States Consultations on Salmon Problems of Mutual Concern (June 17–18, 1971), p. 4; cited in *Balancing Benefits and Burdens: The 1985 Canada/United States Pacific Salmon Treaty Negotiations, 1903 to 1985* (Vancouver: UBC Press), pp. 49–50.
28. Interview with Wayne Shinners (Nov. 1, 2001).
29. Interview with Mike Shepard and Sandy Argue, DFO, Victoria (June 2002).

Chapter 3
1. Geoff Meggs, *Salmon: The Decline of the British Columbia Fishery* (Vancouver: Douglas & McIntyre, 1991), p. 230.
2. Pacific Salmon Treaty hearings before the Committee on Foreign Relations, United States Senate (Feb. 22, 1985).
3. Wendy Long, "Canada–US deal ends 20-year rift over salmon," *Vancouver Sun* (Dec. 15, 1984), p. A1.
4. *Ibid.*
5. Kim Bolen, *Vancouver Sun* (Dec. 17, 1984).
6. Canadian National Discussion Paper, Feb. 10, 1997 (Dept. of Fisheries and Oceans), p. 27.
7. Michael Harris, *Lament for an Ocean* (Toronto: McClelland & Stewart, 1998), p. 131.
8. Richard Cashin, *Charting a New Course: Toward a Fishery of the Future* (Ottawa: Ministry of Supply and Services), pp. vi–vii.
9. Harris, *Lament*, p. 174.
10. Harris. The book is subtitled *The Collapse of the Atlantic Cod Fishery, a True Crime Story: The ecological disaster of the century. The political scandal of a decade.*
11. Miriam Wright, *A Fishery for Modern Times: The State and the Industrialization of the Newfoundland Fishery, 1934–1968* (New York: Oxford University Press, 2001).
12. Julian Beltrame, "Mishap Minister Earns Sympathy," *Vancouver Sun* (Sept. 11, 1990), p. A7.
13. John C. Crosbie, *No Holds Barred* (Toronto: McClelland & Stewart, 1997), p. 37.
14. Gordon Hamilton, "Canada–US Salmon War Looms," *Vancouver Sun* (June 18, 1993), p. A1.
15. Pacific Salmon Commission Annual Report (1993/94), p. 5.

16. "Policing Illegal Fishing Not 'Strictly Legal,' Lawyer Says," *Vancouver Sun* (May 12, 1994), p. A7.

17. Ralph Matthews, "Mere Anarchy? Canada's Turbot War as the Moral Regulation of Nature," *Canadian Journal of Sociology* (Vol. 21, No. 4, 1996).

18. Mark Hume, "Policing Illegal Fishing Not 'Strictly Legal,' Lawyer Says," *Vancouver Sun* (May 27, 1994), p. A1.

19. *Ibid.*

20. *Ibid.*

21. DFO PSC National Discussion Paper, p. 18.

22. Mark Hume, "Anglers Pull Out of Advisory Panel, Claiming Coho Catch is Far Too High," *Vancouver Sun* (Aug. 13, 1994), p. A4.

23. Interview with Mike Shepard and Sandy Argue, DFO, Victoria (June 2002).

24. Pacific Salmon Commission Annual Report (1994/95), p. 47.

25. Robert Williamson, "One Million BC Salmon Missing" *Globe and Mail* (Sept. 15, 1994), p. A5.

26. DFO News Release (Sept. 26, 1994).

27. Miro Cernetig, "BC Salmon Fishery Suffers New Blow," *Globe and Mail* (Oct. 1, 1994), p. A1.

28. Larry Pynn, "Two Million Sockeye Salmon Disappear," *Vancouver Sun* (Oct. 1, 1994), p. A3.

29. *Ibid.*

30. David Hogben, "Conservation to Get 'Priority' in BC Fishery," *Vancouver Sun* (Nov. 2, 1994), p. A3.

31. Pacific Salmon Commission Annual Report (1994/95), pp. 47, 53.

32. Hogben, "Conservation," p. A3.

Chapter 4

1. *R. v Sparrow* (1990) 1 SCR 1075.

2. Terry Glavin, "Musqueam Indians Win Landmark Fish Decision," *Vancouver Sun* (May 30, 1990), p. A1.

3. Terry Glavin, *Dead Reckoning: Confronting the Crisis in the Pacific Fisheries* (Vancouver: Greystone Press, 1996), p. 101.

4. Parsons, *Management*, pp. 425–26.

5. L. Bijsterveld and M. James, *The Indian Food Fishery in the Pacific Region: Salmon Catches 1951 to 1984*, Canadian Data Report of Fisheries and Aquatic Sciences No. 627 (Ottawa: DFO, 1986).

6. Roos, *Restoring*, p. 263.

7. Michael C. Blum and E. Lorraine Bodi, *The Northwest Salmon Crisis: A Documentary History* (Corvallis OR: Oregon State University Press, 1996), p. 193.

8. *Living Treaties: Lasting Agreement: Report of the Task Force to Review Comprehensive Claims Policy* (DIAND, Dec. 1985).

9. Parsons, *Management*, p. 428.

10. Karen Gram and Garry MacDonald, "Dozens of Native Indians Face Illegal Fishing Charges," *Vancouver Sun* (Aug. 22, 1988), p. A1.

11. Glavin, *Dead Reckoning*, p. 115.

12. Interview with Jack Nichol (Aug. 27, 2001).

13. Edwin Blewett, *Compensation Valuation Study: A Study Completed for the Commercial Fishing Industry of Issues Related to Compensation to the Commercial Fishing Industry for Reallocations to the Aboriginal Fishery* (Vancouver, November 1992), p. 32

14. Scott Simpson, "Crosbie Says Changes Won't Hurt the Industry," *Vancouver Sun* (June 30, 1992), p. B12.

15. Parsons, *Management*, p. 429.

16. Standing Committee on Forestry and Fisheries, Minutes and Proceedings and Evidence, May 6, 1993, cited in *The Report of the Standing Committee on Fisheries and Oceans* (June 2003), p. 7.

17. Parsons, *Management*, p. 420.

18. "Calder Raps Unions, Wins Socred Cheers," *The Fisherman* (Mar. 7, 1969), p. 12.

19. Parsons, *Management*, p. 423.

20. *The Fisherman* (Apr.–May 2004), p. 6. Source of data cited: Ministry of Agriculture, Fisheries and Food.

21. Parsons, *Management*, p. 430.

22. Glavin, *Dead Reckoning*, p. 119.

23. Pacific Salmon Commission Eighth Annual Report, p. 32.

24. Peter Pearse (with scientific and technical advice from Peter A. Larkin), *Managing Salmon in the Fraser: Report to the Minister of Fisheries and Oceans on the Fraser River Salmon Investigation* (Ottawa: DFO, Nov. 1992), p. 15.

25. Pearse, *Managing Salmon*, p. 15.

26. Glavin, *Dead Reckoning*, p. 123.

27. Pearse, *Managing Salmon*, p. 29.

28. Peter O'Neil and Mark Hume, "Fisheries Faulted Over Attempts to Stop Poachers," *Vancouver Sun* (Sept. 21, 1994), p. A3.

29. Reasons for Judgement by the Rt. Hon. Antonio Lamer, PC, *Van der Peet v Her Majesty the Queen*, Supreme Court of BC (Aug. 21, 1996), p. 7.

Chapter 5

1. *Fraser River Sockeye 1994, Problems and Discrepancies. Report of the Fraser River Sockeye Public Review Board* (1995), pp. 103–4.

2. *Ibid.*, pp. 37–38.

3. *Ibid.*, p. 46.

4. *Ibid.*, p. 34.

5. A.W.H. Needler, "Evolution of Canada's Fisheries Management Towards Economic Rationalization," *Journal of the Fisheries Research Board of Canada* (No. 36, July 1979), p. 721.

6. Interview with Jim Woodey (Feb. 7, 2002).

7. *Pacific Salmon Commission Run-Size Estimation Procedures: An Analysis of the 1994 Shortfall in Escapement of Late-Run Fraser River Sockeye Salmon*, PSC Technical Report No. 6 (May 1995), p. 32.

8. *Ibid.*, p. 3.

9. *Ibid.*, p. xii.

10. *Ibid.*, p. 75.

11. Glavin, *Dead Reckoning*, p.115.
12. David Taras, *Power and Betrayal in the Canadian Media* (Peterborough ON: Broadview Press, 2001), p. 209.
13. Raymond A. Rogers, *Solving History* (Montreal: Black Rose Books, 1998), p. 28.
14. Fraser River Sockeye Public Review Board, *Fraser River Sockeye 1994: Problems and Discrepancies*, p. 72.

Chapter 6
1. Interview with Geoff Meggs (July 19, 2000).
2. Patricia Marchak, et al. *Uncommon Property: The Fishing Industry and the Fish Processing Industry in British Columbia* (London: Methuen Press, 1987).
3. Wright, *A Fishery*, p. 5.
4. Parsons, *Management*, p. 160.
5. Sol Sinclair, *Licence Limitation: British Columbia, A Method of Economic Fisheries Management* (Ottawa: DFO, 1960), p. 216.
6. James A. Crutchfield and Giulio Pontecorvo, *The Pacific Salmon Fishery: A Study of Irrational Conservation* (Baltimore MD: Johns Hopkins University Press), 1969.
7. G. Hardin, "The Tragedy of the Commons," *Science* (Vol.162, No. 3), pp. 1234–48.
8. Lewis, *Green Delusions*, p. 37.
9. Meggs, *Salmon*, p. 195.
10. This and many other quotes by Jack Davis can be found in Geoff Meggs, "The Privatization Prophet," *The Fisherman* (May 14, 1990).
11. Interview with Jack Nichol (July 11, 2001).
12. UFAWU Licensing Brief, cited in *The Fisherman* (Apr. 18, 1969), p. 11.
13. Parsons, *Management*, p. 162.
14. Brian Hayward, "The BC Salmon Fishery: A Consideration on the Effects of Licensing," *BC Studies* (No. 50), pp. 39–51.
15. Meggs, *Salmon*, p. 198.
16. Sol Sinclair, *A Licensing and Fee System for Coastal Fisheries of BC* (Ottawa: DFO, 1978).
17. Fleet Rationalization Committee Report (Ottawa: DFO), p. 58.
18. Meggs, *Salmon*, pp. 208–9.
19. *Ibid.*, p. 209.
20. *Reforming Regulation: Report of the Economic Council of Canada* (Ottawa: Ministry of Supply and Services, 1981), p. 73.
21. *Ibid.*, p. 74.
22. *Proceedings of the Pearse Royal Commission on Pacific Fisheries Policy* (Vol.1), p. 7.
23. "Pearse Commission Must Deal with Treaty, Industry Control," *The Fisherman* (May 29, 1981), p. 3.
24. *Ibid.*
25. Meggs, *Salmon*, p. 223.
26. Parsons, *Management*, p. 166

27. "Ahoy, Mr. Minister," editorial, *Vancouver Sun* (Dec. 14, 1983), p. A4.
28. Don Cruickshank, *Fleet Rationalization Report* (Ottawa: DFO, Nov. 1982), p. 18.
29. Letter from Don Cruickshank to Minister Pierre De Bane (Jan. 10, 1983); cited in L.S. Parsons and W.H. Lear, *Perspectives on Canadian Marine Fisheries Management* (Ottawa: DFO, 1993), p. 401.
30. Cruickshank, *Fleet Rationalization*, p. 18.
31. *A New Direction for Canada: An Agenda for Economic Renewal* (Ottawa: Department of Finance, Nov. 1984), p. 2.
32. "Fraser SEP 'Is Impossible' Under Tory Budget Plans," *The Fisherman* (Mar. 15, 1985), p. 17.
33. "Privatization, Pearse Still on DFO Agenda," *The Fisherman* (June 21, 1985), p. 1.
34. "1985 Showed Prospects for Future Could Be Good," *The Fisherman* (Dec. 12, 1985), p. 4.
35. Parsons, *Management*, p. 167.
36. Don Cruickshank, *A Commission of Inquiry into Licensing and Related Policies of the Department of Fisheries and Oceans* (1991), pp. 19–20.
37. Terry Glavin, "Processors Edgy About Trade Deal's Fish Fallout," *Vancouver Sun* (Dec. 17, 1987).
38. "Clark Admits Concern About Wineries Future," *Vancouver Sun* (Dec. 17, 1987), p. B5.
39. *West Coast Fisherman* (Oct. 1989), p. 51.
40. *An Inquiry Into Fin Fish Aquaculture in British Columbia*, Public Record, Appendix 1 (Parksville, BC, Nov. 21, 1986), p. 86.
41. Data obtained from the BC Salmon Marketing Council.
42. Meggs, "The Privatization Prophet," p. 5.
43. "Moratorium Demanded," *The Fisherman* (Dec. 17, 1990), p. 11.
44. "Tunnel Vision: Bureaucrats with Chronic Sight Disorder Navigate the Future of Fisheries," *The Fisherman* (June 18, 1990), p. 5.
45. Cruickshank, *Commission of Inquiry*, pp. 9–10.

Chapter 7

1. Mark Hume, "Fisheries Boss Ready to Reel in Licences, Offender Warned," *Vancouver Sun* (Mar. 9, 1995), p. A3.
2. Mike Crawley, "Fishers Won't Get Aid Despite Closure of Harvest," *Vancouver Sun* (Aug. 11, 1995), p. A1.
3. Rogers, *Solving History*, p. 117.
4. *Pacific Fishing Magazine* (Jan. 1997), p. 40.
5. *Outlook for Canada's Pacific Commercial Salmon Fishery* (Ottawa: DFO Economics and Planning Analysis Division, 1995), p. 6.
6. Interview with John Sutcliffe (Oct. 18, 2001).
7. *The Financial Problems of the Pacific Coast Fishery and Some Policy Remedies*, Fisheries Council of BC (Dec. 1993), p. 4.
8. Mike Crawley, *Vancouver Sun* (Dec. 16, 1995), p. B1.

9. Linda McQuaig, *Shooting the Hippo: Death by Deficit and Other Canadian Myths* (Toronto: Viking Penguin, 1995), p. 5.
10. *Pacific Roundtable Discussion Paper on Government Costs* (Ottawa: DFO, Sept. 1995), pp. 2–3.
11. Mark Hume, "Salmon Fishers Issue Storm Warning," *Vancouver Sun* (Dec. 13, 1995), p. B4.
12. Interview with John Sutcliffe (Oct. 18, 2001).
13. Freedom of Information Request on the Mifflin Plan, file 19(1), pp. 000259–62.
14. *Report to the Minister of Fisheries and Oceans on the Renewal of the Commercial Pacific Salmon Fishery,* Pacific Roundtable (Dec. 1995), p. 1.
15. West Coast Sustainability Association, Appendix 3, *Pacific Roundtable Report,* p. 36.
16. UFAWU, Appendix 4, *Pacific Roundtable Report,* p. 40.
17. Barbara Yaffe, "In a Storm of Protest, a Strong Voice Supports Salmon Plan," *Vancouver Sun* (Apr. 15, 1996), p. A3.
18. "Plan targets small boat fleet," *The Fisherman* (Apr. 26, 1996), p. 9.
19. Eric Beauchesne, "Today's Job Losses Tomorrow's Growth, Bank of Canada's Governor Says," *Vancouver Sun* (Mar. 21, 1996), p. A1.
20. Barbara Yaffe, "BC MPs Angling for Changes in Ottawa's Salmon Cutbacks," *Vancouver Sun* (Apr. 11, 1996), p. A3.
21. "Roundtable Members Reject Mifflin Plan," *The Fisherman* (Apr. 26, 1996), p. 8.
22. "Salmon, Survival and Communities," *The Fisherman* (May 20, 1996), p. 1.
23. "Fish Plan Flounders," editorial, *Vancouver Sun* (May 24, 1996), p. A18.
24. L. Pynn, "West Coast Fisheries Head Lambastes Buy-back Foes," *Vancouver Sun* (Apr.15, 1996), p. B4.
25. Interview with Bob Grant (May 19, 2004).
26. "Speaking Out for a Community" and "Protest Mourning Held as Plan Pushed Through," *The Fisherman* (June 24, 1996), pp. 1, 11.

Chapter 8
1. "Fleet Takes First Cuts," *The Fisherman* (July 22, 1996), p. 1.
2. Mark Hume and Peter O'Neil, "BC Fishers to Get $30 Million in Aid," *Vancouver Sun* (Nov. 7, 1996), p. A1.
3. Personal notes from Fryer press conference (Dec. 16, 1996).
4. *The Fisherman* (Feb. 20, 1997), pp. 1–3.
5. "Cutting Back Fishing Fleet Proposed as a Way to Reduce 'Killing Capacity'," *Vancouver Sun* (Aug. 12, 1995), p. A1.
6. Brief from Yves Fortier to Ambassador C. Beeby re: Canada/US PST equity dispute.
7. Interview with Mike Shepard and Sandy Argue, DFO, Victoria (June 7, 2002).
8. Personal notes from Canadian Commissioners meeting (July 12, 1995).
9. Barbara Yaffe, "Clark's Attack on Ottawa Considered to Be Hypocritical," *Vancouver Sun* (June 25, 1996), p. A3.

10. Justine Hunter, "Clark Admits Tough Talk May Have Isolated BC," *Vancouver Sun* (June 25, 1996), p. A4.
11. Personal notes from verbal report by Yves Fortier to the Canadian National Section (Jan. 1997).
12. "Trollers 'Pawns' in Salmon Treaty," *Vancouver Sun* (June 11, 1999), p. B8.
13. Personal notes from report by Canadian northern panel chair Joy Thorkelson, Juneau (Apr. 1997).
14. Personal notes from Pacific Salmon Commission meeting, Vancouver (May 9, 1997).
15. Peter O'Neil, "Ottawa Gives BC a Stake in Fishery," *Vancouver Sun* (Apr. 17, 1997), p. A1.
16. *Ibid.*
17. Personal notes from Pacific Salmon Commission meetings, Seattle (May 21, 1997).
18. Ross Howard, "Talks on Pacific Salmon Collapse," *Globe and Mail* (May 22, 1997), p. A1.
19. G. Middleton, "Is the Coast Toast?" *Province* (May 25, 1997), p. A14.
20. *Ibid.*
21. *West Coast Fisherman* (Sept. 1997), p. 4.
22. Barbara Yaffe, "US Views Nanoose Bay Closure Threat as Scuffle Between BC, Ottawa," *Vancouver Sun* (July 11,1997), p. A3.
23. Peter O'Neil and Justine Hunter, "No Face to Face on Nanoose," *Vancouver Sun* (July 15, 1997), p. A1.
24. *Ibid.*

Chapter 9

1. Dialogue in this chapter is reconstructed from newspaper articles and interviews with Eric Taylor (Feb. 6, 2002), Darlene Wulff (Feb. 6, 2002), John Radosevic (Feb. 6, 2002), Kim Olsen (Feb. 6, 2002), Bob Rezansoff (June 2, 2003), Bob Burkoski and Garth Mirau.
2. Interview with Kim Olsen (Feb. 6, 2002).
3. Interview and correspondence with Bob Burkoski.
4. *Anchorage Daily News* (July 20, 1997).
5. Eric Hobsbawm, *On History* (London: Abacus, 1977), p. 156.
6. Lora Grindlay, "Court Tells Fishermen to End Ferry Blockade," *Province* (July 21, 1997), p. A3.
7. Admiralty action in REM against the ships *Ivory C. D'yermaker* et al *vs The State of Alaska, Alaska Marine Highway System, and Alaska Department of Transportation and Public Facilities*, Federal Court of Canada, Trial Division, Montreal, Quebec (July 20, 1997).
8. Affidavit of Bruce M. Botelho, Registry of the Federal Court of Canada (July 20, 1997).
9. S. Bell and David Hogben, "BC Fishers Defiant Despite Order to End Blockade of Ferry," *Vancouver Sun* (July 21, 1997), p. A3.
10. *Nanaimo Daily News* (July 23, 1997), p. A8.

11. Canoe Preview News, 24 Hour News Top Story, Internet News Agency (July 22, 1997).
12. Ross Howard, "Ottawa Holds Cautious Course in Fish War, Fearing Costly Counter Attacks," *Globe and Mail* (July 21, 1997), p. A1.
13. Interview with Jim Sinclair (May 2002).
14. Bell and Hogben, "BC Fishers Defiant," p. A3.
15. Claire Ogilvie, *Province* (July 20, 1997), p. A3.
16. Diane Rhinehart, "Renegade Fishers Upset Over Layoffs by Fish Processors," *Vancouver Sun* (July 23, 1997), p. A3.
17. CFTK-TV News (July 21, 1997, 8:00 a.m.).
18. David Hogben, Dianne Rhinehart and Jim Beatty, "Prince Rupert Fishboats End Blockade of Alaskan Ferry," *Vancouver Sun* (July 22, 1997), p. A1.
19. Sheila Toony, *Anchorage Daily News*, (July 22, 1997).
20. Paul Koring, "Ferry Blockade May Have Backfired," *Globe and Mail* (July 23, 1997), p. A1.
21. Linda Keene, *Seattle Times* (July 22, 1997).
22. *Ibid.*
23. CKNW News (July 21, 1997, 11:00 a.m.).
24. BCTV Early News (July 21, 1997, 5:00 p.m.).
25. *Ibid.*
26. *Seattle Times*, Associated Press, and Reuters (July 21, 1997).
27. "Salmon Fishermen Issue Ultimatum to Ottawa," *Toronto Star* (July 23, 1997).
28. Ross Howard and P. Koring, "Heat Turned Down on Salmon Stew," *Globe and Mail* (July 23, 1997), p. A1.
29. Ross Howard, "Anderson Becomes Protest Target," *Globe and Mail* (July 22, 1997), p. A1.
30. Barbara Yaffe, "If Only Our Salmon Spoke French, Ottawa Would Listen Harder," *Vancouver Sun* (July 24, 1997), p. A3.
31. CFTK-TV News (July 23, 1997, 9:00 a.m.).

Chapter 10

1. "Daley Sets Out Busy Trade Agenda," *Globe and Mail* (Aug. 7, 1997), p. B9.
2. Ian Mulgrew, "Gillnetters Hold Skeena River Protest Fishery," *Vancouver Sun* (Aug. 5, 1997), p. A3.
3. Peter O'Neil, "Canadian Negotiator Hopeful in Fish War," *Vancouver Sun* (Aug. 6, 1997), p. A3.
4. Rafe Mair, "Where Was Fisheries Minister When BC Needed Him?" *Financial Post* (Aug. 1, 1997), p. 17.
5. Edgar Birch, "Fishermen Keeping Up Pressure on Anderson," *The Fisherman* (Aug. 18, 1997), pp. 1–3.
6. Environics Research, *BC Government Survey on Fisheries, Jobs and Timber Accord, and the Alcan Settlement* (Aug. 19, 1997), p. 5.
7. *Nanaimo Daily News* (Aug. 5, 1997), p. A5.
8. *Thirteenth Annual Report of the Pacific Salmon Commission 1997/98*, Table 14, p. 31.

9. J. Lavoie, "Angry Fishermen Stand and Watch as Salmon Vanish," *Times Colonist* (Aug. 8, 1997), p. A2.

10. See Chapter 8.

11. Trudi Beutel, *Delta Optimist* (Aug. 9, 1997), p. 5.

12. *Ibid.*

13. Interview with Jim Woodey (Feb. 7, 2002).

14. Unpublished open letter to southern fishermen from northern fishermen (July 21, 1997).

15. Press release, West Coast Sustainability Association (Aug. 12, 1997).

16. *Ibid.*

17. Interview with Wilf Caron, Nanaimo (Apr. 8, 2002).

18. Stewart Bell, "Fisheries Officers Threaten Arrests as Trollers Protest Over Salmon Catches," *Vancouver Sun* (Aug. 29, 1997), p. A3.

19. "DFO Minister Silent as Boats Face Seizure," *The Fisherman* (Sept. 22, 1997), pp. 1–3.

20. *Ibid.*

21. David Hogben, "Alaska Refuses to Restore Prince Rupert Ferry Without Apology from Canada," *Vancouver Sun* (Aug. 23, 1997), p. A1.

22. "The Alaska Debacle," Editorial, *Vancouver Sun* (Oct. 4, 1997), p. 20.

23. Don Hauka, "Fish Suits Ask for $325 Million," *Province* (Sept. 9, 1997), p. A14.

Chapter 11

1. Presentation by L. Yves Fortier, CC, QC, Canadian Chief Negotiator for Pacific Salmon Treaty, to David Strangway and William Ruckelshaus (Sept. 29, 1997), p. 2.

2. Pipkin testimony, p. 4.

3. "We Saved Clark From Becoming 'Road Kill' on Nanoose: Anderson," *Vancouver Sun* (Oct. 7, 1997), p. A6.

4. Norma Greenaway, "Tobin Empathizes with BC Over Federal Obsession with Quebec," *Vancouver Sun* (Oct. 7, 1997), p. A3.

5. P. Fong, "BC Could Make or Break Canada, Expert Claims," *Vancouver Sun* (Dec. 5, 1997), p. B3.

6. Peter O'Neil, "Bloc Chief's Trip West Is a Bid to Get Noticed," *Vancouver Sun* (Dec. 4, 1997), p. A1.

7. Chris Montgomery, "We'll Horn In on APEC, Say Fishermen," *Province* (Nov. 6, 1997), p. A23.

8. Peter O'Neil, "US Offers Canada Salmon Fund," *Vancouver Sun* (Oct. 31, 1997), p. A1.

9. *Ibid.*

10. C. Montgomery, *Province* (Nov. 27, 1997), p. A9.

11. Interview transcript Media Q (Oct. 30, 1997), p. 5.

12. Allan Gotlieb, "Getting Attention," *National Post* (May 17, 2002), p. A18.

13. D. Rhinehart, *Vancouver Sun* (Nov. 24, 1997), p. A9.

14. Dan MacLennan, *Campbell River Courier* (Nov. 11, 1997), p. A6.

15. William Ruckelshaus and David Strangway, *Pacific Salmon: A Report to the Prime Minister of Canada and the President of the United States* (Jan. 12, 1998), pp. 4–5.

16. Stephen Thorne, "MPs Panel Urges Ottawa to Fire Top Fish Officials," *Vancouver Sun* (Mar. 2, 1998), p. A5.

17. *The Fisherman* (Jan. 26, 1998), p. 12.

18. "Ottawa Bids $2.75 Million to Cool Fish War," *Globe and Mail* (Jan. 23, 1998), p. A4.

19. *Regina v. Kapp et al, Reasons for Judgement of the Honourable Judge W.J. Kitchen*, file no. 108246, Vancouver (June 28, 2003), pp. 78–79, 89.

20. Letter from L. Yves Fortier to the Honourable David Anderson, PC, MP, and the Honourable Lloyd Axworthy, PC, MP (Jan. 30, 1998), p. 5.

21. T. McDorman, P. Saunders and D.L. VanderZwagg, "The Gulf of Maine Boundary Dispute: Dropping Anchor or Setting Course?" *Marine Policy Journal* (Apr. 1985), pp. 90–106.

22. Personal notes from Portland Pacific Salmon Commission meeting (Feb. 9, 1998).

23. From a copy of the letter from the National Section of the Pacific Salmon Commission on Fortier's resignation, author's collection.

Chapter 12

1. John Van Ameroagen, *The Alaska Fishermen's Journal* (Apr. 1998), p. 12.

2. Bruce Brown, *Mountain in the Clouds* (New York: Simon and Schuster, 1982), p. 85.

3. Lichatowich, *Salmon Without Rivers*, p. 201.

4. Lichatowich, *Salmon Without Rivers*, p. 200.

5. Dianne Rhinehart and Peter O'Neil, "Governor Locke Backs Clark for Fish Talks," *Vancouver Sun* (Mar. 11, 1998), p. A1.

6. Peter O'Neil, "Canada Confronts a Heavy Hitter in Fish Talks," *Vancouver Sun* (Mar. 13, 1998), p. A1.

7. Harris, *Lament*, p. 205.

8. Interview with Mike Shepard and Sandy Argue, DFO, Victoria (June 2002).

9. C. Walters and Josh Korman, "Background Paper No 1999/1b, Salmon Stocks," *1998–99 Annual Report of the Pacific Fisheries Resource Council*, p. 113.

10. Annual Report of the Pacific Fisheries Conservation Council (1998–99), p. 13.

11. M. Roseneau and Mark Angelo, "Freshwater Habitat: Background Paper No 1999/1a," *Pacific Fisheries Resource Conservation Council (1998–99)*, p. 59.

12. *Ibid.*, p. 60.

13. *Ibid.*, p. 61.

14. Interview with Parzival Copes (June 2002).

15. See Parzival Copes, *The Resettlement of Fishing Communities in Newfoundland* (Ottawa: Canadian Council on Rural Development, 1972).

16. Parzival Copes, *Canadian Fisheries Policy and Coastal Community Development: For a Sustainable Fishery with Economic Viability and Social Justice* (Burnaby: Institute of Fisheries Analysis, SFU, Apr. 1999), p. 2.

17. Parzival Copes, *Coping with the Coho Crisis: a Conservation-Minded, Stakeholder-Sensitive and Community-Oriented Strategy* (Victoria: BC Ministry of Fisheries, 1998), p. 4.
18. *Ibid.*, p. 7.
19. *Ibid.*, p. 15.
20. *Ibid.*, p. 36.

Chapter 13

1. Joel Connelly, *Seattle Post-Intelligencer* (May 22, 1998), p. 2.
2. *Business in Vancouver* (May 19, 1998), p. 29.
3. *Port Alberni Times* (June 1, 1998), p. A7.
4. P. Fong, "Cruise Ships a Target, BC's Fishermen Say,"*Vancouver Sun* (June 5, 1998), p. A1.
5. Peter O'Neil and C. Culbert, "Poised to Sign Salmon Deal, Anderson Accused of Sell-out," *Vancouver Sun* (June 26, 1998), p. A1.
6. Dianne Rhinehart, P. Fong, Peter O'Neil and Jim Beatty, "Clark Vows to Kill US–Canada Salmon Deal. 'It's a Travesty,'" *Vancouver Sun* (June 27, 1998), p. A1.
7. Alan Beesley, a former Canadian diplomat, wrote a series of legal briefing notes on this matter for Premier Clark in the fall of 1997.
8. Press release, Washington State Department of Fish and Wildlife (July 1, 1998).
9. Personal notes from DFO Press Conference, Vancouver (July 4, 1998).

Chapter 14

1. Bud Graham, Report for BC Ministry of Fisheries (July 1998). Data source: Pacific Salmon Commission and DFO.
2. DFO-OC489, issued by DFO headquarters (July 2, 1998).
3. Lori Culbert, "Alaska Moves on Coho Deal," *Vancouver Sun* (July 3, 1998), p. A1.
4. Willard E. Ireland, "The Evolution of the Boundaries of British Columbia," *British Columbia Historical Quarterly* (Vol. III, 1939), pp. 281–82.
5. "July 1 Protest: 100 Vessels Fish A–B Line," *The Fisherman* (July 10, 1981), pp. 1–2.
6. Peter O'Neil, "Nuclear subs loom off BC," *Vancouver Sun* (Oct. 3, 1991), p. A1.
7. Frank Rue, Commercial Fisheries Emergency Order (Alaska Fish and Game Department, July 2, 1998).
8. Lori Culbert and Justine Hunter, "Clark Calls Alaska Rogue State After Salmon Talks Collapse," *Vancouver Sun* (July 10, 1998), p. A1.
9. "Politics," CBC Radio (June 30, 1998, 17:23).
10. John Wright, *Bridge News* (June 1, 1998).
11. *Prince Rupert Daily News* (July 15, 1998), p. 3.
12. Personal notes taken at fishermen's rally, Campbell River (Aug. 25, 1998).
13. Paragraph 2, Anderson–Locke agreement (July 2, 1998).

14. Lori Culbert, "Federal Government and Native Fishermen Reach Tentative Deal," *Vancouver Sun* (July 13, 1998), p. A1.
15. Personal notes from Fraser Panel meetings (July 21–Aug. 21, 1998).
16. *West Coast Fisherman* (Sept. 1997), p. 31.
17. *Pacific Salmon Commission Run-size Estimation Procedures: An Analysis of the 1994 Shortfall in Escapement of Late-run Fraser River Sockeye Salmon* (May 1995), p. 9.
18. David Hogben, "Ottawa Suspicious of Fish Inquiry," *Vancouver Sun* (Aug. 29, 1998), p. A1.
19. 14th Annual Report of the Pacific Salmon Commission (1998/99), pp. 17–21.

Chapter 15

1. Brian Peckford, *A Question of Balance: The 1998 Fraser River Sockeye Run* (Initial Report of Peckford Inquiry, Sept. 25, 1998).
2. Robin Junger, Legal opinion re: July 2nd agreement between Federal Fisheries Minister David Anderson and Washington State Governor Gary Locke (Sept. 25, 1998), p. 14.
3. Don Millerd and Jack Nichol, *A Sectoral Strategy for a Sustainable Fish Processing Industry in British Columbia: The Report of the Fish Processing Strategic Task Force* (Victoria: Ministry of Agriculture, Fisheries and Food, Oct. 1994).
4. Glavin, *Last Call*, p. 3.
5. Brian Peckford, *Reaching Out: The Final Report of the Peckford Inquiry* (Nov. 1998), p. 4.
6. Harris, *Lament*, p. 135.
7. "Escapements Show Coho Rebounding," *The Fisherman* (Dec. 18, 1998), p. 7.
8. "Peckford Urges New Management Body for Fisheries," *The Fisherman* (Dec.18, 1998), p. 13.
9. Vaughan Palmer, "McArthur Looks Back on His Time in the Harcourt Era," *Vancouver Sun* (Dec. 10, 1998), p. A20.
10. Judi Tyabji Wilson, *Daggers Unsheathed: The Political Assassination of Glen Clark* (Surrey BC: Heritage House, 2002), p. 138.
11. Peter O'Neil, "Ottawa Vows to Take Over Test Range," *Vancouver Sun* (May 16, 1999), p. A1.
12. Peter O'Neil and C. McInnes, "BC Spurns Ottawa's Offer of $125 Million for Test Range," *Vancouver Sun* (May 14, 1999), p. A1.
13. Peter O'Neil and C. McInnes, "Reform Backs Ottawa in Nanoose Takeover," *Vancouver Sun* (May 19, 1999), p. A12.
14. Lori Culbert and Jim Beatty, "Salmon Pact 'Disappointing,'" *Vancouver Sun* (June 4, 1999), p. A1.
15. *Ibid.*
16. *Ibid.*
17. *An Analysis of the New Rules under the Pacific Salmon Treaty.* (Victoria: BC Ministry of Fisheries, July 4, 1999).
18. Robert Matas and Barrie McKenna, "Deal Aims to End Annual Salmon Wars," *Globe and Mail* (June 4, 1999), p. A1.

Chapter 16

1. K. Pemberton, "$60 Million Salmon Fishery Shut," *Vancouver Sun* (Aug. 7, 1999), p. A1.
2. G.S. Gislason and Associates Ltd., *The 1999 Fraser River Sockeye Fishery: A Lost Year* (Victoria: Ministry of Agriculture, Food and Fisheries), pp. 2–3.
3. Roos, *Restoring*, p. 236.
4. Interview with Dan Edwards (Oct. 17, 2002).
5. S and H Consulting, *The 1999 Salmon Disaster: Poor Forecasting or Natural Disaster?*, (Coastal Community Network, Aug. 1999), p. 3.
6. Gordon Gislason, *Fishing For Direction* (Ottawa: DFO, 1999).
7. "Looking for HRDC Fund? Check out the Corporate Boardroom," *The Fisherman*, (June 19, 2000), p. 5.
8. Mario Procaccini, "Liberal Forest Act a Disaster for Jobs, Environment, say Critics" and "Forest Unions, Ecologists Grapple with Developing Sustainable Forestry Practices," *Columbia Journal* (Vol. 8, No. 2, Apr. 2003), p. 8.
9. James R. McGoodwin, *Crisis in the World's Fisheries: People, Problems, and Policies* (Palo Alto CA: Stanford University Press, 1990).
10. David Ralph Matthews, *Controlling Common Property: Regulating Canada's East Coast Fishery* (Toronto: University of Toronto Press, 1993).
11. Evelyn Pinkerton, ed., *Co-Operative Management of Local Fisheries: New Directions for Improved Management and Community Development* (Vancouver: University of BC, 1989).
12. "MFU Outlines Stand on Burnt Church Fishing," *The Fisherman* (Oct. 2000), p. 5.
13. Tyabji Wilson, *Daggers Unsheathed*, p. 319.

Chapter 17

1. "Fleet Cut Short Despite Huge Run," *The Fisherman* (July 31, 2000), p. 3.
2. *The Fisherman* (July 31, 2000) p. 3.
3. Personal observation at Sointula.
4. Mel Hurtig, *The Vanishing Country* (Toronto: McClelland & Stewart), 2002.
5. Institute For Dispute Resolution, *Independent Review of Improved Decision Making in the Pacific Salmon Fishery: Final Report* (Victoria: University of Victoria, 2001).
6. *The 2001 Fraser River Salmon Fishery*, Report of the Standing Committee on Fisheries and Oceans (June 2003), p. 17.
7. DFO Integrated Fisheries Management Plan, Southern BC Salmon (Apr. 1, 2001–Mar. 31, 2003), pp. 40–41.
8. Personal notes from ad hoc fishermen's meeting, Nanaimo (Apr. 30, 2002).
9. Interview with Bob Rezansoff (Oct. 27, 2004).
10. Question Period Digest (Oct. 22, 2002).
11. Department of Fisheries and Oceans, *Review of the 2002 Fraser River Sockeye Fishery: Report by the External Steering Committee* (Mar. 2003), pp. 82–86. The external steering committee failed to come to the obvious conclusions about the US intervention, but the evidence from the Fraser panel meeting minutes is overwhelmingly clear.

12. Jake Kennedy, "Angry Fishermen Threaten to Drop Lines in Johnstone Strait," *Times Colonist* (Aug. 26, 2002), p. B2.
13. Jeremy Sandler, "'Sold-out' Fishermen Urged to Continue Fishing Illegally," *Vancouver Sun* (Aug.27, 2002), p. A1.
14. *Ibid.*

Chapter 18

1. Catherine Wallace, "New Zealand Fisheries Quota Management: Theory and Experience," unpublished manuscript (School of Government, Victoria University, Wellington, New Zealand, 2004), pp. 9, 11, 15.
2. Jay Sinha, "The Transfer of Fishing Licences in Canada: A Legal Overview," unpublished manuscript (Dec. 1999), p. 1.
3. Personal tape recording of John Fraser's speech at Roderick Haig-Brown Park (Oct. 17, 2002).
4. Annual Report of the Pacific Fisheries Resource Conservation Council (2001–2002), p. 1.
5. David Lane, "Environment a 'Huge Broken Promise'," *The Fisherman* (Dec. 12, 2003), p. 15.
6. Interview with Otto Langer (Nov. 7, 2004).
7. *Pacific Salmon Treaty, 1999 Revised Annexes, Memorandum of Understanding (1985), Exchange of Notes* (Feb. 2000), p. 70.
8. See: http://www.provincialcourt.bc.ca/judgements/pc 2002/02 p035f0217. htm.
9. Matt Volz, "Pacific Salmon Fishermen to Receive Subsidies," *Seattle Post-Intelligencer* (July 17, 2004).

Bibliography

Books

Becker, Lawrence C. *Property Rights: Philosophic Foundations*. London: Routledge and Kegan Paul, 1977.

Bell, Gordon. *Pacific Salmon: From Egg to Exit*. Surrey BC: Hancock House, 1996.

Bijsterveld, L., and M. James. *The Indian Food Fishery in the Pacific Region: Salmon Catches 1951 to 1984*. Canadian Data Report of Fisheries and Aquatic Sciences No. 627. Ottawa: DFO, 1986.

Blum, Michael C., and E. Lorraine Bodi. *The Northwest Salmon Crisis: A Documentary History*. Corvallis OR: Oregon State University Press, 1996.

Brenner, Robert. *The Boom and the Bubble: The US in the World Economy*. London: Verso, 2002.

Brown, Bruce. *Mountain in the Clouds*. New York: Simon and Schuster, 1982.

Cassidy, Frank, and Dale Norman. *After Native Claims? The Implications of Comprehensive Claims Settlements for Natural Resources in British Columbia*. Lantzville BC: Oolichan Books, 1988.

Crosbie, John C. *No Holds Barred*. Toronto: McClelland & Stewart, 1997.

Crutchfield, James, and Pontecorvo Guilio. *The Pacific Salmon Fishery: A Study of Irrational Conservation*. Baltimore MD: Johns Hopkins University Press, 1969.

Forester, Joseph, and Anne Forester. *British Columbia's Commercial Fishing History*. Surrey BC: Hancock House, 1975.

Gilhousen, Philip. *Estimations of Fraser River Sockeye Escapements from Commercial Harvest Data, 1892–1944*. IPSFC, 1992.

Glavin, Terry. *Dead Reckoning: Confronting the Crisis in the Pacific Fisheries*. Vancouver: Greystone Press, 1996.

Greider, William. *Who Will Tell the People: The Betrayal of American Democracy*. New York: Simon and Schuster, 1992.

Groot, Cornelis, and Leo Margolis, eds. *Pacific Salmon Life Histories*. Vancouver: UBC, 1991.

Haig-Brown, Alan. *Fishing for a Living*. Madeira Park BC: Harbour Publishing, 1993.

Harris, Michael. *Lament for an Ocean*. Toronto: McClelland & Stewart, 1998.

Hobsbawm, Eric. *The Age of Capital, 1848–1875*. London: Abacus, 1975.

_____. *On History*. London: Abacus, 1977.

Hume, Mark. *Adam's River*. Vancouver: New Star Books, 1994.

Hurtig, Mel. *The Vanishing Country*. Toronto: McClelland & Stewart, 2002.

Jones, Laura, and Michael Walker. *Fish or Cut Bait*. Vancouver: Fraser Institute, 1979.

Keller, Betty, and Rosella Leslie. *Sea-Silver: Inside British Columbia's Salmon Farming Industry*. Victoria: Horsdal & Schubart, 1996.

Knight, Rolf. *Indians at Work: An Informal History of Native Labour in British Columbia, 1858–1930*. Vancouver: New Star Books, 1996.

Lewis, Martin. *Green Delusions: An Environmental Critique of Radical Environmentalism*. Durham NC: Duke University Press, 1992.

Lichatowich, Jim. *Salmon Without Rivers: A History of the Pacific Salmon Crisis*. Washington DC: Island Press, 1999.

McGoodwin, James R. *Crisis in the World's Fisheries: People, Problems, and Policies*. Palo Alto CA: Stanford University Press, 1990.

McPherson, C.B. *Property: Mainstream and Critical Positions*. Toronto: University of Toronto Press, 1978.

McQuaig, Linda. *Shooting the Hippo: Death by Deficit and Other Canadian Myths*. Toronto: Viking Penguin, 1995.

Marchak, Patricia, et al. *Uncommon Property: The Fishing Industry and the Fish Processing Industry in British Columbia*. London: Methuen Press, 1987.

Martin, Lawrence. *The Presidents and the Prime Ministers: Washington and Ottawa Face to Face, the Myth of Bilateral Bliss, 1867–1982*. Toronto: McClelland & Stewart, 1982.

Matthews, David Ralph. *Controlling Common Property: Regulating Canada's East Coast Fishery*. Toronto: University of Toronto Press, 1993.

Meggs, Geoff. *Salmon: The Decline of the British Columbia Fishery*. Vancouver: Douglas & McIntyre, 1991.

North, George, and Hal Griffin. *A Ripple, A Wave*. Vancouver: Fishermen Publishing Society, 1974.

Parsons, L.S. *Management of Marine Fisheries in Canada*. Ottawa: National Research Council of Canada, 1993.

Phillips, Paul. *No Power Greater: A Century of Labour in British Columbia*. Vancouver: BC Federation of Labour, 1967.

Pinkerton Evelyn, ed. *Co-operative Management of Local Fisheries: New Directions for Improved Management and Community Development*. Vancouver: UBC Press, 1989.

_____, and Martin Weinstein. *Fisheries that Work: Sustainability Through Community-Based Management*. Vancouver: David Suzuki Foundation, 1995.

Rogers, Raymond A. *The Oceans are Emptying: Fish Wars and Sustainability*. Montreal: Black Rose Books, 1995.

_____. *Solving History: The Challenge of Environmental Activism*. Montreal: Black Rose Books, 1998.

Roos, John. *Restoring Fraser River Salmon: A History of the International Pacific Salmon Fisheries Commission 1937–1985*. Vancouver: Pacific Salmon Commission, 1991.

Shepard, M., and W.A. Argue. *The Commercial Harvest of Salmon in British Columbia, 1820–1877*. Ottawa: Department of Fisheries and Oceans, 1989.

_____. *Balancing the Benefits: The 1985 Canada/US Pacific Salmon Treaty Negotiations, 1903 to 1985*. Vancouver: UBC Press, 2005.

Taras, David. *Power and Betrayal in the Canadian Media*. Peterborough ON: Broadview Press, 2001.

Tyabji Wilson, Judi. *Daggers Unsheathed: The Political Assassination of Glen Clark.* Surrey: Heritage House, 2002.

Wilson, V. Seymour. *Canadian Public Policy and Administration: Theory and Environment.* New York: McGraw-Hill Ryerson, 1981.

Wright, Miriam. *A Fishery for Modern Times: The State and the Industrialization of the Newfoundland Fishery, 1934–1968.* New York: Oxford University Press, 2001.

Reports and Articles
(Chronological order)

Sinclair, Sol. *Licence Limitation: British Columbia, A Method of Economic Fisheries Management.* Ottawa: DFO, 1960.

Hardin, G. "The Tragedy of the Commons." *Science*, Vol. 162, No. 3, 1969.

Copes, Parzival. *The Resettlement of Fishing Communities in Newfoundland.* Ottawa: Canadian Council on Rural Development, 1972.

Hewes, Gordon W. "Indian Fisheries Productivity in Pre-Contact Times in the Pacific Salmon Area." *Northwest Anthropological Notes*, Vol. 7, No. 2, 1973.

Sinclair, Sol. *A Licensing and Fee System for the Coastal Fisheries of BC.* Ottawa: DFO, 1978.

Hayward, B. "The BC Salmon Fishery: A Consideration of the Effects of Licensing," *BC Studies*, No. 50, 1981.

Pearse, Peter. *Conflict and Opportunity: Toward a New Policy for Canada's Pacific Fisheries.* Ottawa: Government of Canada, Commission on Pacific Fisheries Policy, 1981.

Pearse, Peter. *Turning the Tide: A New Policy for Canada's Pacific Fisheries.* Vancouver BC: The Royal Commission, 1982.

Cruickshank, Don, et al. *Fleet Rationalization Report.* Ottawa, DFO, 1982.

Coolichan, M. *Living Treaties: Lasting Agreement: Report of the Task Force to Review Comprehensive Claims Policy.* DIAND, 1985.

Shaffer, M., et al. *An Analysis of the Economic Benefits of Recreational and Commercial Fisheries.* Ottawa: DFO, 1986.

DPA Consulting Group, *British Columbia Salmon Fleet Financial Performance, 1981–1985.* Ottawa: DFO, 1988.

An Inquiry into Fin Fish Aquaculture in British Columbia: Public Record, Appendix 1. 1986.

Marchak, Patricia. "What Happens When Common Property Becomes Uncommon?" *BC Studies*, No. 80, 1988/89.

Department of Fisheries and Oceans. *Vision 2000: Pacific Strategic Outlook.* 1989.

Government of Canada. *Green Plan.* 1990.

Schofield, Andrew Mark. *Ideology, Space, and the Dialectics of Union Organization: A Case Study of the United Fishermen and Allied Workers' Union.* Master's thesis, Simon Fraser University, 1990.

Meggs, Geoff. "The Privatization Prophet." *The Fisherman*, May 1990.

Cruickshank, Don. *A Commission of Inquiry into Licensing and Related Policies of the Department of Fisheries and Oceans*. Vancouver and Port Hardy BC: UFAWU et al., 1991.

Department of Fisheries and Oceans. *A Proposal For Reforming Licensing, Allocation, and Sanctions System*. 1991.

Department of Fisheries and Oceans. *Pacific Coast Commercial Fishing Licensing Policy Feedback Report*. 1991.

Pearse, Peter, with Peter Larkin. *Managing Salmon in the Fraser River: Report to the Minister of Fisheries and Oceans on the Fraser River Salmon Investigation*. Vancouver: DFO, 1992.

Blewett, Edwin. *Compensation Valuation Study: A Study Completed for the Commercial Fishing Industry of Issues Related to Compensation to the Commercial Fishing Industry for Reallocations to the Aboriginal Fishery*. Vancouver, November 1992.

ARA Consulting Ltd. *Salmon Enhancement Program Review*. Ottawa: DFO, 1993.

The Financial Problems of the Pacific Coast Fishery and Some Remedies. Fisheries Council of BC, 1993.

Weiler, J., et al. *Building a Sustainable Fishing Industry: A Sectoral Strategy for Prosperity and Resource Health*. Report of the Fish Processing Strategic Task Force, Ministry of Agriculture, Fisheries, and Food, 1994.

Fraser, J.A. *Fraser River Sockeye: Problems and Discrepancies*. Report of the Fraser River Sockeye Public Review Board, 1994.

Pacific Roundtable Discussion Paper on Government Costs. Ottawa: DFO, 1995.

Pacific Salmon Commission Run-Size Estimation Procedures: An Analysis of the 1994 Shortfall in Escapement of Late-Run Fraser River Sockeye Salmon. PSC Technical Report No. 6. Pacific Salmon Commission, 1995.

Walters, C. *Fish on the Line: The Future of Pacific Fisheries*. Vancouver: David Suzuki Foundation, 1995.

Report to the Minister of Fisheries and Oceans on the Renewal of the Commercial Pacific Salmon Fishery. Pacific Roundtable, 1995.

ARA Consulting Ltd. *Fishing for Answers: Coastal Communities and the BC Salmon Industry, a Report to the BC Job Protection Commissioner*. 1996.

Fryer, J., M. Francino, and W. Valentine. *Tangled Lines: Restructuring in the Pacific Salmon Fishery, A Federal–Provincial Review of the Mifflin Plan*. 1996.

Garvey, T., and M. Gianmarino. *Corporate Concentration in the Pacific Salmon Fishery, A Report to the Pacific Salmon Revitalization Plan Review Panel*. 1996.

National Discussion Paper on the Pacific Salmon Treaty. Ottawa: DFO, 1997.

Towards a "Made in BC" Vision to Renew the Pacific Salmon Fishery. Provincial Fisheries Secretariat, 1997.

Glavin, Terry. *Last Call: The Will To Save Pacific Salmon*. Vancouver: David Suzuki Foundation, 1998.

Paul, J., and Associates Ltd. *BC's Tidal and Anadromous Sports Fishery: A Joint Government and Sector Initiative*. Victoria: BC Ministry of Fisheries, 1998.

Gislason, G., et al. *Fishing Communities in Transition*. DFO, 1998.

Government of Canada, *Canada's Coho Recovery Plan and Federal Response Measures*. Ottawa: DFO, 1998.

Copes, Parzival. *Coping with the Coho Crisis: A Conservation-Minded, Stakeholder-Sensitive and Community-Oriented Strategy*. BC Ministry of Fisheries, 1998.

Gislason, G., et al. *Fishing for Money: Challenges and Opportunities in the BC Salmon Fishery*. Report prepared for the BC Jobs Protection Commissioner, 1998.

Duthie, A. *Responsible Fishing in Canada*. Ottawa: DFO, 1998.

Parliamentary Committee on Fisheries. *The West Coast Report*. 1998.

Peckford, Brian. *Reaching Out: Final Report of the Peckford Inquiry*. Prepared for the Government of BC, 1998.

Gislason, G., et al. *The 1999 Fraser River Sockeye Fishery: A Lost Year*. Prepared for BC Ministry of Fisheries, 1999.

Copes, Parzival. *Canadian Fisheries Policy and Coastal Community Development: For a Sustainable Fishery with Economic Viability and Social Justice*. Burnaby, BC: Institute of Fisheries Analysis, SFU, 1999.

S and H Consulting Ltd. *The 1999 Salmon Disaster: Poor Forecasting or Natural Disaster?* Prepared for the Coastal Community Network, 1999.

Brown R. *A Community Fisheries Licence Banking Trust: A Proposal for Community Based Fisheries*. Report for Fisheries Renewal BC, 2000.

We'd Rather Be Fishin': A Review of Transition Programs Designed for the West Coast Fishery. Community Fisheries Development Centre, 2000.

New Directions for Canada's Pacific Salmon Fishery (seven-part series of reports). DFO, Oct. 1998–Jan. 2001.

Independent Review of Improved Decision-Making in the Pacific Salmon Fishery. Victoria: University of Victoria, 2001.

Fruman, S. *How We Lost the Salmon War: A Study of the Press, Politics, and Public Policy*. Master's Thesis, Simon Fraser University, 2001.

Review of the 2002 Fraser River Sockeye Fishery. DFO, 2003.

Report of the Standing Committee on Forestry and Fisheries West Coast Report, June 2003.

Marshall, D. *Fishy Business: The Economics of Salmon Farming in BC*. Canadian Centre for Policy Alternatives, 2003.

Position Paper on BC Salmon Fisheries. Native Brotherhood of BC, 2003.

Index

Abbott Plan, 35
Aboriginal Fishing Strategy (AFS) ; *see also* First Nations, Assembly of; Indian Food Fishery (IFF); Native fishery; Northwest Treaty Tribes, 63–64, 70–79, 84, 118, 207, 234, 236–38, 288, 290, 301, 307, 324–25, 343, 344, 346, 357, 371
Adams River run; *see* sockeye
Agrimarine Industries Ltd., 338
Alaska boundary dispute, 38
Alaska ferry blockade, 182–195, 196–97, 202, 203–4, 213–14, 219, 225, 235, 342
   lawsuit, 203–5, 213–14, 228–30, 233–34, 236
Alaska Ferry Corporation, 182
Alaska Fish and Game Department, 269, 270, 281, 282
Alaska Marine Highways Service, 203
Alaskan fishery, 38, 119, 150–52, 161–62, 177
   treaty negotiations, 47,48, 57–58, 150–52
   interceptions, 38, 49, 57–58, 62, 161–62, 173–74, 177, 188, 192, 197, 226, 267–70, 284, 317, 342, 360
   overfishing, 152–53, 157, 182, 185, 194, 197, 203, 235–36, 247,270, 278, 290, 374
Alaska Trollers Association, 282
Alaskan transit fee, 56–57, 165–66, 282, 369
Albright, Madeline, 167, 240
Alcan; *see also* Kemano; Nechako River, 198–99
Alfred, Pat, 140
Allen, Ron, 166, 274
Allied Pacific Packing Ltd., 179, 187, 189–90
Alverson, Lee, 62
American Fisheries Society, 254, 256
Anderson, David, 9, 135, 147, 155, 160, 168, 170–172, 174, 177, 181, 185, 187–89, 191–95, 197–99, 201, 204–7, 209, 212, 213–215, 220, 227, 231–32,

234–36, 239, 241, 248, 250–54, 257, 260, 263–65, 267–68, 270–77, 278–84, 286–87, 290–91, 293, 296, 302, 310–12, 316–18, 336, 340, 367–69, 373
Anderson-Locke agreement; *see* Pacific Salmon Treaty
Anderson Plan; *see also* Department of Fisheries and Oceans, 26, 251–54, 256–57, 260, 265–66, 277, 278, 297, 316, 332, 342, 343, 344
aquaculture, *see also* DFO, 110, 119, 319–20, 337–38, 341, 374–75
Area G Trollers Association, 209, 289
Argue, Sandy, 29, 39, 150
Arkko, Glen, 373
Arthurs, Harry W., 100
Arvey, Joe, 141
Asia Pacific Economic Co-operation (APEC) Summit, 224–28
Assembly of First Nations, 65
Atlantic Groundfish Subsidy, The (TAGS), 118, 251, 293, 321
Atlantic salmon, 337–38
Atleo, Cliff, 324
Aurora, 229–30
Austin, Dennis, 288
Autumn Venture, 228
Avante, 355
Axworthy, Lloyd, 155–56, 167, 169, 174–75, 191, 197–99, 224–25, 239, 241

Babcock, John Pearse, 32, 34
Beaton, Joyce, 28
BC Aboriginal Fisheries Commission, 67, 169
BC Council of Tourism, 272
BC Fishermen's Survival Coalition (1983), 77
BC Fisheries Survival Coalition (1993), 77, 207, 238, 290, 301, 324–25
BC Maid, 180, 183
BC New Democratic Party, 9
BC Packers Ltd., 10, 19, 72, 96, 132, 179, 319–20

BC Seafood Alliance, 360, 361
BC Seafood Sector Council, 297
BC Sustainable Fisheries Group, 276
BC Wildlife Federation, 169, 311
Beatty, Jim, 304
Beck, John, 54
Becker, Joe, 74
Beeby, Christopher, 154, 159, 164, 218, 375
Belliveau, Mike, 331
Beltrame, Julian, 231
Bennett (Elizabeth) decision, 359–60
Bennett, W.A.C., 39, 323
Benton, David, 159, 162, 173, 215, 219, 233, 240, 269
Binns, Paddy, 10, 21
Binns, William, 10
Birch, Edgar, 73, 199, 364
Birch, Regan, 183
Bird, Tom, 311
Black Fishing Company, 337
Bohn, Glen, 198
Bohunicky, Brian, 170, 221, 271, 273, 279, 292–93
Boldt (George) decision (1977); see also Northwest Treaty Tribes, 66
Botelho, Bruce, 188, 203–4
Bouchard, Lucien, 158
Brander-Smith, David, 62
Brenner (Donald) decision, 237
Brooks, Gord, 202
Broun, Heywood, 278
Brown, Alan, 10, 15–16, 19, 21, 24–25, 60, 64, 88, 372
Brown, Bruce, 244
Brown, Dennis, 136, 149, 151, 207–8, 215, 218–19, 238, 247, 257, 267–68, 274–75, 277, 286, 306–7, 338–39, 341, 352–53, 363
Brown, Kerry, 88–89
Brown, Mavis, 190
Brown, Robert, 261, 375
Bullock, Sandra, 275–76
Burgess, Chloe, 261
Burkoski, Robert, 136, 180, 183, 373
Burns, Nicholas, 166
Burridge, Christina, 360

Calder, Frank, 71
Calgary Declaration, 220, 309
Cameron, Dave, 158
Campbell, Gordon, 139, 169, 305, 341
Campbell, Kim, 52–53
Canada-BC Agreement on the Management of Pacific Salmon Fishery Issues, 163
Canada First Fishing Strategy, *see* Department of Fisheries and Oceans
Canadian Auto Workers Union, 169
Canadian Council of Professional Fish Harvesters, 360, 362
Canadian Fishing Company, 179, 190, 373
Cap Rouge II, 351–52
Carney, Pat, 110, 168, 220–21, 266
Carpenter, Robert, 112, 136
Carr, Nick, 363
Carson, Dick, 207
Cernetig, Miro, 86
Cashin, Richard, 50
Chamut, Patrick, 61, 86, 106, 165, 233, 241, 266, 270–71, 274, 290, 373
Chan, Raymond, 132
Chapple, Rich, 339
Charest, Jean, 281
Charlottetown Accord, 220
chinook (salmon), 22, 32, 40–42, 45, 49, 52, 56, 58, 150–52, 155, 156–62, 171–73, 210, 232, 233, 246, 252, 255, 273, 275–77, 283, 320, 324
Chinook Technical Committee, *see* Pacific Salmon Treaty
Chislett, Jim, 178
Chretien, Jean, 52, 56, 68, 127, 155, 157, 163, 170, 172–74, 195, 197, 221, 224–28, 233, 251, 339–40, 352
Chretien, Raymond, 192, 224
Christiansen, Dave, 136, 324
chum (salmon), 23, 45, 152, 171, 180, 343
Clark, Dale, 308
Clark, Glen, 9, 14, 127–28, 134, 138–39, 148–50, 155–58, 163–175, 191–92, 199, 201, 204–5, 207, 213–15, 219–224, 233–34, 239, 247–49, 265, 267–68, 271–72, 275–77, 282, 284, 289–90,

292, 302, 303–13, 328, 330, 332, 339, 341, 359–60, 373

Clark, Joe, 109, 310

Clark, Mike, 275

Clasby, Bob, 269

Claussen, Eileen, 155, 158, 160

Clayoquot Sound Regional District, 323

Clifton, Heber, 136

Clinton, Bill, 55, 56, 172–74, 191, 199, 214, 224–28, 233, 247

Coalition for Sustainable Forest Solutions, 323

Coastal Community Network (CCN), 133, 168, 169, 259, 276, 316, 319–320

Coastal Fisheries Protection Act, 53

Coastal Navigation Protection Act, 56, 156, 166

cod fishery; *see* East Coast

coho (salmon) 22, 45, 49, 51, 52, 56, 57–58, 150, 152–53, 156, 159–61, 165, 171–72, 174, 202, 203, 206, 210–11, 232, 233, 243, 246, 251–57, 259–61, 266, 268, 269, 270–71, 273–77, 278, 281–84, 311–13, 316, 320, 324, 335–36, 342–43, 344–45, 365

    Thompson River coho stocks, 233, 252, 268, 274–75, 299, 344

    Skeena coho stocks, 252, 270, 278, 281–82, 299, 313, 317, 335, 342

Colson, David, 52

commercial fishing

    abalone fishery, 104

    gillnetting, 21–23, 25, 37, 41, 43, 60, 96, 125, 131, 153, 171, 176–79, 183, 184, 202, 210, 284, 316, 332, 335, 338, 342–43, 352, 353, 357, 370

    purse seining, 21–23, 37, 43, 47, 58, 59–60, 62, 82–84, 96, 98, 111, 125, 131, 171, 174, 185–86, 202, 210, 253, 285–86, 289, 291–92, 316, 319, 332, 343, 350–51, 352, 353, 357, 370

    trolling, 21–23, 41, 42, 45, 47, 48, 60, 82, 111, 125, 131, 157, 159, 160, 171–181, 209, 211–12, 252, 279, 280, 289, 316, 332, 343, 350, 352, 353, 370

reduction herring fishery, 108

roe herring fishery, 90, 97, 107, 108

Community Fisheries Development Centre (CFDC), 204, 316, 360–61

Conroy, Ed, 338

Cook, Chris, 373

Coolican, Murray, 67

Copeland, Lenore, 322

Copes, Parzival, 257–262, 375

Copes Report, 258–61, 297

Coughnour (John) decision, 238–39

Council for Canadian Unity, 222

Cranmer, Bill, 140–41

Crey, Ernie, 58, 74, 76, 238

Crosbie, John, 50–52, 53, 63, 69, 70, 72, 107, 110, 293, 296, 373

Cruickshank, Don, 98, 104–105, 108, 109, 113–15, 334, 375

Cruickshank Report (Fleet Rationalization Committee Report), 104–105, 107, 261

Crutchfield, James, 93–94, 97

Culp, Jim, 202

Cummins, John, 77, 163, 189, 236

Daley, William, 196–97

David Suzuki Foundation, 133, 163, 169, 297, 310, 313, 367

Davidson, Rose, 133

Davis, Jack, 93, 94–95, 115, 132

Davis Plan; *see also* licensing, 39, 94–99, 100, 107, 112, 125, 130, 131, 142

Day, Stockwell, 339

De Bane, Pierre, 102–104

Deep Sea Trawlers Association, 113

Dehaene, Jean-Luc, 173

Delgamuukw case, 238

Department of Fisheries and Oceans (Fisheries and Oceans Canada) (DFO), *see also* licensing *and* Mifflin Plan *and* Anderson Plan, 16, 17, 21, 23–26, 42, 45–46, 56–57, 59–61, 63, 137, 138, 141–43, 144, 146–47, 150, 173, 177, 187, 210, 234, 249, 259–60, 280, 299–302, 332–33, 339–40, 354

    aquaculture, 107, 110, 111, 227–28

    budget cuts, 63, 73, 75, 77–79, 80,

84–85, 107, 121, 123, 126, 256, 302, 366–68
Canada First Fishing Strategy, 171–72, 194, 205, 207, 209–12, 342
chinook conservation program, 41
Coho Recovery Plan, 151–52, 251–52, 257
Economic Programs and Planning Branch, 94, 111, 114, 118, 119–21
environmental politics, 55, 86
fisheries management, 46, 87, 93–100, 104, 107, 112–13, 198, 202–3, 205, 209, 210–13, 251–52, 259–61, 295–96, 300–301, 316–17, 320–21, 326, 335–37, 342–58, 360–64, 370–71
fleet restructuring, 117, 123–25, 128–29, missing fish controversy, 61–63, 73–76, 81–82, 86, 302, 374
Native fishery policies, 65–74, 79, 370–71
No Net Loss Habitat policy, 101, 256
risk-averse management policy, 144, 287,291, 301, 336, 342, 344–45, 353, 358, 366–67
zero mortality policy, 252, 276, 283
Department of Foreign Affairs and International Trade (DFAIT), 214–15
Devereaux, Bruce, 280
Dhaliwal, Herb, 132, 169, 318, 322–23, 328–30, 332–33, 340, 351, 371
Dion, Stephane, 222
Disrupter, 179
Dix, Adrian, 303
Dixon, Alvin, 136
Dixon Entrance boundary dispute, 279–81, 284
Doane, Rusty, 230
Doerksen, Dana, 136
Dominion Fisheries Act (1877), 65
Doogan, Mike, 229
Dosanjh, Ujjal, 308, 321, 332, 338, 340, 341
Doucet, Fernand, 100
Douglas, John W., 167
Douglas, Sam, 288
Drymer, Stephen, 241
Duceppe, Gilles, 222
Duncan, Bill, 352

Duncan, John, 204
Duncan, Josh, 373

East Coast fishery; *see also* Georges Bank dispute, Grand Banks foreign fishing; *Kristina Logos*, North Atlantic Fisheries Organization (NAFO), Northern Cod Assistance and Readjustment Program (NCARP) 26, 212, 302
Easy Come, 181–82, 186, 193
Eby, Phil, 73
Economic Council of Canada (ECC), 98–100, 112
Edwards, Bonnie, 323, 363
Edwards, Dan, 124, 133, 136, 141, 209, 318–19, 321–26, 328–330, 332–33, 340, 363, 371, 373
Edwards, Danielle, 321
Eggleton, Art, 191–92, 201, 310
Eidsvik, Phil, 290
Einarsen, Arthur, 34
Einarson, Dave, 202
Ellis, David, 210
Emes, David, 329
Emes, Mike, 129–30, 131, 137, 213, 373
Endangered Species Act (US), 232, 243–44, 246–47, 276, 312
Environmental Protection Agency (US) (EPA), 199–200
Evans, Corky, 144, 147–48, 234, 309, 323, 332, 338, 339

Farrell-Collins, Gary, 272
Feinstein, Diane, 167
First Ministers Conference on Aboriginal Rights (1987), 67
First Nations, Assembly of; *see* Aboriginal Fishing Strategy; Indian Food Fishery (IFF); Native fishery; Northwest Treaty Tribes
fish traps, 30–31
Fisheries Act, 101
Fisheries and Oceans Canada, *see* Department of Fisheries and Oceans (DFO)
Fisheries Association of BC, 13, 19, 106

Fisheries Council of BC, 87, 118, 122, 151, 163, 164, 169, 187, 193, 225, 262, 264, 271, 324, 341, 360

Fisheries Renewal BC (FsRBC), 163–164, 261, 309, 360, 367

Fishermen's Survival Coalition; *see* BC Fisheries Survival Coalition, 102

Fishers Early Retirement Program, 264

fish farms, *see* aquaculture and DFO

fishing, commercial; *see* commercial fishing; Department of Fisheries and Oceans (DFO)

Fishing Vessel Owners Association, 73, 113, 185

Fitzpatrick, Ross, 133, 221

Fleet Rationalization Report; *see* Cruickshank Report

Fletcher, Kathy, 244

Fonzie, 280

Forest Practices Code (FPC), 304

Forest Renewal BC (FRBC), 163, 367

Forrest, Mike, 73, 136

Fortier, Yves, 52, 55, 150, 154–55, 158–60, 164–66, 172, 174, 205, 217–18, 233, 239–242, 277

Fotheringham, Allan, 201

Four Daughters, The, 165

Fowler, Ron, 48, 136, 307, 339

Francino, Mike, 145–46

Frank, Bill Jr., 244

Fraser, John; *see also* Fraser Report, 26, 44, 62, 81, 82, 84–86, 103, 105–106, 155, 157–58, 212, 302, 355, 365–66

Fraser, Ken, 96

Fraser Report; *see also* Fraser, John, 81–86, 117, 122, 301, 321, 344

Fraser Institute, 112, 138

Fraser River Action Plan, 256

Fraser River Coalition, 210

Fraser River Sockeye Crisis Committee, 319, 320

Fraser Sockeye Public Review Board, 62, 81–84, 87

Free Trade Agreement (FTA), 44, 107, 109, 139, 197, 225, 247–48, 323

Frey, Rick, 228, 338

Fruman, Sheila, 164, 225–26

Fry, Hedy, 132

Fryer, John, 145–46

Fulton, Davie, 38

Fulton, Jim, 133, 169, 280–81, 310, 313

General Agreement on Trade and Tariffs (GATT), 109–10, 151, 234

Gilhousen, Philip, 30

Gislason, Gordon, 253, 319–320

Gitksan Wet'suwe'en, 238

Glavin, Terry, 68, 73, 75, 297–99

Goldenberg, Eddie, 157

Gore, Al, 57, 150

Gorton, Slade, 58, 173, 191

Gosnell, Joe, 306

Gotlieb, Allan, 227

Graham, Bud, 24, 61, 313

Graham, Michael, 93–94

Grant, Bob, 137, 360–61

Gray, Richard, 136

Greene, Paddy, 48, 136, 307, 312

Greenpeace, 133, 210

Greenplan, 152

Greider, William, 176, 199–200

Griswold, Mike, 349–50

Groening, Barbara, 137, 178–79

Groening, Walter, 137, 178–79

Grotius, Hugo, 36

Gulf of Georgia, 11, 16–17, 19, 21, 82, 212

Gulf Trollers Association, 103, 113, 350

Gunton, Tom, 303

Habitat Conservation Stewardship Program, 367

Habitat Restoration Program, 367

Haldane, Hubert, 312, 339, 373

Halton, David, 192

Harcourt, Mike, 164, 238, 303

Hardin, Garrett, 94, 97, 326

Harper, Elijah, 68

Harris, Michael, 50, 220

Hartley, Roland, 32

Harvey, Christopher, 290

Haugan, Richard, 136

Hayward, Brian, 97

Hellberg, Russ, 166, 168, 169, 276, 319
Hells Gate fishways and slide, 31–32, 33, 34, 37, 369
Henderson, John, 286, 332
Henderson, Mike, 121
Heritage Aquaculture Ltd., 320
Hewes, Gordon, 29, 103
Hewison, George, 13, 101
Hird, John, 188, 349
Hobsbawm, Eric, 15, 28, 182, 184, 359
Holdstock, John, 169
Howard, Ross, 194, 276
Hudson's Bay Company, 30
Human Resources Development Canada (HRDC), 144, 222, 321–22, 360
Hume, Mark, 26, 85, 169, 264, 271
Hume, Stephen, 283
hunger strike; *see* Edwards, Dan
Hunt, Christine, 169, 339
Hunter, Justine, 282
Hunter, Mike, 87, 118, 151, 163, 164–65, 169, 187, 193, 225, 262, 271, 307, 324, 341
Hurtig, Mel, 339–40

Ichthyophthirius disease (ICH); *see also* salmon, 153, 335, 337
Indian Fishermen's Assistance Program, 72
Indian fishermen's Emergency fund, 72
Indian Food Fishery (IFF); *see also* Aboriginal Fishing Strategy; Assembly of First Nations; Native fishery; Boldt Decision; Northwest Treaty Tribes, 65–66
Individual Transferable Quotas (ITQs); *see* licensing
International Hake Consortium, 324
International North Pacific Fisheries Commission (INPFC), 36
International Pacific Salmon Fisheries Commission (IPSFC)
  history, 18, 20–21, 30, 31, 32–33, 34–38, 42, 245–246, 301–2, 314, 318, 364
  convention area waters, 33, 38, 46
  Hell's Gate fishways, 34–35
  high seas tagging, 34
  treaty (1937), 9, 23, 66

Nechako River diversion; see also Nechako River, 198–99
Irving, Bill, 324
Iverson, Buddy, 137
Iverson, Ellis, 137
Iverson, Lorne, 124, 136, 228

Jacobs, Gibby, 339
James, Michelle, 72, 120, 190, 361
Jantzen, Jack, 346
Jobs and Timber Accord, 304
John, Edward, 332
Johnson, David, 51
Johnson, Kate, 190
Johnston, Guy, 347, 349–50, 356, 369–370
Johnston, Michelle, 349
Johnstone Strait fishery, 24, 82, 291, 297, 343, 347–49, 352–57, 359
Johnstone Strait protest, 355–56
J.S. McMillan Fishing Company Ltd., 169
Juan de Fuca Strait fishery, 58, 59, 208–10, 343
Junger, Robin, 296

Kadowaki, Ron, 255, 368
Keitlah, Nelson, 324
Kelley, Dale, 282
Kemano; *see also* Alcan; Kenney Dam *and* Nechako River, 198
Kennedy, David, 219
Kenney Dam, 198, 199
Kerley, Doug, 144–45
Kieley, Lawrence, 251
King, Bob, 189, 229, 281, 282
Kitchen (W.J.) decision, 236–37
Kitimat, 199
Kitzhaber, John, 312
Klein, Ralph, 158, 220
Knowles, Tony, 187, 189, 190, 194, 214, 229, 234–35, 281
Koenings, Jeff, 270
Kramek, Robert E., 166
Kristianson, Gerry, 160–61, 339
Kristianson, Thor, 178
Kristina Logos, 53–54
Kwagiulth Fisheries Commission, 169

Ladret, A.S. "Snuffy", 116, 224
land claims; *see* Native land claims
Lande, Brian, 136
Lane, David, 298
Langer, Otto, 367
Larkin, Peter A., 75, 76
Lavoie, Judith, 210
law of the sea; *see* United Nations
  Convention on Law of the Sea
LeBlanc, Romeo, 102, 104
LeBlond, Paul, 62
Lee, Dennis, 144
Lefeaux-Valentine, Bill, *see* Valentine
Lewis, Martin W., 29, 94
licensing; *see also* Davis Plan, 16, 72, 88–92,
  375
  attached cannery licences, 89
  common property, notion of, 88, 90,
    105, 120
  Crown ownership of marine resources, 90
  individual transferable quotas (ITQs),
    89–90, 99–100, 104, 111–12, 123,
    127, 259, 361–62, 373
  licence bank concept, 261
  licence and vessel buy-backs; *see also*
    Pacific Salmon Licence Retirement
    program, 94–105, 111, 114–15,
    120–21, 126–29, 131, 136, 141–42,
    251–52, 260, 332, 372
  licence leasing, 108, 112, 115, 122, 261, 361
  stackable area licensing; *see also* Mifflin
    Plan, 60, 87, 88, 90, 97, 108, 111, 114,
    120, 122–25, 127, 131–133, 136–37,
    140–43, 146–48, 174, 176, 194,
    209–10, 226–27, 235–36, 260, 320,
    361, 373
  licensing the man, 94–95, 108, 112
  UFAWU alternate to Davis Plan, 95
  roe herring licences, 108
Lichatowich, Jim, 245–46
lighthouse destaffing, 140, 170, 222
Lloyd, Jack, 370
Lochbaum, Ed, 346
Locke, Gary, 167, 173, 215, 232, 244, 246–
  47, 265, 268, 270, 272–75, 282–83,
  287, 312

Lower Fraser Fishing Authority, 58, 76, 238
Lowry, Mike, 283
Lubar, John, 368
Lubzinski, Terry, 373
Lunn, Gary, 241, 310
Lynnwood Accord, 40

McArthur, Doug, 157, 234, 247, 249–50,
  267–68, 272, 289, 303–7
McCallum, Brent, 252
McColl, Velma, 157, 177, 221, 274
McCurdy, Earl, 251
MacDonald, Steve, 206, 288
McDonough, Alexa, 167
McEachern, Allan, 238
MacGillivray, Paul, 345–46
McGoodwin, James R., 26–27, 29, 88,
  326–27, 342–43
MacInnes, Dan, 112–13, 375
McIntosh, Dave, 13
McKamey, Bob, 76
McKee, Charles, 287
MacLean, Angus, 20
McLeod, Ron, 210
McMartin, Pete, 321
McMillan, Barry, 169
MacMillan Bloedel, 323
MacPhail, Joy, 250
McQuaig, Linda, 123
McRae, Don, 247, 249, 265–66, 269, 271–
  72, 274, 277, 367
McWhinney, Ted, 132, 340
Magnussen Act, 109
Mair, Rafe, 167, 200, 209
Malispina, 182–195, 203–4, 213
Malling, Eric, 123
Maloney, Aidan, 299
Manning, Preston, 167, 168
Marchak, Patricia, 90–91, 375
Marchi, Sergio, 197, 225
Maritime Fishermen's Union, 331
Marshall (Donald) case, 330
Martin, Keith, 310
Martin, Lawrence, 196
Martin, Paul, 222–23, 309, 352
Martin, Clarence D. 33

Matanuska, 188
Mathias, Joe, 65
Matthews, Ralph, 54–55, 327
May, Art, 103, 106, 373
Mearns, Heather, 178
Meech Lake Accord, 68
Meggs, Geoff, 79, 89, 94, 97, 98, 101, 111, 164, 267
Meltzer, Evelyn, 54
Mentzelopoulos, Athana, 206, 211–12
Meyboom, Peter, 107, 111
Metlakatla, 202
Michelle Rose, 347, 350, 356, 369
Mifflin, Fred, 129–30, 132–33, 135, 140, 144–45, 147–48, 155, 163, 253, 373
Mifflin Plan (Pacific Salmon Fleet Restructuring Program); see also Pacific Roundtable on Fleet Restructuring, licensing, *and* UFAWU vote on licence stacking, 10, 22, 26, 116, 120, 129, 132–33, 134–36, 138, 140–42, 144, 150, 155, 170, 174, 176, 188, 194, 207, 208–9, 211–12, 226–27, 234, 235, 249, 253–54, 259, 260, 297, 303, 305, 309, 316, 325, 332, 341, 347, 371, 372, 374
  DFO office occupation, 136–37, 163
  full Mifflin protest, 263–65
Miller, Dan, 308–9
Millerd, Don, 298
Millman, Tom, 165–66
Minister's Advisory Panel (MAP); see also Pacific Salmon Treaty, 56–58, 81–82
Ministry of Agriculture, Fisheries and Food MAFF), 228, 309, 332, 337–38, 341
Ministry of Fisheries (MoF), 249–50, 257, 299, 332, 360
Mirau, Garth, 136, 177, 352–56, 363
missing salmon; see Pacific Salmon Commission and DFO
Mitchell, David, 221
Montgomery, Chris, 226
Moran Dam, 39, 246
Morley, Rob, 187, 189–90
Morrell, Bill, 131
Morton, Alexandra, 338
Moskovicz, Peter, 347

Mowat, Farley, 81
Mulroney, Brian, 44, 51, 68, 70, 105, 106, 139, 198, 248, 305
Murkowski, Frank, 57, 166, 191, 265, 283, 312
Murray, John, 146
Murray, Patty, 173
Musqueam Indian Band, 65, 74, 206, 237, 288
Mussallem, Jack, 189, 214, 229

Nagy, Arnie, 179
Nahannie, Harold, 64
Nanoose Bay torpedo range, 149, 155–56, 167–69, 171–72, 191–92, 201, 214, 220, 236, 250, 282, 303–5, 309–311, 332, 360
National Infrastructure Program, 251
National Marine Fisheries Service (US) (NMFS), 243–44, 246–47
Native Brotherhood of BC, 67, 71, 111, 133, 202, 237, 335, 339, 352, 373
Native fishery; *see also* Aboriginal Fishing Strategy, Assembly of First Nations; Indian Food Fishery (IFF); Northwest Treaty Tribes, 65–70, 330–31, 357, 370
  food fisheries, 65–67, 72, 290
Native land claims, 67, 78–79, 375
Nechako River; *see also* International Pacific Salmon Commission, 198–99
Needler, A.W.H., 82
Neish, Scotty, 64
Nelson, Ritchie, 19
Newfoundland Fisheries, Food and Allied Workers Union (NFFAWU-CAW), 50, 251
Newman, Edwin, 373
Nguyen, Boi, 136
Nichol, Jack, 13, 48, 69, 76, 101, 102, 151, 162, 169, 298, 307
Nielsen, Erik, 106–7
Nisga'a Treaty, 304–8, 330
Nobels, Des, 184, 188, 202, 230, 373
Nordstrom, Rick, 125, 133, 136
North, George, 36, 37
North America Free Trade Agreement (NAFTA); *see* Free Trade Agreement

Northern Cod Assistance and Readjustment Program (NCARP), 51, 53
northern cod fishery, 50–51, 53, 55, 258
Northern Gillnetters Association, 202
Northern Trollers Association, 339
Northwest Atlantic Fisheries Organization (NAFO), 54
Northwest Indian Fisheries Commission, 244
Northwest Treaty Tribes fishery, 25, 43, 49, 61, 66, 103, 152, 161, 166, 212, 274
Norum, Cynthia, 137
Norum, Mike, 137
Noyes Island, 38
Nyce, Jacob, 133
Nygren, Joan, 225–27
Nygren, Julie, 225–26, 28
Nygren, Wally, 226–28

Oak Bay Marine Group, 42, 118, 215
Ocean Fisheries Ltd., 122
Ocean's Best, 213
Oceanside Cannery, 178–79, 204, 319
Ogden, Frank, 217
Oka standoff, 68–69
Olsen, Kim, 179, 181, 183–188, 193–95, 205, 264, 373
Olson, Pat, 178
Onderdonk, Andrew, 31
O'Neil, Peter, 157, 170, 197, 214, 221, 270, 312
Oppal, Wally, 138
Ordano, Steve, 356
O'Reilly, Terry, 103
Orr, Craig, 58
Ostray, Sylvia, 98
Ostrom, Bob, 112
Ottawa *Sun*, The 189
Owen, Roberts, 248–49, 271, 274, 277
Owen, Stephen, 333, 340

Pacific Area Regional Advisory Committee (PARC), 67
Pacific Fisheries Resource Conservation Council, 255–56, 302, 365–67
Pacific Fishermen's Defence Alliance, 67, 76

Pacific Gillnetters Association, 73, 113, 124, 146
Pacific Roundtable on Fleet Restructuring; *see also* Mifflin Plan, 117–20, 122–26, 128–29, 131–132
Pacific Salmon Commission, 14, 16, 24, 45, 52, 150–52, 155, 173, 212, 232, 241–42, 247, 287, 290, 312, 367–69
    Chinook Technical Committee, 173, 232
    Fraser Sockeye Review Panel, 291, 345, 347–49, 352–54, 357
    missing fish, 61–63, 73
    Northern Boundary Coho Technical Committee, 232
    panel organization 45, 47, 55
    run–size calculations and escapement goals, 46–47, 59–62, 73–74, 76, 81–82, 84, 117, 117–18, 206–7, 218, 287, 288, 291–94, 316–17, 343, 345, 347–48
    Technical Dispute Settlement Board, 158, 239
Pacific Salmon Endowment Fund, 367–69
Pacific Salmon Fleet Restructuring Program; *see* Mifflin Plan
Pacific Salmon Licence Retirement Program; *see also* licensing, 142
Pacific Salmon Seiners Association, 103
Pacific Salmon Treaty; see also Lynnwood Accord, 44–47, 50, 249–50, 269–270, 274, 278, 291, 298, 304, 305, 311–14, 324, 332, 354, 374–75
    agreement (1937) 66
    Anderson–Locke agreement, 273–77, 278, 287, 289, 293, 296
    annexes, 16, 45, 48, 49, 173–74, 217, 275, 282
    Article III (equity), 45, 47, 48, 52, 154–55, 158, 159–160, 165, 172, 217, 224, 231–33, 238–40, 265–66, 268, 274, 298, 311, 314, 360, 368–69, 374
    Article XII (dispute resolution), 239
    BC lawsuit against US overfishing, 214–16, 238–39, 247, 289–90, 309
    Beeby mediation, 154–55

bilateral salmon enhancement
programs, 224, 367–69
conservation endowment fund, 311
negotiations and agreement (1985), 44,
48–49
negotiations and agreement (1999),
139, 151, 154–55, 164–65, 167, 169,
194, 197–98, 232–33, 265, 271–277
stakeholders process, 159–163, 172,
173, 198, 206, 230, 233, 240
special envoys process, 198–202, 215–
16, 217, 219, 227, 228, 230–33, 240,
266–67, 269, 277
Pacific Stock Assessment Review Committee
(PSARC), 266
Pacific Trollers Association, 48, 103, 109,
124, 125, 133, 169, 324
Palmer, Vaughn, 268, 303, 306
Palo, Barry, 136
Parsons, Scott, 67, 70–71, 72, 92, 96, 102,
107, 108
Pattison, Jimmy, 178, 319, 373
Patullo, Duff, 33
Paulsen, Paul, 230
Pearse, Peter, 66, 74, 76, 94, 97, 99, 102,
103, 112, 115, 122, 133, 259, 360, 361
Pearse Report (1983), 66, 101–102, 106,
326
Pearse Report (1992) 74–75, 81
Peckford, Brian, 158, 292–93, 295–96,
299–300, 375
Peckford Inquiry and Report, 292–93,
295–97, 299–300, 302–3
Penikett, Tony, 303
Perry, Tom, 280
Petrachenko, Donna, 211, 286, 339, 366
Petter, Andrew, 309
Pettigrew, Pierre, 250
Pettipas, Randy, 221
pink (salmon), 18, 23, 32, 34, 37–38, 39,
42, 45, 49, 58, 59, 117, 150–52, 174,
181, 202, 203, 207, 212, 254, 311, 343,
373
Pinkerton, Evelyn, 327–28
Pipkin, James, 150–51, 152, 154–55, 160,
162, 217–18, 232–33, 240, 249, 273

Point Henry, 181
Point Roberts, 30
Polar Lady, 179–81, 186
Popovitch, Gilbert, 140–41, 147
Port Essington, 10
Port Simpson, 202
Potvin, Kevin, 284
Prince, Nicholas, 74
Prince Rupert ferry blockade; *see* Alaska
ferry blockade
Prince Rupert Fishing Vessel Owners'
Association 113
Prince Rupert Fishermen's Co-operative
Association, 48, 109, 186
Prince Rupert Fishermen's Co-operative
Guild, 113
Probert, Bruce, 128
Procopation, Bill, 102

Quipp, June, 317

Radosevic, John, 129, 133, 136, 140–41,
164, 177, 184, 186–87, 189, 192–93,
206, 214, 224, 229, 272, 352, 363
Rankin, Harry, 13
Rawson, Bruce, 69–70, 73, 373
Reagan, Ronald, 44, 199
Redekop, John, 195
Reece, Gary, 284
Regional Aquatic Management Society
(RAMS), 323, 326, 328
Reid, David, 98
Reid, Don, 76
Reid, Elsie, 251
Reid, Tom, 20
Reynolds, John, 291
Rezansoff, Bob, 185–89, 205, 351
Ricker, W.E., 35
Riddell, Brian, 156
Rivers, Frank, 64
Rivers Inlet, 11
Roberts, Gerry, 286, 373
Robertson, Glen, 141
Robinson, Ken, 13
Rogers, Raymond A., 86, 118, 243
Romanow, Roy, 168, 304–5

Rombough, Les, 132
Ronneseth, Lawrie, 136–37
Roos, John, 32, 33
Rothstein (Barbara) decision, 152
roundtables; *see* Pacific Roundtable on Fleet
  Restructuring
Routledge, Rick, 62
Royal Proclamation of 1763, 65
Ruckelshaus, William, 199–200, 202, 215,
  217, 227, 231, 233, 241, 277, 296
Rue, Frank, 282
Ruff, Norman, 158

Safeway Caper, The, 179–81
Sainas, Pete, 11
Saito, Wayne, 24, 124, 288, 289, 290, 292,
  349, 354, 357
Salmon Endowment fund, 257
Salmon Enhancement Programs (SEP), 39,
  106, 107, 257, 367
Salmon for Canada Committee, 225
Salmon Watch, 169
Sananin, Don, 64, 353
Sandve, Dave, 178
Saunderson (Brian) decision, 166, 370–71
Saxton, James, 218
Scarfo, Cathy, 209, 211, 268, 289, 373
Schutz, Dave, 24
Scowcroft, Gerry, 239
Scrimger, Joe, 62
Sea Deuce, 15, 372
Secord, David, 124
Seymour Narrows blockade, 285–87, 290–
  92, 296, 303
Sharp, Mitchell, 170
Sheffield, Bill, 49
Shepard, Mike, 29, 39
Shinners, Wayne, 41–43, 106, 373
Siddon, Tom, 51, 67, 107, 110–11, 198,
  373
Sierra Club, 210
Sierra Legal Defence Fund, 257
Siider, Calvin, 346
Silver Spray, 329
Sinclair, James (former fisheries minister),
  19, 37–38

Sinclair, Jim (president, BC Federation of
  Labour), 189
Sinclair, Sol, 92–93, 94, 98
Skeena River, 10
Skeena Watershed Committee (SWC), 152,
  335
Sloan, Gordon, 92
Smallwood, Joey, 51
Smitch, Curt, 215, 246–47, 270, 274
Smith, Joe, 76, 363
Smith, Mel, 325
Smith, Mike, 167–68
Smith, Kendall, 136
Smith, William (premier) 306
Smith, William (Prince Rupert municipal
  clerk), 214
Sockeye Crisis Committee, 322, 328
Sockeye Fusiliers, 337
sockeye, 15, 21, 23–24, 32, 34, 42, 45, 46,
  48, 49, 51, 52,58, 59, 60, 73, 117, 150–
  52, 159–62, 165, 171–73, 174, 176–77,
  180–81, 190, 202, 203, 205–212, 226,
  244, 266, 269, 273, 275–77, 283, 284–
  88, 290–94, 295–96, 297, 299–300,
  311–14, 315, 320, 328, 334–37, 339,
  341–50, 351, 353–58, 363
  Adams River run, 17–21, 24–26, 60–61,
    92, 287, 288, 293, 315, 317–18,
    334–35, 339, 341, 343–44, 346–47,
    354–55, 356–57, 359, 363–66, 368
  early Stuart run, 58, 61, 74, 173, 198,
    206, 207, 288, 300, 316, 344
  escapement, 20–21, 24–26, 35, 46, 59,
    287, 301–2
  ICH disease, 153
  migratory patterns, 17–18, 24, 25, 32,
    47–48, 59–60, 83, 206, 208, 287
  pre-spawn mortality 76, 81, 82, 86, 206,
    300–301, 374
Softwood Lumber Agreement, 323
Souter, Doug, 190
South East Seiners Association (Alaska), 270
Sparrow case (1990), 65, 68, 236
Speak for the Salmon Society, 210
sports fishing, 41, 107, 152, 157, 160, 171,
  215–16, 252, 283, 284, 293, 316, 339, 357

Sports Fishing Advisory Board, 202–3
Sports Fishing Institute of BC, 157, 169, 252, 311–12, 339
Sprout, Paul, 121, 124, 206, 252–53, 290, 339
Squamish Indian Band, 64, 339
Staley, Mike, 160
Stavenes, Steve, 186
Steelhead Society of BC, 58, 210
steelhead sport fishery, 56, 153, 171, 202, 210, 252, 255, 283, 344
Stelle, Will, 243, 247
Stevens, Frank, 169, 265, 283
Stevens, Homer, 13, 18, 19, 36, 71–72, 95, 186
Stevens, John, 178, 184, 228, 235, 373
Stevens, Nick, 178
Stewart, Catherine, 133
Stewart, Gary, 180–81
Stewart, Jane, 308
Stewart, Robert, 162
Stol:lo Native band, 207
Stolt Sea Farms Ltd., 338
Strahl, Chuck, 169
Strangway, David, 198–99, 202, 215, 217, 227, 231, 233, 241, 269, 277, 296
Streifel, Dennis, 249–50, 261, 302–3, 308, 320, 328, 332
Strom, Robert, 136
Superfund Coalition; see also Ruckelshaus, William, 200
Surfline Agreement, 38
survival coalitions; see BC Fisheries Survival Coalition
Sutcliffe, John, 121, 124–25, 133, 136, 205, 253, 302, 364
Suzuki, David ; *see also* David Suzuki Foundation, 134–35
Suzuki, Raymond "Beanie", 181–82
Suzuki, Tatsuro "Buck," ; *see also* T. Buck Suzuki Foundation, 298

T. Buck Suzuki Foundation, 298, 373
Tagore, Rabindranath, 315
Taku, 153, 188
Talbot, Strobe, 197

Taras, David, 85
Tarnoff, Richard, 112
Taaska, 205, 351
Tavaras, Captain Antonio, 53
Taylor, Eric, 178–79
Taylor, Greg, 122, 127
Taylor, Rod, 190–91
Tebb, Terry, 288
Teitelbaum (Max) decision, 188
Terrana, Anna, 132
Terry Lynne, 133, 138
Thames, Lorne, 355–56
Thibault, Robert, 351, 353–54, 371
Thiesen, Gordon, 131
Thomas (Howard) decision, 236, 238
Thompson, E.P., 14
Thorkelson, Joy, 161–162, 273, 276–77, 336
Thorstenson, Bob, 270–71
"Three Amigos", 145–46, 209
Tobin, Brian, 14, 21, 25, 53–57, 61–62, 84, 117, 118, 123, 124, 126, 127–28, 129, 139, 144, 150–51, 155, 171, 174, 193, 201, 303, 369, 373
Todd, Ian, 61, 84
Tousignant, Louis, 117, 118, 121, 123, 124, 127, 128, 129, 133, 136–38, 142, 146, 159, 211, 373
Trade Adjustment Assistance Program (US), 373–74
Tragedy of the Commons, 94
Treaty Negotiations Advisory Committee of BC (TNAC), 306–7
Triggs, Dal, 76
Trudeau, Pierre, 93, 98
Turner, Robert, 166
Turris, Bruce, 361
Tyabji Wilson, Judy, 305

UFAWU-CAW, 133, 146, 148–49, 164, 169, 205, 206, 208, 224, 235, 253, 272, 273, 282, 307, 316, 324, 335, 352, 353, 355, 363, 364
and ferry blockade, 177, 179, 186–93, 214, 228–29,
protest rally, 224
Ulybel Enterprises, 53

United Fishermen and Allied Workers'
Union (UFAWU); *see also* UFAWU–CAW,
9, 12, 14, 16, 19–20, 36, 37–38, 39,
48, 57, 67, 69, 71–73, 76–78, 92–94,
101–103, 108, 109–12, 113, 118, 121,
124, 127–28, 131, 133
   fleet reduction vote, 128–29
   Combines Defence Committee, 13
United Nations Convention on Law of the
Sea (UNCLOS), 36, 39, 45, 259–61
University of Victoria Institute for Dispute
Resolution, 340
Urban Salmon Habitat Program, 367
US National Marine Service, 152
US Naval Underwater War Centre, 310

Valcourt, Bernard, 51, 107
Valentine (Lefeaux-), Bill, 145–46, 250,
257, 267–68, 272–73, 339
Van der Peet case (1996), 78
van Dongen, John, 341, 374
Vianen, William, 30
Viscount, 280
Vision 2000

Wadhams, Greg, 136, 141, 373
Walker, Doug, 311
Walker, Michael, 138
   Walkom, Thomas, 247–48
Wallace, Catherine, 361–62
Walters, Carl, 255
Washington Fish and Game Department, 173
Washington state fishery, 25, 45–47, 49
Washington State Treaty Native fishery; *see*
Northwest Treaty Tribes.
Webb, Lloyd, 361
Weiler, Joe, 177, 298
Weinstein, Bob, 229
Wells, Clyde, 127, 299

West Coast Fleet Development Committee,
97, 122
West Coast Seafood Processors, 169
West Coast Sustainability Association
(WCSA), 126–27, 133, 324–25, 328
West Coast Trollers Association, 268
West, Mary Beth, 160, 162, 164–65, 172,
174
Western Canada Wilderness Society, 210
Weston, Corporation, 319–20
Wet'suwet'en Fisheries Commission, 342
Wetzel, Ross, 133, 136–37, 146
Wheeler, Dave, 290
White, Peter, 222
Wilkerson, Bill, 42
Williams, Percy, 136
Wilson, Michael, 105
Windswept, 183
Wishing Well, 228
Wood, Al, 111
Woodey, Jim, 24, 82, 206
Woolf, 312
Wright, Bob, 42, 118–19, 157, 168, 215–16,
218
Wright, Miriam, 91
Wright, Steven, 124
Wulff, Bob, 176, 373
Wulff, Darlene, 176–79, 373

Yaffe, Barbara, 132–33, 138, 158, 173, 195,
221, 253, 284
Young, Clinton, 136
Young, Don, 56, 283
Young, John, 276
Young, Pat, 184

Zirnhelt, David, 55–56, 140–41
Zyblut, Ed, 361